WTO and World Trade

Contributions to Economics

www.springeronline.com/series/1262

Further volumes of this series can be found at our homepage.

Friedel Bolle/Marco Lehmann-Waffenschmidt (Eds.)
Surveys in Experimental Economics
2002. ISBN 3-7908-1472-5

Pablo Coto-Millán
General Equilibrium and Welfare
2002. ISBN 7908-1491-1

Wojciech W. Charemza/Krystyna Strzala (Eds.)
East European Transition and EU Enlargement
2002. ISBN 3-7908-1501-1

Natalja von Westernhagen
Systemic Transformation, Trade and Economic Growth
2002. ISBN 3-7908-1521-7

Josef Falkinger
A Theory of Employment in Firms
2002. ISBN 3-7908-1520-9

Engelbert Plassmann
Econometric Modelling of European Money Demand
2003. ISBN 3-7908-1522-5

Reginald Loyen/Erik Buyst/Greta Devos (Eds.)
Struggeling for Leadership: Antwerp-Rotterdam Port Competition between 1870–2000
2003. ISBN 3-7908-1524-1

Pablo Coto-Millán
Utility and Production, 2nd Edition
2003. ISBN 3-7908-1423-7

Emilio Colombo/John Driffill (Eds.)
The Role of Financial Markets in the Transition Process
2003. ISBN 3-7908-0004-X

Guido S. Merzoni
Strategic Delegation in Firms and in the Trade Union
2003. ISBN 3-7908-1432-6

Jan B. Kuné
On Global Aging
2003. ISBN 3-7908-0030-9

Sugata Marjit, Rajat Acharyya
International Trade, Wage Inequality and the Developing Economy
2003. ISBN 3-7908-0031-7

Francesco C. Billari/Alexia Prskawetz (Eds.)
Agent-Based Computational Demography
2003. ISBN 3-7908-1550-0

Georg Bol/Gholamreza Nakhaeizadeh/Svetlozar T. Rachev/Thomas Ridder/Karl-Heinz Vollmer (Eds.)
Credit Risk
2003. ISBN 3-7908-0054-6

Christian Müller
Money Demand in Europe
2003. ISBN 3-7908-0064-3

Cristina Nardi Spiller
The Dynamics of the Price Structure and the Business Cycle
2003. ISBN 3-7908-0063-5

Michael Bräuninger
Public Debt and Endogenous Growth
2003. ISBN 3-7908-0056-1

Brigitte Preissl/Laura Solimene
The Dynamics of Clusters and Innovation
2003. ISBN 3-7908-0077-5

Markus Gangl
Unemployment Dynamics in the United States and West Germany
2003. ISBN 3-7908-1533-0

Pablo Coto-Millán (Ed.)
Essays on Microeconomics and Industrial Organisation, 2nd Edition
2004. ISBN 3-7908-0104-6

Wendelin Schnedler
The Value of Signals in Hidden Action Models
2004. ISBN 3-7908-0173-9

Carsten Schröder
Variable Income Equivalence Scales
2004. ISBN 3-7908-0183-6

Wilhelm J. Meester
Locational Preferences of Entrepreneurs
2004. ISBN 3-7908-0178-X

Russel Cooper/Gary Madden (Eds.)
Frontiers of Broadband, Electronic and Mobile Commerce
2004. ISBN 3-7908-0087-2

Sardar M. N. Islam
Empirical Finance
2004. ISBN 3-7908-1551-9

Jan-Egbert Sturm/Timo Wollmershäuser (Eds.)
Ifo Survey Data in Business Cycle and Monetary Policy Analysis
2005. ISBN 3-7908-0174-7

Bernard Michael Gilroy/Thomas Gries/Willem A. Naudé (Eds.)
Multinational Enterprises, Foreign Direct Investment and Growth in Africa
2005. ISBN 3-7908-0276-X

Günter S. Heiduk
Kar-yiu Wong
Editors

WTO and World Trade

Challenges in a New Era

With 47 Figures
and 23 Tables

Physica-Verlag
A Springer Company

Series Editors
Werner A. Müller
Martina Bihn

Editors
Prof. Dr. Günter S. Heiduk
University of Duisburg-Essen
Institute for International and Regional Economic Relations
Campus Duisburg
Lotharstraße 65
47048 Duisburg
Germany
iwbheiduk@uni-duisburg.de

Prof. Kar-yiu Wong, PhD
University of Washington
Department of Economics
Box 353330
Seattle, WA 98195-3330
USA

ISSN 1431-1933
ISBN 3-7908-1579-9 Physica-Verlag Heidelberg New York

Cataloging-in-Publication Data applied for
Library of Congress Control Number: 2005922326

Physica-Verlag is a part of Springer Science+Business Media

springeronline.com

Softcover Design: Erich Kirchner, Heidelberg

SPIN 11393887   88/3153-5 4 3 2 1 0 – Printed on acid-free and non-aging paper

Contents

Part B – Trade Policy

Part C – WTO

Introduction

Günter S. Heiduk* and Kar-yiu Wong**

* Institute of International and Regional Economic Relations, University of Duisburg-Essen, Campus Duisburg, Germany
** Department of Economics, University of Washington, Seattle, USA

The rapid growth of world trade has become one of the most phenomenal features of the international order after the World War. While different countries were experiencing various growth rates of their economies, most of them found out that foreign trade grew much faster than their economies. As a matter of fact, for most economies, foreign trade has been determined to be one of the biggest and the most consistent contributors to economic growth.

Nowadays world trade is a very complicated phenomenon because it is not just an economic but also a social, political, environmental, labour, and legal matter. Economists care about world trade because economies are getting more and more open and world trade is related to the properties of open economies. Government planners care about world trade because it is related to many issues that the economies are facing: Resource allocation, income distribution, employment, production, consumption, government revenue, economic growth, and economic welfare. A right trade policy will enhance the economic welfare and growth of the economy in a more harmonious and equitable way. A wrong policy, however, could spell disaster.

The World Trade Organization (WTO) was established about a decade ago to replace the General Agreement on Tariffs and Trade (GATT). The WTO was set up to help governments to solve some of the trade problems. It not only carries out one of the most important responsibilities of the GATT, conducting multilateral trade negotiations, but also tries to cover more commodities and areas, including the setting up of a dispute settlement process.

The work of the WTO, despite its short history, has already affected world trade in many areas, including government policies, economic growth and welfare, environment, and production and consumption of manufacturing, agriculture, and services. Even though the ongoing Doha Round of trade talks has hit many obstacles so far, it is still very alive. It is expected that some kind of agreements will be signed by the member countries at the end, furthering the work of the GATT and making the world economy a better environment for trade.

In 2002, the Institute of International and Regional Economic Relations, University of Duisburg-Essen, Germany and the Research Center of International Economics, University of Washington, Seattle, USA organized a joint two-day conference in Duisburg on the WTO and world trade, with internationally renowned speakers from all over the world to speak about their views and research results of some of the pressing issues about the WTO, world trade, and their relationship. Some of the papers presented in the conference, after appropriate discussion and revision, have been included in the present volume. There are some additional papers included in the present volume, which we believe will enhance the quality of this volume. All papers provide in-depth analysis of some of the most pressing trade issues facing economists and government planners, and they will certainly help stimulate more research and discussion.

In the opening paper, *Ngo Van Long and Huilan Tian* examine the role of technology transfer within a strategic trade model. They concentrate on non-drastic and costly technology transfer in an international oligopoly and consider factors influencing the equilibrium outcome. They conclude that if the government cannot prove a pre-commitment in the pre-transfer phase for a low tax rate in the post-transfer phase, transfers might not take place that would normally been conducted under a low tax regime. With the governments' commitment, a higher welfare can be achieved. While short-term commitments over several years seem feasible, long-term commitments seem rather unlikely from an empirical point of view. *Theo Eicher's* comment highlights the authors' result that a minor technology gap between countries induces more technology trade than a large gap, confirming the observation that most of the trade in technology takes place between developed countries and not between developed and developing countries. Eicher proposes to embed the model into a general equilibrium framework allowing for endogenous technology costs and to show inter-industry effects.

There has been much written on the income and redistribution effects of international trade and capital movements. Surprisingly, only very few papers are concerned with a quantitative assessment of the issue. In his contribution "Income Redistribution, Trade Prices, and International Capital in Simulated Trade Models", *Henry Thompson* compares the quantitative effects of changing prices and capital endowments on income distributions in a variety of models. Quantitative price effects tend to follow patterns suggested by factor shares. The existing simulations indicate that factor price equalization holds across competitive industries, that foreign capital has only a negligible effect on factor prices and that trade holds more potential than capital in raising wages in low-income countries. In his comment, *Roland Döhrn* points out additional consequences that might arise from free trade and foreign capital. Trade and foreign capital may impact on technology, productivity and prices after trade liberalization, thus influencing income levels as well as income distribution.

Pascalis Raimondos-Møller and *Alan D. Woodland* ask whether establishing customs unions is a way forward in reaching global free trade. Indeed, special focus must be paid to the normative impact of a customs union to the rest of the world. Referring to Kemp and Wan (1976) as well as Kemp and Shimomura (2001), Raimondos-Møller and Woodland are particularly interested in the normative effects of customs unions when not all or none, but only some countries behave optimally. They extend the original proposition so that non-member countries adjust their tariffs in response to the creation of the customs union. Their proposition has important implications for the design of optimal trade policy, for example as in WTO Article XXIV regulating the common external tariff of customs unions. *Ian Wooton* comments the paper and addresses the critical issue of changes in the national production when joining a customs union. He doubts whether a revision of Article XXIV provides any improvements.

Traditional trade and trade policy models neglect institutional characteristics of markets and the trade distortions resulting thereof. *Kala Krishna, Abhiroop Mukhopadhyay* and *Cemile Yavas* overcome this shortcoming by modifying a traditional Ricardian model, a Specific Factor model and a Heckscher-Ohlin model to capture labor market distortions. The modified Ricardian model shows how factor market distortions affect labor allocation and output. In this case, international trade makes existing distortions even worse. Their analysis can be applied to various experiences and reform processes in developing economies, especially transition countries. For example, reforms including privatization can result in inefficiencies in production decisions, which would be worsened through trade. Thus, the urgency with which the WTO pushes forward international trade liberalization needs to be carefully revaluated in the light of these findings. *Kenzo Abe*'s comment is concerned with the fact that the country size of developing countries or transition economies is generally considered to be smaller than that of a developed country and that institutional distortions only have a negligible effect on the national welfare. He also emphasizes the point that it is the labor market distortion that makes a country lose from trade, not trade liberalization itself. Introducing an appropriate policy such as a subsidy could help to ease the negative effects of the market distortion.

K.C. Fung and *Andréa M. Maechler* combine two strands of literature, intra-industry trade and environmental consequences of trade, in a partial-equilibrium setting. In a variety of models, the authors analyze the environmental impact of trade liberalization in the context of intra-industry trade. Their main argument is that while trade expansion has an impact on environmental quality via the composition of national output, the driving force may be international oligopolistic rivalry instead of comparative advantage. Among other interesting results, Fung and Maechler conclude that environmental deterioration is determined by i) which country liberalizes trade and ii) the nature of pollution (local, transboundary or global). They also find that a large number of firms in the liberalized country increases the negative environmental impact of trade liberalization, giving rise to the policy advice not to push anti-trust policies forward because they could harm the environment. *Keith E. Maskus* encourages the authors in his comment to include a technology term into their models that could help to answer the question why openness can improve environmental use. This is especially important for small economies that are open to trade and that enjoy pro-competitive gains.

Julian Emami Namini develops a multi-sectoral model with Heckscher-Ohlin characteristics in order to gain more knowledge on international business cycle transmission that is driven by negative technology shocks. This compares to a situation particularly relevant for developing countries such as China. The author is predominantly interested in the exact process of transmission and its welfare implications. His model uses two countries and four sectors, two of which serve as intermediate input to the other two sectors producing final goods. The sign of the transmission channel seems to depend on the factor intensity of the sector in which the shock occurs. In a so-called trade pattern effect, a country may gain from a domestic temporary technological shock if a higher production of the capital intensive good leads to a future increase of the capital stock. Moreover, if a trade partner is hit by a shock, a country can neutralize the expected negative spillover effect by inducing a domestic technological shock. This neutralization may occur in sectors that are intra-sectoral correlated and do not interfere with the magnitude of comparative advantages. *Roberto A. de Santis* compares Namini's model with the standard two-goods model and highlights the main advantages and disadvantages of the approaches.

Recent years have witnessed the idea that trade protection is "for sale", as described in the eminent paper of Grossman and Helpman (1994). *Theo Eicher* and *Thomas Osang* empirically investigate US trade policy and compare the performance of Contribution Driven models and Political Support models. They find strong evidence confirming that protection is indeed for sale, but reject the Political Support models developed by Hillman (1982). Commenting the paper, *Volker Clausen* takes a closer look at supply-side and demand-side factors and calculates the optimal tariff for both approaches, first for a closed and then for an open economy. This tariff is then utilized to determine the respective production losses and tariff revenues.

Pei-Cheng Liao and *Kar-yiu Wong* examine the policy interactions between two governments in an international duopoly with vertical product differentiation, in which the foreign firm produces a low-quality good and exports it to the home country. Taken this framework, the authors prove that the foreign government has an incentive to set a minimum quality standard. There are situations in which the country with an inferior technology in quality improvement can use such a policy as a strategic instrument, shifting parts of the profit of the advanced firm towards its own firm, thereby increasing its own welfare. Interestingly, the results indicate that both countries' welfare increases. In contrast to other protectionist trade instruments, e.g. an export subsidy, setting a minimum quality standard is not prohibited by WTO regulations. As an extension, *Ngo Van Long* suggests a Bayesian game with two types of politicians (good and bad) and active foreign politicians to cover additional issues as for example certain externalities or reasonable arguments such as health or safety protection.

Udo Kreickemeier focuses on the issue of non-tariff trade barriers restricting imports by imposing a binding upper limit on import quantities and analyzes the welfare implications. Kreickemeier thereby explicitly considers the existence of involuntary unemployment by setting out a specific multi-sector efficiency wage model with unemployment in the equilibrium stage. The underlying idea of this approach stems from the notion that a lot of developed countries are unwilling to further liberalize trade because of concerns for domestic employment. The model's central result is the significance of the labor intensity as decisive variable. *Henry Thompson* offers his comments on the paper and proposes to shift the focus of the model also to the results of changing trade policy and to include political factors, e.g. unionization or labor laws.

The last years have shown an increasing application of the WTO dispute settlement body. The WTO's role in these international trade disputes is simulated in the paper of *Earl L. Grinols* and *Roberto Perrelli*. In a game theoretic model of the dispute settlement process, the authors want to know whether an estimate on the expected results can be obtained. The model's outcome is the prediction that reducing the costs of litigation leads to an increase in infringements and the number of litigated disputes. Especially for small countries, the WTO dispute settlement therefore contains incentives that do actually increase the number of trade disputes. *Henryk Kierzkowski* adds some interesting thoughts by concentrating on the issue of how to measure the size of countries.

Tran van Hoa in his contribution deals with China's accession to the WTO in 2001 in a new flexible Keyesian approach. His objective is to crystallize the effects on investment and growth. A variety of econometrical approaches is compared, thereby focusing on two-stage hierarchical-information estimators. The estimated growth equation seems to be capable of calculating the impact of China's WTO accession on its welfare. Whether or not this new approach dominates other statistical tools, is doubted by *Sweta C. Saxena* who notes that also "simpler" models estimate China's performance concerning trade, investment and growth quite accurately.

Fritz Breuss provides a detailed economic analysis of four recent WTO trade disputes. He not only concludes that the Dispute Settlement Body is biased towards larger countries (US, EU), but also notes that retaliation using tariffs is ineffective, distorts allocation and is difficult to control. Additionally, the calculation of the correct level of damage and also the level of retaliation is practically impossible. One of the reasons is the challenge of a missing hypothetical scenario in which no protectionist measures take place. Thus, Breuss proposes a lump-sum penalty transfer from the government of the non-complying country to the government of the country that has received authorization of compensation from the WTO. The latter government could then redistribute the received transfers to the companies which suffered the concrete loss. *Nicole Pohl* questions whether such a transfer system would work, as it would not allow the complainant to maintain pressure on the defending country. She also points to the global costs of trade disputes that must be included in a general welfare analysis.

We gratefully acknowledge funding from Duisburger Universitäts-Gesellschaft e.V. (DUG) as well as from Gesellschaft von Freunden und Förderern der Universität Duisburg-Essen e.V. (GFF).

We also would like to thank Andreas Eickel, Nadja Kremser and Christian Schabbel for the careful editing of this manuscript.

Duisburg, December 2004
Günter S. Heiduk and Kar-yiu Wong

Non-Drastic Technology Transfer in an International Oligopoly

Ngo Van Long* and Huilan Tian**

* Department of Economics, McGill University, Montreal, Canada
** Division of Management, University of Toronto at Scarborough, Canada

1 Introduction

Technology transfer has often been cited as one of the major contributing factors to the spectacular growth rates of East Asian economies. This paper studies some theoretical aspects of non-drastic and costly technology transfer from an advanced firm in a developed economy to a less advanced firm in a developing country. The two firms are Cournot rivals in a third market. We will examine the parameters that determine the potential gain from technology transfer and the impact of the developing country's government policies on the equilibrium extent of technology transfer.

Technology transfers can take the form of licensing or technological cooperation, such as the training of the technology recipient firm's technicians or managers by the advanced firm's counterparts. Examples of licensing include Samsung's licensing deals with (a) Toshiba for microwave technology, (b) Philips for color TV technology, (c) with JVC and Sony for VCR technology (Hobday 1995). The long term cooperation between Ericsson of Sweden and Intracom of Greece is an example of training to create an indigenous champion. Theoretical models often posit technology licensing as a costless jump in the knowledge level of the recipient firm that allows it to catch up with the advanced firm instantaneously. Costless technology transfer (e.g. licensing of codified knowledge) from an advanced firm to a rival firm has been studied by Marjit (1990), who assumes that the transfer takes place instantaneously, does not use up real resources, and brings the production cost of the laggard firm immediately to the level of the advanced firm. In practice, even licensing involves the transfer of both codified knowledge and tacit knowledge[1], the latter being primarily in the form of know-how, technical services, and training of the technology recipients. Technology transfers typically involve real resource costs that are incurred by both the transferor and the recipient. In order to capture these salient aspects of technology transfer, this paper explicitly introduces the costs of transfer that must be incurred by the transferor and the

[1] A survey by Rostoker (1984) indicated that almost 70% of all licensing agreements involve the transfer of tacit knowledge which is not protected by patents.

technology recipient. The emphasis of our paper is non-drastic[2] and costly technology transfer that aims at reducing production cost of the less advanced firm.

Why might an advanced firm want to transfer its technology to a rival? Such a transfer would increase the gross[3] profit of the rival, and reduce the gross profit of the technology transferor (given that the two firms are Cournot rivals both before and after the transfer). In return, the transferor can extract from the recipient some payment, in the form of a licensing fee, or royalties, or possibly some fraction of the shares issued by the recipient, without making the recipient worse off in comparison with the pre-transfer equilibrium. If the payment exceeds the sum of the real resource costs incurred by the transferor and the expected reduction in its gross profit, then one can presume that the transfer will take place[4].

We focus on the case where it is either not possible, or not desirable, to bring the cost level of the less advanced firm down to the level of the transferor. Non-drastic technology transfer may be the equilibrium outcome if the absorptive capacity of recipient firm's workers is very limited and extensive training is very costly. We seek to provide answers to the following questions: (i) if the two firms can negotiate on a lump-sum transfer[5], what is the equilibrium extent of technology transfer? (ii) how do government policies such as output subsidy or tax affect the equilibrium extent of technology transfer? (iii) what are the welfare implications of the lack of pre-commitment by the government of the developing country? (iv) how do parameters such as the interest rate and the marginal cost of transfer affect the time path of technology transfer?

This paper is organized as follows. In Section 2, we study a static model of technology transfer in the absence of government intervention, using the two-stage game framework of cost-manipulation games (Long and Soubeyran 2001). In Section 3, we examine the impacts (on the equilibrium technology transfer) of taxes that are set by the government of the technology recipient country, under the assumption that the government cannot pre-commit to future tax rates. In Section 3, we compare the results of Section 3 with the "benchmark case" where the government can pre-commit. In Section 4, we extend the model to a fully dynamic setting, using optimal control theory.

---

[2] A technology transfer is said to be "drastic"' if, after the transfer, the technology recipient becomes as efficient as the transferor. Under ideal conditions, i.e., if all the relevant knowledge can be codified, technology licensing may be an example of drastic technology transfer. See Marjit (1990), Mukhopadhyay et al. (1999), Ghosh and Saha (2002) for models of drastic technology transfer.

[3] By "gross profit", we mean the profit before subtracting (i) the fee charged by the transferor, (ii) real resource costs, such as training costs, etc.

[4] It is not always the case, however, that the maximum amount that can be extracted from the technology recipient can compensate for the transferor's expected decrease of gross profit. This point has been made by Marjit (1990) in the case of costless and drastic technology transfer.

[5] The charge for technology transfer can take the form of (i) a fixed fee, (ii) a royalty, (iii) a fixed fee plus a royalty. According to Rostoker (1984), in a survey of US firms, these three modes occurred in 13%, 39%, and 49% of cases, respectively. See Appendix A2 for a brief analysis of the case where both a royalty and a fixed fee are used.

2 The Basic Model

2.1 Assumptions and Notations

There are two firms. Firm i is located in country i, where i=1, 2. Country 2 is called the home country and country 1 is the foreign country. The two firms produce a homogenous good, and compete as Cournot rivals in a third country's market. Firm 1's technology is more advanced. This is reflected in a lower marginal cost, $c_1 < c_2^0$. Here, the superscript 0 denotes the pre-transfer marginal cost. The technology gap, denoted by g, is defined as: $g = c_2^0 - c_1 > 0$.

A transfer of technology from firm 1 to firm 2 is assumed to reduce firm 2's unit cost by the amount $g\gamma$ where γ is a constant, $0 < \gamma \le \gamma_{\max} \le 1$. The quantity γ is called the "extent of the technology transfer" (or degree of technology transfer). The parameter $\gamma_{\max}$ may reflect the impossibility of bringing firm 2's unit cost down to the cost level of firm 1. In what follows, to simplify notation, we assume $\gamma_{\max} = 1$.

In this section, we assume that the transfer takes place in just one instant, and that both before and after the technology transfer, the two firms behave as Cournot rivals. At the time of the transfer of technology, real resources (such as training time and travel costs of technicians) are used up. These are called "direct costs" of the transfer. The direct cost incurred by firm i is denoted by $\Omega_i(\gamma)$. After the transfer, the marginal cost of firm 2 is

$$c_2(\gamma) = c_2^0 - \gamma\left(c_2^0 - c_1\right) = c_2^0 - \gamma g \tag{1}$$

We will use c_2 to denote $c_2(\gamma)$ when there is no risk of ambiguity. The transfer, by narrowing the technology gap, changes the cost structure within the industry. Such a change entails changes in the Cournot equilibrium profits of the two firms. We model the technology transfer as a two-stage game. In stage 1, the two firms cooperatively choose the extent of transfer and the lump sum fee to be paid by the technology recipient. In stage 2, the post-transfer stage, they compete as Cournot rivals. The general framework for this type of two-stage game is set out in Long and Soubeyran (2001).

We assume that firm 2 must pay firm 1 a fixed fee for the transfer, and that there are no royalties[6]. The fixed fee is determined by cooperative Nash bargaining, to be explained later.

In this section, we assume that the governments do not change tax rates after the transfer. For simplicity, tax rates are assumed to be zero both before and after

---

[6] On the assumption that the owner of the patent plays the role of the Stackelberg leader to the licensees, Kamien and Tauman (1986) found that fixed fee licensing is superior to royalty-based licensing from the point of view of the inventor, as well as from the perspective of consumers. For other game theoretic analyses of the patentee's licensing strategies, see Katz and Shapiro (1985, 1986), and Kamien (1992).

the transfer. As usual, we solve the game backwards and begin by considering the post-transfer Cournot equilibrium.

2.2 Stage 2: The Post-transfer Cournot Equilibrium

The inverse demand function in the third market is $P=P(Q)$, where $Q=Q_1+Q_2$. The gross profit function of firm i is $\pi_i=P(Q)Q_i-c_iQ_i$. The equilibrium Cournot gross profits (before subtracting the direct costs and the transfer fee) are denoted by $\pi_1(c_1,c_2)$ and $\pi_2(c_1,c_2)$. These can be computed as follows:
The first order condition for firm i's output choice is

$$P'(\hat{Q})\hat{Q}_i+P(\hat{Q})=c_i \tag{2}$$

(here, the hat denotes Cournot equilibrium outputs, and we assume an interior solution). Summing (2) over $i=1,2$, we get

$$P'(\hat{Q})\hat{Q}+2P(\hat{Q})=C \tag{3}$$

where $C=c_1+c_2$. Equation (3) indicates that the equilibrium industry output, $\hat{Q}$, depends on C alone, as long as both firms produce[7].
From (2), the equilibrium output of firm i is

$$\hat{Q}_i=\frac{P(\hat{Q}(C))-c_i}{-P'(\hat{Q}(C))}=\hat{Q}_i(C,c_i)$$

and the equilibrium gross profit of firm i is

$$\pi_i=\left[P(\hat{Q}(C))-c_i\right]\hat{Q}_i(C,c_i)=\left[-P'(\hat{Q}(C))\right]\left[\hat{Q}_i(C,c_i)\right]^2$$

In what follows, we focus on the case of linear demand, $P=a-bQ$.
Equation (3) becomes: $-b\hat{Q}+2(a-b\hat{Q})=C$
Hence

$$\hat{Q}=\frac{2a-C}{3b} \tag{4}$$

and $P(\hat{Q}(C))=a-\left(\frac{2a-C}{3}\right)=\frac{a+C}{3}$

Firm i's equilibrium output is

$$\hat{Q}_i=\left(\frac{1}{b}\right)\left(\frac{a+C-3c_i}{3}\right)=\left(\frac{1}{3b}\right)(a-2c_i+c_j)\equiv\left(\frac{1}{3b}\right)Z_i \tag{5}$$

[7] Define $\phi(Q)=P'(Q)Q+2P(Q)$. We assume $\phi'(Q)<0$. Then for any given $C\in(0,\phi(0))$, there exists a unique $\hat{Q}=\hat{Q}(C)$ that satisfies the industry equilibrium condition (3).

and its equilibrium gross profit is

$$\pi_i = \left(\frac{1}{b}\right)\left(\frac{a+C-3c_i}{3}\right)^2 = \left(\frac{1}{9b}\right)\left(a-2c_i+c_j\right)^2 \tag{6}$$

In what follows, we assume that firm 2's equilibrium output is positive both before and after the technology transfer. This is ensured if the following condition is satisfied:

Assumption 1:

$$c_2{}^0 < \frac{1}{2}(a+c_1) \tag{7}$$

This assumption ensures $Q_2 > 0$, and also $Q_1 > 0$, because $c_1 \le c_2(\gamma)$. Industry gross profit (in the post-transfer Cournot equilibrium) is

$\Pi(\gamma) = \left(\frac{1}{9b}\right)\left[\left(a-2c_1+c_2\right)^2 + \left(a-2c_2+c_1\right)^2\right]$

We now define the gain in (Cournot equilibrium) industry gross profit as the result of technology transfer at the extent γ as follows:

$G(\gamma) = \Pi(\gamma) - \Pi(0)$

Lemma 1: The gain function is convex in γ, and is given by

$$G(\gamma) = \left(\frac{1}{9b}\right)\gamma g(5\gamma g + 2h) \tag{8}$$

where $h \equiv a - 5c_2{}^0 + 4c_1$

Proof: See Appendix A1.

Remark 1: Let $\hat{Q}_2{}^0$ and $\hat{Q}_1{}^0$ denote pre-transfer Cournot equilibrium outputs. Then h can be expressed as $h \equiv 3b\left(2\hat{Q}_2{}^0 - \hat{Q}_1{}^0\right)$, that is, $h \ge 0$ if and only if at the pre-transfer Cournot equilibrium, firm 1's output is not greater than twice that of firm 2. The marginal gain of the technology transfer is:

$G'(\gamma) = \left(10\gamma g^2 + 2hg\right)\left(\frac{1}{9b}\right)$

Thus $G'(0) \ge 0$ if and only if $h \ge 0$. It follows that there are three cases:

Case 1 (small technology gap): $G(\gamma)$ is positive and increasing for all $\gamma \in (0,1]$ (see Figure 1a). This case applies if and only if

$$5g \le a - c_1 \tag{9}$$

that is,

$$c_1 < c_2{}^0 \leq \frac{1}{5}a + \frac{4}{5}c_1 \tag{10}$$

In this case, if there is no direct cost of transfer (i.e., if technology transfer does not use up real resources), then there are gains for the firms to share at any positive level of technology transfer, and the optimal extent of technology transfer from firm 1 to firm 2 is the maximal extent, i.e., $\gamma^* = \gamma_{\max}$

Case 2 (intermediate technology gap): There exists a value $\bar{\gamma}$ in (0,1) such that $G(\gamma) > 0$ for all $\gamma > \bar{\gamma}$ and $G(\gamma) < 0$ for all $\gamma < \bar{\gamma}$. (see Figure 1b).This case applies if

$$2(a - c_1) > 5g > a - c_1 \tag{11}$$

Or equivalently,

$$\frac{1}{5}a + \frac{4}{5}c_1 < c_2{}^0 < \frac{2}{5}a + \frac{3}{5}c_1 \tag{12}$$

In this case, small levels of technology transfer ($0 < \gamma < \bar{\gamma}$) will reduce industry gross profit, but any level of technology transfer in the interval ($\bar{\gamma}$,1] will raise industry gross profit.

Case 3 (large technology gap): $G(\gamma) < 0$ for all γ in (0,1) (see Figure 1c). This case applies if and only if $G(1) \leq 0$, i.e.

$5g \geq 2(a - c_1)$

or equivalently,

$$\frac{2}{5}a + \frac{3}{5}c_1 \leq c_2{}^0 \tag{13}$$

In this case, the equilibrium industry gross profit in the absence of technology transfer exceeds the equilibrium industry gross profit after any positive level of technology transfer, and hence it is not optimal to have any amount of technology transfer.

The above results are illustrated in Figure 2. Along the horizontal axis, we measure c_1 . The vertical axis measures c_2 . Since $c_2{}^0 < c_1$ by assumption, only points above the 45 degree line are relevant. We are interested in values of c_1 and $c_2{}^0$ that are consistent with positive Cournot equilibrium output. Thus, in view of equation (5), only points inside the triangle defined by the conditions $c_1 \leq a, c_1 \geq 0$ and $c_2{}^0 \geq c_1$, will be considered. Inside this triangle, the region R_1 which is below the line

$$c_2{}^0 = \frac{1}{5}a + \frac{4}{5}c_1 \tag{14}$$

and above the 45 degree line, is the region in which $h>0$. In R_1, technology transfer by any amount $\gamma \in (0, \gamma]$ will improve industry profit. In Region R_2, bounded above by the line

$$c_2^0 = \frac{2}{5}a + \frac{3}{5}c_1 \tag{15}$$

and bounded below by the line described by equation (14), the technology gap is intermediate. Finally, in Region R_3, bounded above by the line

$$c_2^0 = \frac{1}{2}a + \frac{1}{2}c_1 \tag{16}$$

and bounded below by the line represented by equation (15), any positive technology transfer will reduce equilibrium industry profit .

Intuitive explanation: The intuition behind these results is as follows. Recall that the Cournot equilibrium outputs are given by equation (5). Suppose, as a result of the technology transfer, c_2 falls by $\varepsilon = \gamma g$. Firm 2's output will rise by $2\varepsilon/(3b)$ and the output of the more efficient firm will fall by $\varepsilon/(3b)$. Thus the cost saving achieved by producing firm 2's initial output at a lower cost is partially offset by the adverse composition effect: at the new Cournot equilibrium, the more efficient firm produces less than before, and the less efficient firm produces more than before. (There is also a price effect: industry output rises by $\varepsilon/(3b)$, and thus the price falls.) Firm 2's equilibrium profit rises (see Appendix A1), but firm 1's equilibrium profit may fall by a greater amount, if ε is large.

Proposition 1: If the technology gap is small, any positive amount of technology transfer will increase equilibrium industry gross profit. If the technology gap is medium, equilibrium industry gross profit will decrease if the degree of technology transfer is small, and will increase if the amount of technology transfer is large. If the technology gap is large, then any amount of technology transfer will reduce equilibrium industry gross profit.

2.3 Stage 1: Equilibrium Extent of Technology Transfer in the Presence of Direct Transfer Costs

So far, we have not taken into account the direct cost of technology transfer. In practice, technology transfers use up real resources, such as training costs, and these costs may be an increasing function of the extent of transfer. In this subsection, we postulate that both firms incur real costs of transfer. These costs are represented by convex transfer cost functions, denoted by $\Omega_i(\gamma)$:

$$\Omega_i(\gamma) = \frac{K_i}{2}\gamma^2 + F_i$$

where $F_i \geq 0$ is the fixed real resources cost of technology transfer incurred by firm *i*, and $K_i \geq 0$ is the slope of the marginal cost of technology transfer incurred by firm *i*. In stage 1, the two firms cooperatively choose the efficient extent of technology transfer so as to maximize the net gain function

$$N(\gamma) = G(\gamma) - \Omega_1(\gamma) - \Omega_2(\gamma), \quad \gamma \in [0,1] \tag{17}$$

Let γ^* be the solution of the maximization problem (17). The net gain $N(\gamma^*)$ is to be shared between the two firms, and the sharing is achieved by a lump sum transfer fee *f* which is the solution of a Nash bargaining problem. Let us denote the net payoff to firm *i* by V_i, where

$V_1 = \pi_1(\gamma^*) - \Omega_1(\gamma^*) + f$

and

$V_2 = \pi_2(\gamma^*) - \Omega_2(\gamma^*) - f$

The Nash bargaining problem is formulated as follows:

$$\max_{V_1, V_2} \left(V_1 - \pi_1{}^0\right)^{\delta} \left(V_2 - \pi_2{}^0\right)^{1-\delta} \tag{18}$$

subject to the constraint

$V_1 + V_2 = \pi_1(\gamma^*) - \Omega_1(\gamma^*) + \pi_2(\gamma^*) - \Omega_2(\gamma^*)$

i.e.,

$V_1 + V_2 = N(\gamma^*)$

where $\pi_i{}^0$ is firm *i*'s reservation level of payoff, i.e., its Cournot equilibrium profit in the absence of the transfer, and δ is the relative bargaining power of firm 1. ($0 < \delta < 1$.)

The solution to the Nash bargaining problem is given by

$V_1 = \pi_1{}^0 + \delta N(\gamma^*)$

$V_2 = \pi_2{}^0 + (1-\delta) N(\gamma^*)$

This implies that the equilibrium transfer fee is

$f = \pi_1{}^0 + \delta N(\gamma^*) - \pi_1(\gamma^*) + \Omega_1(\gamma^*)$

This means that, if $\delta = 0$, firm 1 (the transferor) will get a fee which is equal to the sum of the direct transfer cost that it incurs, $\Omega_1(\gamma^*)$, and the reduction in profit $\pi_1{}^0 - \pi_1(\gamma^*)$ which is caused by the increased competitiveness of firm 2 after the transfer. At the other extreme, $\delta = 1$ implies that the fee will be so high that the transferee will get a zero net gain. Intermediate values of δ imply both firms have positive net gains.

An interior maximum is possible if the direct cost function of the technology transfer, $\Omega(\gamma)=\Omega_1(\gamma)+\Omega_2(\gamma)$, is more convex than the gain function, $G(\gamma)$, such that the net gain function $N(\gamma)$ is strictly concave. At an interior maximum, we have the first order condition

$$G'(\gamma)-\Omega'(\gamma)=0$$

and the second order condition

$$10g^2-9b(K_1+K_2)<0$$

This gives the solution

$$\gamma^*=\frac{2hg}{9b(K_1+K_2)-10g^2}$$

which is positive if $h>0$ and $K_1+K_2>10g^2$. (Note that $\gamma^*<1$ if K_1+K_2 is sufficiently great.)

Proposition 2: If technology transfer involves real resource costs, and these costs are strictly convex, then the optimal degree of technology transfer may be less than 1.

3 The Effects of Anticipated Government Intervention

So far, we have assumed that neither government imposes taxes or subsidies on the outputs of the firms. We now consider the case where both before and after the technology transfer, the government of the home country (country 2) uses discretionary trade policy to maximize static social welfare. Assume that the home country's government cannot precommit its policy. Before the transfer, the government has a production tax t_2^0 in place (t_2^0 can be positive or negative; if t_2^0 is negative, the firm receives a subsidy). After the transfer, the government will apply a different tax rate, t_2^*. If no transfer takes place, then there is no change in the tax rate.

3.1 Determination of Pre-Transfer Tax

The home country government imposes a tax rate t_2^0 on the output of firm 2 (the laggard firm). Let m_2^0 denote the tax-inclusive marginal cost of output of firm 2 before the technology transfer:

$$m_2^0=c_2^0+t_2^0$$

Similarly, for firm 1, we define

$$m_1=c_1+t_1$$

We assume that t_1 is the same before and after the transfer. The pre-transfer Cournot equilibrium outputs are

$$\tilde{Q}_1 = \frac{1}{3b}\left(a + m_2^0 - 2m_1\right) \equiv \frac{1}{3b}\tilde{Z}_1 \tag{19}$$

where
$\tilde{Z}_1 \equiv a + m_2^0 - 2m_1$

$$\tilde{Q}_2 = \frac{1}{3b}\left(a + m_1 - 2m_2^0\right) \equiv \frac{1}{3b}\tilde{Z}_2 \tag{20}$$

where
$\tilde{Z}_2 \equiv a + m_1 - 2m_2^0$
Firm 2's equilibrium profit is

$$\tilde{\pi}_2 = b\left(\tilde{Q}_2\right)^2 = \frac{1}{9b}\left(\tilde{Z}_2\right)^2 \tag{21}$$

and the home country's tax revenue is
$\tilde{T}_2 = t_2^0 \tilde{Q}_2$
Assume that the home country's government wants to maximize a home welfare function which is a weighted sum of π_2 and T_2:
$W_2 = \tilde{\pi}_2 + \eta \tilde{T}_2$
where $\eta \geq 1$ is the marginal cost of public funds. In the pre-transfer period, the government chooses t_2^0 to maximize the pre-transfer social welfare W_2. The first order condition is

$$\frac{\partial W_2}{\partial t_2^0} = -\frac{4\tilde{Z}_2}{9b} + \eta\left(\frac{1}{3b}\tilde{Z}_2\right) - \eta t_2^0\left(\frac{2}{3b}\right) = 0$$

The second order condition is

$$\frac{\partial^2 W_2}{\left(\partial t_2^0\right)^2} = \frac{8}{9b} - \frac{12\eta}{9b} < 0$$

which is satisfied because $\eta \geq 1$. Thus, the optimal tax rate t_2^0 that maximizes the home welfare function is the solution of

$$-2\eta t_2^0 = \left(\frac{4 - 3\eta}{3}\right)\tilde{Z}_2$$

Lemma 2: In the pre-transfer equilibrium, the host country government's optimal policy is to subsidize its firm (i.e. t_2^0 <0) if $\eta < 4/3$, and to tax its firm (i.e., t_2^0 >0) if η >4/3. The optimal tax that maximizes the home welfare function is given by

$$t_2^0 = \left(\frac{3\eta - 4}{12\eta - 8}\right)\left(a + m_1 - 2c_2^0\right) = v\left(a + m_1 - 2c_2^0\right) \tag{22}$$

where

$$v = \frac{3\eta - 4}{12\eta - 8} \tag{23}$$

The optimal tax is zero if and only if $\eta = 4/3$.

Remark: Note that $v = 0$ if $\eta = 4/3$, and $v = -1/4$ if $\eta = 1$. Since $\eta \geq 1$, v is bounded below and above:

$$-\frac{1}{4} \leq v \leq \frac{1}{4} \tag{24}$$

These bounds will be used to determine the sign of several important terms.

The tax-inclusive *equilibrium* pre-transfer profit of firm 2 is, from (21) and (22)

$$\tilde{\pi}_2^e = \frac{1}{9b}\left(a + m_1 - 2c_2^0\right)^2 \left(\frac{6\eta}{12\eta - 8}\right)^2 \equiv \frac{\phi}{9b}\left(a + m_1 - 2c_2^0\right)^2 \tag{25}$$

where

$$\phi = \left(\frac{6\eta}{12\eta - 8}\right)^2 \tag{26}$$

For firm 1, the profit is

$$\begin{aligned} \tilde{\pi}_1^e &= \frac{1}{9b}\left(a + m_2 - 2m_1\right)^2 = \frac{1}{9b}\left(a - 2m_1 + c_2^0 + t_2^0\right)^2 \\ &= \frac{1}{9b}\left(a - 2m_1 + c_2^0 + v\left(a + m_1 - 2c_2^0\right)\right)^2 \end{aligned} \tag{27}$$

3.2 Post-Transfer Tax

Now assume that once the transfer has taken place, the home government optimizes the post transfer welfare function by setting a post-transfer tax rate t_2^P per unit of output of the home firm (firm 2). Here the superscript p signifies "post-transfer". Let

$m_2^P = c_2^P + t_2^P$

where

$c_2^P = c_2^0 - \gamma\left(c_2^0 - c_1\right) = c_2^0 - \gamma g$

The firms' post-transfer equilibrium outputs are

$$Q_1^P = \frac{1}{3b}\left(a + m_2^P - 2m_1\right) \equiv \frac{1}{3b} Z_1^P \tag{28}$$

$$Q_2^P = \frac{1}{3b}\left(a - 2m_2^P + m_1\right) \equiv \frac{1}{3b} Z_2^P \tag{29}$$

and their post-transfer profits are

$\pi_1^P = \frac{1}{9b}\left(Z_1^P\right)^2$

$\pi_2^P = \frac{1}{9b}\left(Z_2^P\right)^2$

The home government chooses t_2^P to maximize the welfare function

$W_2 = \pi_2^P + \eta t_2^P Q_2^P$

The first order condition yields the optimal post-transfer tax rate

$t_2^P = \left(\frac{3\eta - 4}{12\eta - 8}\right)\left(a + m_1 - 2c_2^P\right) = v\left(a + m_1 - 2c_2^P\right)$

It follows that the equilibrium post-transfer profits are

$$\pi_2^P = \frac{\phi}{9b}\left(a + m_1 - 2c_2^P\right) \tag{30}$$

$$\pi_1^P = \frac{1}{9b}\left(a - 2m_1 + c_2^P + v\left(a + m_1 - 2c_2^P\right)\right)^2 \tag{31}$$

The gain in industry profit that results from the transfer (after taking into account the new optimal tax set by the home government) is

$G^P(\gamma) = \pi_1^P(\gamma) + \pi_2^P(\gamma) - \tilde{\pi}_1^e - \tilde{\pi}_2^P$

Now

$\pi_2^P(\gamma) - \tilde{\pi}_2^e = \frac{\phi}{9b}\left(a + m_1 - 2c_2^P\right)^2 - \left(a + m_1 - 2c_2^0\right)^2$

$= \left(\frac{4\phi}{9b}\right)\left(\gamma^2 g^2 + \gamma g\left(a + m_1 - 2c_2^0\right)\right) > 0$

(where $a + m_1 - 2c_2^0 > 0$, in view of Assumption 1).

Thus we can state the following lemma:

Lemma 3: If the home government imposes a tax (or subsidy) on home firm's output to maximize home welfare, any amount of technology transfer will increase the equilibrium gross profit of the technology recipient.

Now let

$$B = a - 2m_1 + v\left(a + m_1\right) \tag{32}$$

The change in equilibrium profit of the supplier of technology is:

$$\pi_1^P(\gamma)-\tilde{\pi}_1^e=\frac{1}{9b}\left[\left(B+(1-2v)c_2^P\right)^2-\left(B+(1-2v)c_2^0\right)^2\right]$$
$$=\frac{1}{9b}(1-2v)^2\gamma^2g^2-\frac{\gamma g(1-2v)}{9b}\left(2B+2(1-2v)c_2^0\right) \tag{33}$$

which is convex in γ and is negative[8] for all $\gamma>0$.
Thus we obtain the following lemma:

Lemma 4: If the home government imposes a tax (or subsidy) on home firm's output to maximize home welfare, any amount of technology transfer will decrease the equilibrium gross profit of the transferor.

The gain in industry profit, taking into account the fact that the home government will choose t_2^P after the transfer, is

$$G^P(\gamma)=\frac{\gamma^2g^2}{9b}\left[4\phi+(1-2v)^2\right]+\frac{2\gamma g}{9b}\left[2\phi\left(a+m_1-2c_2^0\right)-(1-2v)\left(B+(1-2v)c_2^0\right)\right]$$

This function is strictly convex in γ and $G^P(0)=0$.

Note that in the case η =1 (the marginal cost of public funds is unity, the standard case in the strategic trade literature), we have v =-1/4 and ϕ =9/4, and

$$G^{P\prime}(0)>0 \quad \textit{if and only if} \quad a+\frac{1}{3}m_1-\frac{30}{9}c_2^0>0$$

This is in sharp contrast to the case where the home government is inactive. Recall that in that case

$$G'(0)>0 \quad \textit{if and only if} \quad a+4c_1-5c_2^0>0$$

For example, assume $c_1=m_1=0$. Then, if the initial cost c_2^0 satisfies the inequalities

$$5c_2^0>a>\frac{30}{9}c_2^0$$

We have the result that (i) with an inactive government, it is not in the interest of the two firms to have a small amount technology transfer, as such a transfer would reduce industry profit, but (ii) with an active home government, any amount of technology transfer would improve industry gross profit.

Proposition 3: Technology transfers that would not be undertaken under the laissez-faire regime may be carried out if the home government imposes optimal tax/subsidy on the output of the home firm, provided the marginal cost of public funds is 1 or near 1.

---

[8] Since 1-2v >0, and $c_2^P<c_2^0$, the right hand side of equation (33) is negative even if v>0.

What happens if the marginal cost of public fund η is great? Take the case η =2, so that v=1/8>0 and ϕ =9/4. Then

$G^{P\prime}(0) > 0$ *if and only if* $a + 9m_1 - 10c_2{}^0 > 0$
This condition is more difficult to satisfy than the condition $a + 4c_1 - 5c_2{}^0 > 0$.

Proposition 4: If the marginal cost of public funds is great, so that the government will tax the home firm's output, technology transfers that would be undertaken under the laissez-faire regime may not be carried out when the government cannot precommit to free trade after the technology transfer.

4 Optimal Precommitted Tax

We now study the "benchmark" case where the government of the technology recipient country can pre-commit, prior to the technology transfer, to a tax rate (on the output of the recipient firm) that it will impose after the technology transfer. Let $t_2{}^B$ denote the pre-committed tax rate, which would be applied if a transfer takes place. (Here, the superscript B refers to the "benchmark" case.) If no transfer takes place, the tax rate will be $t_2{}^0$. Here, $t_2{}^0$ is given by equation (22).
Denote by $m_2{}^B$ firm 2's tax-inclusive post-transfer marginal cost:

$$m_2{}^B = c_2{}^0 - \gamma g + t_2{}^B$$

and

$$m_2{}^0 = c_2{}^0 + t_2{}^0$$

For simplicity, we assume that country 1 imposes no tax on firm 1's output. The post-transfer equilibrium outputs are

$$Q_1{}^B = \frac{1}{3b}\left(a + m_2{}^B - 2c_1\right)$$

$$Q_2{}^B = \frac{1}{3b}\left(a + c_1{}^B - 2m_2{}^B\right)$$

and the post-transfer equilibrium profits (given that the transfer takes place) are

$$\pi_1{}^B = \frac{1}{9b}\left(a + m_2{}^B - 2c_1\right)^2$$

$$\pi_2{}^B = \frac{1}{9b}\left(a + c_1 - 2m_2{}^B\right)^2$$

If no transfer takes place, the equilibrium profits are

$$\pi_1{}^0 = \frac{1}{9b}\left(a + m_2{}^0 - 2c_1\right)^2$$

$$\pi_2{}^0 = \frac{1}{9b}\left(a + c_1 - 2m_2{}^0\right)^2$$

The effect of the transfer on the profits is

$$\Delta\pi_1 = \pi_1^{\ B} - \pi_1^{\ 0} = \frac{1}{9b}\left[\left(a + m_2^{\ B} - 2c_1\right)^2 - \left(a + m_2^{\ 0} - 2c_1\right)^2\right]$$

$$\Delta\pi_2 = \pi_2^{\ B} - \pi_2^{\ 0} = \frac{1}{9b}\left[\left(a + c_1^{\ B} - 2m_2^{\ B}\right)^2 - \left(a + c_1 - 2m_2^{\ 0}\right)^2\right]$$

The gross gain in industry profit is

$$\frac{1}{9b}\left[\left(a+m_2^{B}-2c_1\right)^2-\left(a+m_2^{0}-2c_1\right)^2+\left(a+c_1^{B}-2m_2^{B}\right)^2-\left(a+c_1-2m_2^{0}\right)^2\right]$$

and the net gain is

$$N^B\left(\gamma, t_2^{\ B}\right) = G^B\left(\gamma, t_2^{\ B}\right) - \Omega(\gamma)$$

The two firms will choose co-operatively the value γ^* that maximizes $N^B\left(\gamma, t_2^{\ B}\right)$, taking $t_2^{\ B}$ as given. Let $\gamma^*\left(t_2^{\ B}\right)$ denotes the solution of this problem. It can be shown that there exist two values $t_{\min}$ and $t_{\max}$ such that (i) $\gamma^*\left(t_2^{\ B}\right)$ for $t_2^{\ B} \geq t_{\max}$, (ii) $\gamma^*\left(t_2^{\ B}\right) = 1$ for $t_2^{\ B} \leq t_{\min}$, (iii) for $t_2^{\ B} \in \left(t_{\min}, t_{\max}\right)$,

$$0 < \gamma^* < 1 \quad and \quad \frac{\partial \gamma^*}{\partial t_2^{\ B}} < 0$$

The government knows the reaction function $\gamma^*\left(t_2^{\ B}\right)$ and chooses the tax rate $t_2^{\ B}$ to maximize the welfare function

$$W_2^{\ B} = V_2^{\ B} + \eta t_2^{\ B} Q_2\left(c_1, m_2^{\ B}\right)$$

where

$$m_2^{\ B} = c_2^{\ 0} - \gamma^*\left(t_2^{\ B}\right)\left(c_2^{\ 0} - c_1\right) + t_2^{\ B}$$

and

$$V_2^{\ B} = \pi_2^{\ 0} + (1 - \beta) N\left(\gamma^*\left(t_2^{\ B}\right), t_2^{\ B}\right)$$

Let $t_2^{\ B^*}$ denote the solution to this welfare maximization problem. It can be shown that the tax rate $t_2^{\ B^*}$ is lower than the value $t_2^{\ *}$ that would maximize the post-transfer welfare function. This result suggests the possibility of opportunistic behavior on the part of the home government: it can at first announce, before the transfer, that the post transfer tax rate will be $t_2^{\ B^*}$. This relatively low tax rate encourages the firms to agree on a high degree of technology transfer. Once the transfer has taken place, the direct transfer costs have been incurred, and the fee has been paid, these sunk costs are no longer relevant. The government's motive in the post transfer stage is to maximize post transfer welfare; and it will therefore adopt the post transfer tax $t_2^{\ *}$, which is higher than $t_2^{\ B^*}$. This is an instance of the well-known time inconsistency problem, which typically arises when the government can renege on its earlier announcement.

The time inconsistent solution cannot be an equilibrium of a game in which all agents are rational: the firms can anticipate that the government will renege, and therefore they do not believe that the announced value t_2^* will be honoured. In this case, the only possible equilibrium is the one depicted in the preceding section.

5 Optimal Time-Path when Technology Transfer Takes Time

In the real world, technology transfer takes time as well as consumes real resources. It seems more desirable to analyze the transfer in a dynamic setting. Let us modify the basic model by assuming that (i) the transfer of technology uses up time as well as real resources and (ii) the transfer cost becomes prohibitive if the transfer rate is high. We posit the situation where a drastic transfer (interpreted as a jump in γ from the value $\gamma = 0$ to the value $\gamma = 1$) is extremely costly, so that the optimal time path of technology transfer is a gradual one. To model this situation, we consider γ as a continuous function of time: $\gamma = \gamma(t)$. The initial technology gap is $g = c_2^0 - c_1$. We assume c_1 does not change with time. At any time t>0 we have $c_2(t) = c_2^0 - \gamma(t)(c_2^0 - c_1)$.We treat $\gamma(t)$ as a state variable. We interpret $\gamma(t)$as the *cumulative closure* of the technology gap. If at some time T>0, we have $\gamma(T) = 1$, then $c_2(T) = c_1$, that is, the gap is completely closed at time T. We want to find out whether it is optimal to close the gap completely at some future time T. The answer would depend on the cost of reducing the gap. To specify the cost, we introduce a control variable $I(t)$ defined by

$$\frac{\dot{\gamma}(t)}{1-\gamma(t)} = I(t)$$

Thus, $I(t)$ is the rate at which the technology gap is reduced. We call I the "transfer rate". The direct cost of I is assumed to be

$$C(I) = \frac{1}{2}\beta I^2 + \alpha I, \quad where\ \alpha \geq 0\ and\ \beta > 0$$

so that the marginal cost of I is $\alpha + \beta I$.

We assume that (i) at each t, the two firms are Cournot rivals in the product market, but (ii) they cooperate on the choice of the time path of technology transfer, so as to maximize the industry's net gain from the transfer. (This may be justified by the assumption that a transfer fee is charged, as an outcome of Nash bargaining). Here, we assume that the gross gain function $G(\gamma)$ is given by equation (8), and we assume that

$$G'(0) = \left(\frac{1}{9b}\right)2hg > 0$$

Thus, the two firms cooperatively solve the following optimal control problem

$$\max_I \int_0^\infty e^{-rt}\left(G(\gamma) - \alpha I - \frac{1}{2}\beta I^2\right)dt \tag{34}$$

subject to
$\dot{\gamma} = (1-\gamma)I \quad with \quad I \geq 0$
The current-value Hamiltonian is
$$H = G(\gamma) - \alpha I - \frac{1}{2}\beta I^2 + \psi(1-\gamma)I$$
and the Lagrangian is
$L = H + \lambda I$
The necessary conditions are
(i) The control variable I maximizes the Hamiltonian subject to $I \geq 0$

$$\frac{\partial L}{\partial I} = -\alpha - \beta I + \psi(1-\gamma) + \lambda = 0$$
$\lambda \geq 0, I \geq 0, \lambda I = 0$

This condition yields

$$I = I(\gamma,\psi) = \frac{\psi(1-\gamma)-\alpha}{\beta} \quad if\ \psi(1-\gamma) \geq \alpha \quad = 0 \quad if\ \psi(1-\gamma) < \alpha \tag{35}$$

(ii) The rate of change of the shadow price satisfies the differential equation
$$\dot{\psi} = \psi(r+I) - G'(\gamma) \tag{36}$$

Now we proceed with a phase diagram analysis of this problem. In Figure 3, the state variable γ is measured along the horizontal axis and the shadow price ψ is measured along the vertical axis. The curve $\psi = \dfrac{\alpha}{1-\gamma}$ is the dividing line between two regions. In Region A, which is below the curve, the transfer rate is I=0. In Region B, which is above the curve, the transfer rate is positive.

We consider the case in which the initial technology gap is small, as depicted in Figure 1a, and hence $G'(\gamma) > 0$ for all γ in (0,1]. We look for a steady state point (γ_{ss}, ψ_{ss}) where the subscript *ss* indicates steady state values. At a steady state, I=0, hence, setting $\dot{\psi} = 0$ and I=0, we get from (35) and (36):
$$\psi_{ss} = \frac{G'(\gamma_{ss})}{r} = \frac{\alpha}{1-\gamma_{ss}} \tag{37}$$

In the space (γ, ψ), we draw two curves: the curve $\psi_1(\gamma) = G'(\gamma)/r$, and the curve $\psi_2(\gamma) = \alpha/(1-\gamma)$. The intersection of these two curves, point E, gives the equilibrium pair (γ_{ss}, ψ_{ss}). The curve $\psi_1(\gamma)$ is positive, increasing and linear in γ for all $\gamma \in [0,1]$, with vertical intercept $G'(0)/r = 2hg/(9br)$ and slope $G''(\gamma)/r = 10g^2/(9br)$. The curve $\psi_2(\gamma)$ is positive, increasing and strictly convex in γ for all $\gamma \in [0,1]$, with a slope that tends to infinity as γ tends to 1. Its vertical intercept is α. Thus these curves intersect each other at a unique point, which is denoted as γ_{ss} in (0,1) provided $2hg > 9b\alpha r$.

Proposition 5: There exists a unique and positive steady state $\gamma_{ss}<1$ if the interest rate *r* and the marginal cost α are small enough. Thus, under these conditions, it is optimal to transfer technology, but the transfer is partial only: it is not optimal to close the gap completely. At the steady state, firm 2's production cost c_2 remains higher than that of firm 1.

In Figure 3, the curve $\psi_1(\gamma) = G'(\gamma)/r$ intersects the curve $\psi_2(\gamma) = \alpha/(1-\gamma)$ at the point (γ_{ss}, ψ_{ss}). Now, let us determine the shape of the curve $\dot{\psi} = 0$. The equation for this curve is

$$r\psi = G'(\gamma) - \left(\frac{\psi}{\beta}\right)[\psi(1-\gamma) - \alpha] \tag{38}$$

Total differentiation gives

$$\left[r + \frac{2\psi(1-\gamma)-\alpha}{\beta}\right]d\psi = \left[G''(\gamma) + \frac{\psi^2}{\beta}\right]d\gamma$$

Since

$$\frac{2\psi(1-\gamma)-\alpha}{\beta} > \frac{\psi(1-\gamma)-\alpha}{\beta} = I \geq 0$$

we have $\frac{d\psi}{d\gamma} > 0$ along the curve $\dot{\psi} = 0$.

The phase diagram indicates that there exists an approach path that leads to the steady state. Along this approach path, both ψ and γ increase over time. Now, for any constant *I*, consider the iso-transfer-rate curve

$$I(\gamma, \psi) = \frac{\psi(1-\gamma)-\alpha}{\beta} = I$$

This curve is convex and increasing in the space (γ, ψ), and it may intersect the approach path to the steady state at several places. We conclude that along the optimal path, the transfer rate *I(t)* may be non-monotone.

Proposition 6: Along the optimal path, the cumulative closure $\gamma(t)$ increases over time, but the transfer rate $\dot{\gamma}/(1-\gamma)$ may be non-monotone.

Proposition 7: The long-run cumulative closure, γ_{ss}, is a decreasing function of (i) the interest rate, and (ii) the transfer cost parameter α. It is independent of the parameter β.

Proof: An increase in r will shift the curve $\psi_1(\gamma)$ down, and an increase in α will shift the curve $\psi_2(\gamma)$ up. Both shifts move the intersection point E to the left.

6 Concluding Remarks

We have analyzed a simple model of technology transfer and considered factors that influence the equilibrium outcome. In particular, we have shown how government policies might affect the equilibrium degree of transfer. Our analysis indicates that if the government cannot pre-commit, in the pre-transfer stage, to a low tax rate in the post-transfer stage, then transfers that would take place under a low tax regime may not take place. A pre-commitment that no tax (or a very low tax rate) will be imposed in the post-transfer stage (a tax holiday) would encourage a greater degree of technology transfer and may result in a greater welfare sum for the home country, compared with the outcome that obtains when commitment is not feasible. In practice, governments can commit over a short horizon (e.g., five years) to a policy of a zero post-transfer tax, but long term commitments (say over 10 years) seem infeasible. Since technology transfer may take a long time, the assumption of no-commitment may be closer to reality than the assumption of full commitment.

Appendices

Appendix 1

Proof of Lemma A1 and Derivation of the gain function $G(\gamma)$

$$G(\gamma) = \Pi(\gamma) - \Pi(0) = [\pi_1(\gamma) - \pi_1(0)][\pi_2(\gamma) - \pi_2(0)]$$

Now,

$$\pi_1(\gamma) - \pi_1(0) = \frac{1}{9b}\left[\left(a - 2c_1 + c_2{}^0 - \gamma g\right)^2 - \left(a - 2c_1 + c_2{}^0\right)^2\right] \equiv \frac{1}{9b}\left[\left(Z_1{}^P\right)^2 - \left(Z_1{}^0\right)^2\right]$$

$$= -\gamma g\left(2a - 4c_1 + 2c_2{}^0 - \gamma g\right)/(9b) = \frac{1}{9b}\left(\gamma^2 g^2 - 2\gamma g\left(a - 2c_1 + c_2{}^0\right)\right)$$

where $2a - 4c_1 + 2c_2{}^0 - \gamma g = 2\left(a - 2c_1 + c_2{}^0 - \gamma g\right) - \gamma g > 0$. That is, firm 1's profit falls as a result of the transfer, which makes firm 2 more competitive. Similarly,

$$\pi_2(\gamma) - \pi_2(0) = \frac{1}{9b}\left(4\gamma^2 g^2 + 4\gamma g\left(a - 2c_2{}^0 + c_1\right)\right) > 0$$

It follows that

$$G(\gamma) = \left(\frac{1}{9b}\right)\gamma g(5\gamma g + 2h)$$

where $h \equiv a - 5c_2{}^0 + 4c_1 = 2Z_2{}^0 - Z_1{}^0$

Note that h>0 if and only if firm 1's output in the pre-transfer equilibrium is not greater than twice that of the laggard firm. The gain function $G(\gamma)$ is a strictly convex function of γ. Since $G(0) = 0$, the strict convexity of $G(\gamma)$ implies that if $G'(0) > 0$ then $G(\gamma)$ reaches its maximum at the right end of the interval [0,1].

Appendix 2

Combination of a lump sum transfer fee and a royalty

In this Appendix we study the case where the advanced firm charges the transferee a royalty rate R per unit of post-transfer output $Q_2{}^P$, as well as a negotiated lump sum fee prior to the transfer. We want to find out whether this two-part tariff results in a lower extent of technology transfer, and a lower welfare for technology recipient country. We also want to determine how tax rates influence the equilibrium royalty rate.

For simplicity, we assume that the pre-transfer tax rate $t_2{}^0$ and the post-transfer tax rate $t_2{}^P$ have been determined in advanced. (This assumption will be relaxed later.) Given $t_2{}^0$ and $t_2{}^P$, the firms play a two-stage game. In the first stage, the two firms negotiate on the extent of transfer γ, a royalty rate R per unit of output, and a fixed fee f; in the second stage, after the transfer, the firms compete as Cournot rivals by choosing their output levels.

As usual, we solve the second-stage first. Let $m_2{}^0$ (respectively, $m_2{}^P$) denote firm 2's pre-transfer (respectively, post-transfer) marginal cost (inclusive of tax etc.)

$$m_2{}^0 = c_2{}^0 + t_2{}^0$$

$$m_2{}^P = c_2{}^0 - \gamma g + t_2{}^P + R$$

If there were no technology transfer, the Cournot equilibrium outputs of the two firms would be

$$\hat{Q}_2{}^0 = \frac{1}{3b}\left(a - 2m_2{}^0 + c_1\right) \equiv \frac{1}{3b} Z_2{}^0$$

$$\hat{Q}_1{}^0 = \frac{1}{3b}\left(a - 2c_1 + m_1{}^0\right) \equiv \frac{1}{3b} Z_1{}^0$$

and their equilibrium profits would be

$$\hat{\pi}_2^0 = \frac{1}{9b}(a - 2m_2^0 + c_1)^2$$

$$\hat{\pi}_1^0 = \frac{1}{9b}(a - 2c_1 + m_1^0)^2$$

If the technology transfer takes place with extent γ >0 and the royalty rate is R, the post-transfer Cournot equilibrium outputs of the two firms are

$$\hat{Q}_2^{\,P} = \frac{1}{3b}\left(a - 2m_2^{\,P} + c_1\right) \equiv \frac{1}{3b} Z_2^{\,P}$$

$$\hat{Q}_1^{\,P} = \frac{1}{3b}\left(a - 2c_1 + m_1^{\,P}\right) \equiv \frac{1}{3b} Z_1^{\,P}$$

and industry output and price are

$$\hat{Q}^P = \frac{2a - c_1 - m_2^{\,P}}{3b}$$

$$\hat{P}^P = \frac{a + c_1 + m_2^{\,P}}{b}$$

The transferee's profit (after subtracting tax and royalty payments) is

$$\hat{\pi}_2^{\,P} = \frac{1}{9b}\left(a - 2m_2^{\,P} + c_1\right)^2$$

while the transferor's profit (after adding royalty receipts) is

$$\hat{\pi}_1^{\,P} = \left(\hat{P}^P - c_1\right)\hat{Q}_1^{\,P} + R\hat{Q}_2^{\,P} = \frac{1}{9b}\left(a - 2c_1 + m_1^{\,P}\right)^2 + \frac{R}{3b}\left(a - 2m_2^{\,P} + c_1\right)$$

For firm 2, the difference between post-transfer profit and pre-transfer profit is

$$\Delta\hat{\pi}_2 = \frac{1}{9b}\left[\left(Z_2^P\right)^2 - \left(Z_2^0\right)^2\right] = \frac{4}{9b}\left[\gamma^2 g^2 + \gamma g\left(a + c_1 - 2c_2^0 - 2R - 2t_2^P\right)\right] \\ + \frac{4}{9b}\left(t_2^0 - R - t_2^P\right)\left(a + c_1 - 2c_2^0 - R - t_2^P - t_2^0\right) \tag{39}$$

This is a complicated expression. In the special case where $t_2^{\,P} = t_2^{\,0}$, equation (39) reduces to

$$\Delta\hat{\pi}_2 = \frac{4}{9b}\left[\gamma^2 g^2 + \gamma g\left(Z_2^0 - 2R\right) - R\left(Z_2^0 - R\right)\right] \tag{40}$$

which is positive if R is small.
For firm 1, the difference between post-tranfer profit and pre-transfer profit is

$$\Delta\hat{\pi}_1 = \frac{1}{9b}\left[\gamma^2 g^2 + \gamma g\left(2a - 4c_1 + 2c_2^0 + 2c_2^P - 4R\right)\right] \\ + \frac{1}{9b}\left(R + t_2^P - t_2^0\right)\left(2a - 4c_1 + 2c_2^0 + R + t_2^P + t_2^0\right) + \\ \frac{R}{3b}\left(a + c_1 - 2R - 2c_2^0 - 2t_2^P\right)$$

The gain in industry profit is

$$G(\gamma;R) = \Delta\hat{\pi}_1 + \Delta\hat{\pi}_2 = \frac{5}{9b}\gamma^2 g^2 + \frac{\gamma g}{9b}\left(2a + 8c_1 - 10c_2{}^0 - 4R - 10t_2{}^P\right) + \frac{\left(R + t_2{}^P - t_2{}^0\right)}{9b}\left(10c_2{}^0 + 6R + 6t_2{}^P + 6t_2{}^0 - 2a - 8c_1\right) + \frac{R}{3b}\left(a + c_1 - 2R - 2c_2{}^0 - 2t_2{}^P\right) \tag{41}$$

Equation (41) indicates that the effect of the introduction of a royalty rate R on the gain curve $G(\gamma;R)$ (where G is plotted on the vertical axis and γ on the horizontal axis) is (i) to reduce the slope of G by the the amount $4Rg/(9b)$ and (ii) to shift the vertical intercept by the last two terms on the right hand side of (41). In particular, in the case where $t_2{}^0 = t_2{}^P$, the gain function is

$$\begin{aligned} G(\gamma;R) &= \frac{5}{9b}\gamma^2 g^2 + \frac{2\gamma g}{9b}\left(2Z_2{}^0 - Z_1{}^0 - 4R\right) + \frac{R}{9b}\left(2Z_1{}^0 - Z_2{}^0 + 6t_2\right) \\ &= \frac{5}{9b}\gamma^2 g^2 + \frac{2\gamma g}{9b}(2h - 4R) + \frac{R}{9b}\left(2Z_1{}^0 - Z_2{}^0 + 6t_2\right) \end{aligned} \tag{42}$$

For any given R, the firms cooperatively choose γ to maximize the net gain

$$\max_{\gamma} G(\gamma;R) - \frac{K}{2}\gamma^2 - F \tag{43}$$

where $K = K_1 + K_2$ and $F = F_1 + F_2$.

The first order condition is

$$\frac{\partial G}{\partial \gamma} - K\gamma = 0$$

and the second order condition is

$$\frac{\partial^2 G}{\partial \gamma^2} - K < 0$$

(the SOC is satisfied if $9bK > 10g^2$.) To find the effect of an increase in R on the equilibrium transfer extent γ^*, we differentiate the equation (43):

$$\frac{\partial^2 G}{(\partial\gamma)^2}d\gamma^* + \frac{\partial^2 G}{\partial\gamma\partial R}dR - Kd\gamma^* = 0$$

Hence

$$\frac{d\gamma^*}{dR} = -\frac{\dfrac{\partial^2 G}{\partial\gamma\,\partial R}}{\dfrac{\partial^2 G}{(\partial\gamma)^2} - K} < 0$$

because

$$\frac{\partial^2 G}{\partial\gamma\,\partial R} = -\frac{4g}{9b} < 0$$

Thus we obtain the proposition:

Proposition A1: The higher is the royalty rate, the lower is the equilibrium extent of technology transfer.

In particular, in the case where $t_2^{\,0} = t_2^{\,P}$, we obtain

$$\gamma^* = \frac{g(2h - 4R)}{9bK - 10g^2} = \gamma^*(R)$$

The net gain is: $G(\gamma^*(R); R) - \frac{K}{2}\gamma^*(R) - F \equiv \eta(R)$

Now, in the first stage of the game, payoff functions for the firms are

$$V_1 = \pi_1(\gamma^*(R), R) - \Omega_1(\gamma^*(R)) + f$$
$$V_2 = \pi_2(\gamma^*(R), R) - \Omega_2(\gamma^*(R)) - f$$

where *f* is the lump sum fee. The two-part tariff (f^*, R^*) is the solution of the following Nash bargaining problem

$$\max_{R, V_1, V_2} (V_1 - \pi_1^{\,0})^{\delta} (V_2 - \pi_2^{\,0})^{1-\delta}$$

subject to

$$V_1 + V_2 = \pi_1(\gamma^*(R), R) - \Omega_1(\gamma^*(R)) + \pi_2(\gamma^*(R), R) - \Omega_2(\gamma^*(R))$$

i.e.,

$$V_1 + V_2 = \eta(R)$$

The solution is: R^* maximizes the net gain, $\eta(R)$

$$V_1 = \pi_1^{\,0} + \delta\,\eta(R^*)$$
$$V_2 = \pi_2^{\,0} + (1 - \delta)\eta(R^*)$$

This implies that the fixed fee is

$$f^* = \pi_1^{\,0} + \delta\,\eta(R^*) - \pi_1(\gamma^*(R^*), R^*) + \Omega_1(\gamma^*(R^*))$$

From these equations we can determine how changes in the tax rate affect the equilibrium two-part tariff (R^*, f^*) and the equilibrium extent of transfer, $\gamma^*(R^*)$.

References

Ghosh A, Saha S (2002) Trade Policy in the Presence of Technology Transfer. University of New South Wales

Hobday M (1995) Innovation in East Asia: The Challenge to Japan. Edward Elgar

Kamien MI (1992) Patent Licensing. Chapter 11. In: Aumann RJ, Hart S (eds) Handbook of Game Theory 1, Elsevier, pp 332–354

Kamien MI, Tauman Y (1986) Fees versus royalties and the private use of a patent. Quarterly Journal of Economics 101 : 471–91

Katz M, Shapiro C (1985) On the licensing of innovations. Rand Journal of Economics 16 : 504–20

Katz M, Shapiro C (1986) How to license intangible property. Quarterly Journal of Economics 101 : 567–89

Long NV, Soubeyran A (2001) Cost Manipulation Games in Oligopoly, with Cost of Manipulating. International Economic Review 42 : 505–533

Marjit S (1990) On a non-cooperative theory of technology transfer. Economics Letters 33 : 293–298

Mukhopadhyay S, Kabiraj T, Mukherjee A (1999) Technology Transfer in Duopoly: The Role of Cost Asymmetry. International Review of Economics and Finance 8 : 363–374

Rostoker M (1984) A Survey of Corporate Licensing. IDEA 24 : 59–92

Comment

Theo Eicher

Department of Economics, University of Washington, Seattle, USA

Ngo Van Long and Huilan Tian provide a well-crafted analysis of technology transfer within a strategic trade model. The authors characterize the adoption of technology under resource costs, which are assumed to include transfer, time and government policy/tax costs. The question posed is an important one; the authors not only assert a motivation, but also provide crucial empirical support with real world micro evidence. The examples of Toshiba and Samsung are powerful illustrations of the relevance of the model. Aside from the micro evidence there is also abundant cross-country evidence to support the authors' claims that this is an active and important research area. Coe et al. (1994) show the significance of foreign direct investment on economic growth and the associated threshold effects. Benhabib and Spiegel (1994) and Borensztein et al. (1995) prove the importance of human capital in the technology transfer process. In their model and data, technology adoption is a function of general human capital accumulation and training on firm specific technology.

The model developed by the authors is rich and provides intriguing results. The most important one is that technology transfers are shown to be more likely when the technology gap is small (proposition 1). In some sense this proposition, based on a formal model of technology transfer, flies in the face of many of the *assumptions* on technology transfer in growth models. Often it is simply assumed that the farther the country is behind, the faster it catches up, along the lines of Nelson and Phelps (1966). However, the result provides exactly the theoretical evidence to explain why the lion share of foreign investment and licensing and technology transfers occur *among* OECD countries, not between OECD and developing countries.

Another intriguing mechanism explained by the Ngo Van Long and Huilan Tian model is that the technological leader's output falls by less than the laggard's output rises after technology transfer occurs. Price effects, together with the composition effects (depending on the specific demand assumptions), are shown to be crucial to analyze the exact impact of the transfer.

Transfer costs are shown to rule out perfect technology transfer, and optimal government policy might subsidize the host country firm in that case. Of course this introduces an inherent tension between profits handed to a domestic firm and general consumer welfare. The issue of optimality of policy intervention is hard to assess in a model that focuses on one industry to the degree that general predictions about a full-fledged general equilibrium would be impossible.

It would certainly be interesting to embed the model in a rich general equilibrium framework to pick up inter-industry effects to analyze government welfare. In addition, it would be a wonderful extension to move away from fixed technology transfer fees and introduce royalties or allow for technology costs that are endogenous, for example depending on the level of human capital in the host country. My guess is that the results may only be augmented but not qualitatively changed.

Finally, I would be interested to an extension that speaks to endogenous bargaining power between firms. It is certainly conceivable that firms that possess the ultimate technology wield strong bargaining power as to which country or location should produce, especially if this technology allows for high value added and high paying jobs, which are key interests of every locality. My suggestions highlight how rich the current framework that Long and Tien built actually is, and how appealing their existing results are. I am eagerly awaiting further interesting results from future extensions.

References

Benhabib J, Spiegel M (1994) The Role of Human Capital in Economic Development: Evidence from Aggregate Cross-Country Data. Journal of Monetary Economics 34 : 143–173

Borensztein E, DeGregorio J, Lee JW (1995) How Does Foreign Direct Investment Affect Economic Growth?. NBER Working Paper 5057

Coe DT, Helpman E, Hoffmaister AW (1995) North-South R&D Spillovers. CEPR Working Paper 1133

Nelson R, Phelps E (1966) Investment in Humans, Technological Diffusion, and Economic Growth. American Economic Review 56 (2) : 67–75

Income Redistribution, Trade Prices, and International Capital in Simulated Trade Models

Henry Thompson[1]

Economics, Comer Hall, Auburn University, Auburn, USA

Introduction

International trade and capital both increase and redistribute income across domestic factors of production. This income redistribution may explain in part the lack of universal support for free international commerce. In comparative static models of small open economies, price changes due to trade cause factor price adjustments. The Stolper-Samuelson qualitative price link is based on factor intensity but little intuition has developed beyond the two-factor, two-good model. Similarly, income redistribution due to foreign capital has been difficult to generalize beyond simple models. Further, there is little insight into the magnitudes of these general equilibrium effects. The quantitative implications of introducing specific factors of production have not been explored. Finally, there has been no investigation of the quantitative distortions of aggregation. Simulations provide insight into these issues.

The present paper synthesizes a series of simulations of the general equilibrium model of production and trade developed by Jones (1965), Chipman (1966), Jones and Scheinkman (1977), Chang (1979), Ethier (1974), and Takayama (1982), based directly on the classic work of Edgeworth, Heckscher, Ohlin, Vanek, and Samuelson. Underlying assumptions are homothetic neoclassical production functions with constant returns, competitive pricing of homogeneous products in small open economies, and full employment of homogeneous factors of production. The present simulations are more theoretical exercises than the policy oriented computable models such as those of Fullerton et al. (1985) or Hertel and Tsigas (1988).

Factors of production in the present simulations include the various skill groups of labor from the eight skill categories reported by the US Census. Capital input is derived as the residual of industrial value added from the Census of Manufacturing. Clark et al. (1988) show that none of these labor groups can be aggregated and the present aggregations provide insight into the resulting distortions. Simula-

[1] Thanks for suggestions go to Kwan Choi, Roland Döhrn, Panos Hatzipanayotou, Andres Jauregui, Henry Kinnucan, Alexander Sarris, Kar-yiu Wong, and others at the WTO Conference in Duisburg.

tions include models with specific factors of production allowing comparisons with impacts on shared factors.

For notation, let w represent endogenous factor prices, p prices of finished products exogenous to the small open economy, and K the exogenous capital endowment. Analysis begins with estimates of $\delta w_i/\delta p_j$ and $\delta w_i/\delta K$ elasticities, the effects of changing prices and foreign capital on factor prices. A free trade "program" of 1% price changes is multiplied by the matrix of $\delta w_i/\delta p_j$ comparative static elasticities to derive potential percentage changes in factor prices. Similarly, 1% changes in the capital stocks are multiplied by the matrix of $\delta w_i/\delta K$ elasticities to project potential effects of foreign capital.

Theoretical Anticipations

Changing prices of traded products with constant endowments affect factor prices as reflected in the general equilibrium $\delta w_i/\delta p_j$ elasticities, denoted by w_{ij}. In the model with two factors and two products, the Stolper-Samuelson (1941) theorem establishes a qualitative link between prices of products and factors based on factor intensity. The magnification effect of Jones (1965) shows that any ranking of percentage changes in prices of products is flanked by percentage changes in factor prices. Regarding the w_{ij} matrix of comparative static elasticities, for every price p_m there must be a factor h such that $w_{mh} > 1$ and a factor k such that $w_{mk} < 0$. For any ceteris paribus price change, some factor owner must win in terms of real income while another must lose. The w_{ij} elasticities in the present simulations are elastic, illustrating the magnification effect.

A changing capital endowment with prices of traded products held constant affects factor prices as reflected by $\delta w_i/\delta K$ or w_{iK} elasticities. Foreign capital in the present models is assumed to directly add to an exogenous capital endowment with no change in the underlying production function. While national income rises, the entire gain goes to the capital owner due to the competitive envelope property. As a general property, the derived w_{iK} elasticities are nearly zero in all of the present simulations.

Simulations of Factor Proportions Models of Production and Trade

The foundation of factor substitution is a specified cost or production function. Cobb-Douglas (CD) production functions have unitary elasticities of substitution. Balistreri et al. (2001) point out that CD technology cannot be rejected as a null hypothesis for 20 of 28 US manufacturing industries, and all but one of the others have Leontief technology, suggesting Cobb-Douglas is a reasonable starting place for simulations. Flexible translog functions developed by Christensen et al. (1973) allow variation in the elasticity of substitution along isoquants and are typically estimated with systems of partial derivative factor share equations. Uzawa (1962) develops properties of constant elasticity of substitution (CES) production.

In a model with translog production estimated across US states, Thompson (1997b) estimates own factor price elasticities of -1.4 for skilled labor, -1.2 for unskilled labor, and -0.9 for capital. The strongest cross price elasticities are between skilled and unskilled labor, both only about unit value, with capital a weak substitute for both types of labor. Weak substitution between capital and labor is consistent with the literature, including Arrow, Chenery et al. (1961).

Free trade might be expected to lower the US price of aggregated manufactures while raising the relative price of exported business services. Changing prices have elastic effects on factor prices in the comparative statics. Table 1 reports factor price adjustments for a free trade "program" with the price of aggregate manufactures falling 1% and the price of services rising 1%. The extremely elastic wage effects suggest there is a great deal at stake in the move toward free trade. In stark contrast, a change in the stock of capital has negligible wage effects in Table 1. Further, free trade generally causes prices to change much more than 1% while a 1% increase in the capital stock would represent huge investment. These results are robust across a number of simulations of Cobb-Douglas, CES, and translog production.

Table 1. US Factor Price Adjustments to "Trade Program" and Capital Stock Change

	1% price changes [%]	1% increase in K [%]
Three-factor model[a]		
Skilled wage	17	0.3
Unskilled wage	-15	-0.0
Capital	2	-0.3
Disaggregated labor adjustment, translog production[b]		
Professional wage	2	0.1
Technical wage	2	0.1
Service wage	2	0.1
Resource wage	-5	1.3
Craft wage	-1	0.1
Operator wage	-6	0.0
Handler wage	0	0.1
Capital	2	-0.3

[a] Thompson (1997b); Robust For Cobb-Douglas, CES, And Compliments, Thompson (1995a).

[b] Thompson (1990); Robust For CES Production, Thompson (1997a).

Elasticities of factor prices with respect to factor endowments are close to zero in all the present simulations, a result I have called *near factor price equalization* (NFPE). With an equal number of factors and products, FPE holds and $\delta w/\delta K = 0$. When endowments change, outputs serve as "shock absorbers" leaving little impact on factor demands.

In a 3x2 model of the US economy, Thompson (1995a) compares the influence of factor intensity and substitution on comparative static elasticities with Cobb-

Douglas, CES, translog, and production with very strong complements. The w_{ij} elasticities are consistent across all simulations and the w_{iK} elasticities are all nearly identical and close to zero.

Disaggregating the eight labor skill groups, Thompson (1990) reports somewhat larger own translog factor cross price elasticities, between -1 and -3. Factors remain weak substitutes because of the strong influence of factor shares in deriving cross price elasticities. Aggregation lowers the degree of substitution as anticipated in the literature. These disaggregated factor price adjustments in Table 1 are much smaller than in the aggregated model but remain elastic according to the magnification effect. Aggregation exaggerates the w_{ij} elasticities, cofactors of factor shares that increase when aggregated. NFPE holds for the disaggregated labor groups in Table 1 except for the wage of resource workers due to a very high capital share in agriculture.

Thompson (1997a) examines a similar model with CES production and a wide range of substitution for sensitivity. The free trade program has slightly smaller effects than with translog production and the wage of handlers rises slightly. Foreign capital has a weak positive impact on all wages. Regarding robustness, wide variations in the CES have very little impact on the comparative static results.

With CES production in a group of less developed and newly industrialized countries, Thompson (1995b) finds unskilled labor would gain substantially with free trade characterized by higher prices for exported manufactures and lower prices for imported business services. In the 1% free trade program of Table 2, unskilled wages rise up to 18% in Mexico. There should be opponents to free trade, however, with losses of skilled labor ranging up to 13% in Bolivia and capital losses as high as 5% in Argentina and Mexico. While labor disaggregation would lower estimated elasticities, free trade involves sizeable price changes. There is apparently quite a bit at stake inside the NICs and LDCs as they move toward free trade.

Table 2. NIC and LDC Adjustment to 1% Trade Program[a]

	Unskilled wage [%]	Skilled wage [%]	Capital return [%]
Mexico	18	-2	-5
Argentina	13	-2	-5
Ecuador	9	-6	-1
Taiwan	7	-3	-4
Bolivia	6	-13	-5
Korea	6	-4	-1
Venezuela	6	-9	-0
Turkey	4	-10	-0

[a] CES Production, Thompson (1995b).

Relative Influence of Factor Shares and Substitution

The underlying reason for the dominance of factor shares in the w_{ij} elasticities is straightforward. Elasticities of substitution ε_{ik} defined as $\delta ln(a_{ij}/a_{kj}) / \delta ln(w_k/w_i)$ are constant along isoquants with CES production and with CD production they equal 1. Cross price elasticities σ_{ik} defined as $(\delta lna_{ij} / \delta lnw_k)$ depend almost entirely on factor shares θ_{kj}, written as $w_k a_{kj}/p_j$. Sato and Koizumi (1973) show that $\sigma_{ik} = \theta_{kj}\varepsilon_{ik}$. With CD technology, it follows that $\sigma_{ik} = \theta_{kj}$. In the present estimates of translog production, the ε_{ik} are close to unit value.

Relative sizes of the w_{ij} and w_{iK} elasticities are due to properties of cost functions. Cost minimizing factor inputs are positive first derivatives of cost functions by Shephard's lemma, $\delta c/\delta w = a$, and factor shares θ_{kj} are built from these first derivatives. Factor substitution elasticities are based on second derivatives of cost functions, $\delta a/\delta w = \delta^2 c/\delta w^2$. Own effects are negative and the interactive cross terms $\delta a_i/\delta w_k = \delta^2 c/\delta w_i \delta w_k$ are generally small, ensured by addivity and concavity constraints. In the simulations, a derived matrix of cross price elasticities σ_{ik} is combined with a matrix of factor shares θ_{kj} and a matrix of industry shares into a comparative static system. The derived w_{ij} elasticities are cofactors of relatively large factor shares while w_{iK} elasticities are cofactors of smaller substitution terms. Generally, w_{ij} elasticities appear to depend little on substitution and w_{iK} elasticities are nearly zero. In the special case of even models, w_{ij} elasticities are completely independent of substitution and w_{iK} elasticities are all zero.

Simulations of Specific Factors Models

In a specific factors model of the Japanese economy, Thompson (1994) examines the potential effects of protection across industrial wages given Cobb-Douglas production. Protection of an industry has a positive elastic effect on that wage, weak negative effects on other industrial wages, and a weak positive effect on the capital return. The example of a 1% change in the price of iron & steel is reported in Table 3.

Table 3. Japanese Industry Specific Labor[a]

	Δ1% iron & steel price [%]
Iron & steel wage	4
Other industrial wages	-0.5 to -0.01
Shared capital	0.1
	Δ1% in capital stock
Capital return	-0.3
Non-metallic minerals wages	2
Agricultural wages	2
Finance wages	1
Iron & steel wages	1
Other wages	0

[a] Cobb-Douglas Production, Thompson (1994).

Specific factors absorb price shocks. If a specific factor were to become mobile across industries, there would be a dampened price effect. An increase in foreign capital has a slight negative effect on the return to capital, very inelastic effects on most industrial wages, and elastic effects on a few industrial wages.

The NAFTA literature anticipates US industries intensive in production labor will face increased import competition. In a study of the effects of projected NAFTA price changes on 17 Alabama manufacturing industries, Thompson (1996) uses Cobb-Douglas production with industry specific capital, production labor, and nonproduction labor. Testing various vectors of price changes for sensitivity, output effects are found to be inelastic with own output elasticities less than 0.1 as summarized in Table 4. Sector specific capital returns are very sensitive with returns adjusting as much as 20% to the vector of 1% price changes. In the long run, such capital return shocks would significantly affect investment and subsequently outputs. The model then projects long run output adjustments in the range of 20%. Across simulations, production wages fall from 1% to 7% while nonproduction wages increase up to 3%.

Table 4. NAFTA and Alabama Manufacturing with Industry Specific Capital[a]

Short run output effects < 0.1%
Δ specific capital returns, up to 20% - similar long run output effects
(-) labor intensive industries ↓ textiles, apparel, furniture
(+) capital intensive industries ↑ chemicals, equipment, machinery, instruments
-1% < %Δ production wages < -7%
0% < %Δ nonproduction wages < 3%

[a] Cobb-Douglas Production, Thompson (1995), Various Vectors of Price Changes.

In a study of Bolivia's entry into Mercosur, Thompson and Toledo (2001) combine CES production with the government projection of Mercosur price changes in a specific factors model with shared skilled and unskilled labor. Results are summarized in Table 5. Skilled and unskilled labor are projected to suffer moderate wage declines, while sector specific capital returns vary widely. These factor price adjustments are robust over a range of sensitivity analysis. A novel theoretical property is uncovered by these simulations, namely that the w_{ij} elasticities are invariant with respect to the elasticity of substitution given CES production.

Table 5. Mercosur and Bolivia with Industry Specific Capital[a]

Sector-specific capital, shared skilled and unskilled labor		
	Projected price changes [%]	%Δ capital returns [%]
Business services	-20	-25
Agriculture	-12	-25
Mining	4	14
Natural gas	8	23
Manufacturing	30	47
		%Δ shared labor [%]
Skilled wage		-6
Unskilled wage		-1

[a] CES Production, Toledo and Thompson (2001).

Conclusion

Support for free trade is less than universal and the present simulations suggest the high degree of potential income redistribution may be a primary reason. Price changes due to free trade can be expected to substantially alter income distribution following patterns suggested by factor intensity or relative factor shares. While defining factor intensity remains a theoretical challenge with many factors and many products, relative factor shares anticipate the general equilibrium price links.

The theoretical literature has concentrated on isolating conditions under which there would be unambiguous qualitative factor intensity price links but very little intuition has evolved. It is reassuring that quantitative price effects tend to follow patterns suggested by factor shares. Elastic effects of changing prices on factor prices imply substantial income redistribution with a move to free trade, and specific factors are especially sensitive.

Simulations can gauge the quantitative implications of variable returns, nonhomothetic production, various production and cost functions, different utility functions, international monopoly and monopsony power, heterogeneous products and factors, unemployment, elastic factor supply, joint production, and so on. The effects of aggregation can be examined in simulations. Specific policy issues for various countries or regions can be examined. Detailed production data can focus on disaggregated industries.

The present simulations suggest factor price equalization would at least nearly hold across competitive economies and foreign capital has a negligible impact on factor prices. It bears repeating that the move to free trade promises to substantially redistribute income among factors of production. To reach the goal of raising unskilled wages in poor countries, trade holds more potential than foreign capital.

References

Arrow K, Chenery HB, Minhas BS, Solow R (1961) Capital-labor substitution and economic efficiency. Review of Economic Statistics 43 : 225–250

Ballard C, Fullerton D, Shoven J, Whalley J (1985) A General Equilibrium Model for Tax Policy Evaluation. University of Chicago Press, Chicago

Balistreri E, McDaniel C, Wong E (2001) An estimate of US industry level capital-labor substitution elasticities: Cobb-Douglas as a reasonable starting point? USITC Working Paper 2001–12A

Chang W (1979) Some theorems of trade and general equilibrium with many goods and factors. Econometrica 47 : 709–726

Chipman J (1979) A survey of the theory of international trade: Part 3, the modern theory. Econometrica 34 : 18–76

Christensen L, Jorgensen D, Lau L (1973) Trancendental Logarithmic Production Frontiers. The Review of Economics and Statistics 55 : 28–45

Clark D, Hofler R, Thompson H (1988) Separability of capital and labor in US manufacturing. Economics Letters 26 : 197–201
Clark D, Thompson H (1983) Factor movements with three factors and two goods in the US economy. Economics Letters 12 : 53–60
Clark D, Thompson H (1986) Immigration, international capital flows, and long run income distribution in Canada. Atlantic Economic Journal 14 : 24–29
Clark D, Thompson H (1990) Factor migration and income distribution in some developing countries. Bulletin of Economic Research 42 : 131–140
Clark D, Thompson H (1990) International factor migration and the US. Atlantic Economic Journal 18 : 74–78
Ethier W (1974) Some of the theorems of international trade with many goods and factors. Journal of International Economics 4 : 199–206
Harberger AC (1962) The incidence of the corporate income tax. Journal of Political Economy 70 : 215–240
Hertel T, Tsigas M (1988) Tax policy and US agriculture: A general equilibrium approach. American Journal of Agricultural Economics 20 : 289–302
Jones R (1965) The structure of simple general equilibrium models. Journal of Political Economy 73 : 557–572
Jones R, Scheinkman J (1977) The relevance of the two-sector production model in trade theory. Journal of Political Economy 85 : 909–935
Sato R, Koizumi T (1973) On the elasticities of substitution and complementarity. Oxford Economic Papers 25 : 44–56
Shoven J, Whalley J (1972) A general equilibrium calculation of the effects of differential taxation of income from capital in the US. In: Journal of Public Economics 1: 281–322
Stolper W, Samuelson P (1941) Protection and real wages. Review of Economic Studies 9 : 58–73
Takayama A (1982) On theorems of general competitive equilibrium of production and trade: A survey of recent developments in the theory of international trade. Keio Economic Studies 19 : 1–37
Thompson H (1990) Simulating a multifactor general equilibrium model of production and trade. International Economic Journal 4 : 21–34
Thompson H (1994) An investigation into the quantitative properties of the specific factors model of international trade. Japan and the World Economy 6 : 375–388
Thompson H (1995a) Factor intensity versus factor substitution in a specified general equilibrium model. Journal of Economic Integration 10 : 283–297
Thompson H (1995b) Free trade and income redistribution in some developing and newly industrialized countries. Open Economies Review 6 : 265–280
Thompson H (1996) Nafta and industrial adjustment: A specific factors model of production. Growth and Change 27 : 3–28
Thompson H (1997a) Free trade and income redistribution across labor groups: Comparative statics for the US economy. International Review of Economics and Finance 6 : 181–192
Thompson H (1997b) Free trade and income redistribution in a three factor model of the US economy. Southern Economic Journal 64 : 1074–83
Thompson H, Toledo H (2001) Bolivia and South American free trade. International Trade Journal 15 : 113–126
Uzawa H (1962) Production functions with constant elasticity of substitution. Review of Economic Studies 30 : 291–299

Comment

Roland Döhrn

Institute of International Economics, Rhine-Westphalia Institute for Economic Research, Essen, Germany

The paper highlights an interesting aspect of trade liberalization. Its main message is: Free trade will have a strong impact on income distribution. Therefore, it will cause opposition to free trade. So far, the findings fit well into the "political economy"-explanation of protectionism, according to which even small groups that experience losses may be very successful in communicating their losses to decision-making political bodies notwithstanding free trade generates a higher income for the economy as a whole. Those who benefit from free trade, although large by number, will have less influence in the political process, or they are not willing to lobby for free trade, as their gains per capita are small.

The results are calculated under some simplifying assumption: LDC export manufactured goods to industrialized countries and they import business services. Furthermore, constant returns to scale are assumed. Anyhow, most of the simplifications do not reduce the merits of the paper, and they are quite easy to overcome: In the Alabama study, to which the paper also makes reference to, more products are distinguished and a more diversified pattern of price reactions is observed.

To me, the most severe restriction of the paper is its comparative static nature. Thus it neglects the consequences free trade and foreign capital may have on technology, productivity and prices. This will in turn influence income levels as well as income distribution. These effects are relevant in the case LDCs in particular. Firstly, they import investment goods which contain technologies that often are not available in developing countries. Secondly, openness of markets will increase competition and force producers to increase productivity. Imitating best practice and training workers will be additional channels through which these forces will work.

Moreover, as capital is mobile, too, foreign direct investment (FDI) may be an addition channel to influence income. There is ample evidence, that incoming FDI brings in – amongst others – technology, management skills, and market access, and it will create spill-overs to the rest of the economy (for an overview of the effects see e.g. Döhrn and von Westernhagen 2003).

To sum up, income will not be the same before and after opening an economy to international goods, services, and capital. As income will increase, this will mitigate the impact of free trade and foreign capital on income distribution.

Reference

Döhrn R, von Westernhagen N (2003) The Role of Foreign Direct Investment in Transformation. In: Lane T, Oding N, Welfens PJJ (eds) Real and Financial Economic Dynamics in Russia and Eastern Europe. Springer, Berlin : 251–276

On Two Elementary Propositions on Customs Unions

Pascalis Raimondos-Møller and Alan D. Woodland

* Department of Economics, Copenhagen Business School, Denmark
** Discipline of Econometrics and Business Statistics, University of Sydney, Australia[1]

1 Introduction

Enthused by the recent proliferation of regional preferential trade arrangements, old questions concerning the normative implications of preferential trade arrangements have re-surfaced.[2] The present paper focuses on the following question: Are we sure that customs unions (CU) can be formed without destroying the path for achieving worldwide free trade? Or, to put it in a different way, are we sure that customs unions can be enlarged sequentially so as to encompass the whole world?

Similar questions were raised many years ago, when the Vinerian analysis of customs unions – with its picturesque concepts of trade creation and trade diversion – was the standard way of thinking about these issues. At that point, a greatly celebrated paper by Kemp and Wan (1976), entitled "An elementary proposition concerning the formation of customs unions", distanced itself from that literature and answered the above questions in an affirmative, and ingenious, way.

The basic message in the Kemp-Wan proposition was that customs unions can be *designed* to ensure that the path to worldwide free trade is intact, and that the in-

[1] We thank Rick Bond, Ian Wooton and seminar participants in Brussels, Copenhagen and Duisburg for comments on a earlier version of this paper. That version was a substantial revision of notes written by AlanWoodland in 1998 in response to a draft of the Kemp-Shimomura paper. We are grateful to Martin Richardson, who kindly provided his correspondence with Kemp on the Kemp-Shimomura paper and have benefited significantly from having access to it. Our interest on these issues started at early 1996 and developed in 1999/2000, when Raimondos-Møller was on leave at the University of Sydney, the hospitality of which is gratefully acknowledged. Woodland gratefully acknowledges the hospitality and support provided by the Economic Policy Research Unit (EPRU) at the University of Copenhagen, where the paper was completed. The research was supported by a grant from the Australian Research Council and by EPRU, whose activities are financed by a grant from the Danish National Research Foundation. Finally, we thank Thalita Marinho for research assistance.

[2] For an overview of the issues raised in the theory of preferential trade arrangements, see the recent and extensive survey by Panagariya (2000).

strument for doing this was the choice of the common external tariff vector (CET).[3] Once seen and understood, the Kemp-Wan proposition is very intuitive and therefore, perhaps, elementary. However, the Kemp-Wan proposition was never intended as a positive approach to CU formation. As such, it can never be used to address issues concerning what countries – members of a CU or not – actually do. For example, when countries choose their tariff vector optimally, the Kemp-Wan proposition simply does not apply.[4]

The recent interest in the above questions took off from exactly this point. It focused on what we know about the normative effects of customs union formation when *all* countries behave optimally (while, to recapitulate, the Kemp-Wan proposition applies in the case where *no* country behaves optimally). Krugman (1991) presented a story that captured the attention of almost everybody: In short, the enlargement of customs unions will stop when the world contains three trading blocks, at which point the world welfare is at its minimum. Even if further research showed that Krugman's analysis was sensitive to particular functional forms and assumptions (see, e.g., Bond and Syropoulos 1996), the point made was well taken: The normative effects of customs union formation with optimizing countries are in general ambiguous.[5]

Having established that, one can then ask a simpler question: what are the normative effects of customs unions when *some* countries behave optimally? For our purpose, there are two cases:

(i) union members optimally set their CET while non-members do not, and
(ii) the opposite, viz. non-members behave optimally while members do not.

Case (i) turns out to be straightforward. With no retaliation, each enlargement of a union will be beneficial to the members and harmful to the non-members. Each non-member will want to join the union and eventually worldwide free trade will prevail. Case (ii), however, turns out not to be straightforward. On top of that, we will argue below that case (ii) is interesting from a policy perspective.

Richardson (1995) was first to examine case (ii). He presented an example where the adoption of the Kemp-Wan CET, together with optimal behaviour by non-members, proves to be detrimental to the CU member countries. In short, Richardson's point was that allowing for retaliation destroys the nice features of the Kemp-Wan CET. However, and as we emphasized above, the Kemp-Wan CET was

---

[3] The details of the argument will be presented below. Note, however, that Kemp and Wan (1976) were not the first to argue this. Kemp (1964), Vanek (1965) and Ohyama (1972) also discuss, what at that time was called, the tariff-compensating customs union.

[4] Of course, in reality, optimal tariffs may not be chosen. Other, perhaps political economy, arguments for the choice of tariff policy may be more appropriate (see Panagaryia 2000).

[5] The first paper that made exactly this point was Riezman (1985) in what turned out to be a pioneering article within the coalition theory of customs union formation. Recently, Burbidge et al. (1997) developed such a model in more detail. They also present an example where worldwide free trade (the grand coalition) is not an equilibrium outcome in a coalition game.

not designed for a model where countries optimize. It seems then natural to consider the design of a new CET that takes into account optimization by non-members.

To this purpose, and to counter the Richardson argument, Kemp and Shimomura (2001) published "A second elementary proposition concerning the formation of customs unions" in which they argue that it is possible for a customs union to choose its common external tariff policy to ensure a strict Pareto improvement in world welfare – union members gain, while non-members' utilities are unchanged – when non-members react strategically to union behaviour. Specifically, Kemp and Shimomura show that there exists a CET *function* that allows customs unions to be formed without destroying the path towards worldwide free trade. The Kemp-Shimomura CET function, and the policy behaviour it implies, is arguably less intuitive than the Kemp-Wan CET and therefore, perhaps, less "elementary". Nevertheless, we believe that it establishes an important result in the theory of customs unions and that it is potentially important for policy issues.

The reason for our belief in the value of the Kemp-Shimomura result for trade policy is the following. Formation of customs unions, and trade in general, does not occur in a vacuum. The GATT/WTO has for 50 years now been regulating all international trade issues with considerable overall success.[6] Part of this regulation dictates that any customs union formation needs to be approved by the GATT/WTO. Here enters Article XXIV, which imposes conditions on the behaviour of the member countries and on the design of the CET. However, Article XXIV says nothing about the behaviour of the non-member countries, which, therefore, can continue to behave optimally. In other words, what Article XXIV imposes (assuming that it is enforced) is an asymmetry in countries' behaviour that fits exactly case (ii) above. That is precisely the case for which the Kemp-Shimomura proposition was made. Thus, if the Article XXIV was doing what the Kemp-Shimomura CET function describes, then any customs union formation would be beneficial to its members and not detrimental to non-members. Enlargements of this union would eventually lead to worldwide free trade.

The scope of this paper is to pay tribute to both Kemp-Wan and Kemp-Shimomura propositions by: (1) presenting a novel diagrammatic explanation of the Kemp-Wan proposition and (2) showing how the Kemp-Shimomura proposition can easily be proved. The remaining of this paper is organized as follows. Section 2 sets up the framework that we use. Section 3 presents the Kemp-Wan proposition in terms of our model and provides a diagrammatic presentation of their argument. Section 4 is devoted to presenting and proving the Kemp-Shimomura proposition, including a discussion about the issues raised and the implications for a possible reform of the Article XXIV. The paper provides some concluding remarks in section 5.

[6] Bagwell and Staiger (1999) show how important the GATT/WTO rules of reciprocity and non-discrimination are for achieving efficient outcomes in international trade relations.

2 The Model of World Trade

We consider a perfectly competitive general equilibrium model of the world, consisting of a set K of nations trading in a set N of internationally tradeable commodities. The world price vector is denoted by p and the domestic price vectors by p^k for each country $k \in K$. These are connected by tariffs, which may be expressed in specific terms, whence we may write $p^k = p + t^k$.[7] For simplicity, there is just one consumer in each country, who receives a transfer from the government and has utility u^k. We describe each nation by its net revenue function, $S^k(p^k, u^k) \equiv G^k(p^k) - E^k(p^k, u^k)$, which is the difference between the gross domestic product function G^k and the consumer expenditure function E^k. The vector $x^k = S_p{}^k(p^k, u^k)$ denotes the gradient of the net revenue function with respect to prices and is the vector of compensated net export functions for nation k.

Countries are divided into two groups - those that wish to form a customs union and those that do not. The set of countries that form the customs union is denoted by K^U, while K^N is the set of non-union countries. Since attention focuses upon customs union members rather than countries not in the union, the latter's net export functions are written in reduced form as

$X^N(p, t^N) \equiv \sum_{k \in K^N} S_p^k(p + t^k, u^k)$,

where the utility levels solve the national budget constraints

$p^T S_p^k(p + t^k, u^k) \equiv 0, \ k \in K^N$

and t^N is a vector of all tariffs in non-member nations. Using this notation for non-members, the model describing the initial equilibrium prior to the formation of the customs union may be expressed as:

$$\sum_{k \in K^U} S_p^k(p^k, u^k) + X^N(p, t^N) = 0 \tag{1}$$

$$p^T S_p^k(p^k, u^k) = 0, \ k \in K^U \tag{2}$$

where

$$p^k = p + t^k, \ \ k \in K^U \tag{3}$$

These equations consist of the world market equilibrium conditions for internationally traded goods and the budget constraints for each country that later becomes a member of the customs union, together with the price-tariff relationships.

The post-union equilibrium involves the customs union setting a common external tariff, elimination of internal tariffs and a system of intra-union income transfers. Because the customs union is assumed to have a full set of internal income transfers between union members at its disposal, individual country budget con-

---

[7] The model may also be specified in terms of ad valorem tariff rates rather than specific (unit) tariff rates.

straints become irrelevant. Accordingly, the equilibrium conditions under a customs union with internal transfers become simply

$$\sum_{k\in K^U} S_p^k\left(p^U,u^k\right)+X^N\left(p,t^N\right)=0 \tag{4}$$

$$\sum_{k\in K^U} p^T S_p^k\left(p^U,u^k\right)=0, \tag{5}$$

where

$$p^U=p+t^U \tag{6}$$

is the price vector in the union and t^U is the common external tariff vector. Below, we examine a particular form of a customs union – the Kemp-Wan customs union – and show that the constraining equilibrium conditions simplify significantly due to the special structure being imposed.

3 The Kemp-Wan Proposition on Customs Unions

The Kemp-Wan proposition is that any subset of countries can form a customs union agreement comprising internal free trade, a common external tariff and a set of internal income transfers to provide a weak Pareto improvement in welfare for all the countries of the world.[8] If the initial equilibrium has sufficient distortions, the countries in the union will obtain strict welfare improvements. In either case, the Kemp-Wan customs union leaves the non-member countries as well off as before the formation of the union. As Richardson (1995) points out, an implicit assumption is that the non-member countries retain their pre-union tariff schedules and so do not react strategically to the formation of the customs union.

The crux of the Kemp-Wan argument is that the union can choose its common external tariff to ensure that the world price vector (and hence the vector of net trades of the union with the rest of the world) is unchanged as a result of the formation of the union. Accordingly, non-members face exactly the same trading environment as before the formation of the union and so behave exactly as before. They therefore do not experience any change in welfare. The remainder of the argument is to show that union members can gain from the union. This is established from the observations that the vector of net trades of the union with the rest of the world is unchanged, that domestic price vectors for members before the formation of the union are (presumably) different (making the equilibrium Pareto sub-optimal within the union) and that the domestic price vectors for members after the union are identical (because of the common external tariff). As a result, the intra-union equilibrium is Pareto optimal for union members given the external trade and price vectors, a situation we refer to as being conditionally Pareto optimal.[9] Efficiency

---

[8] See also the formulation of this proposition by Ohyama (1972).

[9] The 'conditional' qualification refers to the equilibrium being Pareto optimal for union members (not non-members) and being the result of the Kemp-Wan construction whereby

gains accrue from equalizing domestic prices and lump sum transfers allow these efficiency gains to be redistributed to achieve a Pareto improvement for union members.[10]

3.1 The Proposition

The Kemp and Wan (1976) proposition may be expressed in the context of the model in the present paper and its assumptions, as follows.[11]

Proposition 1 (Kemp-Wan): Any subset of countries may form a customs union that undertakes internal free trade and chooses common external tariffs and internal income transfers in such a way that there results a semi-strict Pareto improvement in world welfare (with a strict Pareto improvement for the union and unchanged welfare for each other country), provided that the rest of the world adopts a passive policy response (the rest of the world's tariffs remain unchanged) and provided that not every member of the customs union has the same (up to a factor of proportionality) domestic price vector and provided that some regularity assumptions about the net revenue functions hold.[12] World prices and the vector of aggregate trade between the union and the rest of the world remain unchanged.

The above discussion indicates that Pareto improvements arise from the removal of differences in pre-union domestic prices. This (well known) idea is now treated more formally. Let the initial equilibrium, before the union is formed, be arbitrarily given and characterized by solution $(p, u) = (p_0, u_0)$ and $(t, b) = (t_0, 0)$. The initial equilibrium might, of course, be a Nash equilibrium in a non-cooperative tariff game but this interpretation is not essential. The post-union equilibrium involves the union setting common external tariffs, elimination of internal tariffs and a system of intra-union income transfers. The Kemp-Wan approach is to choose the external tariffs so that world prices remain at p_0. At this initial price vector p_0 and the initial tariffs in the rest of the world t_0^N, the initial aggregate trade vector for

world prices are held fixed. Conditional upon world prices (and the vector of external) union trade being fixed, the equilibrium is Pareto optimal for union members alone.

[10] Notice that freeing internal trade is not a necessary condition for achieving these gains. Further discussion of this point is contained in our companion paper, Raimondos-Møller and Woodland (2002).

[11] It should be emphasized that we are not attempting to reproduce exactly the Kemp-Wan proposition, nor are we attempting to generalize it. In fact, Kemp and Wan make weaker assumptions and express the outcome in terms of weak Pareto improvements. The stronger version is given here for expositional purposes. It allows us to focus on the essence of the Kemp-Wan argument and on the role of the assumption sufficient for its validity.

[12] The regularity assumptions are not spelt out formally here, but are expressed formally in Raimondos-Møller and Woodland (2002). They are also expressed informally in the discussion of the diagrammatic illustration below.

union members before the union is given, by the market equilibrium conditions, as $x_0^U = -X^N(p_0, t_0^N)$.

For the union to offer this same trade vector after the union is formed and for each union member to gain in welfare, it has to choose common external tariffs and internal transfers such that

$$\sum_{k \in K^U} S_p^k(p^U, u^k) = x_0^U \tag{7}$$

with $u^U >> u_0^U$, where u^U is the vector of utility levels for union members. That is, the union is to choose a common domestic price vector p^U, a vector of transfers b^U and a vector of utilities u^U that generate the same external trade vector as before, satisfy the aggregate balance of trade restriction at the same world prices as before and provide greater utility for all union members. Since the union's balance of trade restriction automatically holds

$$\left(p_0^T x_0^U \equiv -p_0^T X^N(p_0, t_0^N) \equiv 0\right)$$

and internal income transfers are available, only the internal market equilibrium conditions (7) are constraining: any violation of a member's budget constraint can be corrected by an appropriate choice of transfers.[13] Thus, under the Kemp-Wan construction, the union budget constraint (5) can be ignored, simplifying the problem.

Clearly, a particular choice of internal transfers will yield a particular competitive equilibrium solution for utilities and the domestic price vector p^U. This implies a particular common external tariff $t^U = p^U - p_0$. By varying the transfers, therefore, utilities, domestic prices and the common external tariffs also vary. A particular choice of these variables could be made through bargaining between customs union members or by maximizing an admissible social welfare function (as done further below). For the present, we illustrate the proposition and its proof diagrammatically.

3.2 Diagrammatic Illustration of the Kemp-Wan Proposition

The Kemp-Wan construction may be simply illustrated for the case of two goods and two union members in Figure 1. The axes measure the amounts of the two goods. The point y is the union's aggregate production vector (assumed fixed for simplicity) while point c is its aggregate consumption vector before and after the formation of the union. The difference is the net import vector for the union, again both before and after the formation of the union. Thus, the figure reflects the

---

[13] For further details on the modelling of the Kemp-Wan customs union see Woodland (1982) and Raimondos-Møller and Woodland (2002).

Kemp-Wan approach whereby the union ensures that the world price vector and, hence, the aggregate union trade vector with the rest of the world are the same before and after the formation of the union.

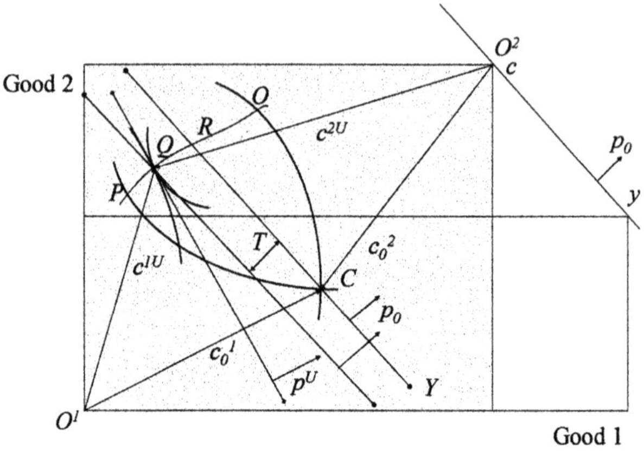

Figure 1. Kemp-Wan Propositions – Transfers Required

The rectangular box formed by the origin and aggregate production point y shows the allocation of production between the union members. Thus, point Y denotes the production points for the members (with origin for the production box at y for member 2).

The rectangular box formed by the origin and the point c is the Edgeworth-Bowley box for the analysis of intra-union exchange between the two union members. Thus O^1 denotes the origin for member 1, while c (labelled O^2) becomes the origin for member 2. Point C is the initial (Nash) consumption point (showing vector c_0^1 from origin O^1 and vector c_0^2 from origin O^2). Clearly, this point is Pareto sub-optimal since the slopes of the indifference curves through this point (hence initial domestic prices) are different.[14]

Consumption points that are Pareto superior to C occur in the cigar shaped area labelled *PCO*. Pareto optimal points that are weakly preferred to C occur on the curve labelled *PO*. Any point on the interior of this curve, such as point Q, is strictly Pareto superior to point C while the endpoints P and O are weakly Pareto superior to C. The essence of the second theorem of welfare economics, as employed by Kemp and Wan, is that any such point can be supported as an equilibrium by the imposition of free internal trade and by an appropriate choice of the common external tariff

[14] The term "optimality" is used here and below to mean optimality conditional upon the Kemp-Wan assumptions (that world prices are kept fixed and the rest of the world does not retaliate) and refers to customs union members.

(equal to the difference between the world price p and the domestic price p^U) and internal lump sum transfers, as is now demonstrated geometrically.

It is now shown that the Pareto optimal point Q may be attained by a suitable choice of the common external tariff for the union and a suitable transfer of income between union members, given free internal trade. In Figure 1 there are two lines passing through point Q. The line passing through point Q with normal vector p^U is a supporting budget line with the post-union price vector p^U since it is tangent to both indifferent curves at point Q. The second line passing through point Q is not a tangent to either indifference curve and corresponds to price vector $p = p_0$ (the world price vector before and after the formation of the union in accordance with the Kemp-Wan approach). However, since this line does not pass through production point Y, the post-union consumption point Q does not satisfy the balance of trade conditions

$$p_0^T S_p^k \left(p^U, u^k\right) = 0, \; k \in K^U .$$

Without internal income transfers, point Q cannot, therefore, be an equilibrium consumption point.

However, there exists a lump sum transfer of income between the union members that allows consumption point Q to be an equilibrium consumption point. The required lump sum transfer of income (T) from nation 1 to nation 2 is indicated by the shift in the balance of trade line

$$p_0^T \left(c^k - y^k\right) = 0, \; k \in K^U ,$$

passing through points Y, C and R, to the new line

$$p_0^T (c^{kU} - y^k) = b^{kU}, \; k \in K^U ,$$

passing through Q and to the south-east of Y (the second of the two lines passing through Q). Country 2 gets a transfer of income

$$b^{2U} = p_0^T \left(c^{2U} - y^2\right) > 0 ,$$

where c^{2U} is consumption by nation 2 at the point Q, while country 1 contributes this amount $b^{1U} = -b^{2U} < 0$.

Thus, the transfer allows the union members to consume at point Q, which is conditionally Pareto superior to the pre-union consumption point C. The union has clearly gained. Since the rest of the world faces the same world prices, it chooses to trade the same amount of each good with the union and so the rest of the world welfare is unchanged. From a world point of view there is a semi-strict Pareto improvement in welfare; from the union's point of view there is a strict Pareto gain (provided that union members' prices are different in the pre-union equilibrium), while non-members' utility levels are unchanged.

Transfers may not be necessary, of course. For example, as illustrated in Figure 2, the balance of trade line passing through Y also passes through the Pareto optimal point R. This consumption point can therefore be supported by a common external tariff yielding a domestic price vector passing through R and tangent to both indifference curves at R without any transfers. Like Q, point R is Pareto superior to the initial Nash consumption point C.[15]

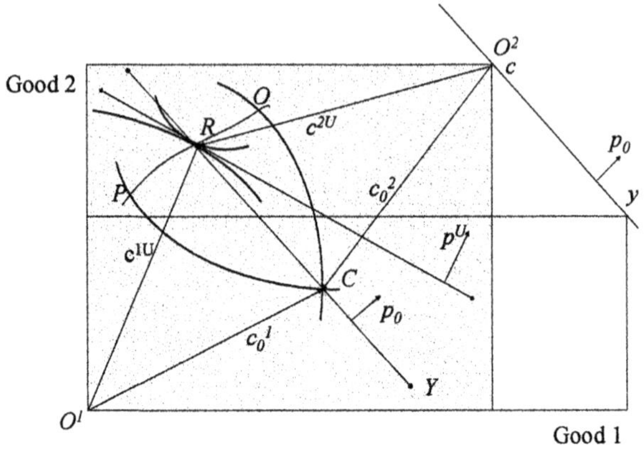

Figure 2. Kemp-Wan Proposition – No Transfers Required

In summary, it has therefore been established that any point on the conditionally Pareto optimal curve *PO* can be supported by internal free trade and by a suitable common external tariff and set of internal transfers. Each such point (with the exception of the end points *P* and *O*) is conditionally Pareto superior to the pre-union consumption point *C*. This is the essence of the Kemp-Wan proposition, which has been diagrammatically illustrated above.

To complete our task, the assumptions behind the diagrammatic proof should be spelled out. At point *C*, the initial consumption point, there are three important features that lead to the welfare improvement. The first is that the indifference curves have smooth curvature – they are not kinked or *L*-shaped. If they both were *L*-shaped, then the cigar shaped area, denoting the potential for welfare improvements, would be empty except for the point *C* itself. The second is that the diagram implicitly assumes that all goods are normal in consumption – higher consumption means higher utility. Again, this ensures that the cigar shaped area indeed represents higher utilities than at initial point *C*. These two conditions form the regularity conditions referred to in the statement of Proposition 1, although the normality assumption can be weakened considerably to simply require that, in each country, higher utility requires higher expenditure.[16]

The final assumption implicit in the diagram is that the initial domestic price ratios in the two countries are different, as indicated by the different slopes of the indifference curves at the initial consumption point, *C*. The difference in slopes of

---

[15] Of course, a point such as R need not exist in general. That is, it may be necessary to use internal transfers to obtain a strict Pareto improvement in welfare.

[16] See the assumption in Raimondos-Møller and Woodland (2002) for details.

the indifference curves means that the cigar shaped area has an interior comprising points Pareto preferred to *C*. If the price ratios had been the same, the indifference curves would have been tangent at *C* and, hence, the initial consumption point would have been Pareto optimal. In this case, no Pareto improvements from the Kemp-Wan customs union would have been possible – each member would have been exactly as well off as before the customs union was formed. Thus, the role of the assumption of different domestic price ratios is to ensure a strict Pareto improvement in welfare for union members.

Thus, we have completed the diagrammatic illustration of the Kemp-Wan proposition by outlining the proof and, in doing so, we have been able to highlight the nature and role of the assumptions used to establish the proposition.

4 The Case of Retaliation by the Rest of the World

The Kemp-Wan proposition establishes that any subset of countries forming a Kemp-Wan customs union experiences a strict Pareto improvement in welfare while the rest of the world is totally unaffected. Thus, there is a semi-strict Pareto improvement from the point of view of the world. As Richardson (1995) demonstrates via an example, this result may break down if the rest of the world does not react passively to the formation of the union but alters its tariffs strategically. To counter this observation, Kemp and Shimomura (2001) have provided a second "elementary proposition on customs unions" whereby the union chooses, not a common external tariff vector, but a common external *tariff function* that ensures a strict Pareto improvement for the union irrespective of the response by the rest of the world.

4.1 An Alternative Interpretation of the K-S Proposition

We offer an alternative interpretation to the Kemp-Shimomura (K-S) proposition and proof. Our approach provides an explanation of the Kemp-Shimomura proposition that fits more comfortably with the traditional characterization of optimal tariff determination using offer curves. As with Kemp and Shimomura, we assume that the initial equilibrium is a Nash equilibrium for a unilateral tariff-setting game. We then consider the new equilibrium arising from the formation of a customs union of a subset of countries in which the rest of the world behaves strategically but the union does not.

The argument rests on the premise that, both before and after the formation of the union, countries in the rest of the world choose tariff vectors non-cooperatively. It is well known that the non-cooperative equilibrium tariffs chosen by a country are optimal for that country, given the tariff choices of all the other countries. Moreover, the optimal tariffs may be viewed as optimal for the country, given the offer surface for trade by all other countries; the optimal tariff vector maximizes a nation's utility subject to trading on the foreign offer curve. One way to induce such a country to choose the same optimal tariffs after the formation of the union as before the formation of the union is to present it with the same offer surface. Then that country will choose the same optimal tariff even though it has the freedom to choose any tariff vector it wishes. The essence of the proof, as presented below, is to characterize the behaviour of the union in this way - ensure that the post-union offer surface is identical to the aggregate pre-union offer surface for the union members.[17]

This argument may be simply presented as follows. As demonstrated above, the Kemp-Wan proposition establishes that the union can set the common external tariff and the internal transfers to ensure a strict Pareto improvement in welfare if it continues to trade the pre-union external trade vector at the pre-union world price vector. The particular solution chosen by the customs union depends upon its social welfare function (or upon the bargaining rule in a bargaining context). Extending Chipman and Moore (1972), we express the social welfare function as

$$W\left(u^U\right) \equiv \min\left\{\left(u^k - u_0^k\right)/a^k, k \in K^U\right\}, \tag{8}$$

where $u_0^{\,k}$ is the initial Nash equilibrium level of utility for nation k and $a^k > 0$ is a parameter. If we let w be the level of social welfare, the levels of member utilities are related to it by $u^k = wa^k + u_0^{\,k}$. Thus, vector a can be thought of as the direction of movement of the customs union's utility vector u^U from the initial utility vector $u_0^{\,U}$.

The Kemp-Wan customs union solution may be interpreted as the solution to the constrained social welfare maximization problem given by

$$\max_{p^U, u^U}\left\{W\left(u^U\right): \sum_{k \in K^U} S_p^k\left(p^U, u^k\right) = x_0^U\right\} \tag{9}$$

where $x_0^U = X^U\left(p_0, t_0^U\right) = -X^N\left(p_0, t_0^N\right)$ is the pre- and post-union trade vector for the union and p_0 is the pre-union world price vector. The resulting common external tariff vector (equal to $t^U = p^U - p_0$) for the union can then be written as

$$t^u = \hat{T}\left(x_0^U, a\right) \tag{10}$$

To deal with potential retaliation by the rest of the world, now consider the complete pre-union net export function for the union (sum of pre-union member's net export functions), which we write as $X^U\left(p, t_0^U\right)$.[18] Now let the union choose its

---

[17] The Kemp-Shimomura proof proceeds by showing that the union can choose its common external tariff as a function of the tariff vectors of the rest of the world. This function is given by $t^u = T\left(t_n^U, t^N, b^U\right)$, which is a function of the pre-union tariffs of member nations, the tariffs selected by the rest of the world and the internal income transfers chosen by the union.

[18] This assumes that there are no transfers in the pre-union equilibrium for simplicity.

common external tariff function by solving the constrained social welfare maximization problem

$$\max_{p^U, u^U} \left\{ W\left(u^U\right) : \sum_{k \in K^U} S_p^k\left(p^U, u^k\right) = X^U\left(p, t_0^U\right) \right\} \tag{11}$$

allowing p to vary parametrically (due to tariff changes in the rest of the world possibly, but not necessarily). Thus, the union solves the maximum social welfare problem (11) for all possible world price vectors p. This yields a *common external tariff function*

$$t^u = T\left(p; t_0^U, a\right), \tag{12}$$

which expresses the common external tariff as a function of the world price vector p, given the pre-union Nash equilibrium tariff vectors of the union members and the weights in the social welfare function. The resulting net export function for the union is denoted as $x^u = X\left(p; t_0^U, a\right)$. The union is able to exactly reproduce its pre-union net export function $X^U\left(p, t_0^U\right)$ as a function of world prices, since, by this construction,

$X\left(p; t_0^U, a\right) = X^U\left(p, t_0^U, a\right)$

for all world price vectors p.

Thus, the union is able to preserve its aggregate pre-union net export function or offer surface. The rest of the world faces exactly the same economic environment as before the union was formed; in particular, it faces the same aggregate offer surface from the union members. Accordingly, the rest of the world will behave exactly as before the union was formed and so choose the same tariffs, trade the same amounts of goods and have the same utility levels. Thus, we obtain the alternative interpretation of the Kemp-Shimomura proposition.

Proposition 2 (Kemp and Shimomura 2001): Starting from an initial Nash equilibrium for a unilateral tariff-setting game, any subset of countries can form a customs union with internal transfers, internal free trade and a common external tariff function $t^u = T\left(p; t_0^U, a\right)$ that yields a net export function (offer surface) identical to the aggregate pre-union net export function for union members. If the rest of the world responds in an optimal fashion, the resulting equilibrium exhibits unchanged world prices, unchanged rest of the world tariffs and utilities, and a strict Pareto improvement in welfare for union members.

4.2 Diagrammatic Illustration

Figure 3 illustrates the essence of the proof in terms of an offer curve diagram. The offer curve labelled U is the aggregate offer curve for the members of the customs union prior to the formation of the union. The equilibrium trading point is denoted by E, at which the rest of the world's (assumed to be one country here for simplicity) highest attainable indifference curve is tangent to the offer curve O. This reflects the characterization of the optimal tariff choice for the rest of the world as one of maximizing utility on the offer curve presented to it.

If a Kemp-Wan union is enacted, the resulting offer curve of the union will certainly pass through the pre-union trading point E. One such possibility is given by the offer curve labelled O^{KW}. Under the Kemp-Wan implicit assumption of no retaliation by the rest of the world, the equilibrium trading point remains at E with world prices unchanged.

However, if retaliation is permitted, the changed offer curve O^{KW} (based upon the union's choice of a common external tariff, calculated on the assumption that the rest of the world does not alter its tariffs) induces the rest of the world to raise its optimal tariff and move to point E^R thereby raising its welfare and reducing the welfare of the union members. Thus, Figure 3 illustrates the importance of the assumption of non-retaliation for the Kemp-Wan outcome.

The Kemp-Shimomura approach to strategic responses by the rest of the world, as expressed here, is for the union to maintain the same offer curve as before the union. It does this by choosing its common external tariff and its internal transfers in response to each possible world price vector p to ensure that its net trade vector lies on its pre-union offer surface, that is, by solving the maximum social welfare problem (11) for all possible world price vectors p. Facing this offer curve, the rest of the world is induced to impose the same optimal tariff as before the formation of the Kemp-Shimomura union. The equilibrium trading point therefore remains at E.

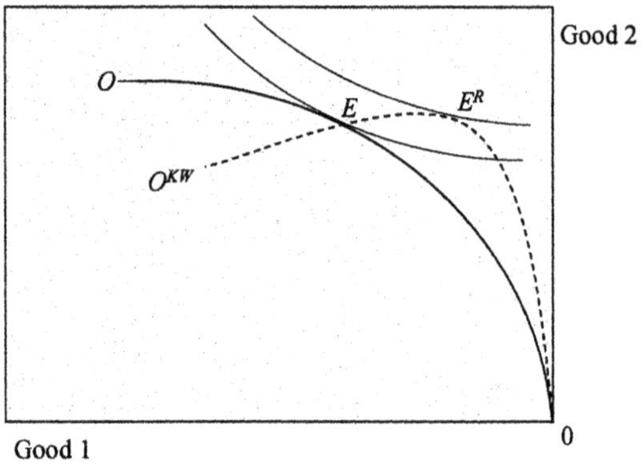

Figure 3. Illustration of Kemp-Shimomura Proposition

Will the union members gain under the Kemp-Shimomura equilibrium? The answer remains "Yes", just as for the Kemp-Wan construction, because the new Kemp-Shimomura construction presents the same offer curve to the rest of the world and so induces the rest of the world to trade at exactly the pre-union trade point, just as under Kemp-Wan. The union members gain, not from any expansion of external trade (there is none) but from the removal of domestic price differentials and the subsequent efficiency gains (possibly associated with greater internal trade). In short, the Kemp-Shimomura common external tariff function or schedule, in conjunction with internal transfers, enables any subset of countries to gain from the formation of a customs union. The Kemp-Wan proposition is thus extended to the case where the rest of the world is allowed to react strategically to the formation of the union; while the rest of the world is *allowed* to react strategically to the formation of the union, the union induces the rest of the world *not to react.*

4.3 Discussion

The argument is that the customs union can present a common tariff function to the rest of the world such that the resulting equilibrium has exactly the same utility levels for all countries, the same world price vector and the same tariff vectors for all non-member countries. Thus, the non-members of the union optimally choose their post-union tariffs to be exactly the same as their optimally chosen pre-union tariffs. In this way, the union of any subset of countries is no worse off than in the initial Nash equilibrium. Some pertinent clarifying remarks about this result are as follows.

1. It is important to note that Kemp and Shimomura introduce a behavioural asymmetry into the model. The union is able to set a *tariff function*, to which the rest of the world reacts. On the other hand, each of the countries in the rest of the world is assumed to present its *tariff vector* to the world. That is, the assumption that the rules of the tariff game have changed is of crucial importance. The game was initially a Nash equilibrium, where each country chose its tariff conditional upon the tariff vectors chosen by all other countries. Now the union presents a tariff function conditional upon the non-members' tariff vectors, while the non-members choose tariff vectors conditional on this tariff function and the tariff vectors of the other non-members. This is a different game. It is akin to the union playing a Stackelberg strategy as leader but not quite: The difference is that the offered tariff function is carefully chosen and does not necessarily coincide with the union's reaction function.[19]
2. Given that behavioral asymmetry, the result has implications for tariff policy. In the Kemp-Wan framework, the Kemp-Wan result may be used to demonstrate the existence of a sequence of customs unions that leads to free trade. Imagine starting from a unilateral tariff setting equilibrium and then consider the formation of a Kemp-Wan customs union. By the Kemp-Wan proposition, this customs union gains with no cost to the rest of the world. The same argument applies to any enlargement to that union. Thus, if the rest of the world remains passive, there is a sequence of Kemp-Wan customs unions that eventually encompass all countries in free trade with internal transfers to ensure that all countries gain. The

[19] Having said that, one should notice that an asymmetry also exists in the Kemp-Wan proposition where the customs union chooses a particular common external tariff policy while the rest of the world remains passive.

same argument applies if the customs unions are formed in the Kemp-Shimomura fashion. At each stage the union members gain, while the non-union members are induced to retain their previous trade policies and so are unaffected. Again, the outcome is free trade with internal transfers.[20]

3. The final point that we discuss here is the reason why the union behaves as assumed when it can do better. WTO's Article XXIV provides one possible answer: any customs union needs to be approved by the WTO, which, by its Article XXIV, imposes restrictions on the common external tariff policy of the union. Thus, customs unions do not freely choose their common external tariff policy. Admittedly, the current specification of Article XXIV focuses more on operational rather than welfare-based considerations of the type discussed here.[21] However, this lack of welfare considerations, together with the apparent imprecision of it, has provoked many scholars to ask for a revision of the Article XXIV (see Bhagwati 1991, McMillan 1993, Sampson 1996, Srinivasan 1997, Syropoulos 1999, Zissimos and Vines 2000). Srinivasan (1997) proposes a revision that is consistent with the Kemp-Wan proposition. One could go a step further and propose a revision that is consistent with the Kemp-Shimomura proposition.

5 Conclusions

The aim of this paper was to emphasize the importance of two normative propositions in the theory of customs unions, viz. the Kemp-Wan proposition and, its recent extension, the Kemp-Shimomura proposition. These are propositions that can answer complicated questions concerning regionalism and multilateralism in a very simple and general way. They both advocate, under different assumptions, the *ex-*

---

[20] Of course, there is an implicit assumption in this extension of the argument that the rest of the world does not form a customs union of its own or break up into several such customs unions. If this is allowed to happen, the asymmetry in tariff policies implicit in the Kemp-Shimomura framework is lost. The problem becomes more complex (as the tariff function of one union will depend on the tariff function of another union) and the solution needs to be worked out.

[21] The Article XXIV writes (see GATT, 1994, pp. 523-524):

"(i)... the duties and other regulations of commerce imposed at the institution of any such union or interim agreement in respect of trade with contracting parties not parties to such union or agreement shall not on the whole be higher or more restrictive than the general incidence of the duties and regulations of commerce applicable in the constituent territories prior to the formation of such a union..." The "general incidence" has been clarified as follows: "... the general incidence of the duties and other regulations of commerce applicable before and after the formation of a customs union shall in respect of duties and charges be based upon an overall assessement of weighted average tariff rates and of customs unions duties collected. This assessment shall be based on import statistics for a previous representative period to be supplied by the customs union, on a tariff-line basis and in values and quantities, broken down by WTO country of origin. For this purpose, the duties and charges to be taken into consideration shall be the applied rates of duty."

istence of a customs union that does not harm the rest-of-the-world (ROW) and that improves the welfare of the member countries.[22] As such, they provide a mechanism under which world-wide free trade can be achieved through a sequential enlargement of a particularly designed customs union.

In reviewing these propositions we provided a diagrammatic exposition and diagrammatic proof of the Kemp-Wan proposition. We then showed how the Kemp-Wan proposition can be extended to the case where the ROW behaves optimally in setting their tariffs, viz. the Kemp-Shimomura proposition. In general, normative results, such as those above, should be used as inspiration to policy prescriptions. With the existence of WTO's Article XXIV, and with the apparent dissatisfaction of its influence, we believe that a revision of it should pay attention to these two important propositions on the formation of customs unions.

References

Bagwell K, Staiger RW (1999) An economic theory of the GATT. American Economic Review 89 : 215–248

Bhagwati J (1991) The World System at Risk. Princeton University Press, Princeton

Bond EW, Syropoulos C (1996) The size of trading blocks: market power and world welfare effects. Journal of International Economics 40 : 411–438

Burbidge J, DePater J, Myles G, Sengupta A (1997) A coalition-formation approach to equilibrium federations and trading blocks. American Economic Review 87 : 940–956

Chipman JS, Moore JC (1972) Social utility and the gains from trade. Journal of International Economics 2 : 157–172

GATT (1994) The Results of the Uruguay Round of Multilateral Trade Negotiation – The Legal Texts. GATT Secretariat, Geneva

Kemp MC (1964) The Pure Theory of International Trade. Prentice-Hall, Englewood Cliffs

Kemp MC, Shimomura K (2001) A second elementary proposition concerning the formation of customs unions. Japanese Economic Review 52 : 64–69

Kemp MC and HY Wan Jr. (1976) An elementary proposition concerning the formation of customs unions. Journal of International Economics 6 : 95–97

Krugman P (1991) Is bilateralism bad? In: Helpman E, Razin A (eds) International Trade and Trade Policy, MIT Press, Cambridge

McMillan J (1993) Does regional integration foster open trade? Economic theory and GATT's Article XXIV. In: Anderson K, Blackhurst R (eds) Regional Integration and the Global Trading System, Harvester Wheatsheaf, Hempel Hempestead

Ohyama M (1972) Trade and welfare in general equilibrium. Keio Economic Studies 9 : 37–73

Panagariya A (2000) Preferential trade liberalization: the traditional theory and new developments. Journal of Economic Literature 38 : 287–331

Raimondos-Møller P, Woodland AD (2002) Non-preferential trading clubs, CEPR Discussion Paper 3572, London

[22] While the Kemp-Wan proposition holds when the ROW does not behave optimally, the Kemp-Shimomura proposition holds when the ROW does behave optimally.

Richardson M (1995) On the interpretation of the Kemp-Wan theorem. Oxford Economic Papers 33 : 135–153
Riezman R (1985) Customs unions and the core. Journal of International Economics 19 : 355–366
Sampson GP (1996) Compatibility of regional and multilateral trading agreements: reforming the WTO process. American Economic Association Papers and Proceedings 86 : 88–92
Srinivasan TN (1997) The common external tariff of a customs union: alternative approaches. Japan and the World Economy 9 : 447–465
Syropoulos C (1999) Customs unions and comparative advantage. Oxford Economic Papers 51 : 239–266
Vanek J (1965) General Equilibrium of International Discrimination: The Case of Customs Unions, Harvard University Press, Cambridge, MA
Woodland AD (1982) International Trade and Resource Allocation, North Holland, Amsterdam
Zissimos B, Vines D (2000) Is the WTO's Article XXIV a free trade barrier? CSGR WP 49/00, University of Warwick

Comment

Ian Wooton

Department of Economics, University of Strathclyde, Glasgow, United Kingdom

This paper gives further consideration to the issue of whether it is possible to form a customs union (CU) that is mutually beneficial to its members and leaves the rest of the world unharmed. The authors develop and illustrate the ideas presented in the seminal paper by Murray Kemp and Henry Wan Jr. and then revisited by Kemp and Koji Shimomura. The paper falls into two parts: First, a novel diagrammatic explanation of the Kemp-Wan result; and, secondly, a demonstration of how Kemp-Shimomura can be easily proved.

The paper sets out the model using the algebra that Alan Woodland has used so effectively in his previous trade writings. I shall also adopt this in my discussion, though with some simplifications. Initially, it is assumed that each of the K nations in the world has imposed non-discriminatory, unilaterally determined tariffs on its trade with the other countries. For country $k \in K$, the vector of its net exports is $x^k = S_p^k\left(p^k, u^k\right)$, where domestic prices are $p^k - p + t^k$ and the utility of the single household is u^k. In this pre-CU setting, equilibrium can be described by the following equations:

$$\sum_{k \in K} x^k = 0, \tag{1}$$

$$p'x^k = 0, \quad k \in K. \tag{2}$$

Thus the world market clears and each country is in budget balance.

On formation of a CU, the world is split into two sets $K^U \cup K^N = K$, where each country in the CU $k \in K^U$ adopts a common external tariff p^U (CET) while the remaining countries $k \in K^N$ continue to set their tariffs independently. For the Kemp-Wan result, it is assumed that these outside countries maintain the same tariffs after the formation of the CU as they did before its creation. That these countries might find it advantageous to change their tariffs in the light of the emergence of the CU is addressed in the Kemp-Shimomura proposition.

The global market-clearing condition (1) continues to hold after the CU is established but, if there are intra-union transfers within the CU, individual members of the CU need not meet their budget constraints, though the CU as a whole must be in balance. Consequently, (2) must be amended to:

$$p'x^k = 0, \quad k \in K^N,$$
$$p'x^U = 0, \quad where\; x^U = \sum_{k \in K^U} x^k. \tag{3}$$

Having established the nature of the equilibrium, the authors then discuss the Kemp-Wan proposition. Assuming that the non-CU countries do not change their tariffs, their welfare can be maintained at the original levels if the formation of the CU does not change the equilibrium world price level p. If the world price is unchanged, the non-union countries will wish to engage in the same trade volumes as before and consequently the net exports of the CU x^U will have to be the same as before the CU was formed. The challenge is then to demonstrate that the CU can raise the welfare of all its members through the combination of the adoption of a CET and intra-CU redistribution, despite there being no change in the CU's external trade volumes. Formally, it is necessary to show that country k's welfare u^k after the formation of the CU is higher than it was beforehand u_0^k. That is:

$$u^k > u_0^k \text{ for all } k \in k^U, \tag{4}$$

where

$$\sum_{k \in k^U} S_p^k\left(p^U, u^k\right) = \sum_{k \in k^U} S_p^k\left(p^k, u_0^k\right) \tag{5}$$

The authors illustrate the solution to this problem in a diagram, showing that it is possible to reallocate consumption within the CU, through the choice of an appropriate CET and redistribution between member states. My problem with the diagram is that it oversimplifies the problem. The authors assume, for the sake of simplicity, that the CU's aggregate production vector remains fixed during the creation of the CU. I am sure that they would not expect this to happen in reality. Unlike those of non-CU nations, the vector of domestic prices in each member country changes as a result of its adoption of the CET ($\Delta p^k = t^U - t^k$) and this will induce adjustments in both national production and consumption. Effectively, the authors are assuming that production does not respond to these price changes and that the welfare improvement is to be achieved entirely through reallocation of consumption. A complete analysis, diagrammatic or otherwise, would include the changes in national production associated with joining the CU. If one thinks back to an older literature and the seminal work of Jacob Viner, the benefits of membership of a CU are closely tied to the changes in the source of supply; trade creation arising when consumers buy more from partners and trade diversion involving the switch from lower cost non-CU countries. These effects are heavily attenuated if only consumption changes are considered.

In the second part of the paper the attention turns to the situation where the non-CU countries are less passive and may change their tariffs in response to the formation of the CU. The authors offer an ingenious interpretation of the Kemp-Shimomura proposition. Effectively, they extend the Kemp-Wan proposition from its original setting to one where non-CU countries can optimally adjust their tariffs in response to the creation of the CU. The novelty is in the CU committing to setting external tariffs contingent upon world prices, such that it is in the interest of non-CU countries to maintain the same tariffs post-CU as before. With no change in external trade, the Kemp-Wan results continue to go through. This analysis and discussion is valuable in making clear the potential gains from CU formation even when outside countries can respond to the internal decisions of the CU.

Finally, the authors discuss the role of the WTO's Article XXIV in influencing the behaviour of newly formed CUs and suggest that a revision consistent with the Kemp-Shimomura proposition might be in order. Here my sceptical nature leads me to doubt the value of such a move. Article XXIV seems largely to be honoured in the breach, given the number of regional trade agreements approved under its auspices yet clearly being inconsistent with its rules.

Trade with Labor Market Distortions and Heterogeneous Labor: Why Trade Can Hurt

Kala Krishna*, Abhiroop Mukhopadhyay** and Cemile Yavas**

* Department of Economics, The Pennsylvania State University, University Park, USA and National Bureau of Economic Research, Cambridge, USA
** Department of Economics, The Pennsylvania State University, University Park, USA

1 Introduction

The latter part of the 20th century saw a surge in trade volumes. Some developing countries liberalized trade hoping to emulate the success of the East Asian miracle economies; others just out of the socialist bloc looked to the world for consumer goods. Most did not perform very well. During the early stages of liberalization, incomes even fell in many transition economies. It would seem appropriate to ask what might lead to such different experiences with trade liberalization.

We argue that labor market distortions and their interactions with trade liberalization might be important in answering this question. Our work is related to the literature in trade on factor market distortions, work in Labor Economics on heterogeneous labor, as well as to work in Development Economics on organizational differences between developing and developed economies.

While factor market distortions and their effect in open economies have been a focus of much work in trade, attention has been targeted for the most part on the effects of minimum wages. See for example, Brecher (1974a, b), which looks at the effect of a minimum wage distortion on an open economy and Davis (1998), which looks at the effects of trade between an economy with a minimum wage distortion (Europe) and one without it (the U.S.) and argues that trade may simultaneously prop up U.S. wages and cause greater unemployment in Europe. The minimum wage distortion in these studies is exogenously specified. Brecher (1992) and Kreickemeier (2003) develop an efficiency wage model with an endogenous factor market distortion which results in unemployment. In contrast, the endogenous distortion in our model results in resource misallocations, not in unemployment.[1]

If firms are unable to identify the ability of workers and workers are unable to fully signal their ability, then wages are positively related to the average ability of the labor pool firms draw from. For example, Weiss (1980) develops such a model

[1] See Rodrik (1987) for some other examples of endogenous distortions and the importance of modelling them in terms of structural parameters.

in a partial equilibrium closed economy setting and argues that job queues or unemployment could occur. Although our model has some common features with these models, we have a general equilibrium model in an open-economy setting.

There is also a large literature in Development Economics on the effects of family farms. However, most of this work deals with homogeneous labor in a closed economy setting. Family farming results in workers earning the average rather than the marginal product in agriculture. When workers are identical in ability and marginal product is diminishing, as has been assumed in this literature, average product exceeds marginal product so that too many workers remain in agriculture. In the development literature this distortion has been linked with the concept of "Disguised Unemployment", see Sen (1960). However, when labor varies in ability, as in our model, only lower ability labor remains in agriculture. The marginal worker obtains a wage below his marginal value product. As a result too few workers remain in agriculture rather than too many!

Differences in the way labor markets work crucially affect how production is organized in various economies. In market economies, workers are paid the value of their marginal product so that labor allocation between sectors is efficient. Such economies can only gain from trade. On the other hand, institutional constraints may prevent an efficient allocation of labor. In this paper we look at a particular kind of factor market distortion that can be interpreted both in the context of an economy making the transition from a socialist to a market economy, and in terms of institutions existing in parts of the developing world.

In the former socialist economies (transition economies), the state owned sectors (the distorted sector) usually pay a wage which is only loosely related to ability. If other sectors are undistorted and pay a productivity based wage, the best workers are attracted to the undistorted sector while the lower ability ones flock to the distorted sector. In developing economies, agriculture is run along family farm lines so that workers in agriculture (the distorted sector) can be thought of as obtaining a fixed wage rather than the value of their marginal product. When workers differ in their abilities, this leads to higher ability workers leaving agriculture.

With either interpretation, the effect of the distortion is the same. In autarky, too little of the distorted good is made and its price is too high. As a result, the distorted economy has a comparative disadvantage in the distorted good which is imported when the economy is opened up. This reduces the output of the distorted good and worsens the distortion. On the other hand, trade results in the usual price effects which raise welfare. Thus, welfare may rise or fall as a result of trade liberalization. However, a large distorted economy always loses from trade as it does not reap any beneficial price effects. This is in line with the literature on the theory of the second best (see Lipsey and Lancaster (1956)), where a recurring theme is that in the presence of existing distortions, reduction or removal of a distortion can lower welfare (see, for example, Ethier 1982).

In autarky, the effect of the distortion on welfare depends on the extent of substitutability in consumption. If the goods are perfect complements, in autarky the consumption levels are the same as in an undistorted economy. However if there is any substitutability, there is too little output in the distorted sector. The more the substitutability, the greater the deleterious effects of the distortion; since the price of the distorted good is higher than in an undistorted economy, consumers substitute away from it a lot when substitutability is high, causing far too little of the distorted good to be produced (as compared to the efficient level).

Trade involves importing the distorted good. With a Constant Elasticity of Substitution formulation of utility, the more substitutable the goods are in consumption, the greater the price effect through trade. As the price effect is beneficial, trade tends to raise welfare.

This paper builds on Krishna and Yavas (2002), which uses a Ricardian setup to show how such labor market distortions in transition and developing countries affect the level and distribution of income and hence the demand for indivisible consumer goods. In their model, effects in transition and developing economies differ, though the basic story is similar. They argue that in the absence of trade, wages are high due to the distortion, and as a result demand for indivisibles is high, which sustains these high wages. However, as the cost of the distorted good is higher in the distorted economy, it tends to be imported, with adverse consequences on the level and distribution of income.

Such factor market distortions have similar effects even when goods are divisible. By modifying the standard trade models, namely the Ricardian, Specific Factors, and Heckscher-Ohlin models, we are able to look at a wider set of issues.

Section 2 develops the Ricardian model and shows how this distortion affects labor allocation and output and why trade always makes existing distortions worse. We also look at the effects of substitutability between goods on the gains from trade for a distorted economy. Section 3 develops the Specific Factors model and argues that similar effects occur when the marginal productivity of labor is diminishing. Section 4 deals with the Heckscher-Ohlin model of trade with an endogenous allocation of capital and shows that this does not alter the flavor of the results. Section 5 contains some final remarks.

2 The Ricardian Model

There are two economies, Home and Foreign, which have access to the same technology, but differ in their institutional arrangements.[2] There are a continuum of individuals, indexed by γ, who are uniformly distributed on the unit interval with density related to the labor size. Type γ is endowed with γ units of effective labor. There are two goods, X and Y, and both goods are produced under competitive conditions. It takes one unit of effective labor, E, to make a unit of either good.

Let Y be the numeraire good with a price of unity. Let I be the total income of the economy, and let P and P^* denote the autarky price of X in Home and Foreign. Let L and L^* be the size of the labor force, i.e., the density of the distribution of γ, in Home and Foreign, respectively. Labor in the Y sector is paid the value of

[2] Since we are looking at the effects of different labor market institutions we abstract from differences in technology. These can be easily added to the model.

its marginal product in both economies. Labor in the X sector is paid its marginal product in Foreign, but is paid a constant wage per worker, independent of ability, in Home.

2.1 Autarky Equilibrium

In the undistorted economy, called Foreign, a worker with productivity γ earns γ if he works in Y and γP^* if he works in X. For both goods to be produced, P^* has to equal 1.

Let $\overline{w}$ be the fixed wage per worker in sector X in the distorted economy. This fixed wage has two interpretations. It can be interpreted as the wage per worker paid by state owned manufacturing firms. Alternatively, it can be interpreted as the income of a worker who works in the family farm and obtains the average product there.[3] The allocation of labor is depicted in Figure 1. At wage w, workers with $\gamma > w$, that is workers in OA, choose to work in X. The remaining workers choose to work in Y. An increase in the wage rate attracts workers with higher ability into X and raises the average quality of labor there.

At wage $\overline{w}$, and assuming γ is uniformly distributed, $\overline{w}L$ workers are employed in X, and total labor cost is $\overline{w}^2 L$. On average, each worker has $\frac{\overline{w}}{2}$ effective units of labor. Total output of X at this wage, denoted by $X(\overline{w})$, is

$$X(\overline{w}) = \frac{\overline{w}^2}{2} L.$$

Per unit cost of good X, and hence its price, P, is 2. In Home, as a result of the fixed wage per worker in sector X, workers (other than the marginal one) earn more than they would in the undistorted sector.[4] This raises the cost of producing good X, and hence its price. This, in turn, implies a lower output of the distorted sector in autarky equilibrium. Thus, there are too few workers in the X sector. This is depicted in Figure 2. The Production Possibility Frontier (PPF) of the distorted economy is the same as that of the undistorted one and given the Ricardian setup, it is linear. The undistorted economy produces at point A where the indifference curve is tangent to the PPF. As there is no unemployment, the distorted economy remains on the PPF. However, it produces at the wrong point, at B, making too little X. At B the price line is flatter than the PPF but is tangent to the indifference curve since consumption decisions are not distorted.[5]

---

[3] We assume that all family farms have the same (average) ability workers.

[4] Note that in the market economy, the productivity of the workers in X is equal to the value of marginal product in Y.

[5] In the extreme case where goods are perfect complements, the consumption and hence output levels in a distorted economy under autarky are the same as in an undistorted

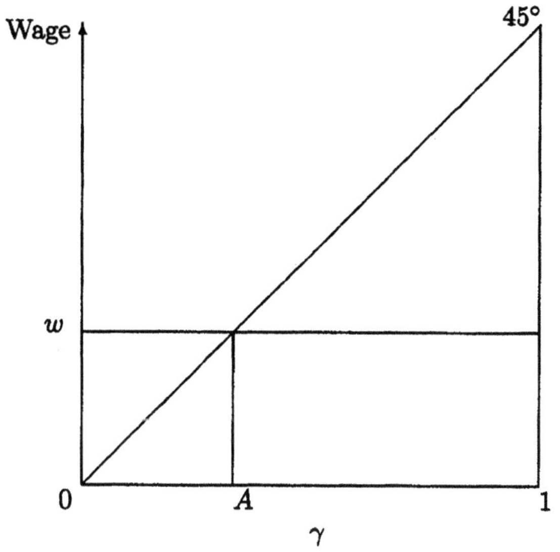

Figure 1. The Allocation of Labor Between Sectors in the Distorted Economy

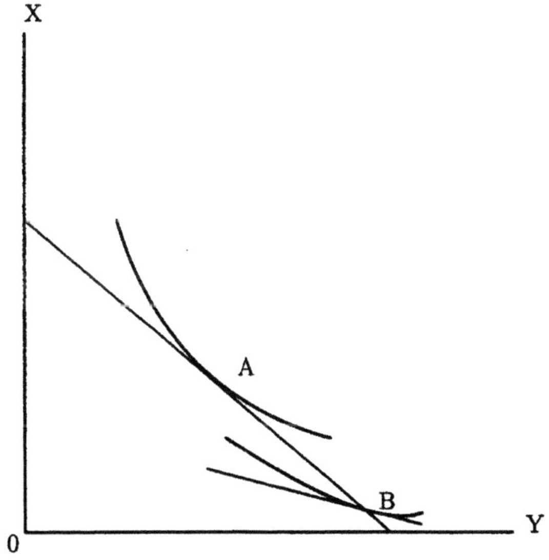

Figure 2. Autarky Equilibrium

---

economy. However as long as there is any substitutability, there is too little output in the distorted sector.

2.2 Trade Equilibrium

Trade equilibrium is best understood using the standard relative demand *(RD)* and relative supply *(RS)* framework. In Figure 3, RS^W depicts the world relative supply. At P=1 the undistorted economy becomes willing to produce good X and it can produce up to $\frac{L^*}{2}$ units while the distorted economy produces only good Y, $\frac{L}{2}$ units of it. Thus, the relative supply of good X at $P = 1$ is, at most, $\frac{L^*}{L}$. For $P \in (1,2)$, $RS^W = \frac{L^*}{L}$. At P=2, the distorted economy also becomes willing to produce good X and RS^W becomes horizontal. Thus, the price under free trade, P^F depends on the relative size of the two countries, L and L^*.

Given identical homothetic preferences across countries, the world relative demand (RD^W) depends on relative prices alone and is identical to that for either country. If, in addition, X and Y enter preferences symmetrically, then $RD^W = 1$ at P=1. Since relative supply at P=1 is at most $\frac{L^*}{L}$, if $\frac{L^*}{L} < 1$, then the intersection of RS^W and RD^W must occur at a point like b or c in Figure 3. Hence P^F must be greater than unity, and the undistorted economy completely specializes in good X. If $\frac{L^*}{L} \geq 1$, then this intersection must occur at a point like a in Figure 3. So $P^F = 1$ and the distorted country completely specializes in good Y.

This pattern makes sense since if $\frac{L^*}{L} < 1$, then Foreign is small relative to Home, and it must specialize in the distorted good, X, in which it has a comparative advantage. On the other hand, if $\frac{L^*}{L} \geq 1$, then Foreign is large relative to Home, it can produce enough to meet world demand of good X, and therefore Home completely specializes in the undistorted good, Y, in which it has a comparative advantage.

2.2.1 Welfare Effects

The undistorted economy never loses from trade. The effects on the distorted economy are varied. There are two effects at play. Recall that the distorted economy produces too little of the distorted good in autarky, and it has a comparative disadvantage in its production. Trade makes this distortion worse as the country produces even less of the distorted good after trade. There may however be a welfare gain through lower prices of X and this effect is strong when σ is large or L^* is large so that the price effect of trade is large. The net effect depends on which one dominates. If substitutability between goods is parameterized using a constant elasticity of substitution (CES) utility function, simulations show that welfare rises due to trade for $(\sigma, \frac{L^*}{L})$ that lie above a weakly downward sloping curve denoted by $\sigma(\frac{L^*}{L})$.

If $\frac{L^*}{L} \geq 1$, then Home makes only Y. Hence, the output effect is adverse. However, as $P^F = 1$, Home has the same price as an undistorted economy, consumes at the same point and obtains the same welfare as that of an undistorted economy. Hence, trade must always raise welfare in Home.

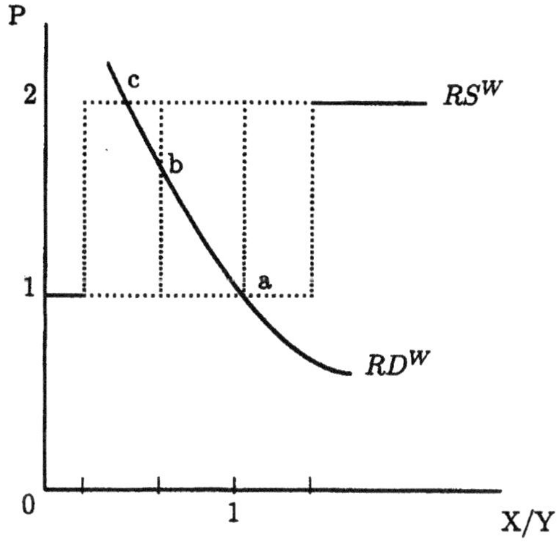

Figure 3. Trade Equilibrium in the Ricardian Model

If $\frac{L^*}{L} < 1$, then P^F must exceed unity, occurring at a point like b or c in Figure 3. For a given $\frac{L^*}{L}$, the lower the substitutability the higher the price in free trade. This occurs because when goods enter preferences symmetrically, the relative demand curve must always go through the point (1,1), i.e., the point a in Figure 3. It is easy to see that when σ is high enough the free trade price is close to unity, so Home welfare under trade approaches that of an undistorted economy. As a result, Home gains from trade. As σ falls from this high value, relative demand becomes steeper, rotating about the point (1,1). Since $\frac{L^*}{L} < 1$, the intersection with relative supply occurs at a higher price. At some level, say $\hat{\sigma}$, P reaches 2. At this level of σ, welfare must fall due to trade since Home makes only Y and prices are its autarky prices. By continuity, at some value of σ in between, $\sigma(\frac{L^*}{L})$, Home neither gains nor loses from trade.

Once σ reaches $\hat{\sigma}$, further decreases in σ do not affect the price in free trade. However, Home starts to produce both X and Y. In this region, Home must lose from trade as there is no positive price effect, and since Home imports X its production of X must be lower than under autarky.[6]

3 Specific Factors Model

Would the results derived above carry through if labor faced diminishing returns as it would in the presence of other factors? In the next two sections we show that their spirit does indeed carry through.

Consider the specific factors model. Each sector has a fixed amount of a specific factor which cannot move across sectors while labor is mobile. We assume that Home and Foreign are identical in every respect except that Home has a labor market distortion in X. Let E^i denote the effective units of labor employed in sector i, and K^i denote the fixed amount of specific factor employed in sector i, for i=X, Y. Let $X(E^X, K^X)$ and $Y(E^Y, K^Y)$ denote the constant returns to scale production functions for the two sectors, and let the price of Y be unity so that P denotes the relative price of X.

3.1 Autarky Equilibrium

As before, X pays a fixed wage per worker regardless of workers' ability while workers earn the value of their marginal product in Y. As a result of this, lower ability workers prefer to work for X while higher ability workers opt for Y. Let $\tilde{\gamma}$ be the worker who is indifferent between working for X and Y.

Let $w^e = Y_1(.)$ be the wage per effective unit of labor in Y (where subscript i denotes the derivative with respect to the ith argument). The earnings of a worker with ability γ in Y are $w^e y$ while the earnings of a worker in X are $\overline{w}$. In equilibrium, the highest ability worker in X, or $\tilde{\gamma}$, is indifferent between the two sectors so that

$$w^e \tilde{\gamma} = \overline{w}. \tag{1}$$

Note that a worker's decision whether to work for X or Y depends on $\frac{\overline{w}}{w^e}$. As this goes up, $\tilde{\gamma}$ rises, and the number of workers as well as the effective labor in X rises while that in Y falls.

What determines the allocation of effective labor in equilibrium? Note that given our assumption that ability is distributed uniformly over the interval [0,1] the average ability of workers employed in X is $\frac{\tilde{\gamma}}{2}$. We assume competition so

---

[6] Suppose its output of X was the same as under autarky. Then as price is the same as Home's autarky price, it must neither import nor export which is a contradiction.

that firms in X take $\overline{w}$ and the average ability of the work force, $(\frac{\tilde{\gamma}}{2})$, as given, and choose only how many such workers to hire.

Thus, the problem faced by firm j in X facing P, $\tilde{\gamma}$ and $\overline{w}$ is

$$\max_{n_j} \; PX(n_j \frac{\tilde{\gamma}}{2}, K_j^X) - \overline{w} n_j$$

where n_j is the proportion of labor force employed by firm j, and hence $n_j \frac{\tilde{\gamma}}{2}$ is the total units of effective labor employed by firm j, denoted by E_j. K_j^X is the amount of the factor specific to X that firm j has. The first order condition of the problem yields

$$PX_1(n_j \frac{\tilde{\gamma}}{2}, K_j^X) \frac{\tilde{\gamma}}{2} = \overline{w},$$

which in turn implies that

$$P = \frac{\overline{w}}{\frac{\tilde{\gamma}}{2} X_1(E_j^X, K_j^X)}. \tag{2}$$

Since all firms face the same prices and wages, their marginal products are equalized. Given constant returns to scale production functions, marginal products are homogeneous of degree zero and depend only on $\frac{E_j^X}{K_j^X}$. Hence, marginal products are equal for all firms and equal to that for the hypothetical aggregate firm. Thus,

$$X_1(E_j^X, K_j^X) = X_1(E^X, K^X). \tag{3}$$

Using equation (3) and substituting for $\overline{w}$ using (1) into (2), and noting that $w^e = Y_1(.)$ gives

$$P = 2 \frac{Y_1(.)}{X_1(.)} \tag{4}$$

as the relation defining the allocation of labor and relative supply in the distorted economy. Also note that when factors are paid in this manner, the value of output exactly equals factor payments.

$$\begin{aligned} PX(E_j^X, K_j^X) &= P[E_j^X X_1(.) + K_j^X X_2(.)] \\ &= P[\frac{\tilde{\gamma}}{2} n_j X_1(.) + K_j^X X_2(.)] \\ &= \overline{w} n_j + r K_j^X. \end{aligned}$$

The first equality follows from constant returns to scale. The second equality follows from the fact that hiring n_j workers of average quality $\frac{\tilde{\gamma}}{2}$ gives the effective labor E_j^X. The last equality follows from (2) and competitive capital markets. As a result, whether one thinks of a fixed wage per person being paid in *X* or whether one thinks of workers in *X* being equal residual claimants to output in *X* (once capital has been paid) gives the same result.

In an undistorted economy the marginal value products of the two sectors are equalized so that

$$PX_1(.) = Y_1(.),$$

and relative supply is given by

$$P = \frac{Y_1(.)}{X_1(.)}.$$

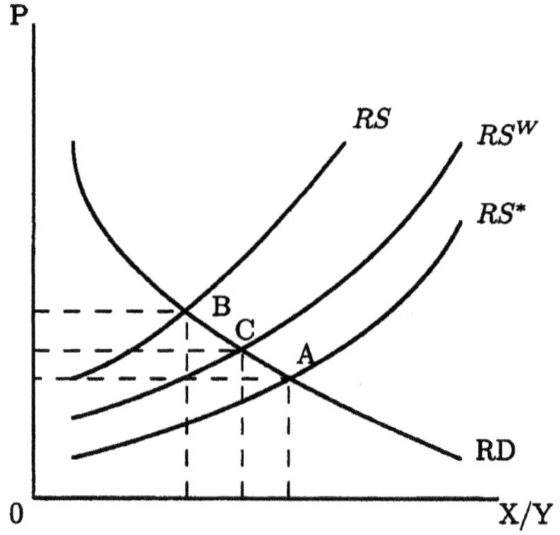

Figure 4. Equilibrium in the Specific Factors Model

Figure 4 illustrates these relative supply curves. For any given allocation of labor, and hence supplies, the price needed to elicit this relative supply in the distorted economy is twice that needed to elicit the same relative supply in the undistorted economy. Hence, at any given horizontal coordinate in Figure 4, the vertical coordinate of *RS* is twice that of RS* Given that preferences are identical and homothetic, relative demand is the same in all economies, so that differences in relative supplies translate to a higher autarky price of *X* in the distorted economy. In Figure 4, point *A* depicts the autarky equilibrium in Foreign, and point *B* depicts the autarky equilibrium in Home.

Given the higher autarky price, the distorted economy's relative demand for, and hence supply of, good *X* is lower than that in an undistorted economy, and therefore sector X in a distorted economy employs too little effective units of labor relative to an undistorted one.

These results can be better understood using Figures 5 and 6. Figure 5 illustrates the allocation of effective units of labor using the standard specific factors diagram. The two ends of the box are the origins for the two sectors and the downward sloping curves (with respect to their origins) depict the value of marginal product of an effective unit of labor in each sector. In the absence of a factor market distortion, the marginal productivity of labor in each sector is equalized. This is represented by point A. On the other hand, with labor market distortions, from (4), it follows that

$$PX_1(.) = 2Y_1(.) \qquad ()$$

and the marginal value product of an effective unit of labor in X equals twice that in Y. In other words, the equilibrium allocation of effective units of labor is such that the vertical length of the $VMPE_X$, denoted by w^X, is twice that of the $VMPE_Y$, denoted by w^Y, as illustrated by point B in Figure 5. Note that at any price, less of X is made and more of Y is made as a result.[7]

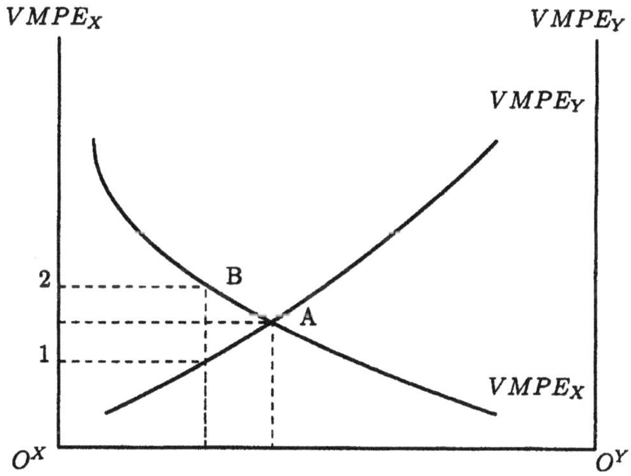

Figure 5. Allocation of Effective Labor

[7] With many sectors the same arguments work. As in Figure 5, draw the horizontal sum of $VMPE$ in each distorted sector using O_X as the origin and the horizontal sum of $VMPE$ in each undistorted sector using O_Y as the origin. In equilibrium, the $VMPE$ in each distorted sector equals the twice that in each undistorted sector.

Figure 6 depicts the production possibilities frontier for the distorted and undistorted economies, as well as production (which equals consumption) in autarky. Both economies have the same production possibility frontier (PPF) by assumption, and they both produce on the frontier as there is no unemployment in either. In the undistorted economy, the autarky relative price of good X (of $\frac{Y_1(.)}{X_1(.)}$) is tangent to both the PPF and to the indifference curve of the economy at point A. On the other hand, the distorted economy has a higher autarky relative price of good X, (of $\frac{2Y_1(.)}{X_1(.)}$) and it consumes and produces less X as depicted by point B. Moreover, the slope of the PPF at B is steeper than the price ratio which equals the slope of the indifference curve through B. Note that as a result its welfare is below that of the undistorted economy.

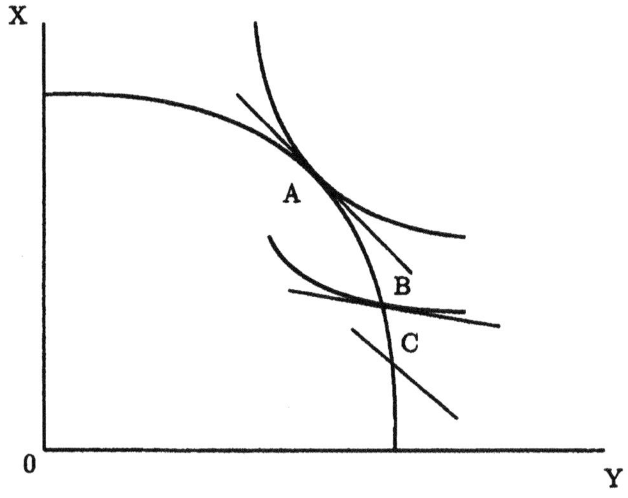

Figure 6. A Comparison of Equilibria

3.2 Free Trade Equilibrium

What will be the effect of trade in this environment? Does the distortion always get worse as in the Ricardian model, or can it get better? The answer follows quite simply. Given the relative supplies of the two economies as depicted in Figure 4, the world relative supply is given by RS^W which must lie in between RS and RS*. As relative demand for the world equals the common relative demand of the two countries, the free trade price must lie in between two autarky prices, as depicted by point C in Figure 4. Therefore, after opening up, Home observes a decline in the relative price of good X and hence its relative supply falls short of its relative demand and it imports good X and exports good Y.

Note that a reduction in the relative supply of X moves Home along its PPF to point C in Figure 6, thereby worsening the distortion in output. At given prices, this reduces welfare. However, the price of X also falls through trade. As Home is an importer of X, this raises welfare. The net effect of trade depends on which of these two effects, the output effect or the price effect, dominates. Under free trade, Home consumption lies along the line through C with slope P^F. It lies to the left of C as X is imported.

As an economy gets larger, the relative price in the free trade equilibrium approaches its autarky price, and therefore the extent of the beneficial price effect falls. If the Home country is very large, then the free trade price will be very close to its autarky price, and the price effect will be negligible. On the other hand, since the other country will export good X and import good Y, the output effect will remain. Therefore, it follows that a large economy must lose from trade.[8]

It is worth noting that trade between two distorted economies, one with a distortion in X and the other with a distortion in Y, causes the distortion in both countries to get worse as each country has a comparative disadvantage in the production of the good in which it has a distortion, and it will import this good in trade equilibrium producing even less of it.

4 Heckscher-Ohlin Model

What makes the Heckscher-Ohlin model different from the specific factors model is the assumption that K as well as E is mobile across sectors. This allows us to ask how the allocation of capital is affected by the distortion in the labor market, the effects of trade on this allocation decision, as well as the consequences of endogenous capital allocation for trade.

Assume, as usual, that there are no factor intensity reversals. Let $c^X(w,r)$ and $c^Y(w,r)$ denote the unit cost functions in the two sectors in the absence of any distortions, where w is the wage per effective unit of labor and r is the rental rate. In equilibrium, $c^X(w,r) = P$ and $c^Y(w,r) = 1$. These conditions are depicted in Figure 7 by the curves X and Y respectively. For both goods to be produced, factor prices must lie at their intersection, namely A.[9] As in the standard model, price cannot exceed cost as profits are zero, and if cost exceeds price, output is zero.

---

[8] Different groups are affected by trade as in the standard specific factors setup. The real return to the specific factor whose relative price goes up rises, while that of the other specific factor falls. The effect on the real return of labor depends on their preferences.

[9] See Mussa (1979) for the classical exposition of the Heckscher-Ohlin model in terms of its dual.

In the presence of the distortion, the wage per efficiency unit of labor will differ between sectors. If the wage per efficiency unit of labor in Y is w^e, then workers choose between earning $w^e\gamma$ in X and $\overline{w}$ in Y. The marginal worker, type $\widetilde{\gamma}$, gets the same in both sectors, so that (1) holds

$$w^Y\widetilde{\gamma} = \overline{w}. \tag{5}$$

Note that each worker in X has an average efficiency of $\frac{\widetilde{\gamma}}{2}$. Let w^X denote the implicit wage per efficiency unit in X. Thus, using (5) gives

$$w^X = \frac{\overline{w}}{\frac{\widetilde{\gamma}}{2}} = 2w^Y.$$

As there is no capital market distortion, r is common to both sectors. Consequently,

$$c^X(2w^Y, r) = P \tag{6}$$

and

$$c^Y(w^Y, r) = 1 \tag{7}$$

give the analogous equilibrium conditions in the distorted economy. The curve X^D which lies halfway between the curve X and the horizontal axis depicts (6) in Figure 7. In the absence of specialization, factor prices are given by the point B for the Y sector and the point C for the X sector. It is worth noting that the factor market distortion can easily lead to specialization in Y at a given price as X^D and Y may not intersect though X and Y do. The specialization in Y can be analyzed along standard lines. Here we focus on the case where both countries produce both goods. We look at how the distortion affects factor prices, capital labor ratios, factor allocations and output in a distorted economy relative to an undistorted one and whether it depends on whether X is capital intensive relative to Y or not.

If X is capital intensive, as depicted in Figure 7(a), then the wage-rental ratio, and hence capital-effective labor ratio, rises in both sectors relative to that in the undistorted economy. Since C is vertically above B, the wage-rental ratio rises by more in X than in Y, and X remains relatively capital intensive. Since total capital and labor is given, the only way for capital intensity to rise in both sectors is for the output of the labor intensive good, Y, along with the allocation of both factors to Y, to rise.

This is easy to verify using the standard Rybczynski box with dimensions K and E, the availability of capital and effective labor in the economy, as depicted in Figure 8. Factor market clearing can be depicted by adding the vector of factor use in X to that in Y (or Y to X) and having this sum reach the other end of the box, i.e., factor markets clear. If X is capital intensive, then the ray denoting the vector of factor use in X is steeper than that in Y, as depicted in Figure 8(a). For given wage-rental ratios, the output levels and factor usages in the two sectors are implicitly given by the intersection of the two rays, at point A. The coordinates of point A give the capital and effective labor usage in X while the remaining factors are used in *Y*. An increase in the wage rental ratio raises the capital-effective labor ratio in both sectors, making both rays steeper. At the new intersection, at point *B*, *X* must use less capital and less effective labor, so that at a given price, relative supply of *X* is lower in the distorted economy.

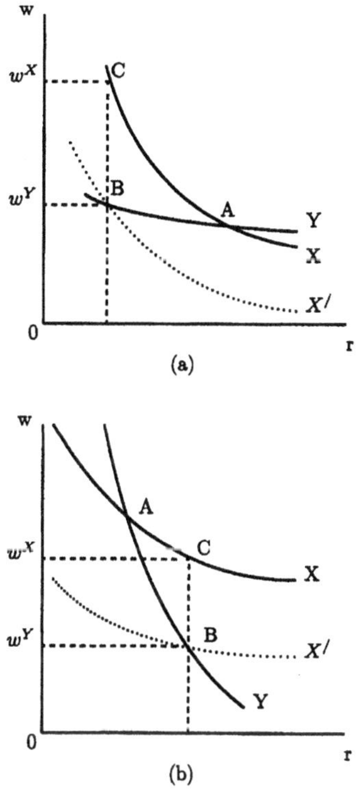

Figure 7. Factor Price Frontier

What if *X* is labor intensive, as depicted in Figure 7(b)? At a given price, if both goods are made, the distorted economy has a lower wage-rental ratio, and hence capital-effective labor ratio, relative to the undistorted economy in both *X* and *Y* since the slope of the line from the origin through *A* exceeds that through *B* or *C*. The only way for capital intensity to fall in both sectors is for the output of the capital intensive good, *Y*, along with the allocation of both factors to *Y*, to rise. Again, this is easy to verify using the Rybczynski box. If *X* is the labor-intensive sector, then the ray denoting the vector of factor usage in *X* is flatter than that in *Y* as illustrated in Figure 8(b). A decrease in the wage-rental ratio will reduce the capital-effective labor ratio in both sectors. In the Rybczynski box, this corresponds to both rays getting flatter. At the new equilibrium, at point *B*, sector *X* uses less capital and less effective labor, and hence relative supply of X is lower in the distorted economy, as earlier.

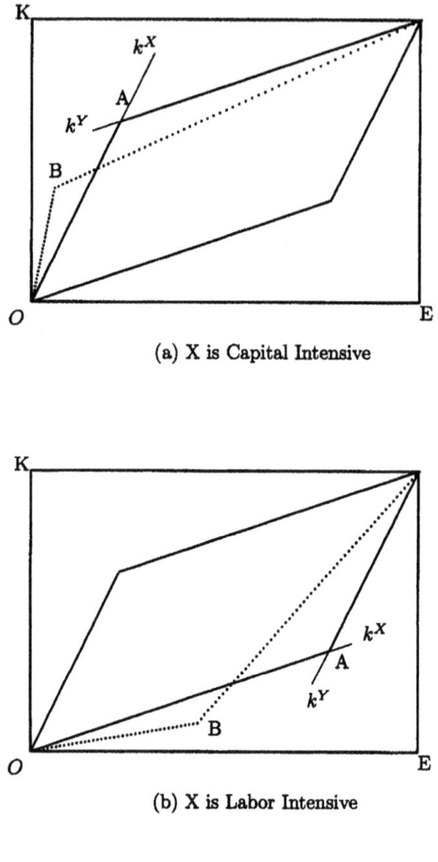

Figure 8. The Rybczynski Box

One might ask at this stage why X must be labor intensive relative to Y in the distorted economy. Since the wage-rental ratio, and hence, one might argue, the capital-effective labor ratio, could rise by more in X than in Y, it seems that X might become the capital intensive sector in the distorted economy, despite the absence of factor intensity reversals. That is, what prevents the slope of X at C from exceeding that of Y at B? We argue that this cannot happen in the absence of factor intensity reversals. The reasoning is simple. Fix a price. Assuming that both goods are made in the undistorted economy, the capital-effective labor ratio in the two sectors in the undistorted economy must bracket the economy's capital-effective labor ratio. As X is labor intensive, its capital-effective labor ratio must lie below *k*, the capital-effective labor ratio of the economy as a whole, while that of *Y* must lie above *k*. Since the wage rental ratio falls in both *X* and *Y*, so do capital labor ratios. If the capital-effective labor ratio in *Y* falls so much that it lies below that in *X*, both sectors' capital labor ratios must lie below *k*. However, this is inconsistent with factor markets clearing in the distorted economy.

Thus, whether *X* is capital or labor intensive, the distortion in the labor market in *X* results not only in a decrease in the allocation of labor to *X* but also a decline in capital allocated to *X* at given prices. In other words, the effects of distortion on the relative supply of *X* is more pronounced than in the specific factors model where capital could not move across sectors. Once again, the relative supply for the distorted and undistorted economies (*RS* and *RS**) are as in Figure 4. As relative demand is the same for both, the points *B* and *A* depict their autarky equilibria. Since *RS* lies to the left of *RS**, the autarky price in the distorted economy must exceed that in the undistorted one and the free trade price lies in between them. As a result, the price of *X* in the distorted economy falls due to trade, and it imports *X* which further reduces its output of it. Once again, while the price effect of trade raises welfare in the distorted economy, the output effect reduces it. The net effect will depend on which of these dominates as earlier.

Our main results are thus independent of which model we choose to use. The factor market distortion creates a comparative disadvantage in *X*. The price of *X* falls through trade for the distorted economy but as *X* is imported so does its output. The fall in the price of *X* raises welfare while the fall in output of *X* makes existing distortion worse.

5 Conclusion

The last decade has seen a large number of countries embracing trade reforms. However, many of them have not been able to emulate the success of the fast growing East Asian countries. Our analysis suggests that labor market distortion prevalent in developing countries might lead to a fall in welfare, especially for a large country, when such economies open up to trade. While the East Asian economies were small, economies that have not done as well tend to be larger.

Our results are consistent with the experiences of some transition economies. Most sectors in the erstwhile socialist economies were state owned in the old regime. This corresponds to all sectors having the labor market distortion. It is easy to verify that in our model if all sectors are distorted, production decisions remain efficient. Reform consisting of privatizing some sectors would however result in inefficiencies in production decisions, which would be worsened through trade. This is yet another example of the Theorem of the Second Best and the dangers of partial reform. Our analysis suggests that a dip in national income occurring in the initial stages of privatization is likely. This is consistent with the initial post reform experience of almost all transition economies; see Figure 1.2 in a recent monograph, World Bank (2002). Boeri and Terrell (2002) argue that part of the reason for the differing experiences in transition of the countries of the Former

Soviet Union (FSU) and those of the Central and Eastern European (CEE) can be explained in part by the different labor market policies they adopted.[10]

While our work here focuses on the implications of a labor market distortion, there are, of course, many other aspects of the experience of both developing and transition economies which are not addressed here. Many reasons have been put forward to explain the differential performance of developing economies. See, for example, Krueger (1984) and Ray (1998) for an overview of some of this literature. Similarly, there have been a number of interesting hypotheses put forward to explain the sharp decline in industrial output and GDP in Eastern Europe and the former Soviet Union countries. These include slow adjustment resulting in unemployment, see Gomulka (1992), investment delays caused by the unwillingness to invest till a good match is found since investment is relation specific, see Roland and Verdier (1999), and the disorganization hypothesis of Blanchard and Kremer (1997), where strong complementarities between inputs allows suppliers to exercise their bargaining power and disrupt production chains.

Our work has some natural extensions. In this paper, we assume that when there are other scarce factors of production, there is a perfect market in land and capital. All those who own land or capital earn the return from it and this is separate from who works with it. However, in many developing countries, leaving the family farm means giving up your rights on the land, and workers who remain in the family farm share the entire output of the farm. The implications of such a labor market distortion are different than the one analyzed here. For one, the factor market distortion could result in too little or too much being produced.

Another natural extension concerns capital flows. There have been large capital flows between market economies and transition and developing economies (see Lucas (1990)). Here we do not allow capital to move between countries. Augmented versions of this model can also help explain the simultaneous occurrence of factor movements and goods trade without resorting to explanations relying on trade barriers (as does the work on Multinationals) or adjustment costs (which results in capital flows being spread out over time). Extending the model in these directions is part of an on-going research agenda.

References

Blanchard O, Kremer M (1997) Disorganization. Quarterly Journal of Economics 112 : 1091–1126

Boeri T, Terrell K (2002) Institutional Determinants of Labor Reallocation in Transition. Journal of Economic Perspectives 16 : 51–76

Brecher R (1974a) Optimal Commercial Policy for a Minimum Wage Economy. Journal of International Economics 4 : 139–149

[10] The CEE countries propped up wages at the bottom of the distribution while the FSU countries allowed greater wage flexibility. As a result, unproductive sectors collapsed more in the former than in the latter.

Brecher R (1974b) Minimum Wage Rates and the Pure Theory of International Trade. Quarterly Journal of Economics 88 : 98–116

Brecher R (1992) An Efficiency-Wage Model with Explicit Monitoring: Unemployment and Welfare in an Open Economy. Journal of International Economics 32 : 179–191

Davis D (1998) Does European Unemployment Prop Up American Wages? National Labor Markets and Global Trade. American Economic Review 88 : 478–494

Ethier W (1982) Decreasing Costs in International Trade and Frank Graham's Argument for Protection. Econometrica 50 : 1243–1268

Gomulka S (1992) The Causes of Recession Following Stabilization. Comparative Economic Studies 33 : 71–89

Kreickemeier U (2003) Efficiency Wages and Unemployment in a Global Economy. The University of Nottingham, Research Paper 2003/33

Krueger A (1984) Trade and Employment in Developing Countries Vol 3 Synthesis and Conclusions, University of Chicago Press, Chicago London

Krishna K, Yavas C (2002) When Does Trade Hurt? Market, Transition and Developing Economies. NBER Working Paper No 8995

Lipsey RG, Lancaster K (1956) The General Theory of Second Best. Review of Economic Studies 24 : 11–32

Lucas RE (1990) Why Doesn't Capital Flow from Rich to Poor Countries? American Economic Review 80 : 92–96

Mussa M (1979) The Two-Sector Model in Terms of its Dual: A Geometric Exposition. Journal of International Economics 9 : 513–526

Ray D (1998) Development Economics. Princeton University Press, Princeton NJ

Rodrik D (1987) Policy Targeting with Endogenous Distortions: Theory of Optimum Subsidy Revisited. Quarterly Journal of Economics 102 : 903–911

Roland G, Verdier T (1999) Transition and the Output Fall. Economics of Transition 7 : 1–28

Sen A (1960) Choice of Technique. Blackwell, Oxford

Weiss A (1980) Job Queues and Layoffs in Labor Markets with Flexible Wages. Journal of Political Economy 88 : 526–538

World Bank (2002) Transition: The First Ten Years. Analysis and Lessons for Eastern Europe and the Former Soviet Union. World Bank, Washington DC

Comment

Kenzo Abe

Graduate School of Economics, Osaka University, Japan

This interesting paper shows that developing countries or transition economies may lose from trade in the modified Ricardian, Specific Factor and Heckscher-Ohlin models that incorporate labor market distortions. The authors present a new mechanism that explains why free trade is not always beneficial to those countries with a distortion or market failure. The WTO pushes forward trade liberalization but it may not be successful without appropriate remedies for institutional constraints in those countries.

The new feature of this paper lies in its formulation of the labor market. Workers differ in their ability or productivity. The distortion arises because workers are paid a flat wage rather than their marginal product in one sector (the distorted sector) while the other sector (the undistorted sector) pays the value of marginal product to each worker. This flat wage means that workers in the distorted sector receive the same wage in spite of the differences in their ability. It differs from the fixed minimum wage regulated by a government. The level of the flat wage is determined by the market demand and supply so that labor is fully employed. An agricultural sector run by family farms in developing countries and a state-owned sector in transition economies are good examples of the distorted sector.

We can see too few workers in the agricultural sector or the state-owned sector in this model, which shows a contrasting result to the well-known "Disguised Unemployment" model where too much workers are in such a sector. If workers differ in their ability, those workers with lower productivity than the flat wage choose to work in the distorted sector. This is because such workers receive the lower wage than the flat wage if they work in the undistorted sector. Then, the average cost or price of the good produced in the distorted sector becomes higher than the social marginal cost, and its production level becomes less then optimal. The economy with this flat wage system (the distorted economy) is inefficient in the sense that there are too few workers or too small production in the distorted sector.

In the distorted economy the welfare effects of opening trade or trade liberalization consist of two effects: the terms of trade effect and the effect of a change in the transition. The former effect increases welfare of trading countries as long as the prices of goods change by opening trade. On the other hand, the latter effect increases (decreases) welfare if the magnitude of the distortion becomes larger (smaller). If the distorted economy trades with the other country (the undistorted economy) where all sectors pay the value of marginal product to workers, the former economy has a comparative disadvantage in the good produced in the distorted sector. Then international trade enlarges the magnitude of the distortion and yields a negative welfare effect since it reduces the amount of production in the distorted sector. If this negative welfare effect is larger than the terms of trade effect, the distorted economy from trade.

The model of this paper is a very simple one, and the argument is very clear and interesting. I just have a few comments on the paper.

My first comment relates to the country size of the distorted economy and the gains from trade. In the modified Ricardian model the distorted economy gains from trade if the amount of labor supply in the distorted economy is smaller than that in the undistorted economy. In this case the consumption bundle of the distorted economy under free trade is identical to that under autarky with no distortion. So trade benefits the distorted economy. The paper points out that the smaller distorted economy tends to gain from trade in the modified Specific Sector Model, too. According to the results of the paper, the small country gains from trade even if the distorted sector remains in the country. In the real world the country size of developing countries or transition economies is considered to be smaller than that of a developed country. Then the institutional constraints like a flat wage in this model may not explain the observed fact that trade liberalization hurts those countries since the welfare effects of such distortion is negligible in small countries.

Second, the countries with the flat wage sector may lose from trade, but it does not mean that trade liberalization is bad for those countries. It is the existence of the labor market distortion that makes the country loose from trade. Then, trade liberalization accompanied by some appropriate policy to reduce the distortion could increase the welfare of the country. For example, consider a direct policy to the distorted labor market like a wage subsidy to the flat wage sector. The subsidy decreases the average cost of production or the price of the good in the distorted sector, and increases its demand and supply. Thus, the wage subsidy to the distorted sector increases the number of workers or the production level in the sector and reduces the magnitude of the distortion. Accompanied by an appropriate wage subsidy to the distorted sector, opening trade or trade liberalization can always increase the welfare of all countries. The distorted economy should not be against trade liberalization, but should consider a good combination of trade liberalization and domestic policies that remove the labor market distortion.

Ma third comment is a rather technical one. In general the relative supply curve in the Heckscher-Ohlin model may not have an upward slope if there is a distortion in factor markets. The production occurs inside of the production possibility frontier and a raise in the relative price of a good does not necessarily increase the relative supply of the good. Then, even if the relative supply curve of the distorted sector's good in the distorted economy lies to the left of that in the undistorted economy, it does not imply that the distorted economy has a comparative disadvantage in the good. In this case some additional assumption like a stability condition will be needed to obtain the result in this paper.

The Impact of Intra-Industry Trade on the Environment

K. C. Fung and Andréa M. Maechler

Department of Economics, University of California, Santa Cruz, USA

1 Introduction

Recent years have witnessed two interesting developments in trade theory, namely, the emergence of intra-industry trade as a widespread phenomenon and a revitalization of the concern about the environmental consequences of international trade.[1] By providing a link between these two strands of the literature, the present paper departs from the standard inter-industry trade approaches used in the trade-environment debate and offers new perspective to revisit this issue in the context of intra-industry trade.

The concept of intra-industry emerged when it became apparent that much of the trade growth experienced over the last fifty years is attributable to an increase in two-way trade within the same industry. This is particularly true for the manufacturing sector, among which rank some of the most pollution-intensive industries, including chemicals, metallurgy, mining, and paper and pulp. Bernhofen (1999), for example, has tested and supported the statistical evidence that a significant share of international trade in certain highly polluting industries, such as the coal market, takes the form of two-way trade.

For illustration, Table 1 presents indexes of intra-industry trade for selected U.S. manufacturing industries in 1993. An index close to one (such as 0.99 for inorganic chemicals) indicates that for this industry the U.S. imports almost as much as it exports, while an index close to zero indicates that for this industry, the U.S. is only an exporter or an importer (such as 0.20 for footwear).[2] While earlier em-

[1] For excellent surveys on the environment-trade nexus, see Anderson and Blackhurst (1992), Beghin, Roland-Holst and van der Mensbrugghe (1994) and Low (1992). See Bhagwati and Hudec (1997) for critical discussions on the international harmonization of environmental standards. Finally, Rauscher (1997) offers an insightful chapter on the interlinkages between trade and the environment in an imperfect competition framework. Although the main focus of his work considers how environmental policies can be used to achieve trade-related policy objectives, he introduces a monopolistic competition model to sketch some of the environmental consequences of intra-industry trade.

[2] For a recent empirical study of intra-industry trade in pollution-intensive homogeneous products, see the recent work by Bernhofen (1999). This paper uses the Brander (1981) model of intraindustry trade in identical commodities to conduct an empirical investigation in the context of the petrochemical industry in Germany and the United States.

pirical work focuses on industrial countries, more recent studies suggest that this phenomenon is not limited to industrialized countries and can be significant in developing countries.[3] In fact, a new consensus is emerging from recent experience suggesting that trade liberalization has been a powerful vehicle for the growth of intra-industry trade in a wide range of countries.[4]

Table 1. Intra-Industry Trade for U.S. Industry, 1993 [values in percent]

Inorganic Chemicals	0.99
Power-Generating Machinery	0.97
Electric Machinery	0.97
Organic Chemicals	0.96
Medical and Pharmaceutical	0.86
Iron and Steel	0.43
Footwear	0.29

Source: Krugman and Obstfeld (1997)

The observation that an increasing share of trade expansion is taking the form of intra- rather than inter-industry trade is of particular importance when examining the far-reaching environmental consequences of trade liberalization. For example, the literature recognizes that the adjustment costs associated with shifting resources across industries (i.e., from import-competing industries to export-competing industries) are generally much larger than those associated with switching resources across different product lines within the same industry.[5] Following the same argument, trade liberalization is also likely to yield very different effects on the environment depending on whether the underlying structure of trade leads to inter- or intra-industry trade expansion. This suggests that, in the presence of intra-industry factor movements, the interactions between international trade and the quality of the environment need to be analyzed in their own right, that is, independently of what occurs in the presence of inter-industry factor movements.

So far, however, the question of international trade and the environment has not been addressed in the context of intra-industry trade. Thus, the purpose of this paper is to fill this gap in the literature and to add elements of intra-industry trade to the current debate on trade and the environment.

Broadly, the literature on the environmental consequences of international trade distinguishes between three effects, namely, the *scale* effect that always increases

---

[3] For a comprehensive survey of the literature on intra-industry trade, see Greenaway and Milner (1986) and Helpman (1987). Tharakan (1984) provides evidence on intra-industry trade between OECD countries and the developing world.

[4] For example, Hoekman and Djankov (1996) presents evidence for trade liberalization-induced intra-industry trade expansion in Eastern Europe, Lee and Lee (1993) in Korea and Menon (1994) in Australia.

[5] Krugman (1981), for example, shows that in the context of intra-industry trade it is possible for all factors of production to gain, which can alleviate adjustment costs. See Menon and Dixon (1996, 1997) for a general discussion on factor market disruption under inter- versus intra-industry trade.

pollution (trade induces more output, which means more pollution); the *technique* effect that always decreases pollution (trade makes cleaner technologies available, which reduces pollution) and the *composition* effect (trade alters the pattern of production).[6] To isolate the link between intra-industry factor relocation and environmental damage, we put aside both, the technique and the scale effects and focus on the third and largely contentious effect, that is, the composition effect of trade.[7]

The composition effect of trade relies on the theory of comparative advantage to predict how trade alters the composition of national output and thereby, the quality of the environment.[8] For example, trade may deteriorate the quality of the environment if it causes, say, the relatively capital-abundant countries to specialize in the (dirty) capital-intensive goods.[9] Trade may also deteriorate the quality of the environment if it induces the dirty industries to relocate away from the industrialized countries imposing tougher environmental standards towards the lower-income countries requiring lower environmental standards.[10] According to these arguments, global trends in environmental degradation are explained by inter-industry factor relocation.

The present paper, however, offers a very different approach to address the trade-environment nexus. It focuses on intra-industry trade as the main culprit of environmental degradation. In this context, the composition effect of trade generates a very different kind of change in the pattern of production, namely, one that alters an industry's output mix across international oligopolies rather than modify-

[6] This decomposition is first introduced in Grossman and Krueger (1993, 1995), elaborated in Copeland and Taylor (1994, 1995) and then tested in Antweiler, Copeland and Taylor (1998). Note that the scale and the technique effects can incorporate the income effect, which is discussed in Copeland (1995), Copeland and Taylor (1994) and Grossman and Krueger (1993).

[7] The technique effect relies on a very different set of theoretical premises dealing with the role of technological progress. The scale effect requires a general equilibrium analysis, while our model, which follows the tradition of the new oligopoly literature, is set in a partial equilibrium framework. It is important to keep in mind, however, that whatever the environmental consequences of trade via the composition effect are (which Antweiler, Copeland and Taylor (1998) finds to be only slightly negative), the full impact of trade may be either positive or negative, depending on the relative strength of the (positive) technique and the (negative) scale effects.

[8] The theory of comparative advantage predicts that a country tends to export products that use intensively the factors of production with which it is relatively well endowed, and import those that use intensively its scarce factors. With respect to the environment, the effects of trade depend on whether a country becomes an exporter or an importer of pollution-intensive goods in the postliberalization situation. In the absence of transboundary pollution, trade is good for the domestic environment in the former case, while it is bad in the latter case.

[9] This hypothesis, which is refered to as the "simple factor endowment" hypothesis, relies on factor-abundance to explain the link between trade and the environment.

[10] The literature refers to this hypothesis as to the "pollution-haven" or "dirty industry migration".

ing a country's commodity mix across industries. In particular, we find that global trends in environmental deterioration are determined largely by two factors, namely: (i) by which trading partner liberalizes trade, and (ii) by the nature of pollution (i.e., whether pollution is local, transboundary or global). For example, our model predicts that the global environment can benefit from trade liberalization, provided that the most pollution-intensive country liberalizes trade.

By restricting our analysis to the context of oligopolistic intra-industry trade, our model isolates the source of trade to be determined solely by the strategic interactions of oligopolistic polluting firms and not by cost differences and/or by economies of scale.[11] In reality, of course, the determinants of trade are manifold, including differences in factor endowments, income levels, technological capabilities and regulatory and institutional frameworks. But given the strong empirical evidence in support of a substantial and ever-growing volume of intra-industry trade, it remains useful to analyze the likely impact of international trade on the quality of the environment in this limited context.

This paper is organized as follows. Section 2 presents our basic duopoly model of intra-industry trade and derives the environmental consequences of trade liberalization under local, transboundary and global pollution. Section 3 extends the basic model to verify the validity of our results in the presence of multiple ...rms. In Section 4, we examine how trade collusion alters our basic results. In Section 5, we introduce foreign direct investment (FDI) to discuss the impact of trade liberalization on the quality of the environment when one of the trading partners engages in FDI activities. Finally, concluding comments are provided in Section 6.

2 Basic Model

2.1 Framework

We develop a standard intra-industry trade model in the tradition of Brander (1981) and Brander and Krugman (1983). There are two countries, a home country and a foreign country, each holding one polluting firm. Consumers consume goods which are produced both at home and abroad. Because most intra-industry trade occurs between similar economies, it is safe to assume that the two countries have similar tastes and endowments. The home (foreign) country produces a pollution-intensive good which is sold in the home (foreign) market and which can also be exported to the foreign (home) market. The profit function of, respectively, the home and the foreign firm is written as:

$$\pi_x = x_1 p_{x1} + x_2 p_{x2} - e_x(x_1 + x_2) - t_x x_2 \tag{1}$$

[11] Note, however, economies of scale would be a key determinant of environmental deterioration in the context of monopolistic competition.

$$\pi_y = y_1 p_{y1} + y_2 p_{y2} - e_y (y_1 + y_2) - t_y y_1 \tag{2}$$

where x_i (i = 1,2) represents a pollution-intensive good that is produced in the home country and y_i (i = 1,2) represents a pollution-intensive good that is produced in the foreign country. The subscripts indicate whether a good is sold in the home market (1) or in the foreign market (2).

For example, while the first term in equation (1) represents the domestic sales of the home firm, the second term represents its export sales. The third term represents the home pollution tax e_x; which the home country imposes on all home-produced pollution-intensive goods, regardless of whether they are sold at home or abroad. Finally, the fourth term represents the foreign import tariff t_x; which the home country faces when exporting its pollution-intensive production abroad. Similarly for the foreign profit function in equation (2), where the first term represents its export sales to the home country, the second term represents its domestic sales to the foreign market, the third term represents the foreign pollution tax ey imposed on the foreign produced pollution-intensive good and the fourth term represents the home import tariff t_y imposed on foreign exports.

To highlight the environmental effects of trade liberalization, we assume zero production and transportation costs and focus solely on pollution taxes and/or trade protection. While the assumption of zero production and transportation costs greatly simplifies the interpretation of the results, it does not affect its general conclusions.

We assume a symmetric linear demand structure and allow for differentiated goods (that is, we assume $\beta_1 = \beta_2 \neq \gamma$)[12]:

$$p_{xi} = \alpha_1 - \beta_{xi} - \gamma y_i$$

$$p_{yi} = \alpha_2 - \beta_{yi} - \gamma x_i$$

where $\alpha_i (i = 1,2) > 0, \beta > 0, and\ \gamma > 0$. Assuming that the firms are Cournot-Nash players, the first-order profit maximization conditions yield the following outputs:

$$x_1^{CN} = \frac{2\beta(\alpha_1 - e_x) - \gamma(\alpha_2 - e_y - t_y)}{D} \tag{3}$$

$$x_2^{CN} = \frac{2\beta(\alpha_1 - e_x - t_x) - \gamma(\alpha_2 - e_y)}{D} \tag{4}$$

[12] This demand structure is associated with the following aggregate utility function: $U_i = w_i + m_i$,where $w_i = \{\alpha_1 x_i + \alpha_2 y_i - \frac{1}{2}(\beta(x_i^2 + y_i^2) + 2\gamma x_i y_i)\}$ represents the expenditure on x_i and y_i and m_i the expenditures on all other goods in country *i*.

$$y_1^{CN} = \frac{2\beta(\alpha_2 - e_y - t_y) - \gamma(\alpha_1 - e_x)}{D} \tag{5}$$

$$y_2^{CN} = \frac{2\beta(\alpha_2 - e_y) - \gamma(\alpha_1 - e_x - t_x)}{D} \tag{6}$$

where $D = (4\beta^2 - \gamma^2)$. Note that the concavity assumption of the aggregate utility function U_i associated with the above demand functions implies that $(\beta^2 - \gamma^2) > 0$ Furthermore, we assume that the own-price effects are greater than the cross-price effects, that is, $\beta > \gamma$.

2.2 Conditions for Intra-Industry Trade

The existence of intra-industry trade requires that $x_2^{CN} > 0$ and $y_1^{CN} > 0$. Thus, the conditions for intra-industry trade can be expressed as:

$$x_2^{CN} > 0 \; iff \; \frac{2\beta}{\gamma} > \frac{(\alpha_2 - e_y)}{(\alpha_1 - e_x - t_x)}$$

$$y_1^{CN} > 0 \; iff \; \frac{2\beta}{\gamma} > \frac{(\alpha_1 - e_x)}{(\alpha_2 - e_y - t_y)}$$

According to the above conditions, intra-industry trade is more likely to occur in the presence of: (i) greater product differential (high β/γ); (ii) low import tariffs, t_i; and (iii) lower environmental standards imposed on the exporting country i (high $\alpha_i - e_i$), where i represents the liberalized country.[13]

2.3 Unilateral Trade Liberalization

Assume that the home (foreign) country implements a unilateral trade liberalization, such that $dt_y < 0$ (dtx < 0): The impact of such a trade policy on the demand for pollution-intensive goods is given in the following equations:

$$\frac{\partial x_1^{CN}}{\partial t_y} = \frac{\gamma}{D} > 0 \tag{7}$$

[13] The results in the present paper are derived under the assumption that the pollution-intensive goods are differentiated goods $(i.e., \beta_1 = \beta_2 \neq \gamma)$: Assuming homogenous goods $(i.e., \beta_1 = \beta \neq \gamma)$; however, would not alter significantly our results, except that the conditions for intra-industry trade become stricter, requiring an even lower import tariff and/or an even higher environmental differential between the two countries for our results to hold.

$$\frac{\partial y_1^{CN}}{\partial t_y} = -\frac{2\beta}{D} < 0 \tag{8}$$

For example, by unilaterally liberalizing trade, the home country facilitates the access of foreign pollution-intensive goods into the home market. Given our earlier assumption that the own-price effects exceed the cross-price effects, i.e. $\beta > \gamma$, the increase in imports exceeds the fall in the demand for the domestically produced good $(i.e., |\partial y_1^{CN} / \partial t_y| > |\partial x_1^{CN} / \partial t_y|)$. Thus, on aggregate, a unilateral trade always increases the domestic consumption of the pollution-intensive good and reduces its domestic production.

Similarly for a foreign trade liberalization, which increases the demand for the imported good by more than it decreases the demand for the domestically-produced polluting good, raising the aggregate foreign consumption of the pollution-intensive good and reducing its foreign production.

$$\frac{\partial y_2^{CN}}{\partial t_x} = -\frac{\gamma}{D} > 0 \tag{9}$$

$$\frac{\partial x_2^{CN}}{\partial t_x} = -\frac{2\beta}{D} < 0 \tag{10}$$

In summary, a unilateral trade liberalization ($dt_i < 0$) raises the pollution-intensive output in the country benefiting from trade liberalization and lowers it in the liberalizing country. Furthermore, the liberalizing country increases its aggregate consumption of the pollution-intensive good.

Although these results set the stage for our analysis, we need to go one step further and to model how the volume effects of trade liberalization presented in equation (7)-(10) above translate into the environmental impact of trade liberalization. This is what we do next.

2.4 Environmental Damage

In this section, we focus on how a unilateral trade liberalization affects the environment in a world where the quality of the environment is a by-product of the production of pollution-intensive goods.[14] To tackle this question, we assume that pollution harms consumers without affecting the production possibility frontier and that the source of pollution may lie outside of national boundaries. We differ-

[14] Although most of the existing theoretical work focuses on production-generated pollution, Copeland and Taylor (1995, 1999) examine, respectively, pollution as a by-product of consumption and pollution as it affects productivity.

entiate between three types of pollution, namely: (i) local pollution; (ii) transboundary pollution; and (iii) global pollution.[15]

Although no strict line delimiting local pollution from transboundary or even global pollution does exist, the impact of various types of production-generated pollutions on the environmental quality may be very different in scope. When pollution is local, a country's environmental damage is determined entirely by its domestic polluting production. Examples of local pollution abound and include urban air pollution, local soil erosion and local contamination of water, air and land. When pollution is transboundary, environmental damage spills across national boundaries and the quality of a country's environment is determined by the sum of two components, namely, the pollution generated by its own domestic polluting production and a fraction of the pollution generated during the polluting production abroad. Acid rain, for example, is often cited as an illustration of transboundary pollution. The production of certain pollution-intensive goods releases pollutants in the air, which are then carried by winds hundreds of miles away from their production site before being deposited again in the atmosphere through rain, fog or snow. In this situation, a country cares about the type and the quantity of pollution generated abroad. Finally, when pollution is global, a country's environmental damage is determined by the aggregate pollution-intensive production, regardless of the country of production. Examples of global pollution include the deterioration of the ecosystem, the depletion of the ozone layer and global warming.

The environmental damage of, respectively, the home and the foreign country, can be written as:

$$Ed_x = d_x(x_1 + x_2) + \eta_y d_y(y_1 + y_2)$$

$$Ed_y = d_y(y_1 + y_2) + \eta_x d_x(x_1 + x_2)$$

where d_i (i = x, y) represents the environmental damage associated with the pollution-intensive goods produced, respectively, in the home (x) country and in the foreign (y) country. η_i represents the pollution spillover parameter and illustrates the extent to which pollution generated in one country damages the environment in the other country.[16]

[15] Although there is an extensive literature on transboundary pollution (see Dean 1992 for a survey), there is little work examining the environmental consequences of trade in an imperfect competitive framework and even less in an intra-industry setting (see Rauscher 1997).

[16] While there is an extensive literature on transboundary pollution, it is mostly concerned with how environmental regulations affect trade, rather than how trade affects the quality of the environment (Siebert, 1977 and Baumol and Oates, 1988). See Copeland and Taylor (1993, 1995) for a discussion on the role of transboundary pollution in the debate over trade and the environment.

At one extreme, η_i is zero and one country's pollution does not affect the quality of the environment in the other country. This is the case of local pollution. At the other extreme, η_i is equal to one and pollution produced in either country affects both countries equally. This is when pollution is global. Finally, if η_i lies somewhere between zero and one, pollution is transboundary. In this case, no country is completely insulated from the other country's pollution and pollution incurred in one country spills over to the other country. Since the pollution parameter is between zero and one, the damage that a country incurs from its own pollution is greater than the damage it incurs from the pollution generated abroad.

To clarify our analysis, we assume that the home country is the 'clean' country, in the sense that it imposes a higher pollution tax than the foreign country, or, $e_x > e_y$. Furthermore, we also assume that the stricter environmental standards induce the clean country to generates less pollution than the foreign country or, $d_x < d_y$. These assumptions allow us to focus on a particular scenario, without compromising the generality of our results. Henceforth, we will use interchangeably the terms of home and clean country on the one hand, and of foreign and dirty country on the other hand.

We can turn now to the effects of a unilateral trade liberalization on the environment.

2.4.1 Local Pollution

When pollution is local, the environmental damage of, respectively, the home and the foreign country, is given by:

$$Ed_x^l = d_x(x_1 + x_2)$$

$$Ed_y^l = d_y(y_1 + y_2)$$

Clearly, under local pollution, there is a direct link between a country's level of polluting production and the quality of its environment: a country raises (lowers) the quality of its environment if it decreases (increases) its pollution-intensive production. The effects of a unilateral trade liberalization by the clean country on the environmental damage of, respectively, the clean and the dirty country, are given by:

$$\frac{\partial Ed_x^l}{\partial t_y} = \frac{\gamma d_x}{D} > 0$$

$$\frac{\partial Ed_y^l}{\partial t_y} = -\frac{2\beta d_y}{D} < 0$$

We have seen above that a unilateral trade liberalization raises the polluting output in the country benefiting from the liberalization and reduces it in the liberalizing country. Thus, a trade liberalization by the clean country transfers the production of the pollution-intensive good away from the clean country towards the dirty country. This lowers the environmental damage in the clean country and raises it in the dirty country, or, put differently, this raises the quality of the environment in the clean country and deteriorates in the dirty country.

Similarly, if the dirty country liberalizes trade, the production of the pollution intensive good is shifted away from the dirty country towards the clean country. Thus, a unilateral trade liberalization by the dirty country lowers the environmental damage in the dirty country (which produces now less of the pollution-intensive good) and raises it in the clean country (which produces now more of the pollution-intensive good). This can be seen in the following equations:

$$\frac{\partial Ed_x^l}{\partial t_x} = -\frac{2\beta d_x}{D} < 0$$

$$\frac{\partial Ed_y^l}{\partial t_x} = \frac{\gamma d_y}{D} > 0$$

These equations highlight one very interesting point, namely, that a unilateral trade liberalization actually improves the quality of the environment in the country that liberalizes trade, regardless of which country is liberalizing. This is a very different outcome than the one generally predicted under standard inter-industry trade models, where comparative advantage generally drives the economic consequences of trade liberalization. This result can be formalized in the following terms.

Proposition 1: Assuming that pollution is local, a unilateral trade liberalization improves the quality of the environment in the liberalizing country and deteriorates it in the country benefiting from trade liberalization. This proposition holds regardless of whether the clean country or the dirty country is liberalizing trade in the pollution intensive goods.

2.4.2 Transboundary Pollution

In the presence of transboundary pollution, the environmental damage of, respectively, the home and the foreign country, can be written as:

$$Ed_x^t = d_x(x_1 + x_2) + \eta_y d_y(y_1 + y_2) \tag{11}$$

$$Ed_y^t = d_y(y_1 + y_2) + \eta_x d_x(x_1 + x_2) \tag{12}$$

where $0 < \eta_i < 1$ (for i = x,y): Because now pollution produces in one country spills over to the other country, the effects of a unilateral trade liberalization by the home country on the environmental damage of, respectively, the home and the foreign country, are given by:

$$\left(\frac{\partial Ed_x^t}{\partial t_y}\right)^{CN} = \frac{1}{D}\{\gamma d_x - 2\beta\eta_y d_y\} \tag{13}$$

$$\left(\frac{\partial Ed_x^t}{\partial t_y}\right)^{CN} = \frac{1}{D}\{\gamma d_x - 2\beta\eta_y d_y\} \tag{14}$$

To simplify their interpretation, these equations can be re-written in the following conditional expressions:

$$\frac{\partial Ed_x^t}{\partial t_y} > 0 \; iff \; \frac{d_x}{\eta_y d_y} > \frac{2\beta}{\gamma} \tag{15}$$

$$\frac{\partial Ed_y^t}{\partial t_y} > 0 \; iff \; \frac{d_y}{\eta_x d_x} > \frac{\gamma}{2\beta} \tag{16}$$

For notational purposes, we refer to the left-hand side of the above conditional statements as country i's "relative pollution differential" effect. This effect is measured by the pollution borne by country i due to its own pollution damage over the pollution it bears due to the pollution spillover from country j. On the right-hand side, we define $2\beta/\gamma$ as the "product differential" effect, which is always positive according to our earlier assumption regarding the magnitude of the own- and cross-price effects.

We have seen that a unilateral trade liberalization by the clean country shifts the pollution-intensive production away from the clean country towards the dirty country. As long as the home country does not bear a large fraction of the foreign pollution (i.e., as long as the pollution spillover from abroad, η_y is not too large), the clean country (which benefits from lower production and hence, lower domestic pollution) improves the quality of its environment by unilaterally liberalizing trade. The quality of the environment in the foreign country, however, always deteriorates following a unilateral trade liberalization by the home country. This can be seen from equation (16), where the conditional statement never holds. Assuming that the home relative pollution differential exceeds the product differential, we can summarize the results as follows:

Proposition 2: Assuming that pollution is transboundary, the clean country can improve its environment by unilaterally liberalizing trade. But the higher environmental quality in the clean country is always achieved at the expense of a deterioration in the environmental quality of the dirty country.

So far, we have considered the case where the clean country liberalizes trade. However, once pollution is no longer local, the effects of a trade liberalization on the quality of the environment are sensitive to which country is liberalizing trade. Thus, we turn now to the case where the dirty country is liberalizing trade.

$$\frac{\partial Ed_x^t}{\partial t_x} > 0 \text{ } iff \text{ } \frac{\eta_y d_y}{d_x} > \frac{2\beta}{\gamma}$$

$$\frac{\partial Ed_y^t}{\partial t_x} > 0 \text{ } iff \text{ } \frac{d_y}{\eta_x d_x} > \frac{2\beta}{\gamma}$$

A foreign unilateral trade liberalization shifts the pollution-intensive production away from the dirty country towards the clean country. Again, as long as the foreign country does not bear a large fraction of the home pollution (i.e., as long as the pollution spillover parameter from home, η_x is sufficiently small), the dirty country can improve the quality of its environment by unilaterally liberalizing trade.

The interesting point here is that when the foreign country liberalizes trade, the clean country does not necessarily suffer from higher pollution in the postliberalization equilibrium. Indeed, the quality of its environment can improve, even though it ends up producing a greater quantity of the polluting good. This is possible if its new level of clean production generates less pollution than that borne previously under the foreign pollution spillover. For this to be true, d_x must be relatively low and $\eta_y d_y$ relatively large.

Again, provided that the foreign relative pollution differential exceeds the product differential, we can summarize these results as follows:

Proposition 3: Assuming that pollution is transboundary, the dirty country can improve simultaneously its own environment and that of the clean country by imposing a unilateral trade liberalization in the pollution-intensive goods. This proposition holds when the production process in the dirty (clean) country generates a sufficiently large (small) amount of pollution spillover.

2.4.3 Global Pollution

When pollution is global, the environmental damage is determined by the aggregate production of pollution-intensive good (regardless of whether it is produced at home or abroad) and it is identical in both countries. This global environmental damage can be expressed as:

$$Ed^g = d_x(x_1 + x_2) + d_y(y_1 + y_2)$$

According to this expression, the effects of, respectively, a home and a foreign trade liberalization on the global environmental damage are given by:

$$\frac{\partial Ed^g}{\partial t_y} > 0 \text{ iff } \frac{d_x}{d_y} > \frac{2\beta}{\gamma} \tag{17}$$

$$\frac{\partial Ed^g}{\partial t_x} > 0 \text{ iff } \frac{d_y}{d_x} > \frac{2\beta}{\gamma} \tag{18}$$

As before, we refer to the right-hand side of these conditional statements as the product differential effect. But in the presence of global pollution, we refer to the left-hand side as the "absolute pollution differential" (equation (17) refers to the home absolute pollution differential, while equation (18) refers to the foreign absolute pollution differential).

By unilaterally liberalizing trade, the clean country transfers the production of the pollution-intensive good away from the clean country towards the dirty country. Since the rise in dirty production exceeds the reduction in clean production, the unilateral trade liberalization by the clean country always raises the global environmental damage. This is expressed in equation (18), where the conditional statement never holds and hence, $\partial Ed^g / \partial t_y < 0$.

This result may be reversed if the dirty country reduces its trade barriers, in which case a unilateral trade liberalization shifts the pollution-intensive production away from the dirty country towards the clean country, possibly raising the quality of the environment. While the aggregate production is higher in the post-liberalization equilibrium (which tends to support higher global pollution), the rise in the clean production exceeds the reduction in the dirty production. Thus, with a sufficiently large pollution differential, the dirty country can still improve the quality of the environment by unilaterally liberalizing trade.

Assuming that the foreign relative pollution differential exceeds the product differential, these results can be summarized as follows:

Proposition 4: Assuming that pollution is global, a unilateral trade liberalization by the clean country deteriorates unambiguously the global environment. But a unilateral trade liberalization by the dirty country can still improve the quality of the global environment, provided a large pollution differential.

In this section, we show that when the driving forces of the environmental damage associated with trade expansion are fueled by oligopolistic competition, there is no justification for the traditional inter-industry factor-relocation hypotheses. Indeed, according to our model, the environmental consequences of trade liberalization depend largely on two factors, namely, on which country initiates trade liberalization and on the nature of pollution (as opposed to comparative advantage). For example, under local pollution, the liberalizing country always benefits from trade liberalization, while the liberalized country always suffers from it, regardless of whether it is the clean country or the dirty country that liberalizes trade. This result, however, depends strongly on the nature of pollution. As pollution crosses borders, the global economy is better-off when the dirty country liberalizes trade than when the clean country does so. These results support the inconclusive empirical evidence found in support of the inter-industry effects of trade.[17]

2.5 Multilateral Trade Liberalization

So far, we have discussed the effects of a unilateral trade liberalization on the quality of the environment. Assume now that the home and the foreign countries implement a multilateral trade liberalization, such that $dt_x = dt_y = d\tau < 0$: Under this scenario, it is easy to show that a trade liberalization always affects negatively the quality of the environment, regardless of whether pollution is local, transboundary or global. The main reason for this result is that a multilateral trade liberalization raises the domestic production geared towards exports by more than it reduces the domestic production geared towards domestic consumption. This is illustrated in the following expressions:

$$\frac{\partial x_1^{MTL}}{\partial_\tau} + \frac{\partial x_2^{MTL}}{\partial_\tau} = \frac{\gamma - 2\beta}{D} < 0$$

$$\frac{\partial y_1^{MTL}}{\partial_\tau} + \frac{\partial y_2^{MTL}}{\partial_\tau} = \frac{\gamma - 2\beta}{D} < 0$$

Thus, a multilateral trade liberalization raises each country's overall pollution intensive production, and hence, deteriorates each country's environmental quality. This is shown in the following equations:

$$\frac{\partial Ed_x}{\partial \tau} = \frac{1}{D}\left[\left(d_x + \eta_y d_y\right)\left(\gamma - 2\beta\right)\right] < 0 \tag{19}$$

$$\frac{\partial Ed_y}{\partial \tau} = \frac{1}{D}\left[\left(\eta_x d_x + d_y\right)\left(\gamma - 2\beta\right)\right] < 0 \tag{20}$$

According to equations (19) and (20), a multilateral trade liberalization always deteriorates the quality of the environment, regardless if whether pollution is local ($\eta_i = 0$), transboundary ($0 < \eta_i < 1$) or global ($\eta_i = 1$). But the magnitude of this deterioration, however, depends positively on the size of the pollution spillover parameter η_i. These results can be summarized in the following terms:

Proposition 5: A multilateral trade liberalization always deteriorates the quality of the environment in both, the clean and the dirty country. This proposition holds

[17] For a recent survey on the empirical literature, see Rauscher (1997). An excellent collection of papers is provided in Low (1992), where various aspects of this issue are discussed and reviewed.

regardless of whether pollution is local, transboundary or global, although its detrimental environmental effects are smallest when pollution is local.

Note, however, that although a multilateral trade liberalization raises the aggregate level of pollution, it is important to keep in mind that the environmental damage under intra-industry trade is not as localized as predicted under standard inter-industry trade. This is an interesting finding, since the literature has long argued that different countries have different pollution assimilation capacities. Thus, as long as the environmental degradation borne by each country does not exceed its absorptive capacity, the positive variety and pro-competition effects may well outweigh the negative environmental effect.[18]

So far, we make the assumption that the polluting firms are quantity-setting oligopolists. However, we know from standard textbooks of industrial organization that this is not the only possible mode of competition. To test the robustness of our previous results, we have also considered the case where the polluting firms are pricesetting producers, rather than quantity-setting producers. It is easy to show that under standard assumptions, the presence of a price-setting competition does not alter the results derived under a quantity-setting competition and all of the propositions derived in Section 2.4 carry over to the case of Cournot-Nash competition.

3 Multiple Firms

In this section, we extend the previous analysis and examine how our earlier results change when each country holds a number of firms producing the pollution-intensive good, as opposed of having a single polluting firm. In particular, we allow for m (n) firms to produce good x (y), where (m; n) > 1: Under this new specification, the profit function of, respectively, the home and the foreign firm needs to be modified as follows:

$$\pi_x^i = x_1 p_{x1}(X_1, Y_1) + x_2 p_{x2}(X_2, Y_2) - e_x(x_1 + x_2) - t_x x_2$$

$$\pi_y^i = y_1 p_{y_1}(X_1, Y_1) + y_2 p_{y_2}(X_2, Y_2) - e_y(y_1 + y_2) - t_y y_2$$

where $X_i = x_i + (m-1)\, v_i$ and $Y_i = y_i + (n-1)\, z_i$ (for i = 1,2): While both x and v are produced in the home country, good x is produced by a single oligopolistic firm and good v is produced by the remaining (m–1) oligopolistic firms in the domestic industry: Similarly for the foreign country, where good y is produced by a single

[18] Excellent discussions on countries' different pollution absorptive capacities can be found in Bhagwati and Srinivasan (1997) and Low and Safadi (1992). Note that while the authors highlight countries' variable capacities to assimilate pollution in defense against an international harmonization of environmental regulations, they both recognize that not all pollution is unacceptably bad for the environment.

foreign firm, while good z is produced by the remaining (n–1) foreign firms in the industry: If we assume now that all the firms in a given country produce a homogenous good, we can now drop the inter-firm product differential and focus on the international product differential, such that $x_i = v_i$ and $y_i = z_i$: As before, the subscripts indicate whether a polluting good is sold in the home market (1) or in the foreign market (2).

In the presence of multiple firms, the optimal outputs require:

$$x_1^{CN} = \frac{(n+1)\beta(\alpha_1 - e_x) - n\gamma(\alpha_2 - e_y - t_y)}{E}$$

$$x_2^{CN} = \frac{(n+1)\beta(\alpha_1 - e_x - t_x) - n\gamma(\alpha_2 - e_y)}{E}$$

$$y_1^{CN} = \frac{(m+1)\beta(\alpha_2 - e_y - t_y) - m\gamma(\alpha_1 - e_x)}{E}$$

$$y_2^{CN} = \frac{(m+1)\beta(\alpha_2 - e_y) - m\gamma(\alpha_1 - e_x - t_x)}{E}$$

where $E = \left[(m+1)(n+1)\beta^2 - mn\gamma^2\right]$, which is assumed to be positive.[19]

3.1 Conditions for Intra-Industry Trade

The existence of two-way trade requires that xCN 2 > 0 and yCN 1 > 0. Thus, the conditions for intra-industry trade can be expressed as:

$$x_2 > 0 \; iff \left(\frac{n+1}{n}\right)\frac{\beta}{\gamma} > \frac{(\alpha_2 - e_y)}{(\alpha_1 - e_x - t_x)}$$

$$y_1 > 0 \; iff \left(\frac{m+1}{m}\right)\frac{\beta}{\gamma} > \frac{(\alpha_1 - e_x)}{(\alpha_2 - e_y - t_y)}$$

Similarly to the conditions derived under the basic case in Section 2, intra-industry trade is more likely to occur in the presence of: (i) greater product differential (high β/γ); (ii) low import tariffs, ti; and (iii) lower environmental standards im-

[19] When comparing the optimal outputs derived in the presence of a single firm (equations (7)–(10) in Section 2.3) with those presented here in the presence of multiple firms, we note that the denominator in the former is smaller the denominator in the latter, or, E > D for (m, n) > 1.

posed on the exporting country i (high $\alpha_i - e_i$). Note, however, that since (q + 1) =q < 2 (for q = m, n) the conditions for intra-industry trade are more binding in the m × n case than under the basic case. Thus, when the polluting good is produced by multiple firms rather than by a single firm in each country, at least one of the three conditions stated above must be stronger for intra-industry trade to occur and hence, for our analysis to be relevant.

3.2 Unilateral Trade Liberalization

The impacts of a trade liberalization on the demand for pollution-intensive goods are given by the following equations:

$$\frac{\partial x_1^{CN}}{\partial t_y} = \frac{n\gamma}{E} > 0 \tag{21}$$

$$\frac{\partial y_1^{CN}}{\partial t_y} = -\frac{(m+1)\beta}{E} < 0 \tag{22}$$

$$\frac{\partial x_2^{CN}}{\partial t_x} = -\frac{(n+1)\beta}{E} < 0 \tag{23}$$

$$\frac{\partial y_2^{CN}}{\partial t_x} = \frac{m\gamma}{E} > 0 \tag{24}$$

Clearly, the presence of multiple firms does not alter the proposition stated in Section 2.3. It is interesting to point out, however, that it is not clear whether the effects of a unilateral liberalization on the environment will be larger or smaller (in absolute value) in the presence of multiple firms than in the presence of a single domestic firm. This will depend on the respective magnitude of two conflicting effects. While, on the one hand, the determinant in the single firm case is smaller than the determinant in the multiple firm case (E > D), on the other hand, the numerator increases with the number of firms (m, n). This can be seen by comparing equations (7)-(9) with equations (21)-(24).

3.3 Environmental Damage

Assuming that each country holds multiple firms producing the pollution-intensive good, the impact of a unilateral trade liberalization by the home country on the quality of the environment can be summarized in the following expressions:

$$\left(\frac{\partial Ed_x}{\partial t_y}\right)^{m\times n} = \frac{mn}{E}\left\{\gamma d_x - \left(\frac{m+1}{m}\right)\beta\eta_y d_y\right\} \tag{25}$$

$$\left(\frac{\partial Ed_y}{\partial t_y}\right)^{m\times n} = \frac{mn}{E}\left\{\gamma\eta_x d_x - \left(\frac{m+1}{m}\right)\beta d_y\right\} \tag{26}$$

The various scenarios under local, transboundary or global pollution can be represented by substituting η_i with the relevant pollution spillover parameter ($\eta_i = 0$ for local pollution, $0 < \eta_i < 1$ for transboundary pollution and $\eta_i = 1$ for global pollution): Similarly in the case of a foreign trade liberalization,

$$\left(\frac{\partial Ed_x}{\partial t_x}\right)^{m\times n} = \frac{mn}{E}\left\{\gamma\eta_y d_y - \left(\frac{n+1}{n}\right)\beta d_x\right\} \tag{27}$$

$$\left(\frac{\partial Ed_y}{\partial t_x}\right)^{m\times n} = \frac{mn}{E}\left\{\gamma d_y - \left(\frac{n+1}{n}\right)\beta\eta_x d_y\right\} \tag{28}$$

While the presence of multiple firms does not alter significantly the general conclusions derived in Section 2.4, both the direction and the magnitude of the environmental effffects of a trade liberalization can be different in the $m \times n$ case than in the basic case, depending on the specific parameter values of the model. In particular, the overall effect will depend on the relative size of two effects:

i. First, the second term in the brackets of equations (25)-(28) is smaller in the $m \times n$ case than in the basic case, because $(q + 1) = q < 2$ (for q = m, n): This means that, in the presence of transboundary pollution, a trade liberalization is more likely to be good for the environment in the presence of a large number of firms than in the presence of a single firm in the liberalizing country. Note that the direction of the environmental impacts of a trade liberalization depends only on the number of firms in the liberalizing country and not on the number of firms in the liberalized country.[20]
ii. Second, the multiplier in front of the brackets in equations (21)-(24) is larger in the $m \times n$ case than in the basic case (mn=E > 1=D). According to this effect, whatever the direction of the environmental effects of a trade liberalization, these effects are magnified in the presence of multiple firms. Thus, the presence of multiple firms magnifies the impact of a trade liberalization on the quality of the environment: If a trade liberalization is good (bad) for the environment, its impact on the environment will be better (worse) under the $m \times n$ case than under the basic case.

---

[20] This is because following, say, a home trade liberalization, the foreign country produces a higher level of the pollution-intensive production. In equilibrium, the extent to which the foreign country increases its production depends on the number of firms in the home country. This is shown in equations (21)-(24).

These results can be summarized in the following proposition:

Proposition 6: Generally, the presence of multiple polluting firms does not alter the direction of the environmental effects of trade liberalization, although it magnifies their impact. Nevertheless, if pollution is transboundary, there exists a range of parameter for which a trade liberalization is more likely to be good for the environment when a large number of polluting firms (as opposed to a single firm) are located in the liberalizing country.

Note the interesting implication of this observation in the context of competition policy. According to our model, anti-trust policies can be pro-environment. This statement is particularly true for the liberalized country and in the case of global pollution.

3.4 Multilateral Trade Liberalization

In the presence of multiple firms, the effect of a multilateral trade liberalization on the environmental damage of country i is given by:

$$\frac{\partial Ed_x}{\partial_\tau} = \frac{mn}{E}\left\{\left(\gamma - \left(\frac{n+1}{n}\right)\beta\right)d_x + \left(\gamma - \left(\frac{m+1}{m}\right)\beta\right)\eta_y d_y\right\} < 0$$

$$\frac{\partial Ed_y}{\partial_\tau} = \frac{mn}{E}\left\{\left(\gamma - \left(\frac{n+1}{n}\right)\beta\right)\eta_x d_x + \left(\gamma - \left(\frac{m+1}{m}\right)\beta\right)d_y\right\} < 0$$

where η_i, the degree of pollution spillover, can be substituted with the appropriate parameter value to illustrate the environmental damage under local, transboundary, and global pollution.

As in Section 2.5, a multilateral trade liberalization always raises the overall level of polluting production, which necessarily deteriorates the quality of the environment. The number of firms, however, magnifies the detrimental environmental effect of trade liberalization.

Proposition 7: As in the basic case presented in Section 2.5, a multilateral trade liberalization always deteriorates the quality of the environment in both, the clean and the dirty country. The number of oligopolistic firms, however, magnifies the detrimental environmental effects of a multilateral trade liberalization. This proposition holds regardless of whether pollution is local, transboundary or global, although the degradation of the environment is smallest when pollution is local.

4 The Repeated Game

4.1 Collusion

In the previous sections, we examine the potential compatibility between liberalizing trade and improving the quality of the environment in a one-shot game. In reality, of course, firms interact more than once, in which case it becomes more relevant to work within the framework of repeated interactions. In this context, it is well-known that producers can cooperate for certain parameters of the discount rate. Collusive intra-industry trade, however, is only feasible if the goods are imperfect substitutes (Fung 1991). Thus, in the presence of intra-industry trade, an additional condition is required, namely, the imperfect substitutability of the polluting goods. In the present section, we continue to assume that the polluting firms produce a heterogeneous good and interact in an infinitely repeated game and that there exists a focal equilibrium around which they can cooperate.[21]

Assuming cooperation, it is easy to determine the equilibrium levels of output at which the firms produce, namely,

$$x_1^{COL} = \frac{\beta(\alpha_1 - e_x) - \gamma(\alpha_2 - e_y - t_y)}{F} \tag{29}$$

$$x_2^{COL} = \frac{\beta(\alpha_1 - e_x - t_x) - \gamma(\alpha_2 - e_y)}{F} \tag{30}$$

$$y_1^{COL} = \frac{\beta(\alpha_2 - e_y - t_y) - \gamma(\alpha_1 - e_x)}{F} \tag{31}$$

$$y_2^{COL} = \frac{\beta(\alpha_2 - e_y) - \gamma(\alpha_1 - e_x - t_x)}{F} \tag{32}$$

where $F = 2(\beta^2 - \gamma^2) > 0$. Since the determinant is higher under the basic Cournot-Nash case than under collusion ($D > F$), it is not clear whether firms produce more or less under collusion than under a Cournot-Nash game.

4.2 Unilateral Trade Liberalization

Assume that the home (foreign) country implements a unilateral trade liberalization, such that $dt_y < 0$ ($dt_x < 0$). Relative to the basic case, the impact of such a

---

[21] Since the existence of explicit cartels is an illegal practice in many countries, we focus on implicit collusion, that is, collusion that is sustainable in a non-cooperative setting.

trade policy on the demand for pollution-intensive goods is given in the following equations:

$$\frac{\partial x_1^{COL}}{\partial t_y} = \frac{\gamma}{D} > \frac{\partial x_1^{CN}}{\partial t_y} \tag{33}$$

$$\frac{\partial x_2^{COL}}{\partial t_x} = -\frac{\beta}{D} >< \frac{\partial x_1^{CN}}{\partial t_y} \tag{34}$$

$$\frac{\partial y_1^{COL}}{\partial t_y} = -\frac{\beta}{D} >< \frac{\partial y_1^{CN}}{\partial t_y} \tag{35}$$

$$\frac{\partial y_2^{COL}}{\partial t_x} = \frac{\gamma}{D} > \frac{\partial y_2^{CN}}{\partial t_x} \tag{36}$$

When comparing the results derived under trade collusion with those derived under the Cournot-Nash case, equations (33)-(36) show that a trade liberalization has a larger (ambiguous) volume effect on the liberalizing (liberalized) country. For example, while a home trade liberalization lowers the level of home (foreign) production more under collusion than under Cournot-Nash, it has an ambiguous effect on the level of foreign production, depending on the specific parameters of the model.

4.3 Environmental Damage Under Collusion

Assuming that a trade liberalization does not affect the sustainability of the trade cartel, the effects of a trade liberalization on the quality of the environment under trade collusion follow closely those derived in the basic Cournot-Nash case. These effects can be summarized as:

$$\left(\frac{\partial Ed_x}{\partial t_y}\right)^{COL} = \frac{1}{F}\{\gamma d_x - \beta \eta_y d_y\} \tag{37}$$

$$\left(\frac{\partial Ed_y}{\partial t_y}\right)^{COL} = \frac{1}{F}\{\gamma \eta_x d_x - \beta d_y\} \tag{38}$$

$$\left(\frac{\partial Ed_x}{\partial t_x}\right)^{COL} = \frac{1}{F}\{\gamma d_y - \beta \eta_x d_x\} \tag{39}$$

$$\left(\frac{\partial Ed_y}{\partial t_x}\right)^{COL} = \frac{1}{F}\{\gamma\eta_y d_y - \beta d_x\} \tag{40}$$

where the pollution spillover parameter, η_i, can be substituted with the relevant parameters to represent, respectively, local, transboundary or global pollution. According to equations (37)-(40), two general results can be highlighted:

i. A trade liberalization is more likely to be good for the environment under trade collusion than under the basic Cournot-Nash case (i.e., it is easier to satisfy the condition $\partial Ed_y / \partial t_x > 0$ under trade collusion than under Cournot-Nash). This can be seen by comparing, for example, the (larger) terms in the brackets of equations (37)-(38) with the (smaller) ones in equations (13)-(14). This result suggests that antitrust policy may hurt the environment in the case of oligopolistic pollution-intensive industries.
ii. The environmental effects of trade liberalization are magnified in the presence of collusion. This is because the multiplier is greater under Cournot-Nash competition than under trade collusion (i.e., 1/D > 1/F): Thus, if trade liberalization is environment-friendly, its positive impact on the environment is greater under collusion than under Cournot-Nash. If, however, trade liberalization is environment-unfriendly, collusion magnifies its deteriorating effects.

Proposition 8: Assuming that a unilateral trade liberalization does not affect the sustainability of the existing trade cartel, it is more likely to be pro-environment in the presence of trade collusion than in the standard Cournot-Nash competition case presented in Section 2.4. Furthermore, regardless of whether trade liberalization is good or bad for the environment, collusion magnifies its impact on the quality of the environment.

4.4 Environmental Damage Under a Regime Shift

So far, we assume that the trade liberalization does not affect the sustainability of the existing trade cartel. In reality, however, a sufficiently large trade liberalization can threaten the viability of the cartel, forcing firms to revert from a cartel regime to a competition regime. The central question of this sub-section is to determine whether a trade liberalization, which can generate a shift away from trade collusion toward trade competition, is likely to improve or worsen the quality of the environment. To answer this question, we need to consider two separate issues, namely: (i) the effect of a trade liberalization on the sustainability of the trade collusion; and (ii) in the presence of a regime shift (say, from trade collusion to Cournot-Nash competition), the effect of this shift on the quality of the environment.

We now turn to the first issue concerning the sustainability of trade collusion.

4.4.1 Sustainability of Collusion

We know that cooperation is self-enforcing as long as the one-period gain from cheating dominates the punishment discounted infinitely into the future. Let's consider the following simple set of trigger strategies: the polluting firms produce at the collusion output levels (given in equations (29)-(32)) until some firm cheats. As soon as one firm deviates, all firms move back to the Cournot-Nash output levels (given in equations (3)-(6)). Although these trigger strategies yield sub-game perfect equilibria, they are arguably not the most satisfactory way to model repeated interactions. But for our purpose, they allow to highlight the possible impact of trade liberalization on the quality of the environment in a simple dynamic setting.

We know from standard literature on game theory that the condition for sustainability can be expressed as:

$$\rho < \frac{\pi_{s_i}^{COL} - \pi_{s_i}^{CN}}{\pi_{s_i}^{CH} - \pi_{s_i}^{CN}} \equiv r_{s_i}^{c} \quad (s = x, y \; and \; i = 1,2) \tag{41}$$

where ρ is the discount rate, r_{si}^{c} the critical interest rate, and π^{COL}, π^{CN} and π^{CH} the profits under, respectively, trade collusion, Cournot-Nash and cheating. According to this expression, trade collusion is feasible as long as the discount rate is smaller than the critical interest rate, and becomes less sustainable as the critical interest rate decreases. In other words, the firm with the smallest critical interest rate is the firm most likely to switch back to non-collusive trade and is often referred to as the 'weak link'.

Although there are four critical rates, r_{xi}^{c} and r_{yi}^{c} (i = 1,2), it is easy to show that in the presence of tariffs, $r_{x1}^{c} > r_{x2}^{c}$ and $r_{y2}^{c} > r_{y1}^{c}$, such that there remains only two relevant critical rates r_{x2}^{c} and r_{y1}^{c}. With symmetric demand functions, the following relationship can be established:

$$\left[r_{y_1}^{c}\right] \gtreqless \left[r_{x_2}^{c}\right] \; iff \; \left[2(\alpha_2 - e_y) - t_y\right] \gtreqless \left[2(\alpha_1 - e_x) - t_x\right] \tag{42}$$

Clearly, the firm with the greatest competitive disadvantage has the smallest critical interest rate. Assuming that both countries start with an identical level of trade protection ($t_x = t_y$), the clean country (with stricter pollution control) represents the weak link of the trade cartel and hence, the most likely to defect in the case of a widening of its competitive disadvantage. Thus, according to equation (42), a unilateral trade liberalization by the clean country ($dt_y < 0$) weakens the trade cartel; while a trade liberalization by the dirty country ($dt_x < 0$) strengthens the trade cartel. Finally, in the case of a multilateral trade liberalization, both critical rates decrease by the amount of the tariff reduction, making collusion less sustainable, as either both or only the weakest country defect the collusive equilibrium and revert to trade competition.

4.4.2 Environmental Damage Differential

In order to analyze the effects of a change in the competition regime on the quality of the environment, we need to compare the environmental damage under a trade collusion regime with that under a Cournot-Nash competition regime:

$$\Delta Ed_s \equiv \left[Ed_s^{COL} - Ed_s^{CN} \right] \overset{>}{\underset{<}{=}} 0 \text{ for } s = x, y \tag{43}$$

We refer to the expression in equation (43) as the environmental differential (between a trade collusion regime and a Cournot-Nash competition regime). If this term is positive, the environmental damage is higher under trade collusion and a trade policy that breaks the cartel is beneficial to the environment. If, however, equation (43) is negative, a trade competition regime supports a higher level of environmental damage and a trade policy that promotes trade collusion is an environmental-friendly policy.

The environmental damage differential of, respectively, the home and the foreign country is given by:

$$(Ed_x^{COL} - Ed_x^{CN}) = d_x[\Delta x_1 + \Delta x_2] + \eta_y d_y [\Delta y_1 + \Delta y_2] \tag{44}$$

$$(Ed_y^{COL} - Ed_y^{CN}) = \eta_x d_x[\Delta x_1 + \Delta x_2] + d_y [\Delta y_1 + \Delta y_2] \tag{45}$$

$$\Delta x_1 > 0 \text{ } iff \text{ } A < \frac{\alpha - e_x}{\alpha - e_y - t_y} \tag{46}$$

$$\Delta x_2 > 0 \text{ } iff \text{ } A < \frac{\alpha - e_x - t_x}{\alpha - e_y} \tag{47}$$

$$\Delta y_1 > 0 \text{ } iff \text{ } A < \frac{\alpha - e_y - t_y}{\alpha - e_x} \tag{48}$$

$$\Delta y_2 > 0 \text{ } iff \text{ } A < \frac{\alpha - e_y}{\alpha - e_x - t_x} \tag{49}$$

$$[\Delta x_1 + \Delta x_2] > 0 \text{ } iff \text{ } A < B \equiv \frac{2(\alpha - e_x) - t_x}{2(\alpha - e_y) - t_y} \tag{50}$$

$$[\Delta y_1 + \Delta y_2] > 0 \text{ } iff \text{ } A < C \equiv \frac{2(\alpha - e_y) - t_y}{2(\alpha - e_x) - t_x} \tag{51}$$

$$A = (2\beta^2 + \gamma^2)/3\beta\gamma \geq 1 \tag{52}$$

The first termon the right-hand side of equation (44) represents the pollution associated with the production differential in the home country associated with switching from trade collusion to Cournot-Nash competition. The second term represents the foreign pollution spillovers associated with the production differential abroad. Similarly for equation (45), where the first term represents the home pollution spillovers associated with the production differential abroad and the second term represents the pollution associated with the production differential in the foreign country.

For future reference, we refer loosely to A as the "product differentiation" effect and to C as the "environmental standards" effect (B is simply the inverse of C). For the sake of tractability, we impose three further restrictions, which we assume to hold unless specified otherwise. First, we assume that both countries start with an identical level of trade protection ($t_x = t_y$). This assumption implies that C is always greater than 1, given our earlier assumption that the clean country has also higher environmental standards[22]. Second, we assume that the environmental standards effect exceeds the product differentiation effect (A < C). Finally, we assume that the pollution differential between the two countries is large, that is, that d_x is relatively small and d_y is relatively large.

We now turn to the analysis of how a trade liberalization, by strengthening or weakening the trade collusion, affects the environmental damage under local, transboundary and global pollution.

Local Pollution: When pollution is local, the environmental damage differential between a collusion and a competition regime for, respectively, the home and the foreign country, is given by:

$$\Delta Ed_x^l = (\Delta x_1 + \Delta x_2)d_x < 0$$

$$\Delta Ed_y^l = (\Delta y_1 + \Delta y_2)d_y > 0 \; iff \; A < C$$

According to these equations, a unilateral trade liberalization by the home country, which weakens the trade cartel, is likely to worsen the quality of the environment in the home and to improve it in the foreign country.

It is interesting to note that, as far as the home country is concerned, a sufficient condition for trade liberalization to be environmentally-damaging is e_x to exceed (e_y+ t_y). This can be seen from equation (47), which indicates that Δx_2 is always negative given our assumptions. Thus, when the home firm has a competitive disadvantage in its own market, a shift from trade collusion to trade competition is bad for its environment.

While the result on the home environment is unambiguous, the impact of a trade liberalization on the foreign environment depends heavily on the assumption

[22] Note also that an increase in the pollution tax seems to be twice as important as an increase in the import tariff.

that the environmental standards effect exceeds the product differentiation effect: Indeed, if we relax this assumption and allow A > C, a trade liberalization by the home country (which weakens the trade cartel) is likely to deteriorate the quality of the environment in both countries.

Similarly in the case of a foreign unilateral trade liberalization (which strengthens the trade cartel), where the environmental quality in the home country benefits from lower pollution, while the foreign country (again, provided that A < C) suffers from higher environmental degradation.

Transboundary Pollution: When pollution is transboundary, the environmental damage differential between a collusion and a competition regime for, respectively, the home and the foreign country is given by:

$$\Delta Ed_x^t = (\Delta x_1 + \Delta x_2)d_x + (\Delta y_1 + \Delta y_2)\eta_y d_y \tag{53}$$

$$\Delta Ed_y^t = (\Delta x_1 + \Delta x_2)\eta_x d_x + (\Delta y_1 + \Delta y_2)d_y \tag{54}$$

We have already seen above that, according to our initial assumptions, the first term of the right-hand side of equation (53) is always negative, while the second term is positive, provided that A < C. In this case, a home trade liberalization can be beneficial to both countries, provided that the relative pollution differential between the two countries is sufficiently large. If, however, we relax our assumption that the environmental standards effect is greater than the product differentiation effect and assume that A > C, a trade liberalization by the home country, which weakens the trade cartel, is likely to deteriorate the quality of the environment in both countries, and more so the higher the foreign pollution spillover effect.

Alternatively, under the assumption A < C, a trade liberalization by the foreign country, which strengthens the trade cartel, can be beneficial to both the home and the foreign environment, provided that the relative pollution differential is sufficiently large (that is, a relatively small $d_x/\eta_y d_y$ for the home country and a relatively large $d_y/\eta_x d_x$ for the foreign country). If, however, A > C, a foreign trade liberalization always supports a lower-pollution regime in both, the home and the foreign country.

Global Pollution: When pollution is global, the environmental damage differential between a collusion and a competition regime is given by:

$$\Delta Ed^g = (\Delta x_1 + \Delta x_2)d_x + (\Delta y_1 + \Delta y_2)d_y$$

Again, while the first term of the right-hand side is always negative, the second term is positive if we assume that A < C. Provided that the absolute pollution differential d_y/d_x is large, the environmental damage is higher under collusion than under competition and a trade liberalization by the home country, which weakens the trade cartel, is likely to improve the quality of the global environment. If, however, we relax our assumption that the environmental standards effect is greater than the product differentiation effect and assume that A > C, a home trade liberalization deteriorates unambiguously the environment.

Alternatively, a trade liberalization by the foreign country, which strengthens the trade cartel, is likely to deteriorate the quality of the global environments, provided that the absolute pollution differential is large and that A < C.

Note that while the focus of the present paper concerns the effects of a trade liberalization on the quality of the environment, this model also highlights the way in which stricter environmental policies may not always produce the desired effects on the environment. For example, if the clean country were to increase its pollution tax to a point where it would break the trade cartel and revert to trade competition, an environmental-friendly policy (i.e., higher pollution control) would actually deteriorate the environmental quality.

Finally, if we assume that the home country is the dirty country (in the sense that $d_x > d_y$), while keeping our assumption that the home country imposes higher pollution taxes ($e_x > e_y$), a home trade liberalization always deteriorates the environment, while a foreign trade liberalization always improves the environment. Assuming that the absolute pollution differential between the two countries is large and that A < C; we can summarize the results in the following terms:

Proposition 9: A unilateral trade liberalization by the clean country, which weakens the trade cartel, is likely to improve the quality of the environment in both countries, while a unilateral trade liberalization by the dirty country, which strengthens the trade cartel, is likely to deteriorate the quality of the environment in both countries.

5 In the Presence of Tariff-Jumping FDI

5.1 Framework

When tariff barriers are high, rather than producing the pollution-intensive good at home and exporting it abroad, a firm may choose to serve the foreign market by engaging in foreign direct investment (FDI) and setting up production plants abroad, so as to 'jump' these high tariff barriers. For exposition, we present only the case where the foreign firm engages in FDI activities, while the home firm continues to produce the pollution-intensive good at home and to export part of its production to the foreign market.

Throughout this section, we assume that the foreign firm uses the same production technology, regardless of whether the goods are produced at home or abroad. The corresponding profit function of, respectively, the home and the foreign firms is given by:

$$\pi_x^{FDI} = x_1 p_{x1} + x_2 p_{x2} - e_x(x_1 + x_2) - t_x x_1 \tag{55}$$

$$\pi_y^{FDI} = y_1 p_{y1} + y_2 p_{y2} - e_x y_1 + e_y y_2 - F_y \tag{56}$$

The profits of the FDI host country (i.e., the home country) increase with total sales revenues (from both, the domestic and the export market) and decreases with both the home pollution tax (e_x) and the foreign tariff (t_x). The profit function of the FDI source country (i.e., the foreign country) differs in two aspects. First, the foreign firm pays the home pollution tax (e_x) on the polluting good it produces in the home country and the foreign pollution tax (e_y) on the polluting good it produces in the foreign country. Second, it incurs a lump-sum set-up cost F_y to engage in FDI activities.

The first-order profit maximization conditions yield the following optimal supply functions:

$$x_1^{FDI} = \frac{2\beta(\alpha_1 - e_x) - \gamma(\alpha_2 - e_x)}{D} \tag{57}$$

$$x_2^{FDI} = \frac{2\beta(\alpha_1 - e_x - t_x) - \gamma(\alpha_2 - e_y)}{D} = x_2^{CN} \tag{58}$$

$$y_1^{FDI} = \frac{2\beta(\alpha_2 - e_x) - \gamma(\alpha_1 - e_x)}{D} \tag{59}$$

$$y_2^{FDI} = \frac{2\beta(\alpha_2 - e_y) - \gamma(\alpha_1 - e_x - t_x)}{D} = y_2^{CN} \tag{60}$$

where $D = 4\beta^2 - \gamma^2$. As in the basic case presented in Section 2, the concavity assumption of the aggregate utility function associated with the above demand functions implies that $\beta^2 - \gamma^2 > 0$. We continue to assume that the own-price effects are greater than the cross-price effects, that is, $\beta > \gamma$. While the presence of foreign FDI activities in the home country does not alter the sales in the foreign market (i.e., $x_2^{FDI} = x_2^{CN}$ and $y_2^{FDI} = y_2^{CN}$), it affects those in the home market. In particular, whether the home market sales are higher or lower under a FDI regime than under the standard Cournot-Nash regime described in Section 2.1 depends crucially on the relationship between e_x and ($e_y + t_y$). In particular,

$$\left[x_1^{FDI}\right] \overset{>}{\underset{<}{=}} \left[x_1^{CN}\right] \text{ if } e_x \overset{>}{\underset{<}{=}} \left[(e_y + t_y)\right] \tag{61}$$

$$\left[y_1^{FDI}\right] \overset{>}{\underset{<}{=}} \left[y_1^{CN}\right] \text{ if } e_x \overset{>}{\underset{<}{=}} \left[(e_y + t_y)\right] \tag{62}$$

5.2 Condition for FDI

The foreign country chooses to engage in FDI activities in the home country if its profits are higher under a FDI regime than under an intra-industry trade regime. The relative profitability between these two regimes is given by:

$$\pi_y^{FDI} - \pi_y^{CN} = \beta[(y_1^{FDI})^2 - (y_2^{CN})^2] - F_y \tag{63}$$

If this expression is positive, it is profitable for the foreign firm to invest abroad and hence, to incur the initial set-up cost necessary to produce y1 in the home country.

If $(\pi_y^{FDI} - \pi_y^{CN}) = 0$, the foreign firm is indifferent between producing y_1 in the foreign country (and paying import tariffs to the home country) and incurring the initial setup cost to produce y_1 in the home country (and evading the home country's import tariffs). Finally, $\pi_y^{FDI} - \pi_y^{CN} < 0$ corresponds to the situation in which it is in the foreign firm's best interest to produce y_1 at home and to export its production abroad, rather than to invest and produce abroad.

The conditional expressions given in (61) and (62), together with the foreign profit differential function given in (63) indicate that foreign export sales and hence, foreign profits, are always smaller under a FDI regime than under an exports regime when $e_x > (e_y + t_y)$. In this situation, it is never profitable for the foreign firm to engage in FDI activities. Indeed, the foreign firm engages in FDI only when $e_x < (e_y + t_y)$, that is, when a smaller tax burden is levied on the foreign good produced in the home country than on the foreign good produced in the foreign country and subsequently exported to the home country. While $e_x < (e_y + t_y)$ is a necessary condition for the foreign firm to consider FDI activities, it is not a sufficient one. This can be seen from equations (63), where the firm's relative profitability requires not only to produce a higher level of output under a FDI regime than under an exports regime but also to cover its initial set-up cost F_y associated with FDI. Thus, we need an additional condition to determine under which conditions it is profitable for the foreign firm to engage in FDI activities.

For given pollution taxes, there exists a critical tariff rate at which the foreign firm is indifferent between undertaking FDI in the home country and exporting y_1 to the home country. This critical tariff rate t_y^c can be determined by differentiating the foreign profit differential given in equation (63) with respect to the home import tariff t_y, and by solving for the following quadratic solution:

$$t_y^2 - At_y - B = 0 \tag{64}$$

where

$$A = \left\{2(\alpha_2 - e_y) - \left(\frac{\gamma}{B}\right)(\alpha_1 - e_x)\right\}$$

$$B = \left\{[e_x^2 - 2\alpha_2(e_x - e_y) - e_y^2] + \frac{\gamma}{\beta}(\alpha_1 - e_x)(e_x - e_y)\right\}$$

The foreign firm engages in FDI if the tariff level exceeds this critical tariff rate. Thus, the sufficient set of conditions for the foreign country to undertake FDI requires e_x to be smaller than $(e_y + t_y)$ and t_y to be greater or equal to t_y^c.

Proposition 10: The foreign country engages in FDI activities under the following two conditions, namely: (i) if e_x is smaller than $(e_y + t_y)$; and (ii) if t_y is greater or equal to t_y^c.

5.3 Unilateral Trade Liberalization

In the previous section, we have shown that when $e_x \geq (e_y + t_y)$, it is never profitable for the foreign firm to engage in FDI activities, in which case the foreign firm exports y_1 to the home country. In the context of the present paper, this is not an interesting situation since a unilateral trade liberalization by the home country ($dt_y<0$) does not alter the foreign country's initial decision to export and thus, yields the same results as those already derived earlier in Section 2.3.

If, however, $e_x < (e_y + t_y)$, the foreign country may choose to either undertake FDI activities or export, depending on whether $t_y \gtrless t_y^c$. In particular, when $t_y > t_y^c$, it is more profitable for the foreign firm to incur the costs associated with FDI and to produce y_1 abroad. But when $t_y < t_y^c$, it becomes more profitable for the foreign firm to produce y_1 at home and to export its production to the home market. This highlights an interesting implication for trade policy in the context of intra-industry trade.

Assuming that the environmental damage generated under a FDI regime is significantly different from that generated under an exports regime, a unilateral trade liberalization by the home country can affect the quality of the environment if it induces the foreign country to switch away from a FDI regime toward an exports regime. Clearly, the extent to which one country benefits from trade liberalization depends on several factors, including which country is liberalizing, which country is experiencing inward FDI, which regime is more harmful to the environment and which type of pollution is occurring.

We turn now to the environmental damage generated under a FDI regime.

5.4 Environmental Damage Differential

Assuming that the foreign country engages in FDI, the environmental damage borne by, respectively, the home and the foreign country is given by:

$$Ed_x^{FDI} = [d_x(x_1^{FDI} + x_2^{CN}) + d_y y_1^{FDI}] + \eta_y d_y y_2^{CN} \tag{65}$$

$$Ed_y^{FDI} = d_y y_2^{CN} + \eta_x [d_x(x_1^{FDI} + x_2^{CN}) + d_y y_1^{FDI}] \tag{66}$$

Again, by substituting the appropriate value for η_i, the degree of pollution spill-over, the above expressions illustrate the environmental damage under local (η_i=0), transboundary (0<η_i<1), and global (η_i=1) pollution.

According to equation (65), the home country suffers from two sources of pollution. While the first source is caused by the polluting production taking place in the home country (generated by both, the home and the foreign firm), the second source is generated by the foreign pollution spillovers. Similarly for the foreign country, which suffers from the pollution caused by the polluting production taking place in the foreign country and from the pollution spillovers associated with the production taking place in the home country (generated by both, the home and the foreign firm). By comparing the environmental damage produced under a FDI regime (given in equations (65) and (66)) with that produced under an intra-industry trade regime (given in equations (11) and (12)), it is now possible to determine which regime supports a higher level of pollution and hence, to examine the environmental consequence of a given trade policy. In particular, we are interested in solving the expression $Ed_i^{FDI} - Ed_i^{BN}$ for i = x,y under, respectively, local, transboundary and global pollution.

If this expression is positive, the environmental damage associated with the production of pollution-intensive goods is higher under an FDI regime than under a Cournot-Nash exports regime and a trade liberalization, which discourages the foreign country to engage in FDI activities, is good for the environment. If, however, it is negative, the environmental damage is higher under a trade regime than under an FDI regime and a trade liberalization is bad for the environment.

5.4.1 Local Pollution

Assuming that pollution is local, the environmental damage differential between an FDI regime and an exports regime of the home country is given by:

$$\left[(Ed_x^{FDI} - Ed_x^{CN})^l\right] = \left[(x_1^{FDI} - x_1^{CN})d_x + y_1^{FDI} d_y\right] \gtrless 0 \tag{67}$$

We have already shown above that if the foreign country engages in FDI activities, it must be true that $e_x < (e_y + t_y)$; which in turn implies that $x_1^{FDI} < x_1^{CN}$. Thus, the sign of equation (67) is ambiguous. But it is possible to solve for the condition under which the environmental damage of the clean country is higher under an FDI regime than under an intra-industry trade regime. This is shown in equation (68) below.

$$(Ed_x^{FDI} - Ed_x^{CN})^l > 0 \; iff \; \frac{d_x}{d_y} > \frac{2\beta(\alpha_2 - e_x) - \gamma(\alpha_1 - e_x)}{\gamma(e_y + t_y - e_x)} \tag{68}$$

From a trade policy perspective, for the parameter range over which the condition in equation (68) holds, the home country can improve its environment by liberalizing trade to a point where $t_y < t_y^c$. Indeed, by reducing its tariff level below the foreign critical level, the home country discourages FDI and thereby, redirects the pollution-intensive production towards the foreign country. This policy improves the environmental quality in the home country, while deteriorating it in the foreign country. The latter result is shown in equation (69), where the environmental damage for the foreign country is always lower under an FDI regime than under a intra-industry trade regime.

$$(Ed_y^{FDI} - Ed_y^{CN})^l = -y_1^{CN} d_y < 0 \tag{69}$$

Proposition 11: There exists a parameter range under which a trade liberalization by the home country, which induces the dirty country to switch from an FDI regime to an exports regime, improves the environmental quality in the clean country. Such a regime shift, however, unambiguously deteriorates the environmental quality in the dirty country.

5.4.2 Transboundary Pollution

When pollution is transboundary, the environmental damage differential between an FDI regime and an exports regime of, respectively, the home and the foreign country is given by:

$$(Ed_x^{FDI} - Ed_x^{CN})^t = \left[(x_1^{FDI} - x_1^{CN})d_x + (y_1^{FDI} - y_1^{CN}\eta_y)d_y\right]\substack{< \\ >} 0 \tag{70}$$

$$(Ed_y^{FDI} - Ed_y^{CN}) = \left[(x_1^{FDI} - x_1^{CN})\eta_x d_x + (y_1^{FDI}\eta_x - y_1^{CN})d_y\right]\substack{< \\ >} 0 \tag{71}$$

Assuming that the foreign country engages initially in FDI activities, we know that the first bracket in equation (70) is negative, while the second bracket is positive. Thus, the sign of equation (70) depends on the relative size of these two conflicting effects. But it is easy to see that in the presence of a relatively small pollution spillover from the foreign country (i.e., a small η_y), the second (positive) bracket becomes very large, making it possible for the home country to improve the quality of its environment by liberalizing trade. In particular, the environmental damage is always higher under an FDI regime than under a Cournot-Nash trade regime, in which case a trade liberalization is always good for the environmental quality of the home country, under the following condition:

$$(Ed_x^{FDI} - Ed_x^{CN})^t > 0 \text{ iff}$$

$$\frac{d_x}{d_y} > \frac{(1-\eta_y)[2\beta(\alpha_2 - e_x) - \gamma(\alpha_1 - e_x)] + 2\beta(e_y + t_y - e_x)\eta_y}{\gamma(e_y + t_y - e_x)} \tag{72}$$

Thus, in the presence of transboundary pollution, a regime shift can produce either positive or negative environmental consequences for the clean country, depending on the size of the foreign pollution spillover parameter.

As far as the foreign country is concerned, equation (73) shows that there exists also a parameter range under which a trade liberalization by the home country, which induces the foreign country to switch from FDI activities to exports, improves the quality of the foreign environment. In particular, the condition necessary for a trade liberalization to be good for the environment is given by:

$$(Ed_y^{FDI} - Ed_y^{CN})^t > 0 \text{ iff}$$
$$\frac{d_x}{d_y} > \frac{(\eta_x - 1)[2\beta(\alpha_2 - e_x) - \gamma(\alpha_1 - e_x)] + 2\beta(e_y + t_y - e_x)\eta_y}{\gamma(e_y + t_y - e_x)\eta_x} \tag{73}$$

According to equation (73), the environmental damage borne by the foreign country is lower under an FDI regime than under a trade regime when η_x is relatively small. Clearly, as long as pollution does not cross borders easily, the foreign country does not have to bear the full pollution externality generated by its dirty production plants located in the home country and it benefits from a higher environmental quality under an FDI regime.

Proposition 12: Under transboundary pollution, a trade liberalization by the home country, which induces the dirty country to switch from an FDI regime to an exports regime, can improve the environmental quality in both, the clean and the dirty country. For this proposition to be true, the foreign country must generate a relatively large pollution spillover, while the home country must generate a relatively small pollution spillover.

5.4.3 Global Pollution

When pollution is global, the environmental damage differential between an FDI regime and an exports regime for the global economy is given by:

$$(Ed^{FDI} - Ed^{CN})^g = \left[(x_1^{FDI} - x_1^{CN})d_x + (y_1^{FDI} - y_1^{CN})d_y\right] \lessgtr 0$$

Again, assuming that the foreign country engages initially in FDI activities, we know that the first brackets is negative, while the second bracket is positive, making the sign of the environmental differential damage ambiguous. Thus, under global pollution, there exists a parameter range under which a trade liberalization by the home country, which induces the dirty country to switch from an FDI regime to an exports regime, improves the global environmental quality. In particular, the necessary condition for the global environmental damage to be higher under an FDI regime than under an intra-industry trade regime is given by the following equation:

$$(Ed^{FDI} - Ed^{CN})^g > 0 \; iff \; \frac{d_x}{d_y} > \frac{2\beta}{\gamma} \tag{74}$$

A sufficient condition for the conditional expression in equation (74) to hold true is that the home absolute pollution differential exceeds the product differential. Thus, as long as the pollution differential is sufficiently large, a trade liberalization by the home country, which induces the dirty country to switch from an FDI regime to an exports regime, unambiguously improves the global environmental quality. The intuition for this result is as follows. Assuming that the foreign country engages initially in FDI activities, we know from equation (61) and (62) that $x_1^{FDI} < x_1^{CN}$ and that $y_1^{FDI} > y_1^{CN}$. Thus, a trade liberalization, which induces a regime shift away from FDI activities towards trade activities, is good for the environment, because such a regime shift allows producing more of the clean good and less of the dirty good. These results can be summarized as follows:

Proposition 13: Under global pollution, a unilateral trade liberalization by the clean country, which induces the dirty country to switch from an FDI regime to an exports regime, improves unambiguously the quality of the global environment.

We find that under certain conditions the results derived in the previous section can be reversed if one of the firm is engaging in FDI activities in the pre-liberalization equilibrium. For example, assuming that pollution is global, we have seen in Section 2.4 that a unilateral trade liberalization by the clean country deteriorates unambiguously the global environment. If, however, the foreign country is circumventing high tariff barriers by engaging in FDI activities, a unilateral trade liberalization by the clean country, which induces the dirty country to switch from an FDI regime to an exports regime, improves unambiguously the quality of the global environment. While these contradicting results are driven by very different forces, they both highlight the relevance of recognizing the underlying trade structure and of examining the environmental damages of trade liberalization in their appropriate context.

6 Conclusion

In this paper, we offer a new causal mechanism linking international trade to changes in the quality of the environment. We argue that while trade expansion alters the composition of national output and hence, its environmental quality, its driving force may be international oligopolistic rivalry rather than comparative advantage. We do not claim to offer a complete resolution of the debate over trade and the environment. Our contribution is to take a first step toward clarifying the role of intra-industry trade in determining how trade liberalization affects the quality of the environment.

First, our results show that when the driving forces that determine the environmental damage associated with trade expansion are fueled by neither comparative advantage nor cost differences but rather by oligopolistic competition, there is no justification for the traditional inter-industry factor-relocation hypotheses. In particular, we find that environmental deterioration is largely determined by two factors, namely (i) by which country liberalizes trade, and (ii) by the nature of pollution (i.e., whether pollution is local, transboundary or global). This result offers a potential explanation for why the composition effect of trade has only found inconclusive empirical evidence.

Second, this paper sheds light on the question as to whether there are still positive gains from trade when environmental degradation matters. In the context of intra-industry trade, a unilateral trade liberalization induces three effects, namely, a product variety effect, a pro-competition effect and an environmental effect. While the first two effects are positive, we show that the third effect is not necessarily negative. For example, when pollution is transboundary, the global environment can benefit from trade liberalization, provided that the most pollution-intensive country liberalizes trade.

Furthermore, our model presents interesting insights about the relative severity of pollution under, respectively, intra- and inter-industry trade. Because pollution is less localized under intra-industry trade than under inter-industry trade, the environmental damage associated with trade liberalization is not going to be as severe as under the former than under the latter trade structure. This is noteworthy, for the literature has long argued that different countries have different pollution assimilation capacities. Thus, as long as the environmental degradation borne by each country does not exceed its absorptive capacity, the positive variety and pro-competition effects may well outweigh the negative environmental effect.

Our results also offer a new perspective on the role of competition policy in the context of highly polluting industries. Our model suggests that the presence of a large number of firms in the liberalized country magnifies significantly the (negative) environmental impact of trade liberalization. Thus, anti-trust policies may not always be good for the environment.

Finally, we find that our basic results can be reversed if polluting firms are either colluding or engaging in FDI activities in the pre-liberalization equilibrium. Assume, for example, that high tariff barriers in the home country induce the foreign polluting firms to engage in FDI activities in the home market. Then, even when pollution is global, a unilateral trade liberalization by the clean country (which induces the dirty country to switch from an FDI regime to an exports regime) improves unambiguously the quality of the global environment.

It is important, however, to recognize the limitations of our analysis. Our analysis is limited to the channel linking trade and the environment to the composition effect via intra-industry trade, ignoring other channels such as technological transfers and income effects. Also, our model suffers from extreme stylization. Nevertheless, the simple structure of our model can also be a virtue since it lays bare the basic relationship driving our results and enhances our understanding of the relationship between pollution and trade in the context of intra-industry trade. If anything, this paper highlights how much remains to be done in advancing our understanding of the many complex factors that influence the environmental consequences of trade liberalization in an increasingly integrated world economy.

References

Anderson K, Blackhurst R (eds) (1992) The Greening of World Trade Issues. Harvester Wheatsheaf, New York

Antweiler W, Copeland BR, Taylor MS (1998) Is Free Trade Good for the Environment? NBER Working Paper Series, WP 6707

Beghin J, Roland-Holst D, van der Mensbrugghe D (1995) Trade Liberalization and the Environment in the Pacific Basin: Coordinated Approaches to Mexican Trade and Environment Policy. American Journal of Agricultural Economics 77 : 778–786

Beghin J, Potier M (1997) Effects of Trade Liberalization on the Environment in the Manufacturing Sector. The World Economy 20 : 435–456

Beghin J, Roland-Holst D, van der Mensbrugghe D (1994) A Survey of the Trade and Environment Nexus: Global Dimensions. OECD Economic Studies 23 : 167–192

Bernhofen DM (1999) Intra-Industry Trade and Strategic Interaction: Theory and Evidence. Journal of International Economics 47 : 223–244

Bhagwati JN, Srinivasan TN (1997) Trade and the Environment: Does Environmental Diversity Detract form the Case for Free Trade? In: Bhagwati JN, Hudec RE (eds) Fair Trade & Harmonization: Prerequisites for Free Trade? Volume 1: Economic Analysis. The MIT Press, Cambridge MA

Brander JA (1981) Intra-Industry Trade in Identical Commodities. Journal of International Economics 11 :1–14

Brander J, Krugman P (1983) A "Reciprocal Dumping" Model of International Trade. Journal of International Economics 15 : 313–321

Burniaux JM, Martin JP, Oliveira-Martins J (1992) The effects of Existing Trade Distortions in Energy Markets on the Costs of Policies to Reduce CO2 Emissions: Evidence from GREEN. OECD Economic Studies 19 : 141–166

Cole MA, Rayner AJ, Bates JM (1998) Trade Liberalization and the Environment: The Case of the Uruguay Round. The World Economy 21 : 337–347

Copeland BR (1996) Pollution Content Tariffs, Environmental Rent Shifting, and the Control of Cross-Border Pollution. Journal of International Economics 40 :459–476

Copeland BR, Taylor MS (1999) Trade, Spatial Separation and the Environment. Journal of International Economics 47 : 137–168

Copeland BR, Taylor MS (1995) Trade and the Environment: A Partial Synthesis. American Journal of Agricultural Economics 77 : 765–772

Copeland BR, Taylor MS (1995) Trade and Transboundary Pollution. American Economic Review 85 : 716–737

Copeland BR, Taylor MS (1994) North-South Trade and the Environment. Quarterly Journal of Economics 109 : 754–787

Durbin AC (1995) Trade and the Environment: The North-South Divide. Environment 37 : 16–25

Fung KC (1991) Collusive Intra-Industry Trade. Canadian Journal of Economics 24 : 391–405

Fung KC (1988) Strategic Trade Policies, Differentiated Duopoly and Intra-Industry Trade. International Economic Journal 2 : 19–34

Greenaway D, Torstensson J (1997) Back to the Future: Taking Stock on Intra-Industry Trade. Review of World Economics 133 : 249–269

Greenaway D, Milner C (1987) Intra-Industry Trade: Current Perspectives and Unresolved Issues. Review of World Economics 123 : 39–57

Greenaway D, Milner C (1986) The Economics of Intra-Industry Trade. Basil Blackwell Ltd, Oxford

Greenaway D, Tharakan PKM (eds) (1986) Imperfect Competition and International Trade: The Policy Aspects of Intra-Industry Trade. Wheatsheaf Books Ltd, Sussex

Grossman G, Krueger AB (1995) Economic Growth and the Environment. Quarterly Journal of Economics 110 : 353–377

Grossman G, Krueger AB (1993) Environmental Impacts of a North American Free Trade Agreement. In: Garber P (ed) The U.S.-Mexico Free Trade Agreement. MIT Press, Cambridge MA

Hauer G, Runge FC (1999) Trade-Environment Linkages in the Resolution of Transboundary Externalities. The World Economy 22 : 25–39

Helpman E (1987) Imperfect Competition and International Trade: Opening Remarks. European Economic Review 31 : 77–81

Helpman E, Krugman P (1985) Market Structure and Foreign Trade. MIT Press. Cambridge MA

Hoekman B, Djankov S (1996) Intra-Industry Trade, Foreign Direct Investment and the Reorientation of East European Exports. CEPR Discussion Paper, No.1377

Krugman P (1981) Intra-Industry Specialization and the Gains from Trade. Journal of Political Economy 89 : 959–973

Krugman P, Obstfeld M (1997) International Economics: Theory and Policy. 4th edition Addison–Wesley, New York

Lee HH, Lee YY (1993) Intra-Industry Trade in Manufactures: The Case of Korea. Review of World Economics. 129 : 159–171

Levinson A (1997) Environmental Regulations and Industry Location: International and Domestic Evidence. In Bhagwati JN, Hudec RE (eds) Fair Trade & Harmonization: Prerequisites for Free Trade? Vol 1: Economic Analysis. MIT Press, Cambridge MA

Low P (ed) (1992) International Trade and the Environment. World Bank Discussion Papers No. 159, The World Bank, Washington DC

Menon J (1994) Trade Liberalization and Intra-Industry Specialization: the Australian Experience. Centre of Policy Studies Monash University, General paper G–107

Menon J, Dixon PB (1997) Measures of Intra-Industry Trade as Indicators of FactorMarket Disruption. The Economic Record 73 : 233–247

Menon J, Dixon PB (1996) How Important is Intra-Industry Trade in Trade Growth? Open Economics Review 7 : 161–175

Rauscher M (1997) International Trade, Factor Movements, and the Environment. Clarendon Press, Oxford

Tharakan PKM (1984) Intra-Industry Trade Between the Industrial Countries and the Developing World. European Economic Review 26 : 213–226

Thompson P, Strohm LA (1996) Trade and Environment Quality: A Review of the Evidence. Journal of Environment & Development 5 : 363–388

Tussie D (1999) The Environment and International Trade Negotiations: Open Loops in the Developing World. The World Economy 22 : 535–545

Venables AJ (1985) Trade and Trade Policy with Imperfect Competition: The Case of Identical Products and Free Entry. Journal of International Economics. 19 : 1–19

World Bank (1992) World Development Report 1992: Development and the Environment. Oxford University Press, Oxford

Comment

Keith E. Maskus

Department of Economics, University of Colorado, Boulder, USA

I am pleased to have this opportunity to discuss the paper by K.C. Fung and Andreá Maechler, which begins to fill a gap in the literature on trade policy and environmental protection. Specifically, they develop a series of straightforward models of oligopolistic competition between two countries in symmetric goods, permitting reductions in tariffs in either or both countries to affect trade and outputs of polluting firms. I appreciate the comprehensive set of cases they consider, involving local pollution, cross-boundary pollution, and global environmental damage subject to both unilateral tariff cuts and multilateral liberalization. They also permit foreign direct investment (FDI) of a horizontal nature between countries, which affects payoffs to firms.

As befits models of this kind, there are no definitive answers and virtually anything can happen as a result of competition pre- and post- trade liberalization. However, the authors do isolate some important parametric relationships that have much to do with the possible outcomes. Ultimately, however, the ambiguity of results suggests that the questions they ask really are empirical and the framework they set out could be usefully taken to the data in further work.

In my comments I essentially wish to point out that, despite the complexity of the models, there remain a number of important omissions or extensions that would be interesting and important to pursue. The authors are aware of these issues, so the intent of this commentary is simply to encourage them to push this research forward.

First, I think the omission of at least a technique effect as an outcome of trade liberalization is serious. After all, tariff cuts in the Cournot-Nash quantity-setting environment may be expected to raise real incomes in both countries due to additional competition between firms. To the extent that techniques respond positively to income gains (and this was the main empirical result in Antweiler et al. 2001), the authors have failed to describe an important reason why openness can improve environmental use. Indeed, the result could be significant for small economies that open to trade and enjoy significant pro-competitive gains.

Second, it is unfortunate that welfare analysis cannot be performed within the model. In part this is because it is a strictly partial-equilibrium setup, but mainly there are exogenous "environmental damage" functions that cannot be assessed within well specified utility functions. Moreover, these damage functions are kept remarkably simple in order to be tractable. In truth, this is a virtue of the model, because this tractability permits the identification of such key exogenous ratios as the "pollution differential" between national firms and even this simplicity generates almost endless complexity. Nonetheless, I wonder if the results would hold up in a context where environmental damages were strictly convex in output (that is, went up at an increasing rate).

A final comment is that the policy analysis is limited. Specifically, the only policies considered are marginal tariff cuts. This eliminates consideration of large episodes of trade liberalization, including a shift to free trade. More significantly, it fails to account for the interesting possibility that tariff cuts and environmental taxes could be set jointly to affect certain outcomes. For example, both governments could offset the environmental damages generated by trade liberalization through an appropriate re-balancing of pollution taxes. Alternatively, the pollution taxes could be set to reduce the competitive pressures from tariff cuts. Most interestingly, within the model set out here the government in the clean country might well wish to subsidize output in the dirty country, if pollution is local, in order to drive out its own polluters. Most fundamentally, a comparison of tariff cuts with unchanged environmental taxes to the case of tariff cuts with "optimal" environmental taxes (designed to reduce environmental damage imposed by domestic production to some specified level) would seem appropriate here.

Of course, these latter policy experiments would require some kind of national welfare function for the government to maximize in order to settle on appropriate or optimal policies. Without a fuller setup in this context, the policies considered would be ad hoc, if interesting, just as they are in the model at hand.

Despite these reservations, I think the chapter is interesting and well-done. It sets out an important question, particularly in light of the dominance of intra-industry trade in the world economy. The models are simple but sharply illuminate both important parameters and the inherent ambiguities arising in this second-best world. In future work I hope the authors can bring some empirical evidence to bear on the ambiguities they identify.

International Business Cycle Transmission in a Dynamic Multi-Sectoral Heckscher-Ohlin Model

Julian Emami Namini[1]

Department of Economics, University of Duisburg-Essen, Campus Essen, Germany

1 Introduction

Both, the popular opinion and the academic literature share the belief that the ongoing globalization with deepening trade channels is at least partly responsible for the appearance of a common business cycle across countries.

While the cross-country dependence of the business cycle might be relatively less dangerous for developed economies with sound economic institutions, it is regarded as more critical for economically less developed countries with fragile economic institutions. The most recent significant step toward forming integrated world markets, China's accession to the WTO in 2001, has produced several country-studies for this emerging country that intend to assess the economic consequences of the resulting trade liberalization.[2] These studies mostly emphasize the potential static and dynamic efficiency gains, which might result from a less distorted allocation of economic resources and an increased competition on the world markets. However, some authors also highlight China's short term risks from being exposed to the cyclical fluctuations in the economically more developed trading partners.[3]

Back to economic theory, one can also observe a large and still growing literature that is concerned with trade as a medium of international business cycle transmission in general.[4] One strand of this literature is completely empirical. Kose et al. (2003), for example, investigate annual data of a sample consisting of 75 industrial and developing countries over the last four decades. They demon-

---

[1] For helpful comments I am grateful to Volker Clausen, Bernd Hayo, Clemens Reinhold and seminar participants at the Universities of Duisburg-Essen, Hamburg and Kiel. I alone am responsible for any remaining errors and shortcomings. The extended working paper version is downloadable from http://www.uni-essen.de/fb5/pdf/132.pdf.

[2] Cf. Frazier/Hansen (1999) or U.S. International Trade Commission (1999) for an early economics based assessment of China's potential joining of the WTO; Christensen (2001) and Fewsmith (2000, 1999) judge China's respective benefits from the viewpoints of political scientists.

[3] Cf. Christensen (2002), Shadwick (2000) or Yang/Tyers (2000).

[4] More recent studies are, e.g., Kose et al. (2003), Imbs (2003), Ambler et al. (2002), and Backus et al. (1995, 1992).

strate that the strength of the trade linkage with the *G7* countries increases the correlation of domestic macroeconomic variables with the respective world variables. Typically, the empirical literature on trade as a means of international shock transmission does not reveal the particular characteristics of the trade linkage that can be seen as the causes for the certain sign of the transmission channel.[5]

A second strand of the literature draws conclusions from dynamic general equilibrium trade models. These models mostly intend to solve the puzzle of the so-called *quantity anomaly* described by Backus et al. (1995, 1992). The *anomaly* refers to the size of the correlation of macroeconomic variables between countries: Standard one-good aggregated dynamic general equilibrium models predict a cross-country correlation of output that is smaller than the cross-country correlation in the technology shocks, the latter in turn being smaller than the cross country correlation in consumption. Empirical investigation, however, results in a reversed ranking of cross-country correlations. Ambler et al. (2002) partly succeed in removing this discrepancy between theoretical models and reality. By constructing a dynamic *multi*-sectoral general equilibrium model, they exploit the features that may result from a shock-induced change in the production structure. Anyhow, Ambler et al. (2002) only demonstrate *that* a certain correlation of macroeconomic variables between countries may exist.

Both these contributions, however, are completely silent on the exact process of transmission and its welfare consequences. This is the starting point of the present study. By analyzing a dynamic multi-sectoral general equilibrium model numerically, it intends to reveal the actual character and causes of a positive or a negative transmission channel between two countries that are linked via goods trade. The base case model is characterized by Heckscher-Ohlin assumptions. This base case model is then extended by incorporating the households' labor supply decisions into the model and assuming imperfect substitutability between home and foreign produced goods.

Section *2* describes the model setup, section *3* the calibration procedure and simulation results. Section *4* concludes.

2 The Model

2.1 Production

Production in both countries, which are indexed with *H* (home country) and *F* (foreign country), is represented by two intermediate and two final product sectors. The intermediate product sectors use only labor and capital as factors of pro-

[5] The word *sign* refers to the assessment of the transmission channel. If, e.g., a home country *H* suffers an inefficiency shock and its trading partner, a foreign country *F*, gains – however gains are measured –, the sign of the transmission channel is termed *positive*. If, on the other hand, country *F* looses, the sign of the transmission channel is termed *negative*.

duction, while the two final product sectors use both intermediate goods as well as labor and capital as inputs. Households demand both final products and divide the total amounts demanded between consumption and investment. Investment then raises the depreciable capital stock.[6] A graphical illustration of the production sides of both economies is given in the following Figure 1.

2.2 Production Technologies

In general, the production technologies for both countries are specified such that no reversal in the factor intensity ranking of the sectors occurs at all possible relative factor prices, neither in the intermediate goods sector, nor in the final goods sector. This restriction on the production technologies is fulfilled, if all technologies are of the constant elasticity of substitution (*CES*)-form.[7] The production technologies of the intermediate goods sector n, $n = 1, 2$, and the final goods sector m, $m = 1, 2$, are then described by the following equations:[8]

$$x_{nit} = A_{nit}^{x}\left(\varphi_{nL} L_{nit}^{1-1/\sigma_{x_n}} + (1-\varphi_{nL}) K_{nit}^{1-1/\sigma_{x_n}}\right)^{\frac{\sigma_{x_n}}{\sigma_{x_n}-1}} \tag{1}$$

$$y_{mit} = \left(\varphi_{mX}\left(X_{1mit}^{\gamma} X_{2mit}^{1-\gamma}\right)^{1-1/\sigma_{y_m}} + (1-\varphi_{mX})\left(A_{mit}^{y} L_{mit}^{\theta_m} K_{mit}^{1-\theta_m}\right)^{1-1/\sigma_{y_m}}\right)^{\frac{\sigma_{y_m}}{\sigma_{y_m}-1}} \tag{2}$$

where x_{nit} denotes the output of intermediate good n in country i, $i = H, F$, in period t, y_{mit} the gross output of final good m in country i in period t. σ_{x_n} and σ_{y_m} represent the elasticities of substitution between the factor inputs in the production of intermediate good n and final good m. L_{nit}, K_{nit}, L_{mit} and K_{mit} stand for labor and capital input in the production of good n and good m. X_{nmit} denotes the input of intermediate product n into the production of final good m, γ and θ are both strictly between zero and one. The capitalized variable X_{nmit} stands for an aggregate of home and foreign produced intermediate good n. The aggregation procedure is described in detail below. Later it will be exploited that the weighting parameters φ_{nL}, $(1 - \varphi_{nL})$, φ_{mX} and $(1 - \varphi_{mX})$ equal the value shares of labor and capital in the base case equilibrium, which is characterized by all relative prices equal to one and $\sigma_{x_n} = \sigma_{y_m} = 1$, $n, m = 1, 2$, in order to simplify calibrating the model to this benchmark.

---

[6] The production side of the present model is therefore identical to that used by Ambler et al. (2002) and Kouparitsas (1998).

[7] This property of an irreversibility in the factor intensity ranking for *CES*-technologies is shown and proven in Wong (1990), p. 438-439; the invariable ranking in factor intensities will turn out to be crucial for the model results.

[8] This specification of the intermediate goods production technology deviates from Ambler et al. (2002), but is in line with Kouparitsas (1998). Ambler et al. (2002) include the possibility of the final goods to be input factors for the production of the intermediate goods. However, this deviation should not be central for the model results.

The business cycle in the model, i.e. the temporary deviation from the balanced growth path, is caused by a negative technology shock. This technology shock is implemented by means of an inefficiency parameter in each sector, A^x_{nit}, $A^y_{mit} < 0$, that gives rise to greater capital and labor requirements for a given amount of output. The inefficiency parameters evolve according to a first order autoregressive process, i.e. $\ln A^l_{kit} = \rho \ln A^l_{ki(t-1)} + \varepsilon^l_{kit}$, $k = 1, 2$, $l = x, y$, with $0 < \rho < 1$ and ε^l_{kit} denoting a white noise disturbance for sector k, production stage l, country i in period t. The ε^l_{kit} are assumed to be uncorrelated across sectors in order to disentangle the exact shock transmission mechanism, but may be correlated across countries. If the ε^l_{kit} are uncorrelated across countries, they give rise to a *national* shock, if the ε^l_{kit} are correlated across countries, they give rise to a *global* shock. As identical production technologies for both countries are assumed, the *national* shock could represent a shock to the quality of production factors, whereas the *global* shock could represent a shock to the production technology.

The total supply of labor and capital is fully employed in both intermediate goods sectors and both final goods sectors. This gives two resource constraints for country i on the balanced growth path, which is characterized by a growth of actual labor supply and total capital supply at an identical rate:

$$\left(\overline{L}_{i0} - S_{i0}\right)\left(1+g\right)^t \geq \sum_{n=1}^{2} L_{nit} + \sum_{m=1}^{2} L_{mit} \tag{3}$$

$$\overline{K}_{i0}\left(1+g\right)^t \geq \sum_{n=1}^{2} K_{nit} + \sum_{m=1}^{2} K_{mit} \tag{4}$$

where g denotes the exogenously given growth rate of the potential labor force. $\overline{L}_{i0}$ represents the potential labor force in the initial period, S_{i0} the consumption of leisure in the initial period – leisure consumption is determined exogenously in

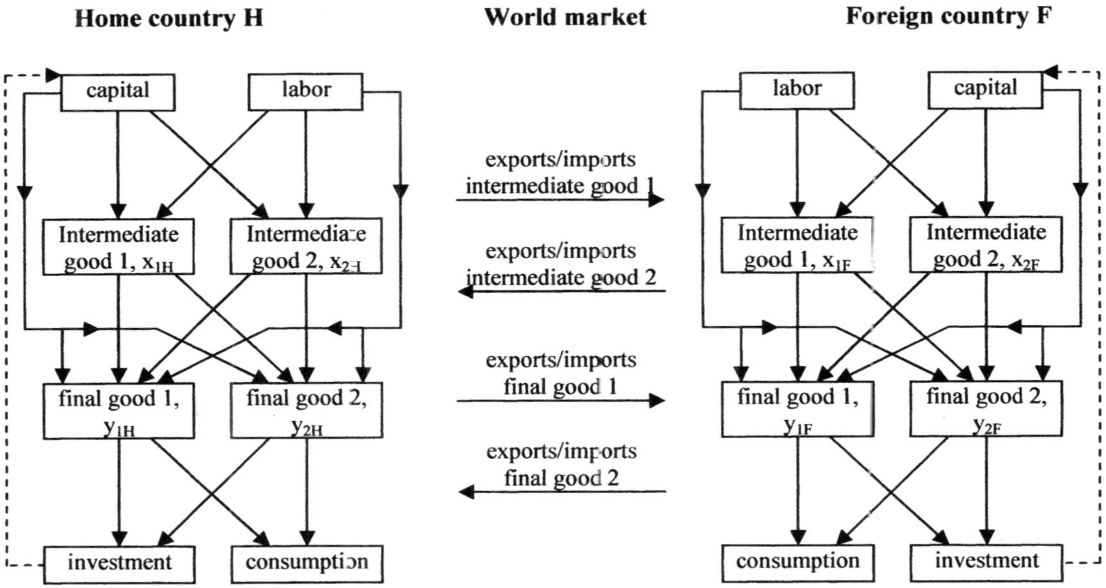

Figure 1. The Production Sides of Both Economies

the base case model – and $\bar{K}_{i0}$ the supply of capital in the initial period.[9] The actual evolution of the capital stock depends on the rate of depreciation and on investment. Both countries possess an investment technology that is characterized by a one period *it time to build* structure. In both countries, the capital stock in period *t* equals the capital stock in the previous period less depreciation plus investment in the previous period *(t-1)*. The capital formation process for country *i* is then described by

$$\bar{K}_{it} = (1-\delta)\bar{K}_{i(t-1)} + \left(\varphi_I I_{Y_{1i(t-1)}}^{1-1/\sigma_I} + (1-\varphi_I) I_{Y_{2i(t-1)}}^{1-1/\sigma_I}\right)^{\frac{\sigma_I}{\sigma_I - 1}} \tag{5}$$

where δ denotes the rate of depreciation and σ_I the elasticity of substitution between the amounts of the final goods invested at time *(t-1)*, $I_{Y_{mi(t-1)}}$, *m = 1, 2.*[10] Obviously, the amount invested of good *m* in country *i* at time *t*, $I_{Y_{mit}}$, equals total availability of this good, Y_{mit}, minus total consumption, C_{mit}, i.e. $I_{Y_{mit}} = Y_{mit} - C_{mit}$.

2.3 Households

All households in both countries are each represented by one single and infinitely lived household. The representative household in country *i* gains utility in period *t* from consuming an aggregate consumption good C_{it} and leisure S_{it}. While the base case model supposes leisure consumption to rise with the exogenously given rate *g*, one of the counterfactual analyses endogenizes the households' labor supply decisions. Nevertheless, the base case version of the model sets S_{it} equal to zero during the solution procedure. An additional adjustment of the parameters in the households' utility functions then guarantees constant returns to scale utility functions with respect to goods consumption, which is determined endogenously. The discounted lifetime utility of household *i* is thus given by

$$U_{i0} = \sum_{t=0}^{\infty} \frac{u_{it}(C_{it}, S_{it})}{(1+\rho)^t} \quad \text{with } u_{it} = \frac{1}{1-1/\sigma_T} \cdot C_{it}^{1-1/\sigma_T} \tag{6}$$

for the base case model and

---

[9] It should be emphasized that the evolution of the capital stocks in both countries is determined endogenously, via the households' saving decisions. Solely the growth rates of the potential labor forces are given exogenously. Growth of both factor endowments at an identical rate only results on the balanced growth path, i.e. as soon as the steady state capital endowment per worker is reached. The base case model obviously assumes that leisure consumption grows at an identical rate as the potential labor force. Actual labor supply therefore also grows with the rate *g*.

[10] This specification of the expansion of the capital stock is standard in real business cycle theory. Backus et al. (1995), p. 337, extend the *time to build* structure to *j = 1, ...,J* periods and introduce a variable s_{it}^j, denoting investment projects in *t* that are *j* periods away from adding to country *i's* capital stock. The present model therefore assumes *j = 1.*

$$u_{it} = \frac{1}{1-1/\sigma_T} \cdot \left(\left(\varphi_{U_i} \cdot C_{it}^{1-1/\sigma_U} + \left(1-\varphi_{U_i}\right) \cdot S_{it}^{1-1/\sigma_U} \right)^{\frac{\sigma_U}{\sigma_U - 1}} \right)^{1-1/\sigma_T}$$

for the counterfactual analysis that endogenizes the households' labor supply decisions. C_{it} is specified as $C_{it} = C_{1it}^{\psi} C_{2it}^{1-\psi}$, $0 < \psi < 1$. C_{mit} represents total consumption of good m for country i in period t, σ_U the elasticity of substitution between both inputs in the upper nest of utility production, σ_T the constant intertemporal elasticity of substitution and ρ the rate of time preference. The φ_{Ui} receive a country index to allow for different shares of goods and leisure consumption in the respective counterfactual analysis. The lifetime utility function is specified without an expectations operator, because perfect foresight is assumed.

Both representative households maximize their lifetime utility subject to the evolution of the capital stock and the following budget constraint:

$$\sum_{t=0}^{\infty} \sum_{m=1}^{2} \frac{p_{Y_{mit}}}{(1+r)^t} \left(C_{mit} + I_{Y_{mit}} \right) \leq \sum_{t=0}^{\infty} \left(\frac{w_{it}}{(1+r)^t} \left(\sum_{n=1}^{2} L_{nit} + \sum_{m=1}^{2} L_{mit} \right) + \frac{r_{it}}{(1+r)^t} \left(\sum_{n=1}^{2} K_{nit} + \sum_{m=1}^{2} K_{mit} \right) \right), \quad (7)$$

where w_{it} denotes the wage rate for country i in period t, r_{it} the respective capital rental rate and $p_{Y_{mit}}$ the consumer price of good Y_{mit}. Parameter r denotes the time invariant real interest rate that is assumed to be identical across both countries. This inequality simply states that the total discounted value of goods consumption and investment can not exceed the total discounted value of factor income over the entire time horizon.[11]

2.4 Armington Assumption

Both producers and consumers in the model may regard products which are produced at different locations as imperfect substitutes, i.e. the Armington assumption is valid.[12] Producers and households in both countries aggregate domestic and foreign produced intermediate and final goods according to the following CES functions:

$$X_{nit} = \left(\varphi_{nA} \left(x_{niit} \right)^{1-1/\sigma_{x_{nA}}} + \left(1-\varphi_{nA}\right) \left(x_{njit} \right)^{1-1/\sigma_{x_{nA}}} \right)^{\frac{\sigma_{x_{nA}}}{\sigma_{x_{nA}} - 1}} \quad (8)$$

$$Y_{mit} = \left(\varphi_{mA} \left(y_{iit} \right)^{1-1/\sigma_{y_{mA}}} + \left(1-\varphi_{mA}\right) \left(y_{jit} \right)^{1-1/\sigma_{y_{mA}}} \right)^{\frac{\sigma_{y_{mA}}}{\sigma_{y_{mA}} - 1}} \quad (9)$$

---

[11] This equation implicitly permits a temporary trade imbalance for either country. However, sensitivity analyses showed that formulating the budget constraint for each single period, i.e. requiring a zero trade balance for each period, does not change the central model results, but increases the time which is required for solving the model.

[12] See Armington (1969) for this way of rationalizing "two-way trade" in a single good.

with X_{nit} denoting the total quantity of intermediate good n, $n = 1, 2$, that is at country i's disposal in period t, Y_{mit} denotes the respective quantity of final good m, $m = 1, 2$. The parameters $\sigma_{x_{nA}}$ and $\sigma_{y_{mA}}$ represent the elasticities of substitution between home and foreign produced intermediate good n and final good m, respectively. The subscripts ij denote the country of production, i, and the country of sale, j. Both the weighting factors φ_{nA} and φ_{mA}, $m, n = 1, 2$, might reflect a home bias concerning the preferences of consumers and producers. Obviously, the total amount of intermediate good n produced in country i in period t, x_{nit}, equals total supply of this good to country i and country j, i.e. $x_{nit} = x_{niit} + x_{nijt}$. The same equality has to hold for the total amount of final good m produced in country i in period t, y_{mit}, i. e. $y_{mit} = y_{miit} + y_{mijt}$.

2.5 The Dynamic General Equilibrium

The dynamic general equilibrium is now fully described by the equations of the production technologies in each country, the respective resource constraints, which include the equations for the capital stock evolvement, the shock equations, the households' intertemporal maximization problems and the Armington aggregation functions. It is now possible to formulate the constrained welfare-maximization problem for each of both representative households and to set up the necessary first order conditions that describe the dynamic general equilibrium as a mixed complementary problem. The model to be solved then consists of several zero profit conditions for each production sector in both countries, several goods and factor market clearing conditions for both countries and the world markets, and – assuming strict monotonous references of both representative households – one income-balance condition per country.[13]

3 Solving the Model

3.1 Calibration and Simulation

The model is solved with the help of numerical solution methods. Calibrating the model parameters is carried out by the use of a synthetic database. The choice of synthetic data is due to achieving easily interpretable results. Several other general

[13] The transformation f the constrained maximization problem, which is explained above, into a *mixed complementary problem* consisting of the mentioned zero profit conditions, additional market clearing conditions and two income balance equations is described in detail by Mathiesen (1985) and, on a more general level, by Kuhn and Tucker (1951). The detailed derivation of all zero profit conditions, all market clearing conditions and the numerical representation of the period zero base case equilibrium is left to the working paper version of this model.

equilibrium trade models exist, whose benchmark is calibrated to real data.[14] These models, which aggregate their economies to a limited number of sectors, use averaged values for the labor share in production costs that range from under *10%* to almost *50%*. Detailed input-output tables, however, reveal values for this labor share that may well vary between under *10%* to *85%* for certain sectors.[15] The present study assumes cost shares for the primary factors of *10%* (*5%*) and *90%* (*45%*) in the intermediate (final) goods sectors. Therefore, the chosen cost shares are in line with real data and – at the same time – are located at the margins of the empirical = relevant range.

A larger home country *H*, which represents the industrialized North, is relatively well endowed with capital, the smaller foreign country *F*, which represents the economically less developed emerging country, is relatively well endowed with labor.[16] All units on the balanced growth path are chosen so that the relative prices in this benchmark equal one. The parameters of all production functions are then already specified via the cost shares of the production factors. Moreover, elasticities of substitution in all production technologies and the households' utility functions – the intertemporal elasticity of substitution σ_T included – are fixed at values of one. This leads to the following specification of the model parameters that are taken both for the base case scenario and the counterfactual analyses:

Intermediate goods production:

L_{1it}/x_{1it}:	$\varphi_{1L} = 0.1$	K_{1it}/x_{1it}:	$1-\varphi_{1L} = 0.9$
L_{2it}/x_{2it}:	$\varphi_{2L} = 0.9$	K_{2it}/x_{2it}:	$1-\varphi_{2L} = 0.1$

Final goods production:

$X_{11it}/\left(X_{11it}^{\gamma}X_{21it}^{1-\gamma}\right)$:	$\gamma = 0.5$	$X_{21it}/\left(X_{11it}^{\gamma}X_{21it}^{1-\gamma}\right)$:	$1-\gamma = 0.5$
$X_{12it}/\left(X_{12it}^{\gamma}X_{22it}^{1-\gamma}\right)$:	$\gamma = 0.5$,	$X_{22it}/\left(X_{12it}^{\gamma}X_{22it}^{1-\gamma}\right)$:	$1-\gamma = 0.5$,

[14] These models are, i.a., Dervis et al. (1982) for Turkey, Kouparitsas (1998) for a sample of northern and southern countries and Ambler et al. (2002), who mainly rely on U.S. input-output tables.

[15] Cf. the input-output tables for the OECD countries at http://www.oecd.org/document: In the United States, for example, the labor share in the textile and apparel sector is about *85%*, whereas the labor share in the agricultural sector is about *20%*. The input-output table for China, for example, which is available at http://www.stats.gov.cn/yearbook, gives higher values for the labor share in China's agricultural sector, namely slightly more than *50%*. China's textile and apparel sector, in contrast, has a labor share of only *14%*.

[16] The difference in the size of the countries is mainly chosen for illustrative reasons. As all production technologies are specified with constant returns to scale and preferences are homothetic, the trade pattern between the countries is only determined by relative factor endowments. It can be shown that the size of a country only influences the model results in a quantitative sense.

$L_{1it}/\left(L_{1it}^{\theta_1}K_{1it}^{1-\theta_1}\right)$:	$\theta_1 = 0.9$,	$K_{1it}/\left(L_{1it}^{\theta_1}K_{1it}^{1-\theta_1}\right)$:	$1\text{-}\theta_1 = 0.1$,
$L_{2it}/\left(L_{2it}^{\theta_2}K_{2it}^{1-\theta_2}\right)$:	$\theta_2 = 0.1$,	$K_{2it}/\left(L_{2it}^{\theta_2}K_{2it}^{1-\theta_2}\right)$:	$1\text{-}\theta_2 = 0.9$,
$\left(X_{11it}^{\gamma}X_{21it}^{1-\gamma}\right)/y_{1it}$:	$\varphi_{1X} = 0.5$,	$\left(L_{1it}^{\theta_1}K_{1it}^{1-\theta_1}\right)/y_{1it}$:	$1-\varphi_{1X} = 0.5$,
$\left(X_{12it}^{\gamma}X_{22it}^{1-\gamma}\right)/y_{2it}$:	$\varphi_{2X} = 0.5$,	$\left(L_{2it}^{\theta_2}K_{2it}^{1-\theta_2}\right)/y_{2it}$:	$1-\varphi_{2X} = 0.5$,

Investment technology:

I_{Y1it}/I_{it} :	$\varphi_I = 0.5$,	I_{Y2it}/I_{it} :	$1-\varphi_I = 0.5$,

Instantaneous utility function, base case:

$\left(C_{1Ht}^{\psi}C_{2Ht}^{1-\psi}\right)/u_{Ht}$:	$\varphi_{U_H} = 1$,	S_{Ht}/u_{Ht} :	$1-\varphi_{U_H} = 0$,
$\left(C_{1Ft}^{\psi}C_{2Ft}^{1-\psi}\right)/u_{Ft}$:	$\varphi_{U_F} = 1$,	S_{Ft}/u_{Ft} :	$1-\varphi_{U_F} = 0$,

Instantaneous utility function, counterfactual analysis:

$\left(C_{1Ht}^{\psi}C_{2Ht}^{1-\psi}\right)/u_{Ht}$:	$\varphi_{U_H} = 0.77$,	S_{Ht}/u_{Ht} :	$1-\varphi_{U_H} = 0.23$,
$\left(C_{1Ft}^{\psi}C_{2Ft}^{1-\psi}\right)/u_{Ft}$:	$\varphi_{U_F} = 0.83$,	S_{Ft}/u_{Ft} :	$1-\varphi_{U_F} = 0.17$,

Instantaneous utility function, aggregation of consumption goods:

$C_{1it}/\left(C_{1it}^{\psi}C_{2it}^{1-\psi}\right)$:	$\psi = 0.5$,	$C_{2it}/\left(C_{1it}^{\psi}C_{2it}^{1-\psi}\right)$:	$1-\psi = 0.5$.

Furthermore, the time preference rate ρ is equated with the real interest rate r, which is set equal to 0.05.

The base case model assumes that both domestic and foreign produced goods are regarded as perfect substitutes by consumers and producers. One of the counterfactual analyses, in contrast, supposes imperfect substitutability between domestic and foreign produced goods and sets the Armington elasticity of substitution equal to one for both countries. This counterfactual analysis then assumes $\phi_{1A} = 0.95$, $\phi_{2A} = 0.5$ for intermediate goods supply to country *H*, $\phi_{1A} = 0.1$ and $\phi_{2A} = 0.95$ for final goods supply to country *H*, $\phi_{1A} = 0.1$ and $\phi_{2A} = 0.8$ for intermediate goods supply to country *F* and finally $\phi_{1A} = 0.8$ and $\phi_{2A} = 0.1$ for final goods supply to country *F*.

With respect to the countries' factor endowments, the capital rich northern country is twice as big as the labor rich emerging country. Total factor income in $t=0$ equals 1000 for the northern country and 500 for the emerging country. The potential labor force in both economies is fixed at a level of $\bar{L}_{i0} = 500$ in $t = 0$.[17] This potential labor force grows at an exogenously given rate of $g = 0.02$ p.a. In the base case model, it is assumed that actual labor supply is fixed and equals $340(1+g)^t$ in the northern country in t and $410(1+g)^t$ in the emerging country in period t. Therefore, the base case model is characterized by a labor's share value of 0.34 in the northern country and 0.82 in the emerging country.[18] A counterfactual analysis will relax the fixed labor supply restriction and allow the households to choose between goods and leisure consumption.

The trade pattern between both countries on the balanced growth path is characterized by exports of the capital intensive intermediate good x_1 from the northern to the emerging country, exports of the labor intensive intermediate good x_2 from the emerging to the northern country, exports of the labor intensive final good y_1 from the emerging to the northern country and exports of the capital intensive final good y_2 from the northern to the emerging country.

In order to avoid the trade flows to be indeterminate, additional *iceberg* trade costs are introduced.[19] These trade costs account for 4% of the quantity shipped and occur for each trade linkage that is not active on the balanced growth path. These trade costs might be justified as well with higher per unit transport-costs for any trade linkage that is not established since long.

Period 1 is the only period in which a negative technological shock may occur. The shock equation $\ln A_{kit}^l = \rho \ln A_{ki(t-1)}^l + \varepsilon_{kit}$, $k = m, n, l = x, y$, is specified with $\rho = 0.5$ and $\varepsilon_{ki1} \approx 0.051$ for the sector in which the shock occurs. This implies that labor and capital contribute only 95% of the base case level to output in $t=1$, if the shock occurs in the respective sector. In a first scenario, technological shocks are assumed to be *national* shocks, i.e. only the northern country is hit by a shock. In a second scenario, the shocks are assumed to be *global* shocks, i.e. the cross-country correlation of the technological shocks is assumed to be perfect and the emerging

---

17 The exact specification of absolute factor endowments is unimportant for the qualitative model results, as constant returns to scale technologies and homothetic preferences are assumed; Ambler et al. (2002), p. 284, Kouparitsas (1998), p. 10, for example, choose normalized factor endowments and set potential labor force endowment per period equal to one.

18 See Ambler et al. (2002), p. 287. They assume identical countries with respect to relative factor endowments. Nevertheless, there is trade in the Ambler et al. (2002) model, as they assume imperfect substitutability between home and foreign produced goods. The base case version of the present model, in contrast, must assume endowment differences, if trade shall not cease. Baxter and Kouparitsas (2002), p. 4, argue that it is indeed comparative advantage based on relative factor endowments, which is central for the explanation of international trade. Furthermore, a ratio of northern capital per worker to capital per worker in the emerging country of roughly 10:1 seems realistically; cf. the values for the United States and those for the Philippines or Thailand in Summers and Heston (1991), p. 352–3.

19 The problem of *indeterminacy of trade flows* and the possibility of introducing trade costs is discussed by Ginsburgh and Keyzer (2002), p. 147–55.

country is hit by exactly the identical shock as the northern country. The intersectoral correlation of the shocks is set equal to zero. This will certainly simplify discovering the exact shock transmission mechanism.

To capture the welfare consequences that result from the shock, the periodic change in total factor income of each country, $\Delta\Pi_{it}$, is calculated.[20] Decomposing the periodic change in total factor income into its components and weighting with the balanced growth path factor income in period zero results in

$$\frac{\Delta\Pi_{it}}{\Pi_{i0}^0}=\frac{w_{it}^0\Delta L_{it}}{\Pi_{i0}^0}+\frac{L_{it}^0 w_{it}}{\Pi_{i0}^0}+\frac{r_{it}^0\Delta K_{it}}{\Pi_{i0}^0}+\frac{K_{it}^0\Delta r_{it}}{\Pi_{i0}^0}+\frac{\Delta L_{it}\Delta w_{it}}{\Pi_{i0}^0}+\frac{\Delta K_{it}\Delta r_{it}}{\Pi_{i0}^0}, \tag{10}$$

where the superscript 0 denotes the values on the balanced growth path and the operator Δ the difference between the values in the shock scenario and those on the balanced growth path. Adding up the $\Delta\Pi_{it}/\Pi_{i0}^0$ over the entire model horizon and indicating every component only by the respective difference operator for saving space results in

$$\Delta\Pi_i=\Delta L_i+\Delta w_i+\Delta K_i+\Delta r_i+\Delta L_i\Delta w_i+\Delta K_i\Delta r_i. \tag{11}$$

Finally, the numerical solution of the model is determined with the help of the *mixed complementary problems*-solver, which is integrated into the software *GAMS*.[21] Using this solver permits a model solution without linearizing the model around its steady state. Thus, the present model may in principle evolve with discontinuities. Solving the model numerically, however, requires reducing the model horizon from infinity to a finite number of periods.[22] In the present analysis, the model is run for 101 periods.

---

[20] As the zero profit conditions are always fulfilled, the periodic change in total factor income certainly equals the periodic production gain/loss. As all factor and goods prices are shadow prices, these changes reflect changes in a country's welfare. Displaying the total periodic changes in the value of production seems not appropriate for the present study, as they hardly allow for tracing back the shock-induced welfare changes to their exact causes. Furthermore, explicitly calculating cross-country correlations in macroeconomic variables would only make sense with technological shocks that may occur in each period.

[21] Cf. Brooke et al. (1998) for a general description of the software *GAMS* and Rutherford (1998) for an introduction into general equilibrium modelling with the *mixed complementary problems*-solver in *GAMS*.

[22] The adjustments which are necessary for solving a model with an infinite horizon numerically are described in detail by Lau et al. (2000), p. 9–12, Paltsev (2000), p. 14: E.g., the households are not allowed to consume these resources in period $t = 100$, which they would need for production in period $t = 101$, if this period would be observed.

Table 1. Simulation Results, Base Case Model and Counterfactual Analyses

Country H, base case							
sector of shock	$\Delta\Pi_H$	ΔL_H	Δw_H	ΔK_H	Δr_H	$\Delta L_H \Delta w_H$	$\Delta K_H \Delta r_H$
X_{1H}	-434.22		-3.89	-425.09	-7.16		1.91
X_{1H} & X_{1F}	-2.57		-1.03	-1.88	0.34		0.00
X_{2H}	48.83		-1.9	51.00	-0.24		-0.03
X_{2H} & X_{2F}	-3.07		-1.03	-2.38	0.34		0.00
Y_{1H}	43.59		-1.15	44.46	0.26		0.02
Y_{1H} & Y_{1F}	-1.31		0.14	-2.55	1.10		0.00
Y_{2H}	-435.68		-5.68	-422.41	-10.75		3.16
Y_{2H} & Y_{2F}	-4.77		-2.23	-2.13	-0.41		0.00
labor supply endogenous							
X_{1H}	-433.70	0.01	-3.70	-425.00	-6.81	0.00	1.79
Y_{1H}	43.83	-0.29	-1.13	44.95	0.27	0.01	0.00
Armington elasticity = 1							
X_{1H}	-2.70		-0.96	-2.05	0.32		0.00
Y_{1H}	-0.55		0.22	-1.25	0.47		0.00
sector of shock	$\Delta\Pi_H$	ΔL_H	Δw_H	ΔK_H	Δr_H	$\Delta L_H \Delta w_H$	$\Delta K_H \Delta r_H$
X_{1H}	835.02		-8.96	847.85	-0.79		-3.08
X_{1H} & X_{1F}	-3.63		-2.48	-1.24	0.09		0.00
X_{2H}	-97.26		3.78	-100.85	-0.26		0.08
X_{2H} & X_{2F}	-2.63		-2.48	-0.24	0.09		0.00
Y_{1H}	-87.25		2.84	-89.99	-0.07		-0.03
Y_{1H} & Y_{1F}	0.29		0.33	-0.34	0.30		0.00
Y_{2H}	822.97		-14.11	843.41	-1.27		-5.06
Y_{2H} & Y_{2F}	-5.95		-5.37	-0.47	-0.11		0.00
labor supply endogenous							
X_{1H}	835.41	-0.11	-8.52	847.58	-0.70	0.00	-2.84
Y_{1H}	-88.21	0.24	2.89	-91.24	-0.06	0.01	-0.04
Armington elasticity = 1							
X_{1H}	-2.82		-2.33	-0.58	0.09		0.00
Y_{1H}	-0.93		-0.75	-0.06	-0.11		-0.01

Note: Values in Per Cent

3.2 Results

The main simulation results are displayed in the following Table 1. These values, which are denoted in per cent, correspond to those specified in equation (11). Of course, the magnitude of these numerical results depends both on the specific factor endowments the countries are assigned in period 1 and the chosen parameters for all functions. In a qualitative sense, however, these results are independent from the specific numerical values described above.

The set up of the model implies that these values already account for the households' time preference rate and therefore represent present values of the periodic income change over the entire model horizon.

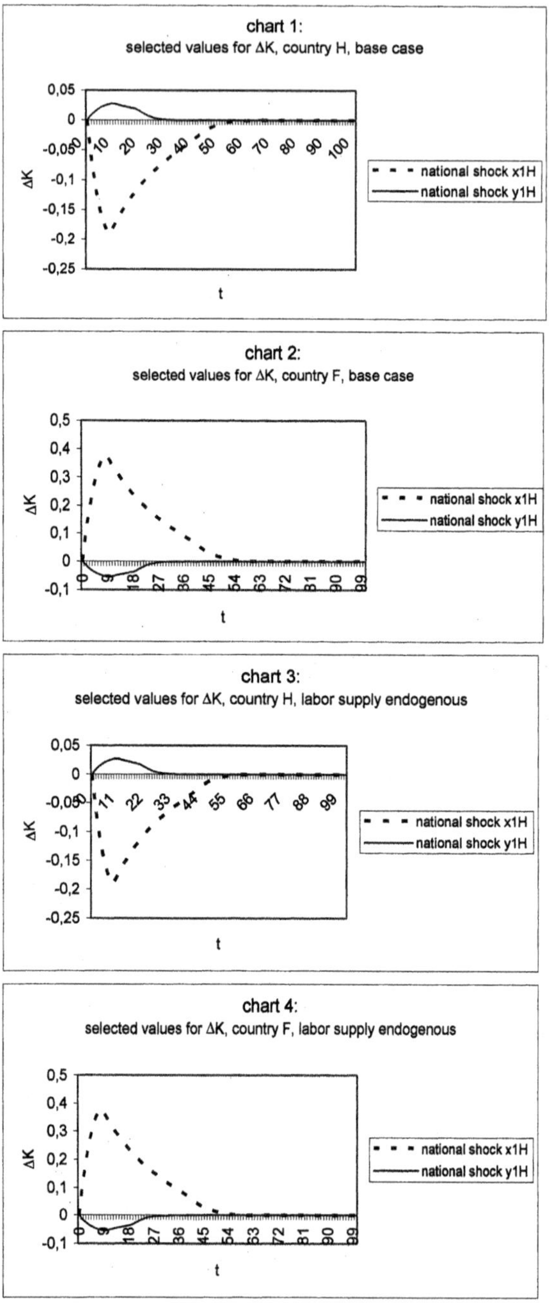

Figure 2. The Evolution of ΔK Variables

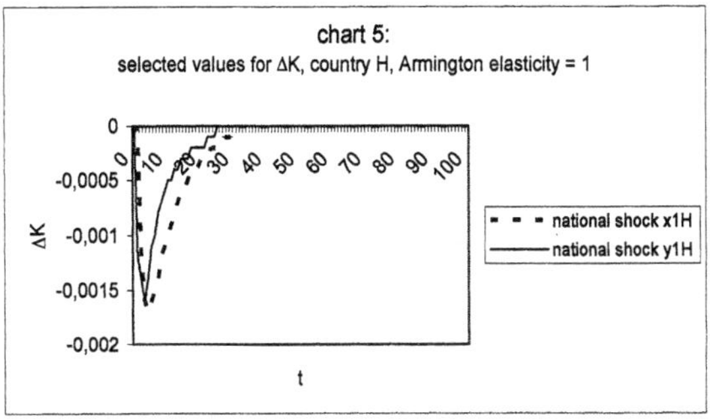

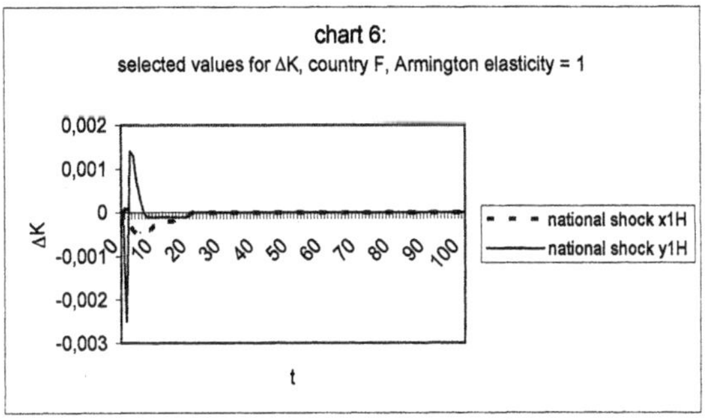

Figure 2. [cont.] The Evolution of ΔK Variables

Table 1 demonstrates that the capital stock variables ΔK_H and ΔK_F are the driving forces behind the significant changes in total periodic factor income, which occur in the cases of a national shock in country *H*.[23] The charts in Figure 2 illustrate the evolution of these ΔK variables for selected shock scenarios in the base case and the counterfactual analyses.

Both, the values in Table 1 and the graphs in Figure 2 reveal several basic characteristics of the shock transmission mechanism. First, if the technology shock is global, the change in total periodic factor incomes is always smaller in absolute value, compared to the situation with a national shock only. Second, country *H* may even gain in the cases in which it experiences a negative national shock on its own. This result occurs whenever country *H* is hit by a national shock in the labor intensive sectors x_{2H} and y_{1H}, in which it possesses a comparative disadvantage. Third, in the cases where country *H* is hit by a national shock, the gain (loss) in total periodic factor income for both countries can almost completely be attributed to an increase (decrease) in the respective capital endowment. In exactly these

[23] Table 1 reveals as well that the Δw variables may in some cases explain at least an observable part of the change in total periodic factor income. Although the evolvement of every variable, which is explained endogenously, could be reconstructed, the present study will restrict attention on ΔK. Sensitivity analyses revealed at least that an increase in the inefficiency shock leads to a rising contribution of the ΔK variables to the change in total periodic factor income.

cases of a national shock in country *H*, the sign of the change in total periodic factor income is always different between both countries.

Because of limited space, only three representative cases shall now be observed in greater detail, namely a national shock in sectors x_1 and y_1 and a global shock in sector x_1. At first, the potential causal chains will be described. These causal chains for these scenarios will be confirmed subsequently by a graphical illustration of the behavior of all explanatory model variables. Again, limited space restricts this graphical illustration to the first shock scenario. The figures for the remaining scenarios are displayed in the working paper version of this model.

National shock occurs in sector x_{1H}: Country *H* suffers a negative technology shock in one of those sectors, in which it possesses a comparative advantage. The temporary diminished efficiency in producing good x_1 leads to a transient breakdown of x_1 exports to country *F*. Consequently, a *shock effect* as well as a *trade pattern effect* brings about the observed results. Resources of country *H* are reallocated toward sector x_2, which uses labor more intensively in production. Both the reduction in investment for smoothing consumption and the temporary structural change in production lead to a significant overall decline in investment. The absolute and relative capital endowment of country *H* falls subsequently.

Country *F*, in contrast, increases the production of the capital intensive good x_1, as it can not revert to imports of x_1 any more. Hence, country *F* is forced to augment its own capital stock and rises investment to absorb the corresponding decline of the capital stock in country *H*. The relative capital endowments of both countries accordingly converge toward each other. The introduction of trade costs for those trade linkages that are inactive on the balanced growth path now prevents a hysteresis-like situation, in which country *F* reaches a higher relative capital endowment than country *H* and the trade pattern is permanently reversed. Once the immediate influence of the shock is vanished, both countries return to their initial investment behavior and converge to their initial balanced growth path. However, the temporary change in absolute capital endowment brought about a loss in the present value of total factor income in country *H* and a corresponding gain in country *F*.

These model results are well in line with work by Samuelson (1975), Srinivasan and Bhagwati (1980) or Grossman and Helpman (1995). All these papers describe additional gains from trade – besides the traditional static efficiency gains – that may result from changes in a country's investment behavior and therefore its capital stock.

The principal dynamics for this shock scenario are summarized in Figures A1 to A4 in the appendix. Figure A1 illustrates the evolvement of x_1 exports from country *H* to country *F* in the shock scenario, relative to the balanced growth path. Figure A2 depicts total investment in country *H* in the shock scenario, relative to the balanced growth path – a value less than one obviously denotes a temporary decline in total investment. Figure A3 illustrates the same investment ratio for country F.[24] Figure A4 describes the evolution, and hence the temporary convergence of the relative capital endowments of both countries.

The first counterfactual analysis endogenises the households' labor supply decisions. However, with respect to the total periodic income change over the entire model horizon, no significant differences to the base case model can be observed. Figure A5 in the appendix merely reveals a stronger reaction of total factor income in period zero, relative to the base case model, for both countries. If labor supply is determined endogenously, an immediate adjustment in total periodic factor supply is possible – an adjustment that is ruled out in the base case model, as *current* investment only influence the total factor supply in the *future* period.[25]

The second counterfactual analysis reduces the elasticity of substitution between home and foreign produced goods from infinity to one. The income changes for both countries attenuate sharply, compared to the base case model. Obviously, if both countries depend on both versions of a single good, i.e. the domestic and the foreign produced variant, the shock influences the trade pattern much less, the *trade pattern effect* is reduced. Figure A6 in the appendix representatively illustrates the x_1 exports of country H, relative to the balanced growth path. If the shock leaves the production pattern in both countries nearly unaffected, the absolute factor endowments of both countries accordingly remain fairly stable.

Global shock occurs in sectors x_{1H} *and* x_{1F}: Both countries are hit by one and the same technological shock. Thus, none of either country experiences a change in the size of its comparative advantages. No *trade pattern effect*, only a *shock effect* brings about the observed results. Figure A7 in the appendix of the working paper version underpins this result by representatively showing the x_2 exports of country F in this shock scenario, relative to the balanced growth path.

Investments are reduced only for smoothing consumption. They are not reduced because of a temporary change in the production structure, additionally. Therefore, neither country goes through the considerable change in its absolute capital endowment that significantly influenced its total factor income in the previous shock scenario.

National shock occurs in sector y_{1H}: This scenario probably deserves particular consideration, as country H gains from a domestic negative shock and any adverse

---

[24] Figure A2 and Figure A3 reveal three stages for the adjustment process. Periods 0 to 6 are characterized by high investment for country F and no investment at all for country H. Country F has to build up an additional capital stock for increasing its x_1-production, whereas country H reduces its capital stock, as it produces x_1 only for domestic requirements in the near future. From period 7 until period 42, investment fall in country F and rise in country H. Both countries now have to maintain capital stocks that allow producing x_1 for domestic requirements. Periods 43 onwards are characterized by the immediate convergence to the initial balanced growth path. Investment in country F is temporarily equal to zero, in country H temporarily higher than on the balanced growth path – both countries now return to their initial capital stocks.

[25] It should be noted, that the total change in the real factor income is an incomplete indicator of the welfare change a country undergoes in this counterfactual analysis with "leisure consumption".

consequences are transmitted to country *F*. The detrimental shock transmission takes place via the opposite forces that lead to the advantageous shock transmission described in the first shock scenario. As the shock leads to a temporary less efficient production of y_1 in country *H*, the comparative advantage of country *H* in producing the capital intensive good y_2 gains in size. The extended comparative advantage of country *H* in producing y_2 is synonymous with an increase in the comparative advantage of country *F* in producing y_1. After all, both a *shock effect* and a *trade pattern effect* drive the model results in this scenario. The shock leads to a temporary rise of the capital intensive production in country *H* and the labor intensive production in country *F*. For a certain period, country *H* accordingly builds up an additional capital stock, compared to the balanced growth path. Country *F*, in contrast, temporarily reduces its investment below the break-even level. The subsequent temporary change in absolute capital endowments leads to a gain in the present value of total factor income in country *H* and a corresponding loss for country *F*.

The results for this shock scenario are visualized in Figures A8 to A10 in the appendix. Figure A8 illustrates the transitional increase of y_2 exports from country *H* to country *F*, relative to the balanced growth path. Figure 9 shows this same ratio for y_1 exports of country *F* to country *H*. Figure 10 finally depicts total investment, both for country *H* and country *F* in this shock scenario, relative to the balanced growth path.

The interpretation of the counterfactual analyses is similar to those in the first shock scenario. Most notably, assuming imperfect substitutability between home and foreign produced goods prevents the favorable evolution in the capital endowment of country *H*, which was described above. Thus, country *H* suffers only from the negative technological shock in this second counterfactual. The loss for country *F*, which can be mainly attributed to a decline in the wage rate, results from temporary lower exports of its labor intensive good y_1. *Figure A11* in the appendix illustrates these temporary lower y_1 exports of country *F*.

4 Conclusion

This paper presents a dynamic Heckscher-Ohlin model for analyzing international trade as a business cycle transmission mechanism. The business cycle is driven by negative technology shocks. Two observed countries are characterized by a 4-sector production structure, in which the output of two sectors is used as an intermediate input in the other two sectors that each produce one final good. The countries as well as the technologies for producing both intermediate and final goods are most different with respect to relative factor endowments and factor intensities.

The results show that the *sign* of the transmission channel depends on the factor intensity of the sector in which the shock occurs. A base case model, which assumed perfect substitutability between foreign and domestic produced goods, generated two mentionable results. First, a country may gain from a domestic temporary technological shock, if this shock influences the trade pattern such that the production of the capital intensive sector rises. Consequently, this *trade pattern effect* induces higher investment and therefore a rise of the capital stock in subsequent periods. Second, if the trade partner of a country is hit by a shock, such that the own production of the labor intensive good c.p. rises, a country may neutralize a negative spill-over by a domestic technological shock. This neutralization occurs if the shocks are intra-sectoral correlated and do not influence the magnitudes of comparative advantage. Such correlated shocks may prevent a country from specializing in the labor intensive good and neglecting the development of its own capital endowment. This country then only suffers from a *shock effect*, not from an additional *trade pattern effect*.

The above mentioned results were mostly confirmed by one of the counterfactual analyses, which assumed a limited substitutability between domestic and foreign produced goods. With this limited substitutability, a negative technological shock in the foreign country influences the own production structure and therefore the own capital accumulation only moderately. The possibly negative transmission channel, i.e. the {\it trade pattern effect} is dampened.

These findings point to possible extensions of the current model. Incorporating real world features like capital adjustment costs, sector specific capital or involuntary unemployment should refine the present results. A more subtle analysis could expand the model to analyze trade policy measures for immunizing a country against a negative shock transmission via the trade channel.

Appendix

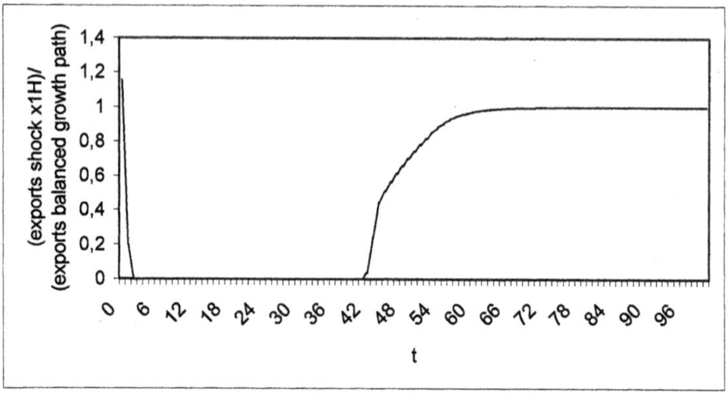

Figure A1. National Shock in Sector x_{1H} Country H Exports of x_1, Relative to Balanced Growth Path.

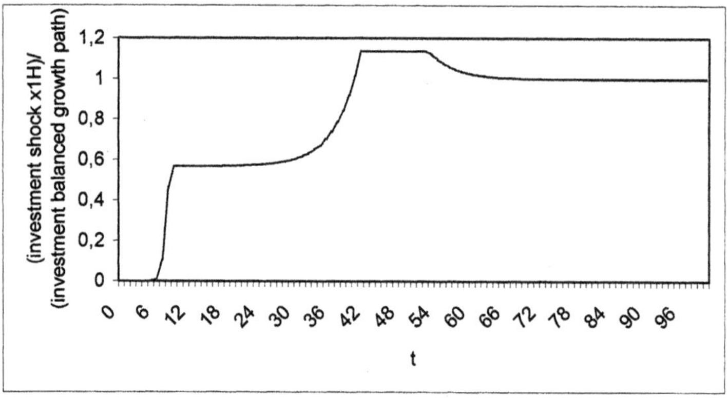

Figure A2. National Shock in Sector x_{1H}, Total Investment Country H, Relative to Balanced Growth Path

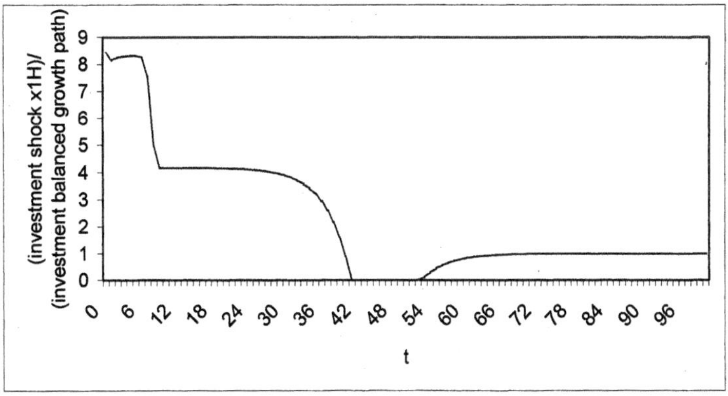

Figure A3. National Shock in Sector x_{1H}, Total Investment Country F, Relative to Balanced Growth Path

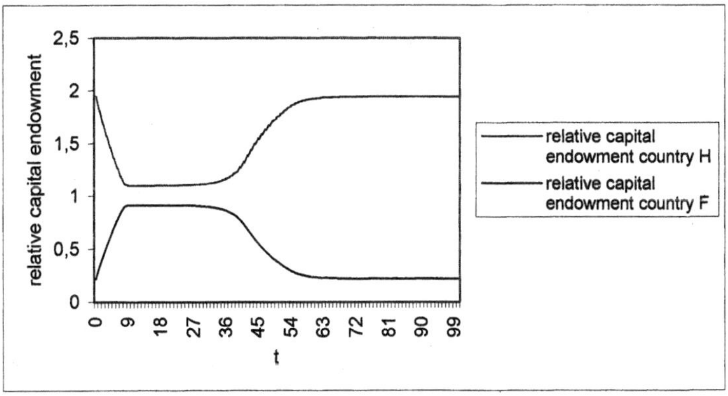

Figure A4. National Shock in Sector x_{1H}, Relative Endowments of Both Countries

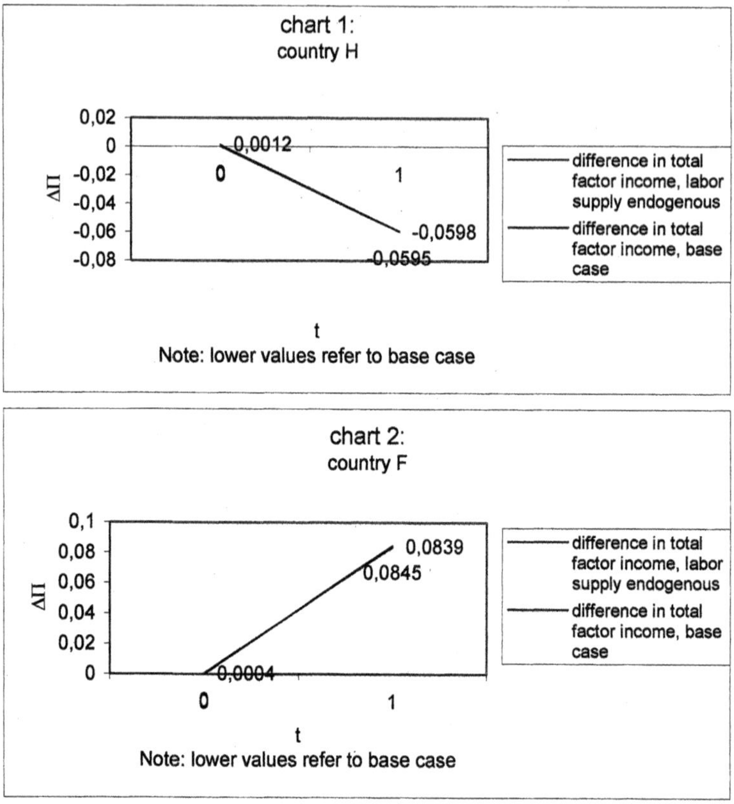

Figure A5. National Shock in Sector x_{1H}, $\Delta\Pi$, Both Countries, Labor Supply Endogenous vs. Base Case

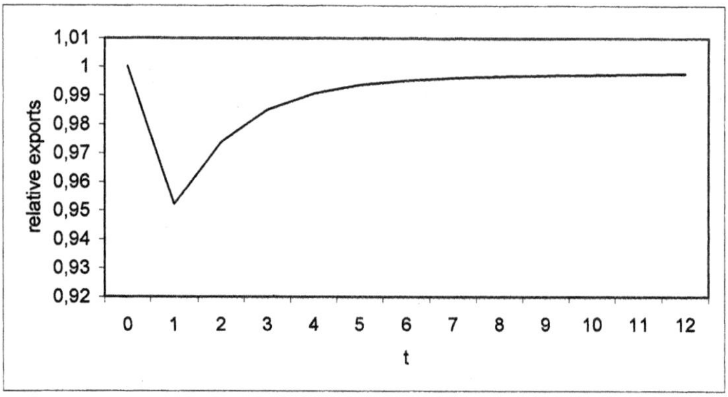

Figure A6. National Shock in Sector x_{1H}, Armington Elasticity = 1, Country H Exports of x_1 Relative to Balanced Growth Path, Periods 0 to 12

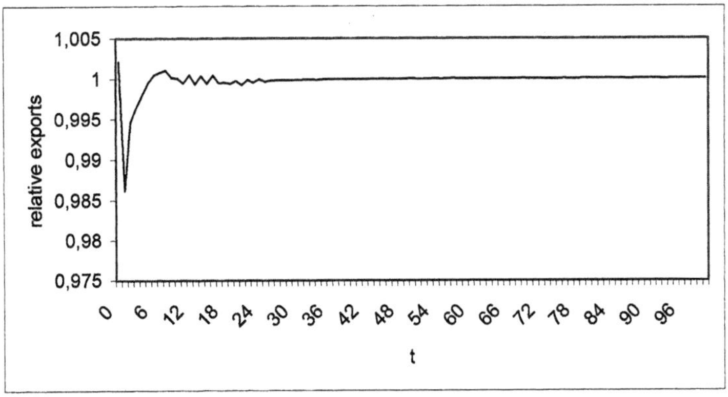

Figure A7. Global Shock in Sector x_{1H} and x_{1F}, Country F Exports of x_2 Relative to Balanced Growth Path

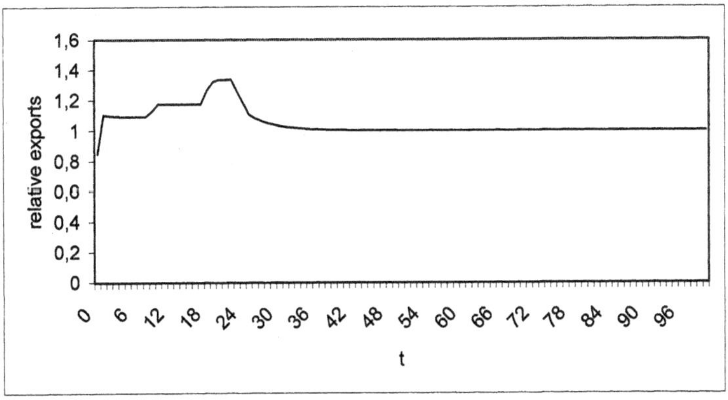

Figure A8. National Shock in Sector y_{1H}, Country H Exports of y_2 Relative to Balanced Growth Path

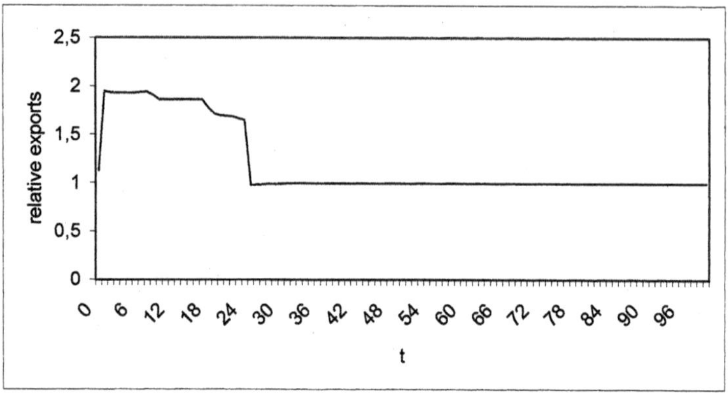

Figure A9. National Shock in Sector y_{1H}, Country F Exports of y_1 Relative to Balanced Growth Path

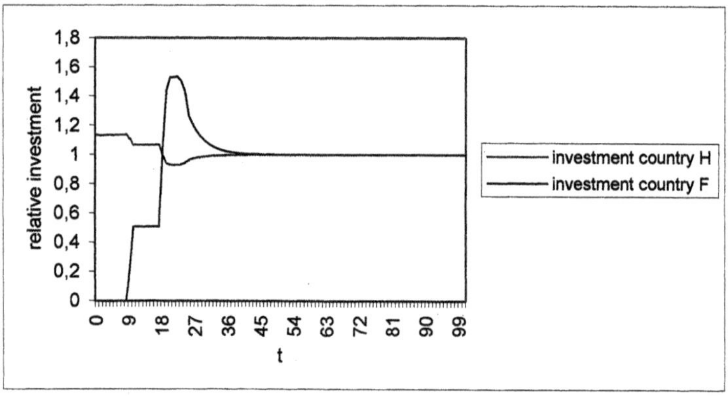

Figure A10. National Shock in Sector Y_{1H}, Total Investment in Both Countries, Relative to Balanced Growth Path

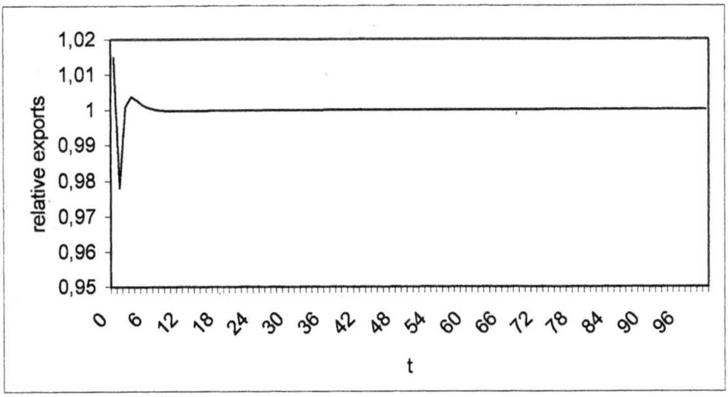

Figure A11. National Shock in Sector Y_{1H}, Armington Elasticity = 1, Country F Exports of Y_1, Relative to Balanced Growth Path

References

Ambler S, Cardia E, Zimmermann C (2002) International transmission of the business cycle in a multi-sector model. European Economic Review 46 : 273–300

Armington P (1969) A Theory of Demand for Products Distinguished by Place of Production. International Monetary Fund Staff Papers 27 : 488–526

Backus DK, Kehoe PJ, Kydland FE (1995) International business cycles: Theory and evidence. In: Cooley TF (ed) Frontiers of Business Cycle Research, Princeton, 331–356.

Backus DK, Kehoe PJ, Kydland FE (1992) International real business cycles. Journal of Political Economy 101, 745–775.

Baxter M, Kouparitsas MA (2002) Trade structure, industrial structure, and international business cycles. Federal Reserve Bank of Chicago Working Paper 2002/30

Brooke A, Kendrick D, Meeraus A, Raman R (1998) GAMS. A user's guide. Washington

Christensen TJ (2002) China. Strategic Asia 3 : 51–94

Christensen TJ (2001) China. Strategic Asia 2 : 27–69

Dervis K, de Melo J, Robinson S (1982) General equilibrium models for development policy. Cambridge et al.

Fewsmith J (2000) The impact of WTO/PNTR on Chinese politics. NBR Analysis, Essay 2

Fewsmith J (1999): China and the WTO: The politics behind the agreement. NBR Analysis, Essay 2

Frazier MW, Hansen PM (1999) China's accession to the WTO: A candid appraisal from U.S. industry. NBR Briefing

Ginsburgh V, Keyzer M (2002) The structure of applied general equilibrium models. Cambridge MA London

Grossman GM, Helpman E (1995) Technology and trade. CEPR Discussion Paper No. 1134

Imbs J (2003) Trade, finance, specialization and synchronization. IMF Working Paper 03/81

Kose MA, Prasad ES, Terrones ME (2003) How does globalization affect the synchronization of business cycles? American Economic Review, Papers and Proceedings 93 : 57–62

Kouparitsas MA (1998) North-South business cycles. Federal Reserve Bank of Chicago Working Paper 96/9

Kuhn HW, Tucker AW (1951) Nonlinear Programming. In: Neyman J (ed) Proceedings of the 2nd Berkeley symposium on mathematical statistics and probability. Berkeley, 481–492.

Lau MI, Pahlke A, Rutherford T (1997) Modelling economic adjustment: A primer in dynamic general equilibrium analysis [available at http://nash.colorado.edu/tomruth/primer/paper.htm]

Mathiesen L (1985) Computation of economic equilibrium by a sequence of linear complementary problems. Mathematical Programming Study 23 : 144–162

Paltsev SV (2000) Moving from static to dynamic general equilibrium economic models. mimeo, University of Colorado

Rutherford T (1998) Economic equilibrium modelling with GAMS. mimeo, University of Colorado

Samuelson P (1975) Trade pattern reversals in time-phased Ricardian systems and intertemporal efficiencies. Journal of International Economics 5 : 309–364

Shadwick M (2000) Globalisation: Economic policy challenges for China. Presentation at the "Greater China an the World Economy" Conference, Hong Kong, July 2000

Srinivasan TN, Bhagwati JN (1980) Trade and welfare in a steady state. In: Chipman JS, Kindleberger CP (eds) Flexible exchange rates and the balance of payments. Amsterdam, 341–353

Summers R, Heston A (1991) The Penn World Table (Mark 5): An expanded set of international comparisons. Quarterly Journal of Economics 106 : 327–368

U.S. International Trade Commission (1999) Assessment of the economic effects on the United States of China's accession to the WTO. Washington, DC

Wong KY (1990) Factor intensity reversal in a multi-factor, two-good economy. Journal of Economic Theory 51 : 434–42

Yang Y, Tyers R (2000) GTAP-based comparative static macroeconomics: An application to China's policy options. Working Paper No. 384, Australian National University

Comment

Roberto A. de Santis[1]

European Central Bank, Frankfurt, Germany

Namini's paper aims at investigating the mechanisms of transmission of country-specific productivity shocks on countries' business cycles and welfare. This study is carried out by means of a dynamic applied general equilibrium model with two countries, two final goods, two intermediate goods, labor and capital. Therefore, this paper fits within the literature that investigates the discrepancies between standard calibrated international business cycles and real data generally called *anomalies* (Backus et al. 1992, 1993; Baxter and Crucini, 1995; Stockman and Tesar, 1995).

Two main anomalies have been investigated in the literature: the *quantity anomaly* and the *price anomaly*. As to the *quantity anomaly*, cross-country correlations in calibrated models are much higher for consumption than for output, while the empirical evidence suggests the opposite; and cross-country correlations of employment and investment are negative, while in the data they are positive. As to the *price anomaly*, the standard deviation of the terms of trade is considerably smaller in calibrated economies than the data would suggest.

Given the fact that Kehoe and Perri (2002) resolved the *quantity anomaly* by incorporating the credit market friction in a standard international business cycle model, I would have expected in Namini's paper much more emphasis on the ability of the model to resolve the *price anomaly*. Indeed, the richer structure of Namini's model characterized by four tradable goods could be used to check if it resolves the *price anomaly* for a wide range of parameter values. More generally, the author should check how good the model is in replicating the empirical moments related to exports, employment, output, consumption, investment and terms of trade.

To understand the strength and the possible weakness of Namini's model, I have summarized in Table 1 the key features of a standard two-goods model often used in the literature and the model suggested by Namini. For simplification, I used the notation of Namini's paper and I have eliminated some redundant subscripts, such as countries (i,j) and time frequency (t).

[1] The opinions expressed herein are those of the author and do not necessarily represent those of the European Central Bank. All errors are author's responsibility.

Table 1. Calibrated International Business Cycle Models

	Standard two-good model	Namini's paper
Demand side:		
Preferences	$u_t = E\sum_{t=0}^{\infty}\frac{U(C_t^1, C_t^2, S_t)}{(1+\rho)^t}$	$u_t = E\sum_{t=0}^{\infty}\frac{U(C_t^1, C_t^2, S_t)}{(1+\rho)^t}$
Final goods	-	$Y_m = \Omega^d(y_m^1, y_m^2)$
Intermediate goods	-	$X_n = \Phi^d(x_n^1, x_n^2)$
Investment	Tobin's q	$I_m = Y_m - C_m$
Supply side:		
Final goods	$y_m = \Omega^s(A_m^y, L_m, K_m)$	$y_m = y_m^1 + y_m^2 = \Omega^s(X_m^1, X_m^2, A_m^y, L_m, K_m)$
Intermediate goods	-	$x_n = x_n^1 + x_n^2 = A_n^x \Phi^s(L_n, K_n)$
Monetary side:	Risk-free real bond	-

Note: The intermediate goods sector is denoted by n. The final goods sector is denoted by m. Countries are denoted by 1 and 2.

The main difference between the standard models in the literature and Namini's model is that in the latter capital accumulation does not face any adjustment costs. In a bond economy without capital adjustment costs, capital would flow rapidly to the country with the higher productivity shock. This would result in volatility of investment and net exports being much higher than in the data. This problem does not exist in Namini's paper, because he rules out the possibility of capital flows. However, by so doing, trade balance in each period is a strong constraint of this model. I would rather prefer a model with capital adjustment costs and with an intertemporal current account used to equilibrate the savings-investment decisions of households/firms.

The same model could also be used to explore a typical issue investigated with the econometric method, that is: "How much does international trade affect business cycle synchronization"? The latter is a title of a recent paper by Gruben, Koo and Millis (2003) at the Federal Reserve Bank of Dallas. Triggered by the strong results obtained by Frenkel and Rose (1998) and Gruben et al. (2003) by refining Frenkel-Rose specification corroborates the results that increased trade leads to increased business cycle correlation. The advantage of Namini's model is that he could run numerical simulations to investigate how the calibrated model would answer the above question under alternative model specifications: intra-industry trade in final goods, intra-industry trade in intermediate goods and inter-industry trade. In addition, Namini could evaluate what type of trading relationship favour a more synchronized business cycle. These exercises would create a bridge between the questions addressed in the macro-econometric trade literature and the *anomalies* often discussed with calibrated dynamic stochastic general equilibrium models.

All in all, the idea of introducing linkages among sectors with intermediate inputs is very interesting. However, Namini should verify if its model is able to resolve the discussed *quantity* and *price anomalies*.

References

Backus DK, Kehoe PJ, Kydland FE (1992) International Real Business Cycles. Journal of Political Economy 100 : 745–775

Backus DK, Kehoe PJ, Kydland FE (1993) International Business Cycles: Theory vs. Evidence. Federal Reserve Bank of Minneapolis Quarterly Review 17 : 14–29

Baxter M, Crucini MJ (1995) Business Cycles and the Asset Structure of Foreign Trade. International Economic Review 36 : 821–854

Frenkel JA, Rose AK (1998) The Endogeneity of the Optimum Currency Area Criteria. Economic Journal 108 : 1009–1025

Gruben WC, Koo J, Millis E (2003) How Much Does International Trade Affect Business Cycle Syncronization. Federal Reserve Bank of Dallas Working Paper 203

Kehoe PJ, Perri F (2002) International Business Cycles With Endogenous Incomplete Markets. Econometrica 70 : 907–928

Stockman AC, Tesar L (1995) Tastes and Technology in a Two-Country Model of the Business Cycle: Explaining International Comovements. American Economic Review 85 : 168–185

Political Support or Contributions: An Empirical Investigation of US Trade Policy

Theo Eicher* and Thomas Osang**

* Department of Economics, University of Washington, Seattle, USA
** Department of Economics, Southern Methodist University, Dallas, USA[1]

1 Introduction

The trade literature offers a variety of competing explanations for the prevailing trade policies. In contrast to the traditional commercial policy models that analyze trade policy in terms of economic efficiency, the lion's share of the recent literature is based on distributional considerations. In these endogenous protection models, self-interested politicians use trade policy to transfer income to particular interest groups. Given that contributions from lobbies and Political Action Committees figure prominently in the political landscape where tariffs, quotas, and voluntary export restraints exist in spite of their large social costs, this recent literature seems to provide particularly intuitive explanations for the observed pattern of protection.

Since the early 1980's, several alternative political economy approaches to endogenous protection have been advanced. Previous empirical studies of the political economy determinants of trade protection are numerous. However, a large share of these studies relies on reduced forms (see Rodrik 1995, for an excellent survey). The reduced form approach introduces ambiguity as to which model is actually tested, and as to the choice of independent variables.[2] With the exception of Eicher and Osang (2002), the distinct differences in the theoretical structures of

[1] We thank Kishore Gawande, Francois Laisney, Myong-jee Lee, Essie Maasoumi, Ravi Yatawara as well as seminar participants at SMU and Texas Camp Econometrics for helpful comments and suggestions. Kirhore Gawande and Daniel Treffler kindly provided their datasets. During part of this project, Osang was visiting the University of Washington, while Eicher was visiting Nuffield College and the University of Tübingen. Both thank their respective host universities for their hospitality. Financial support for Eicher was provided by the von Humboldt Foundation.

[2] For the most extensive comparison of endogenous tariff formation models within this traditional framework see Gawande (1998). Aside from significance, his measure of validity is "that at least some subset of variables representing [any one] theory is shown to have the correct sign."

the models have to date not permitted a comprehensive assessment as to exactly which approach to endogenous protection is empirically the most relevant.[3]

The lack of comparative empirical tests can be attributed to the absence of a unified theory. In a recent paper, however, Helpman (1997) developed a comprehensive framework that was utilized in Eicher and Osang (2002) to derive an empirical model that allows for the juxtaposition of the Contribution Driven Model with the Tariff Function Model. In this paper we extend the unified framework to test the tariff formulas that are predicted by the political equilibria of the Influence Driven (Grossman and Helpman 1994) and the Political Support Function (Hillman, 1982) approaches. This allows us to extend the tests of the Influence Driven model by Goldberg and Maggi (1999) (G-M from hereout) and Gawande and Bandyopadhyay (2000) (G-B from hereout) and Eicher and Osang (2002) to compare the performance and significance of the two approaches.

Helpman's (1997) theoretical framework holds clear implications for empirical testing: The sectoral import elasticities and the levels of import penetration are crucial variables for both models. Depending on the nature of the specific approach, these variables are augmented with additional explanatory variables suggested by the theory. This allows us to estimate key parameters, and to test the models' respective significance for endogenous protection. In the Political Support Model we introduce measures of sectoral profits and welfare to estimate the marginal rate of substitution between the two in the government's political support function. In contrast, for the Influence Driven model we follow the results of Eicher and Osang (2002) who utilize a measure of organization to test whether contributions or the existence of a lobby matter and to estimate the model's key parameters.

Our estimation takes into account the possible endogeneity of independent variables. Using a Tobit, instrumental variable approach and a GMM minimum distance estimator (MDE), the empirical results yield little ambiguity. The Political Support model disappoints on multiple levels, which may be due to imperfect data proxies (especially profit measures). Alternatively, the weakness of the Political Support model may be a function of the model's inability to account for the extensive lobbying that is observed in the US. The one interesting aspect about the estimation of the Political Support model is that the weight that the government places on welfare, relative to profits, is large and of similar magnitude as the one we estimate for the Influence Driven approach. Following the methodology of Eicher and Osang (2002) the Influence Driven model is strongly confirmed, with all coefficients exhibiting the correct sign and strong statistical significance.

---

[3] For example, Goldberg and Maggi (1999) and Gawande and Bandyopadhyay (2000) develop excellent tests of the "Influence Driven Contributions" approach popularized by Grossman and Helpman (1994). The pattern of protection in the data seems to be consistent with the model's predictions. No matter how significant the results of one model may be, there still remains interest in ascertaining its predictive power relative to alternative models of endogenous protection. Eicher and Osang (2002) juxtapose the Influence Driven model only with the Tariff Function model.

Since the difference in the performance of the two models is so dramatic, the question arises a) how the power of the models compare to each other and b) if a combination of the two models improves the estimation of either models, or if one of the variables holds relatively more explanatory power. We find that the key variable of the Influence Driven model (an indicator variable that identifies the existence of an organized lobby) is significantly more powerful than any political support, profit or welfare measure. To formally juxtapose both models we employ J-Tests. We cannot reject the null hypothesis of correct specification of the Influence Driven model, but find evidence of significant misspecification in the Political Support Function approach. The results provide additional evidence as to the strength and robustness of the Influence Driven model and to the weakness of the political support model.

Our tests of the strict theories add to the voluminous empirical literature on protection that focused on heuristic or general factor endowment approaches, such as Ray (1981), Baldwin (1985), or Trefler (1993). Especially interesting is the comparison of our results to the findings of previous reduced form juxtapositions of endogenous tariff formation models in Gawande (1998). He finds, similar to our results, that the political-self-interest/special-interest model performs best against alternative models, while the public-interest/political-altruism type model associated with Hillman (1982) evidence is at best weak.

The remainder of the paper is organized as follows. The theoretical framework of endogenous protection is reviewed in section 2. We discuss the empirical methodology used to estimate the three models in Section 3. Data issues and empirical results are discussed in sections 4 and 5, respectively. Section 6 concludes the paper. All tables are relegated to the appendix.

2 Theoretical Approaches to Endogenous Protection

We commence by outlining the common theoretical framework that serves as the basis for our empirical analysis. This framework was used in the comparison of the Influence Driven Model and the Tariff Formation Model in Eicher and Osang (2002). The analysis is a succinct representation of Helpman (1997), who discusses both the motivations and derivations in detail. The critical advantage of Helpman's (1997) model is that the derived equations for endogenous protection are sufficiently similar to allow for comparative testing of the various approaches. In addition, the model nicely highlights the common fundamental structure that the models share.

Consider a continuum of individuals, j, populate an economy whose population size is normalized to unity. Each individual possesses a utility function

$$u(c) = c_0 + \sum_{i=1}^{n} u_i(c_i) \qquad (1)$$

where c_i is consumption of product i. A numeraire good, indexed 0, is produced using only one unit of labor per unit output. All other products are produced with labor and a sector-specific input.

An individual owns l^j of the aggregate labor supply, and γ_i^j of the sectors' specific input. The wage rate then equals one, and the return to a sector specific input, $\Pi_i(p_i)$, is an increasing function of the producer price, p_i. Let aggregate imports be denoted by M_i, and normalize all foreign prices to unity, which implies $p_i = \tau_i$, and $\tau_i > 1$ for positive rates of protection. Finally, suppose that the government redistributes tariff revenue lump-sum, and uniformly to all individuals. The reduced form of the indirect utility function can then be written as an additive composite of the incomes derived from labor, transfer and the specific factor incomes, plus the consumer surplus, S_i:

$$\hat{v}(\tau,\gamma^j) = l^j + \sum_{i=1}^{n}(\tau_i - 1)M_i(\tau_i) + \sum_{i=1}^{n}\gamma_i^j\Pi_i(\tau_i) + \sum_{i=1}^{n}S_i(\tau_i) \qquad (2)$$

By integrating over all individuals (2), the aggregate welfare is given by

$$W(\tau) = 1 + \sum_{i=1}^{n}(\tau_i - 1)M_i(\tau_i) + \sum_{i=1}^{n}\Pi_i(\tau_i) + \sum_{i=1}^{n}S_i(\tau_i) \qquad (3)$$

From these general definitions of the indirect utility and welfare we can derive three distinct models of endogenous protection based on different specifications of the political economy process.

2.1 The Political Support Function Approach

The Political Support Function approach was developed by Hillman (1982) and generalized by Van Long and Vousden (1991). In this approach the government trades off political support from consumers against higher industry profits. The support for the government from the industry increases in industry's profits, while consumers raise their support when product prices decline. The exact mechanics by which either group provides support are not specified. Much like in Staiger and Tabellini (1987), the government does not have a self-interested motive, other than to redistribute in order to minimize the loss to either constituency. It is thus possible to interpret the model as one in which an altruistic government chooses a tariff to maximize aggregate support from its constituents.

Following Hillman (1982), the government's generic political support function

$$\Theta[\tau] = \Theta[\Pi[\tau], W[\tau]],$$

contains domestic welfare and industry profits, both as functions of the tariff. Higher support from the industry and from the general population is forthcoming if profits and welfare increase, $\Theta_{\Pi}, \Theta_W > 0$. However, profits increase with tariffs, while welfare decreases. The government maximizes the political support by choosing a tariff that maximizes the political support function, or

$$\frac{d\Theta}{d\tau} = \frac{d\Pi}{d\tau}\frac{\partial\Theta}{\partial\Pi} + \frac{dW}{d\tau}\frac{\partial\Theta}{\partial W} = 0 \tag{4}$$

which implies

$$-\frac{d\Pi}{dW} = \frac{\partial\Theta}{\partial W} \Big/ \frac{\partial\Theta}{\partial\Pi} \equiv \delta_P$$

Helpman (1997) defines δ_P as the marginal rate of substitution between aggregate welfare and profits of special interests in the government's political support function. The greater δ_P, the more likely is the government to give up industry profits to increase aggregate welfare. Extending Hillman (1982) to many sectors, i, and using a specific functional form, Helpman (1997) rewrites the political support function as

$$\hat{\Theta}[\tau] = \sum_{i=1}^{n} \frac{1}{\delta_i}\left(\Pi_i[\tau_i] - \Pi_i[1]\right) + \left(W[\tau] - W[1,1,\dots,1]\right) \tag{5}$$

Using (3) and (5), the government chooses the optimal tariff to maximize its political support, which implies the tariff rate[4]

$$\tau_i - 1 = \frac{\partial\Theta/\partial\Pi}{\partial\Theta/\partial W}\frac{X_i}{(-M_i')} = \sigma_{W,\Pi_i}\frac{W}{\Pi_i}\frac{X_i}{(-M_i')} \tag{6}$$

where $\sigma_{W,\Pi_i} = -(dW/d\Pi_i)(\Pi_i/W) > 0$ is the support function's elasticity of substitution between profits and aggregate welfare in sector i. From the definition of δ_P, we know that σ_{W,Π_i} also equals the ratio of the profit and welfare elasticities in the political support function, or

$$\sigma_{W,\Pi_i} = (\partial\Theta/\partial\Pi_i * \Pi_i/\Theta)/(\partial\Theta/\partial W * W/\Theta) \tag{7}$$

Hence σ_{W,Π_i} can be loosely interpreted as the weight the government places on profits, relative to aggregate welfare.

The tariff increases in the sector's output level, X_i, because the larger the domestic output, the greater the benefits to domestic producers when the domestic price increases. The tariff decreases in the elasticity of the import demand function, since the welfare loss increases and the government is less willing to impose excess burden on society. In addition, the more likely the government is to trade off sectoral profits for national welfare, the lower the tariff in that sector.

---

[4] The derivation uses the properties of the utility that $M = -[S' + \Pi']$ and that $X = \Pi'$.

While the theory does not provide insights into the determinants of the elasticity of substitution between aggregate welfare and special interest profits, we can utilize the data to obtain an estimate. Using proxies for wealth, as well as for industry profits, we can derive estimates for σ_{W,Π_i}. How relevant this estimate is will depend on the power of equation (6) to predict endogenous protection.

2.2 The Influence-Driven Contributions Approach

The Political Contributions approach, developed by Grossman and Helpman (1994), and tested formally against the tariff function approach in Eicher and Osang (2002). In this approach to tariff formation interest groups that maximize benefits to their members offer politicians campaign contributions to influence their policy stance. Accordingly, politicians seek to maximize a political objective function that depends on contributions and on the well being of the general public. Knowing how contributions from constituents depend on the selected policies, politicians choose their policy stance.

Suppose the political objective function that the policy maker maximizes is $(1-\beta)C+\beta W$, where $C=\sum_i C_i$ stands for the sum of campaign contributions from all sectors, W represents aggregate welfare, and β is a parameter that represents the weight the government places on welfare considerations. If a sector does not contribute to the campaign, the policy maker disregards that sector's special interest concerns.

Suppose that in some subset of the sectors, $L\subset\{1,2,\ldots,n\}$, the owners of the sector-specific inputs form lobbies. The aggregate welfare of the interest group is then given by

$$W_i(\tau)=l_i+\Pi_i(\tau_i)+\alpha_i\sum_{j=1}^{n}[(\tau_j-1)M_j(\tau_j)+S_j(\tau_j)] \tag{8}$$

which again includes labor and specific factor incomes as well as the tariff rebates and consumer surplus. The lobby maximizes $W_i(\tau)-C_i$ and takes the contribution functions of all the other interest groups $j\neq i$, $C_j(\tau)$, as given. If lobby i wants to generate a tariff, it must offer a contribution. The size of the contribution is determined by the condition that the lobby must contribute sufficiently to raise the policy maker's welfare above $G_{-i}=\max_\tau[(1-\beta)\Sigma_{j\neq i}C_j(\tau)+\beta W(\tau)]$, which is the level generated in the absence of lobby i's contribution. In short, the standard participation constraint in principal-agent problems requires that in equilibrium contributions equal

$$C_i(\tau)=G_{-i}-[(1-\beta)\sum_{j\neq i}C_j(\tau)+\beta W(\tau)]\,. \tag{9}$$

This implies that interest groups lobby not only for their own cause, but also for an entire tariff policy vector, that maximizes each lobby's objective function $W_i(\tau)-C_i$

$$\tau^i \in \arg\max_{\tau} W_i(\tau) + \left[(1-\beta) \sum_{j \neq i} C_j(\tau) + \beta W(\tau) \right].$$

When politicians maximize their welfare function, subject to L interest groups' optimal policy vectors, the resulting tariff formula is

$$\tau_j - 1 = \frac{I_j - \alpha_L}{\frac{\beta}{(1-\beta)} + \alpha_L} \frac{X_j}{-(M'_j)}, \tag{10}$$

where $\alpha_L = \sum_{j \in L} \alpha_j$ stands for the fraction of people that own sector specific inputs and I_j is a dummy that takes the value of one if $i \in L$, that is, if the sector is organized, and zero otherwise.

In the extreme case, when all sectors have organized pressure groups and every individual has a stake in some sector, there is free trade. From (10) we find that the rate of protection in sector i increases in the concentration of the ownership in that sector's specific factor, since the greater the concentration, the less the lobby cares about dead weight loss. The tariff also increases in the weight the policy maker places on contributions relative to welfare, since it becomes "cheaper" to influence the policy maker with contributions. The effects of output and of the slope of the import demand function are the same as in the formulas that derived for both the Political Support Function approach, and the Tariff Function approach. However there is an added twist to the model. For protected sectors, $I = 1$, the tariff rate should decrease in the import penetration ratio. This is because the larger the domestic output, the more owners of specific factors gain from an increase in the domestic price, while the economy as a whole incurs fewer inefficiency losses when the volume of imports is low, *ceteris paribus*. For unprotected sectors, the relationship between tariffs and import penetration is positive.

In comparing the Influence Driven approach with the previous ones, we observe several similarities. The effect of the degree of concentration of ownership is similar to the Tariff Function approach, while the role of the marginal rate of substitution between welfare and contributions plays a similar role to the marginal rate of substitution between welfare and profits in the Political Support Function approach.

3 Empirical Methodology

To allow for the estimation of the three competing approaches contained in equations (6), and (10), we must introduce several simplifying assumptions. First, for each model we follow the procedure of G-M and Eicher and Osang (2002) and move the import elasticities to the left-hand side, to counter measurement errors.[5]

[5] G-B improved the estimation procedure by utilizing the standard errors on the elasticities. We maintain the G-M methodology for comparison purposes.

Measurement errors in the dependent variable cause a loss of efficiency, while measurement errors in the exogenous variables cause biased and inconsistent coefficient estimates. Second, we assume that the elasticities in (6) are constant across sectors. We use the Wald Test to check the validity of this assumption, and it can already be said that parameter instability will be rejected in either model.

Therefore, the two empirical models that will be tested are given by

Political Support Function

$$\frac{\tau_i^*}{\tau_i^*+1}e_i = a_1\frac{W}{\Pi_i}\frac{1}{z_i}+\varepsilon_{1i}, \tag{6a}$$

Influence Driven Contributions

$$\frac{\tau_i^*}{\tau_i^*+1}e_i = a_4 I_i\frac{1}{z_i}+a_5\frac{1}{z_i}+\varepsilon_{3i}, \tag{10a}$$

where $\tau_i^* = \tau_i - 1$, e_i is the import demand elasticity, and $z_i = \frac{M_i}{X_i}$ is the import penetration ratio. Since we employ stochastic versions of (6) and (10) in the econometric analysis, a disturbance term, ε_{ji}, was added. A Tobit estimation is necessary for (6a) and (10a) due to the censoring of the dependent variable at zero.

There are both theoretical and empirical reasons to question the exogeneity of the independent variables in (6a) and (10a) (see Trefler 1993 and G-M for a discussion). To correct for the possible bias in the estimates caused by the endogeneity of the explanatory variables, we use the same set of exogenous (instrumental) variables as in G-M, which allows us to directly compare our results to the results reported in G-M.

In contrast to the maximum likelihood estimator (MLE) used in G-M, we apply a minimum distance estimator (MDE). The MDE approach is useful in estimating simultaneous equations (see Lee 1996, chapter 5 and 9) and can be easily extended to models with censored and/or binary dependent variables. The main problem the MDE answers is how to optimally impose the overidentifying restrictions. The MDE is a two-step estimator. In the first step, the relationship between each of the K endogenous variables and the set of exogenous variables is estimated. In the second step, the parameter vector of interest, *a*, is consistently estimated with feasible GLS using only the first-step coefficient estimates. The reason why we can apply GLS to a data set with only K "observations" is that the error term in the second step estimation has a degenerate distribution converging to 0. Finally, in the case that the reduced form estimator is MLE and the overidentifying restrictions are linear, MLE applied directly to the estimation of *a* and the two-step MDE are identical.

4 Data[6]

We follow G-M in the construction of the key data, Political Action Committee contributions, non-tariff barriers, import penetration ratios and import elasticities. We thus use U.S. data for 106 manufacturing industries at the three-digit SIC level for 1983. Estimates of import demand elasticities are not available at the four-digit SIC level, hence we base this study on three-digit level data. The data on non-tariff barriers (NTBs), τ_i, import penetration ratio, z, and the instrumental variables used in the Tobit IV estimates are taken from Trefler (1993), but aggregated to the three-digit level using as weights the share in value of shipment. TOTALSALES$_i$ denotes the value of shipments per industry, obtained from the 1996 NBER productivity database, and TOTALSALES is the value of shipment aggregated over all industries and scaled by 10,000. Import demand elasticities, e_i, are taken from Sheills et al. (1986).[7] Political Action Committee contributions by firms and unions in each sector were obtained from Gawande (for details on how these data were constructed, see the appendix in G-B). The data, covering contributions over four Congressional election cycles 1977-78, 1979-80, 1981-82, and 1983-84, measure spending per firm and union divided by value added. Multiplying by value added as well as by the number of contributing firms and unions, we obtain total contributions by firms and unions per industry. TOTALCONTRIBUTIONS$_i$ represents the sum of firm and union contributions in a sector, while TOTALCONTRIBUTIONS is measured as the sum of all sector-specific contributions by firms and unions. For the organization dummy, ORGANIZED, in the Influence Driven approach we use a contribution threshold level similar to the one used in G-M.

Our data set deviates from G-M since we have to construct additional variables to test the alternative endogenous protection approaches. We construct two different profit measures. The first profit variable, PROFITS1, is based on the latest version of the 1996 NBER productivity database, from which we derive profits per industry as value-added minus total labor cost. The second profit measure, PROFITS2, was obtained from pre-tax income for 1983 as derived from the IRS source book, after converting the IRS data from SOI classification to three-digit SIC level. Both measures are imperfect. PROFITS2 is a direct profit measure, while PROFITS1 is an indirect measure that includes the regular return to capital as well as true industry profits. While PROFITS1 is a precise three-digit SIC industry measure, PROFITS2 contains the usual conversion error. The correlation between profit measures is 0.4, which confirms substantial differences between the two proxies. However, if we were to remove one outlier (industry 291; Petroleum Refining), the correlation coefficient would increase to 0.7.

---

[6] See the appendix for an overview.

[7] There is a small number of industries with positive import demand elasticities in our sample. Following G-M, we set these elasticities to zero.

5 Empirical Results

5.1 Political Support Function

The first round of estimates of the theoretical models is provided in Table 1. In the Political Support Function model, we estimate the elasticity of substitution between profits and aggregate welfare in the political support function. We attempted several specifications of welfare for the political support function. None worked as well as TOTALSALES and still the results are not satisfactory.[8] Test results using either profit measure (PROFITS1_i or PROFITS2_i) disappoint, the coefficient estimates are statistically insignificant. In addition, only the direct profit measure, PROFITS2_i exhibits the expected positive sign.

Despite the insignificant estimates, we venture to remark that the elasticity of substitution between aggregate welfare and profits is extremely low in either regression, indicating that the policy makers' political support function places significantly larger weight on aggregate welfare than on profits. Using a Cobb Douglas Support Function with constant returns akin to the functional form used in Grossman and Helpman, the value of 0.028 implies an elasticity of the support function with respect to welfare of about 0.97. This value of the implied weight on welfare is strikingly similar to the one we derive in the Influence Driven model below.

The fact that these regressions also exhibit the lowest log-likelihood ratio values may serve as additional evidence that the model is either misspecified or missing key elements. We will discuss this issue further when we compare the models in section 6. Alternatively one could argue that governments do not in fact maximize their political support (because of bounded rationality, or imperfect information).

5.2 Influence Driven

The influence driven estimates are from Eicher and Osang (2002) and summarized here for comparison purposes. As the theory predicts, the estimates show that in addition to the positive effect of import penetration on the dependent variable, there is a negative effect of import penetration on non-tariff barriers for organized industries (i.e. for industries with firm contributions above a certain, exogenously determined threshold). The Grossman and Helpman (1994) propositions are thus confirmed at the 1 percent significance level that whether or not a sector is organized plays a crucial role in explaining the relationship between import penetration and protection.

Based on the coefficient estimates, the implied value for the government weight on welfare, β, is 0.96, while the fraction of the population that owns sector specific inputs, α_L, is 0.26. Using a slightly improved estimation technique, com-

[8] Any welfare measure is only going to affect the scale but not the qualitative results.

pared to GM , Eicher and Osang improved the efficiency of the estimation to be able to prove that $a_5 + a_4 > 0$ is significant at the 1 percent significance level.

The goodness of fit of the Influence Driven model is certainly better than that of the Political Support Model. This adds empirical evidence to the discussion of the effect of import penetration on endogenous protection.

5.3 Parameter Stability

To test for structural change of the estimated coefficients, we separate the samples and perform a Wald test for each approach to endogenous protection. The Wald statistic,

$$\Lambda_1 = (\hat{\theta}_1 - \hat{\theta}_2)'(V_1 + V_2)^{-1}(\hat{\theta}_1 - \hat{\theta}_2),$$

has a chi-squared distribution with k degrees of freedom where k=1 in (6a), k=2 in (7a) and (10a), and k=4 in (11). To estimate Λ_1, we replace V_1 and V_2 by their estimated values, a procedure that is valid in large samples. The test statistics and the corresponding p-values for each model are provided in the last row of Table 1.

We cannot reject the null hypothesis of parameter stability at the one percent significance level for either model. Since the Wald test for parameter stability has the property in small and medium-sized samples that the probability of type I error is larger than the chosen critical value, a larger critical value is appropriate to correct for this problem. We therefore conclude that parameter instability is not a problem in the Political Support or Influence Driven models.

6 Model Comparisons

Eicher and Osang have shown that the Influence Driven model outperforms the Tariff Function, the above presents additional evidence of the Influence driven model, as the Political Support estimates disappoint. The fully compare the models formally, however requires non-nested hypothesis testing in form of J tests, which we provide in Section 6.2. A second question to ask leads us away from strict theory and concerns the explanatory power of each individual exogenous variable in the two models. It is natural to inquire if the fit and the explanatory power of the regression can be improved by combining variables from both approaches in one regression. This question is not entirely devoid of theory. In a sense the generic Political Support model is augmented in the Influence Driven model by contributions and by the influence of lobbies. This question is tackled in Section 6.1.

6.1 General Models

We can compare the power of the variables suggested by the strict theoretical models in a "General" model that combines all variables in one regression.

General1(a & b)

$$\frac{\tau_i^*}{\tau_i^*+1}e_i = a_6\frac{W}{\Pi_i}\frac{1}{z_i} + a_7\frac{C_i^S}{C_i^O}\frac{1}{z_i} + a_8 I_i\frac{1}{z_i} + a_9\frac{1}{z_i} + \varepsilon_{4i}. \tag{11}$$

Where the relative contributions of supporters and opponents (C^S, C^O) are included as an alternative to the step function generated by the indicator variables, I. The results from the Tobit MDE estimation of General1a and General1b (using our two profit measures) are reported in the first column of Table 2. The results show that little explanatory power is derived from either profit measure, PROFITS1 or PROFITS2. In General1a the relative contribution variable from the Tariff Function model is significant (at the 10 percent level), all other variables are statistically insignificant. The alternative profit measure in General1b yields a highly significant organization variable and an excellent fit, but no other significant variables. Since either contributions or organization were significant, but never the profit measures, we proceed by excluding profit measures and basically combine the Tariff Function and the Influence Driven approach in

General2

$$\frac{\tau_i^*}{\tau_i^*+1}e_i = a_{10}\frac{C_i^S}{C_i^O}\frac{1}{z_i} + a_{11} I_i\frac{1}{z_i} + a_{12}\frac{1}{z_i} + \varepsilon_{5i}. \tag{12}$$

General2 generates by far the best fit of all regressions, including the strict theoretical approaches in Table 1. As expected, in the absence of contributions or organization, import penetration is positively related to tariffs, and statistically significant at the 1 percent level. However, only the Influence Driven and not the contribution variable from the Tariff Function model is significant at the 1 percent level. The lack of significance of the estimate of the contribution variable suggests that organization is indeed more important than outright contributions. In summary, we find that the political support model's weakness is confirmed in the general model approach. New information, however, is that relative contributions of supporters and opponents of tariffs hold weaker explanatory power than the organization indicator function.

6.2 Non-Nested Hypothesis Testing

In keeping with the objective of the paper, we return to the models that were suggested by the theory. Section 6.1 provides heuristic evidence that political support variables hold little explanatory power compared to the Influence Driven variables. In this section we seek to further evaluate the relative strength of each exact theoretical model in explaining endogenous protection, by performing a series of non-nested tests. Our methodology is to test the relative strength of each model against each of the two competing alternatives. We follow the test procedure for non-nested J tests developed by Davidson and MacKinnon (1981, 1993).[9] An insignificant coefficient estimate in Table 3 implies that the null hypothesis can be rejected, implying that the alternative does not add significant estimation power to the null hypothesis.[10]

Table 3 reports the J test statistics, and the results of the first four rows provide further strong evidence in favor of the Influence Driven model and against the Political support model. In rows one the J test rejects the null hypothesis that the Political Support Model (with PROFITS1) is the true model. It is shown that the addition of the Influence Driven model's variables - specifically the information whether a sector is organized or not - adds significant information in estimating endogenous protection. The second row repeats the experiment in reverse, where the J test report that the Political Support model does not add relevant information to the Influence Driven model in estimating endogenous protection. The null hypothesis of the Influence Driven model being the "true" model cannot be rejected. Both test statistics are at an astonishing 1 percent significance level. The interpretations of the J test results are in line with the results in Table 1 and Table 2. The Influence Driven model had the best fit in Table 1 and survived as the only significant estimate in Table 2. Hence it is not surprising that it "beat" the Political Support Model in the J test.

7 Summary and Conclusions

The contribution of this paper is the exact empirical investigation of two prominent endogenous protection models. In the absence of reduced forms and extraneous variables to the regression we find that the simple testable implications of the models yield powerful results. There exists a profit measure for which the estimated coefficients in the Political Support Function model have the correct sign. The Influence Driven model exhibits the best overall fit among the models, however. Further evidence for the superiority of the Influence Driven model comes

---

9 The intuition of the J tests is the following. Suppose the truth (the null hypothesis) we wish to test is $H_0 = y_i = f_i(\lambda_i, a) + \varepsilon_{0i}$ where a is a vector of parameters to be estimated and λ_i is a vector of observations on exogenous variables. Suppose theory suggests an alternative hypothesis $H_1 = y'_i = g_i(\lambda_i', a') + \varepsilon_{1i}$ where a' and λ_i' are different vectors of parameters and observations. The J test tests for $\kappa = 0$ in $y_i = \kappa f_i(\lambda_i, a) + (1-\kappa) g_i(\lambda_i', \hat{a}') + \varepsilon_i$ where $\hat{a}'$ is the ML estimate of a'. See Davidson and MacKinnon (1981) for details.

10 For this class of tests, the non-nested alternative hypothesis need not be true. Nor does a rejected null hypothesis imply that the alternative is accepted.

from non-nested misspecification tests that indicate that the Influence Driven model, when tested against the Political Support Model, cannot be rejected.

Overall the Political Support Function approach disappoints. This may be because of shortcomings in the data. Profit data are notoriously noisy, and even using two alternative measures does not help the results. The results give rise to the strong impression that the Political Support Function approach suffers from its exclusion of the explicit modeling of the incentives of agents to lobby or contribute, as it focuses exclusively on the political interests.

Appendix: Description of Variables

TOTALSALES$_i$, value of shipments per industry, 1996 NBER productivity database.

TOTALSALES, is the aggregation over all industries' value of shipments.

Import demand elasticities, e_i, are taken from Sheills, Stern, and Deardorff (1986). Following G-M, the small number of industries with positive import demand elasticities are set to zero.

Non-tariff barriers (NTBs), τ_i, (Trefler 1993), aggregated to the three-digit level using as weights the value of shipments.

Import penetration ratio, *z*, (Trefler 1993), aggregated to the three-digit level using as weights the value of shipments

Instrumental variables, (Trefler 1993), aggregated to the three-digit level using as weights the value of shipments. The list of instrumental variables is identical to the one used by G-M: Physical capital, inventories, engineers and scientists, white-collar, skill, semiskilled, cropland, pasture, forest, coal, petroleum, minerals, seller concentration, buyer concentration, seller number of firms, buyer number of firms, scale, capital stock, unionization, geographic concentration, tenure.

Political Action Committee contributions, total firm and union contributions by industry obtained for the 1983-84 congressional elections (Gawande 1998); firm and union spending is multiplied by the number of firms and unions to obtain totals.

TOTALCONTRIBUTIONS$_i$, the sum of firm and union contributions per industry.

ORGANIZED, firm contribution dummy, set to zero if industry-level contribution is smaller than 10 million and 1 if it is larger.[11]

PROFITS1, value-added minus total labor cost, 1996 NBER productivity database.

PROFITS2, 1983 pre-tax income from IRS source book, converted from SOI classification to three-digit SIC level.

Table 1. Strictly Theory Based Tests of Endogenous Protection Models IV Tobit Estimations

Dependent Variable $\frac{\tau_i^*}{1+\tau_i^*} e_i$	Political Support 1	Political Support 2	Influence Driven
$\frac{1}{\text{Import Penetration}\,(z_i)}$			-.0098*** (4.3073)
$\frac{\text{TOTALSALES}(W)}{\text{PROFITS1}_i\,(\Pi_i)} \frac{1}{\text{Import Penetration}\,(z_i)}$	-.008 (.693)		
$\frac{\text{TOTALSALES}(W)}{\text{PROFITS2}_i\,(\Pi_i)} \frac{1}{\text{Import Penetration}\,(z_i)}$		.028 (.536)	
$\text{ORGANIZED}(I) * \frac{1}{\text{Import Penetration}\,(z_i)}$			.0374*** (7.265)
Log-Likelihood	-54.82	-55.78	-51.66
Wald Test, Λ	5.2867	5.9576	7.7385
(p-value)	(.0215)	(.0147)	(.0209)

***/**/*: 1 percent/ 5 percent/ 10 percent significance level, t-statistics in parentheses

[11] We use GM's 10 million threshold. They do, however, report their threshold as 100 million, which is a typo (there is not one sector that contributed 100 million)

Table 2. „General“ Endogenous Protection Models IV Tobit Estimations

Dependent Variable $\frac{\tau_i^*}{1+\tau_i^*}e_i$	General 1a	General 1b	General 2
$\frac{1}{\text{Import Penetration}\left(z_i\right)}$	-.0032	-.008	-.007***
	(1.02)	(1.63)	(2.09)
$\frac{\text{TOTALSALES}(W)}{\text{PROFITS1}_i\left(\Pi_i\right)}\frac{1}{\text{Import Penetration}\left(z_i\right)}$	-.030		
	(1.56)		
$\frac{\text{TOTALSALES}(W)}{\text{PROFITS2}_i\left(\Pi_i\right)}\frac{1}{\text{Import Penetration}\left(z_i\right)}$		.026	
		(.18)	
$\frac{\text{TOTALCONTRIBUTIONS}_i\left(C_i^S\right)}{\text{TOTALCONTRIBUTIONS}\left(C_i^O\right)}\frac{1}{\text{Import Penetration}\left(z_i\right)}$	1.91*	-.97	-.98
	(1.89)	(.96)	(1.00)
$\text{ORGANIZED}(I)*\frac{1}{\text{Import Penetration}\left(z_i\right)}$	.003	.055***	.055***
	(.15)	(2.68)	(2.79)
Log-Likelihood	-53.90	-50.58	-50.58

***/**/*: 1 percent/ 5 percent/ 10 percent significance level, t-statistics in parentheses

Table 3. Non-Nested Hypothesis Testing

Null Hypothesis	Alternative Hypothesis	J-Test Statistic	Interpretation
Political Support 1	Influence Driven	.148	Reject null hypothesis
Influence Driven	Political Support	7.89***	Cannot reject null hypothesis

***/**/*: 1 percent/ 5 percent/ 10 percent significance level, t-statistics in parentheses
Note: Not being able to reject the null hypothesis implies that the model associated with the null hypothesis is the "correct model" in the sense that information added by the alternative hypothesis does not improve the estimation of the dependent variable.

References

Baldwin R (1985) The Political Economy of U.S. Import Policy. MIT Press, Cambridge

Baldwin R, Magee C (1998) Is Trade Policy for Sale? Congressional Voting on Recent Trade Bills. NBER Working Paper 6376

Davidson R, MacKinnon JG (1981) Several Tests for Model Specification in the Presence of Alternative Hypothesis. Econometrica 49 : 781–793

Davidson R, MacKinnon JG (1993) Estimation and Inference in Econometrics. Oxford University Press, Oxford

Eicher TS, Osang T (2002) Protection for Sale: An Empirical Investigation. Comment. American Economic Review 92 : 1702–1711

Feenstra R, Bhagwati J (1982) Tariff Seeking and the Efficient Tariff. In: Bhagwati J (ed) Import Competition and Response. University of Chicago Press, Chicago

Finger JM, Harrison A (1996) The MFA Paradox: More Protection and More Trade? In: Krueger AO (ed) The Political Economy of American Trade Policy. NBER Project Report Series. University of Chicago Press, Chicago

Findlay R, Wellisz S (1982) Endogenous Tariffs, the Political Economy of Trade Restrictions, and Welfare. In Bhagwati J (ed.) Import Competition and Response. University of Chicago Press, Chicago

Gawande K (1998) Comparing Theories of Endogenous Protection: Model Comparisons Using Gibbs Sampling Output. Review of Economics and Statistics 80 : 128–40

Gawande K, Bandyopadhyay U (2000) Is Protection for Sale? Evidence on the Grossman-Helpman Theory of Endogenous Protection. Review of Economics and Statistics 82 : 139–152

Goldberg PK, Maggi G (1999) Protection for Sale: An Empirical Investigation. American Economic Review 89 : 1135–1155

Greene WH (1997) Econometric Analysis, Third Ed., Prentice Hall, New York

Grossman G, Helpman E (1994) Protection for Sale. American Economic Review 84 : 833–850

Grossman G, Helpman E (1996) Electoral Competition and Special Interest Politics. Review of Economics Studies 63 : 265–86

Helpman E (1997) Politics and Trade Policy. In: Kreps D, Wallis K (eds) Advances in Economics and Econometrics: Theory and Application. Cambridge University Press, Cambridge

Hillman AL (1982) Declining Industries and Political-Support Protectionist Motives. American Economic Review 72 : 1180–1187

Hufbauer G, Berliner D, Kimberly E (1986) Trade and Protection in the US: 31 Case Studies. Institute for International Economics, Washington DC

Lee JW, Swagel P (1997) Trade Barriers and Trade Flows across Countries and Industries. Review of Economics and Statistics 79 : 372–382

Lee M (1996) Methods of Moments and Semiparametric Econometrics for Limited Dependent Variable Models. Springer Verlag, New York

Magee SP, Brock A, Young L (1989) Black Hole Tariffs and Endogenous Policy Theory. Cambridge University Press, Cambridge

Maggi G, Rodriguez-Clare A (2000) Import Penetration and Politics of Trade Protection. Journal of International Economics 51 : 287–305

Mayer W (1984) Endogenous Tariff Formation. American Economic Review 74 : 970–985

Ray E.J (1981) The Determinants of Tariff and Non-Tariff Trade Restrictions in the United States. Journal of Political Economy 89 : 105–121

Rodrik D (1995) Political Economy of Trade Policy. In: Grossman GM, Rogoff K (eds) Handbook of International Economics III. North-Holland, Amsterdam

Staiger R, Tabellini G (1987) Discretionary Trade Policy and Excessive Protection. American Economic Review 77 : 340–348

Stern PM (1988) The Best Congress Money can Buy, Pantheon, New York

Shiells CR, Stern RM, Deardorff AV (1986) Estimates of the Elasticities of Substitution between Imports and Home Goods for the United States. Weltwirtschaftliches Archiv 122 : 497–519

Trefler D (1993) Trade Liberalization and the Theory of Endogenous Protection: An Econometric Study of U.S. Import Policy. Journal of Political Economy 101 : 138–160

Van Long N, Vousden N (1991) Protectionist Responses and Declining Industries. Journal of International Economics 30 : 87–103

Comment

Volker Clausen[1]

Department of Economics, University of Duisburg-Essen, Campus Essen, Germany

The paper by Theo Eicher and Thomas Osang represents a valuable and substantive contribution to the empirical literature on the motivation of US trade policy. Their econometric design is theory-driven and draws on Helpman (1997). Eicher and Osang spell out clearly the different implications of alternative models and use state-of-the-art econometric techniques in order to test the contrasting approaches. They find overwhelming empirical support for the "protection for sale" model by Grossman and Helpman (1994) and clearly reject the political support model by Hillman (1982).

Overall, this paper belongs to a series of very mature contributions by both authors and others. Rather than trying to spot any remaining weaknesses, this comment takes an alternative route and offers in a somewhat complementary fashion a general equilibrium analysis, which serves to produce a quantitative framework in order to evaluate trade policy measures. More specifically, this comment designs a general equilibrium model, which is fully consistent with Helpman (1997) and allows us to illustrate some theoretical results graphically.

Both approaches to explain tariff formation are compared with respect to their welfare consequences. This is done by calculating the production loss by moving from free trade to the respective tariff-distorted equilibrium. Using the concept of a *compensated equilibrium* (cf. Dixit and Norman (1980), p. 79) we know that the level of the production loss fully describes the welfare loss associated with the transition to the tariff-distorted equilibrium. According to this concept, the government is assumed to impose appropriate consumption and employment taxes and subsidies such that households still face the *initial* price vector. Firms, in contrast, base their decisions on the *new* price vector. With this compensation scheme, households do not change their factor supply and consumption decisions, while the trade policy by the government causes an excess burden that equals the production loss. As the new situation is characterized by an import tariff,[2] the additional tariff revenue has to be subtracted from the production loss. The resulting

---

[1] I thank my PhD student Julian Emami Namini for numerous, substantive and extremely stimulating discussions on the subject and, in particular, for performing the below-mentioned simulations using GAMS.

[2] This import tariff may well be an export subsidy, depending on the initial and the new trade pattern. If the imposition of the import tariff, which raises the domestic price of the respective good, leads to exports of this good, the *import tariff* becomes an *export subsidy*.

total burden of the government may now be financed by a lump sum tax. The larger this total burden and therefore the lump sum tax, the larger the general welfare burden for the households from the transition to the tariff-distorted equilibrium.

This comment proceeds as follows: First, it specifies the underlying supply and demand side of the economy. Then, the economy opens up to world markets and the optimal tariffs for the *Political Support Function* and the *Influence Driven Contributions* approach are calculated. This tariff is then taken in order to determine the production loss and tariff revenues.

The Supply Side of the Economy

First, the closed economy is analysed in order to provide insights into the properties of the specific model set up in Helpman (1997) and used in the paper by Eicher and Osang (2004). To keep the model easily tractable, the numbers of factors and goods are both restricted to two. Note that capital is assumed to be sector-specific and only used in the production of good one. The supply side of the economy is then fully described by two factor market equilibrium conditions and two zero profit conditions:[3]

$$a_{L0}(w,r)\cdot q_0 + a_{L1}(w,r)\cdot q_1 \leq \overline{L} \tag{1}$$

$$a_{K1}(w,r)\cdot q_1 \leq \overline{K} \tag{2}$$

$$a_{L0}(w,r)\cdot w \geq p_0 \tag{3}$$

$$a_{L1}(w,r)\cdot w + a_{K1}(w,r)\cdot r \geq p_1, \tag{4}$$

where $a_{ij}(w,r)$ denotes the Hicksian demand for factor i per unit of good j, q_j the amount of good j produced, $\overline{L}$ and $\overline{K}$ the total supplies of labor and the sector-specific factor capital, which are assumed to be completely price inelastic, w and r the prices for labor and capital and p_j the price for good j.[4] The production technology for good zero, which acts as the numéraire, is specified in Ei-

[3] Each sector earns zero profits in equilibrium, which is implied by the following arguments: On the one hand, given a non-competitive sector with positive profits, this sector could not be foreign-owned as profits of all sectors enter the government objective function (cf. Eicher and Osang (2004), eq. (5)). On the other hand, in the case of a domestic-owned sector with profits, the equation $p_i = \tau_i, \forall i$ (cf. Eicher and Osang (2004), p. 5) could not hold.

[4] The Hicksian per unit demand functions for the factors of production only depend on relative factor prices because constant returns to scale are assumed. Increasing or decreasing returns to scale are ruled out in the present model, however: Increasing returns to scale are excluded by the condition that no domestic firm can influence market prices; decreasing returns to scale are excluded by stability conditions.

cher/Osang (2004), p. 5, as $L_0 = q_0$. This implies $a_{L0}(w,r) = 1$ and $w = p_0 = 1$ if good zero is produced in a strictly positive amount. Furthermore, total labor endowment and the total endowment of the sector-specific factor capital are specified to equal one.[5] Producing good one requires both production factors, labor and capital. These factors are aggregated here according to the following Cobb-Douglas production function:[6]

$$q_1 = L_1^{\alpha} K^{1-\alpha} \left(\left(\frac{1-\alpha}{\alpha} \right)^{\alpha} + \left(\frac{\alpha}{1-\alpha} \right)^{1-\alpha} \right). \tag{5}$$

This particular specification of the production technology has the advantage that the per unit Hicksian factor demands simply result as $a_{L1} = (r/w)^{1-\alpha} \cdot \alpha$ and $a_{K1} = (w/r)^{\alpha} \cdot (1-\alpha)$. Assuming that all factor markets clear and both goods are produced in strictly positive amounts now leads to the following convenient representation of the supply side of the economy:

$$q_0 = 1 - \frac{\alpha}{1-\alpha} \cdot r \tag{6}$$

$$q_1 = \frac{1}{1-\alpha} \cdot r^{\alpha} \tag{7}$$

$$w = p_0 = 1 \tag{8}$$

$$r^{1-\alpha} = p_1. \tag{9}$$

In addition, this up to now *closed* economy is characterized by the equality of output q_j and consumption c_j of good j. The consumption of good zero is then determined as $q_0 = 1 + r - p_1 q_1$, with $1 + r$ denoting total factor income and $p_1 q_1$ the amount of total factor income that is spent on good one. Having four linearly independent equations – two factor market equilibrium conditions, two zero profit conditions, the demand equation for q_0 is just the sum of the zero profit conditions, each multiplied with the amount of each good produced – and five variables

[5] These total factor endowments can be deduced from eq. (2) and (3) in Eicher and Osang (2004): Summing the individual labor endowments over all individuals results in $L = 1$. A certain variable γ_i^j is defined as follows: "An individual owns... γ_i^j of the sector specific input" (Eicher and Osang (2004), p. 5); aggregating γ_i^j across all individuals results in $K = 1$. The Eicher and Osang (2004) version of this model therefore slightly deviates from the Helpman (1997) version, which defines γ_i^j as a *fraction* of the sector specific factor an individual owns. Normalizing both factor endowments to equal one, simplifies the model exposition, however.

[6] Cf. Emami Namini (2004) for this particular specification of a Cobb-Douglas production function, which serves to justify the calibrated share form in applied general equilibrium models.

q_0, q_1, p_1, r, w – one has to incorporate the demand side to construct a general equilibrium for this economy.

The Demand Side of the Economy

Preferences of the representative household in the economy are represented by the additive separable utility function $u(c) = c_0 + u_1(c_1)$, with $u_1(c_1)$ strictly concave in c_1. $u_1(c_1)$ is assumed here as $u_1(c_1) = \phi \cdot \ln c_1$, $1 < \phi$.[7] Utility maximizing behavior of the representative household then leads to $p_1 = \phi / c_1$. One can now show that a situation with $p_0 = 1, p_1 \geq 1, w = 1, r = 1, q_0 = 1 - \alpha/(1-\alpha)$ and $q_1 = 1/(1-\alpha)$ leads to a general equilibrium in the economy:

$$1 \cdot 1 = 1 \text{ (zero profits sector 0)} \tag{10}$$

$$\left(\frac{1}{1}\right)^{1-\alpha} \cdot \alpha + \left(\frac{1}{1}\right)^{\alpha} (1-\alpha) = 1 \text{ (zero profits sector 1)} \tag{11}$$

$$1 \cdot \left(1 - \frac{\alpha}{1-\alpha}\right) + \alpha \cdot \left(\frac{1}{1-\alpha}\right) = 1 \text{ (market equilibrium } \overline{L}\text{)} \tag{12}$$

$$\frac{1}{1-\alpha} \cdot \left(\frac{1}{1}\right)^{\alpha} \cdot (1-\alpha) = 1 \text{ (market equilibrium } \overline{K}\text{)} \tag{13}$$

$$2 - \frac{1}{1-\alpha} \cdot 1 = 1 - \frac{\alpha}{1-a} \text{ (market equilibrium } q_0\text{)} \tag{14}$$

$$\frac{\phi}{p_1} = \frac{1}{1-\alpha} \cdot p_1^{\alpha/(1-\alpha)} \text{ (market equilibrium } q_1\text{),} \tag{15}$$

---

[7] Finding a sub-utility function for good 1 that is adequate for the model requires the following considerations: First, all world market prices are set equal to one. A utility function of the form $u_1(c_1) = c_1^{\phi}, 0 < \phi < 1$, would not work: This utility specification leads to marginal utility of consumption equal to $\phi \cdot c_1^{\phi-1}$ and a demand function of $c_1 = (p_1/\phi)^{1/(\phi-1)}$. In autarky, a price $p_1 = 1$ – which already implies no trade in the *free trade* situation – would lead to the market clearing condition for this good $(1/\phi)^{1/(\phi-1)} \leq 1/(1-\alpha)$, which would imply that for every values of both ϕ and α strictly between zero and one, supply would always exceed demand. A price $p_1 < 1$ could circumvent this excess supply problem in autarky, but would imply exports of good one in the *free trade* situation – the *import tariff* would then be an *export subsidy*. Second, the utility function could be specified as $u_1(c_1) = \theta \cdot c_1^{\phi}$ and the excess supply problem in autarky would disappear if θ is chosen appropriately. But this specification would lead to *two* additional parameters that are free to choose. Third, a Cobb-Douglas utility function would bring about the problem that the demand for good one is influenced by factor income and the model would be hard to solve by hand. The logarithmic form of the utility representation has the advantage that equilibrium prices in autarky are easily determined.

where the last equation leads at a given price p_1 to a unique relationship between α and ϕ:

$$\alpha = 1 - \frac{p_1^{1/(1-\alpha)}}{\phi} \tag{16}$$

In order to simplify the following calculations, p_1 is set to equal one in autarky. This leads to $\alpha = 1 - 1/\phi$ from the market equilibrium condition for q_1. *Both* equilibrium prices in the closed economy will then equal one in absolute value – as they do in the world markets. Obviously, opening up the economy will not bring about any trade. The *import tariff* therefore could be redefined as a *consumption tax*, and the *tariff revenue* then would become a *subsidy burden.* The market clearing condition for q_1 and $p_1 = 1$ imply that α can only be positive, i.e., good one uses labor as an input factor with positive productivity, if $\phi > 1$. A further restriction may be imposed on ϕ by supposing that *both* goods are produced in autarky. This restriction leads to $1/2 > \alpha$.[8] Combining this inequality with $\alpha = 1 - 1/\phi$ from the market equilibrium condition for good one in autarky leads to $2 \geq \phi$.

The Open Economy

Provided that the *political support function* approach describes the political process of this economy, the government will chose the tariff $\tau_1 - 1 = \frac{\partial\Theta/\partial\Pi}{\partial\Theta/\partial W} \cdot \frac{q_1}{-M_1'}$ for sector one, with $\Theta(\tau_1) = \Theta\left(\Pi(\tau_1), W(\tau_1)\right)$ denoting the government's political support function, $\Pi(\tau_1)$ the rewards to the sector specific factor and $W(\tau_1)$ the economy's aggregate welfare. The *influence driven contributions* approach would give rise to $\tau_1 - 1 = \frac{I_1 - \alpha_L}{\beta/(1-\beta) + \alpha_L} \cdot \frac{q_1}{-M'_1}$ for this sector. In order to allow for a straight comparison between the two different approaches, the objective function of the government is defined as $\Theta(\tau_1) = (1-\beta) \cdot C_1(\tau_1) + \beta \cdot W(\tau_1)$ in *both* situations and total campaign contributions of sector one, $C\,(\tau_1)$, are to equal total tariff-induced profits in this sector, $\Pi(\tau_1)$. This leads to the following tariff-included prices for the *political support function* approach, *PS*, and the *influence driven contributions* approach, *ID*:

$$\tau_1^{PS} = \frac{1-\beta}{\beta} \cdot \frac{q_1}{-M_1'} + 1$$

[8] This restriction results from eq. (8): $q_0 > 0$ implies $1 - \alpha/(1-\alpha) > 0$, if $p_1 = 1$ in autarky.

$$\tau_1^{ID} = \frac{I_1 - \alpha_L}{\frac{\beta}{1-\beta} + \alpha_L} \cdot \frac{q_1}{-M_1'} + 1. \tag{18}$$

In what follows, only an *organized* (Eicher and Osang (2002), p. 8) sector one will be considered, i.e., $I_1 = 1$. The parameter α_L, which represents the fraction of households that own sector specific factors, will be redefined, as only one sector specific factor is assumed, preferences are not homothetic and the household specific consumer price index therefore depends on the households' factor income: Below, α_L will represent the fraction of households that own *only* labor, where the other part of the households possesses *only* sector specific capital. If a tariff is implemented, p_1 rises and if all households consume *both* goods, a tariff will be conflict generating as it reduces the real factor income of the households that belong to α_L. For the open economy, the value of total production, evaluated at world market prices, is given by

$$Y = p_0 \cdot \frac{1 - 2 \cdot \alpha}{1-\alpha} + p_1 \cdot \frac{1}{1-\alpha} = 2.$$

The change in the value of production that results from the imposition of the tariff is then described by $\Delta Y = 2 - q_0^T - q_1^T$, with q_0^T and q_1^T as the quantities that are produced in the tariff-distorted equilibrium.[9] As

$$q_0 = 1 - \frac{\alpha}{1-\alpha} \cdot r \text{ , } q_1 = \frac{1}{1-\alpha} \cdot r^{\alpha} \text{ and } r^{1-\alpha} = p_1 = \tau_1 \text{ ,}$$

the changes in the value of production in both situations can be computed as

$$(\Delta Y)^{PS} = -1 - \frac{\alpha}{1-\alpha} \cdot \left(\tau_1^{PS}\right)^{1/(1-\alpha)} + \frac{1}{1-\alpha} \cdot \left(\tau_1^{PS}\right)^{\alpha/(1-\alpha)} \text{ and}$$

$$(\Delta Y)^{ID} = -1 - \frac{\alpha}{1-\alpha} \cdot \left(\tau_1^{ID}\right)^{1/(1-\alpha)} + \frac{1}{1-\alpha} \cdot \left(\tau_1^{ID}\right)^{\alpha/(1-\alpha)}.$$

Both changes equal zero, if the tariff is equal to zero and $\tau_1^k = 1, k = PS, ID,$ of course.

For the purpose of determining $q_1/(-M_1')$ in the free trade equilibrium, the utility function was specified as $u(c) = c_0 + \phi \cdot \ln c_1$. Maximizing utility with respect to the budget constraint at given prices results in $c_1 = \phi / p_1$. As

$M_1 = c_1 - q_1$ and

$q_1 = 1/(1-\alpha) \cdot p_1^{\alpha/(1-\alpha)}, M_1' = c_1' - q_1'$ equals $-\phi / p_1^2 - \alpha/(1-\alpha)^2 \cdot p_1^{(2\alpha-1)/(1-\alpha)}$.

This leads to

---

[9] The term *production loss* is now substituted by *change in the value of production* in order to avoid any confusion: If the *loss* is *positive*, it hurts the country. The *change*, however, may be defined to be *negative* and is then *added* to the undistorted income of the country.

$$\frac{q_1}{-M_1'} = \frac{1/(1-\alpha)\cdot p_1^{\alpha/(1-\alpha)}}{\phi/p_1^2 + \alpha/(1-\alpha)^2 \cdot p_1^{(2\alpha-1)/(1-\alpha)}} \tag{19}$$

Evaluated at the initial free trade equilibrium, i.e., $p_1 = \tau_1 = 1$, and considering that α is specified as $\alpha = 1 - 1/\phi$ from the autarky market equilibrium condition for q_1 results in the following simplification for $q_1/(-M_1')$:

$$\frac{q_1}{-M_1'} = \frac{1/(1-\alpha)}{\phi + \alpha/(1-\alpha)^2} = \frac{1}{\phi}, \tag{20}$$

where this transformation results from $1-\alpha = 1/\phi$ and $\alpha/(1-\alpha) = \phi - 1$.

Political Support versus Influence-Driven Contributions

First of all, both tariffs are identical, if $\alpha_L = 0$. The tariff of the *Influence Driven Contributions* approach will be lower than the tariff of the *Political Support Function* approach, if $\alpha_L > 0$. Thus, as the free trade equilibrium is Pareto-optimal, one can directly infer that the *Influence Driven Contributions* approach is Pareto-superior to the *Political Support Functions* approach, if $\alpha_L > 0$. Therefore, only the situation for $\alpha_L = 0$ will be considered further. With $\alpha_L = 0$, the tariff-included price is given by $\tau_1 = \frac{1-\beta}{\beta}\cdot\frac{1}{\phi} + 1$. Obviously, if β increases, the first ratio and therefore τ_1 decreases – the higher the weight the government places on the households' welfare, the smaller the tariff. The second ratio in the formula for τ_1 obviously decreases, if ϕ rises. This response of τ_1 on ϕ can be explained by the fact that the fraction of total income that is devoted to good one, $c_1\big|_{p_1=1} = 1/(1-\alpha) = \phi$ increases in ϕ. A higher ϕ therefore implies a stronger distorting effect of a given tariff and a lower τ_1 for a given weight to government places on the households' welfare.

The total burden B the government suffers from imposing the tariff, while holding all domestic consumer prices constant, equals the change in the value of production ΔY, plus total tariff revenues T, i.e.,

$$B = -1 - (\phi - 1)\cdot\tau_1^{\phi} + \phi\cdot\tau_1^{\phi-1} + (\tau_1 - 1)(c_1(\tau_1) - q_1(\tau_1))$$

$$= -1 - (\phi-1)\left(\frac{1-\beta}{\beta}\cdot\frac{1}{\phi}+1\right)^{\phi} + \phi\cdot\left(\frac{1-\beta}{\beta}\cdot\frac{1}{\phi}+1\right)^{\phi-1}$$

$$+\frac{1-\beta}{\beta}\cdot\frac{1}{\phi}\left(\frac{\phi}{(1-\beta)/\beta\cdot 1/\phi+1} - \phi\cdot\left(\frac{1-\beta}{\beta}\cdot\frac{1}{\phi}+1\right)^{\phi-1}\right). \tag{21}$$

The first term, the change in the value of production is always negative, as the initial free trade equilibrium is Pareto-optimal and any deviation of the home production structure from the Pareto-optimum leads to a decrease in the value of production, evaluated at undistorted prices. The second term, total tariff revenue, is negative either. If a tariff is introduced, i.e., the domestic price for good one increases, consumption of good one will decrease and its production will increase – additional production that will be sold on world markets. The government then offers an export subsidy to sector one. Figure 1 illustrates these results for different values of β and ϕ.[10] The upper left chart 1 displays the resulting tariff-included price τ_I, the upper right chart 2 displays total tariff revenue T, the lower left chart 3 displays the change in the value of production ΔY and the lower right chart 4 finally displays the total burden B:

[10] ϕ was chosen to vary between 1 and 2, β to vary between 0.3 and 1. If $\beta < 0.3$, certain combinations of β and ϕ exist that lead to a negative production of q_0 - the production loss could then be greater than 2 in absolute value.

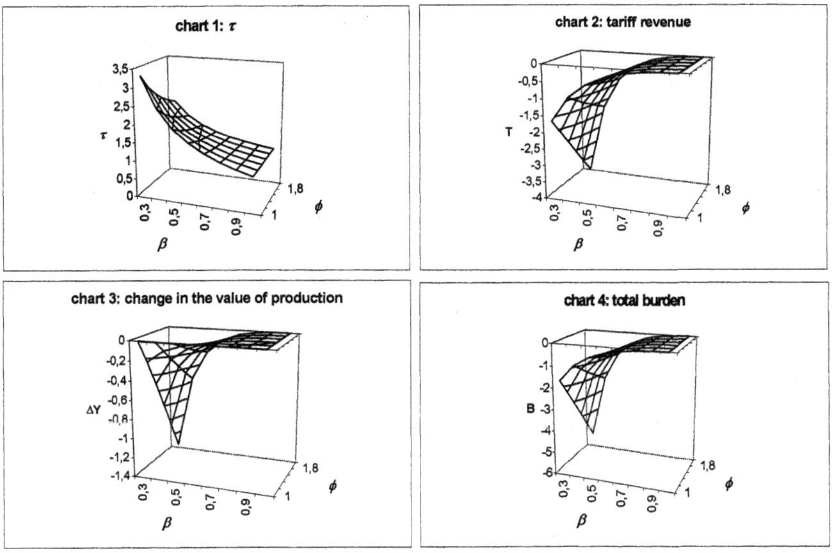

Figure 1. A Graphical Presentation of the Tariff Distortion

References

Dixit A, Norman V (1980) Theory of International Trade. Cambridge University Press, Cambridge

Eicher T, Osang T (2005) Political Support or Contributions: An Empirical Investigation of US Trade Policy. In Heiduk G, Wong K (eds) WTO and World Trade: Challenges in a New Era, Springer, Heidelberg New York

Emami Namini J (2004) The Calibrated Share Form in Applied General Equilibrium Models: A Formal Justification. *Mimeo*, University of Duisburg-Essen

Grossman G, Helpman E (2002) Interest Groups and Trade Policy. Princeton University Press, Princeton

Helpman E (1997) Politics and Trade Policy. In: Kreps D, Wallis, K. (eds) Advances in Economics and Econometrics: Theory and Application. Cambridge University Press, Cambridge

Minimum Quality Standard and International Rivalry in Quality and Price

Pei-Cheng Liao* and Kar-yiu Wong**

* Department of Accounting, National Taiwan University, Taiwan
** Department of Economics, University of Washington, Seattle, USA

1 Introduction

The use of strategic trade policy to promote trade has been proven to be disruptive in world trade. One of the achievements of the GATT and the WTO is to prohibit the use of subsidies to promote trade performance of domestic firms, and it regulates the actions countries can take to counter the effects of subsidies, including settlement by the WTO and imposition of countervailing duties. The Agreement on Subsidies and Countervailing Measures ("SCM" Agreement) defines what constitute subsidies that governments are not allowed to impose. The definition contains three basic elements: (i) a financial contribution (ii) by a government or any public body within the territory of a member country (iii) which confers a benefit. The first part, a financial contribution, seems to be a crucial part in the measure.[1] Thus, there could be no government subsidy unless there was a charge on the public account; for example, grants, loans, equity infusions, loan guarantees, fiscal incentives, the provision of goods or services, and the purchase of goods. It turns out that there are many other government policies that do not involve financial contributions but that can be used strategically to confer a benefit. This paper considers one such policy: minimum quality standard.

Minimum quality standards (MQS) are usually used in closed economies to improve the quality of goods produced in the market; for example, the requirement of air bags, anti-lock brake systems, fuel-economy standards and automobile emissions standards in the car industry. Usually the use of MQS is justified by the existence of moral hazard or the cost of inspection by the government, and appropriate use of MQS is welfare improving.[2]

There has also been work on analyzing the use of MQS for open economies. One of the earlier papers was Krishna (1987), who analyzes the effects and desirability

---

[1] Some member countries suggested that all forms of government interventions that have the purpose of directly promoting the trade performance of domestic firms, whether or not they involve expenses of the government, should be included in the agreement and be banned. However, this stronger approach has not been approved.

[2] See, for example, Ronnen (1991), Crampes and Hollander (1995), and Ecchia and Lambertini (1997). Ecchia et al. (2001) provide good surveys on the regulation and welfare consequence of MQS.

of quotas, tariffs, and MQS when the foreign firm is a monopolist in the home market. In a model of international duopoly, Das and Donnenfeld (1989) analyze the effects of quotas and MQS when both firms choose quality and quantity simultaneously to compete in the home market. They show that a MQS above the free trade level on the low-quality imports is welfare deteriorating to the home country. Boom (1995) considers the effects of different MQS levels set by two countries, with both firms competing in both countries. Compared to the identical MQS case, if one country sets a higher MQS than the other country, both firms are hurt while consumers in both countries benefit, but the welfare effect is ambiguous. Polavarapu and Vaidya (1996a, b) analyze the effects of tariffs, taxes/subsidies and MQS when a home firm and a foreign firm compete in the home market. They show that a MQS imposed on the foreign firm makes the home firm upgrade quality, and this benefits the home welfare. Lutz (2000) analyzes and compares the two alternative standard-setting treatments of full harmonization and mutual recognition in a two-country, two-firm model. Under the condition that both firms must stay in the market, mutual recognition is always the optimal policy.

However, little work has been done to analyze MQS when used as a strategic trade policy. As the above papers show, MQS is often imposed on industries that are characterized by imperfect competition. When the quality levels of firms' outputs are determined endogenously, and when firms compete in quality (and possibly in price as well), the policy of MQS could have important effects on firms' profits and national welfare of the economies. This means that there could be situations in which MQS can be used strategically to improve a country's national welfare. It is thus the purpose of this paper to find out some of these situations, and to analyze the impacts of this policy.

Like other strategic policies, MQS is likely detrimental to its trading partner, and thus will likely draw retaliation. This paper will also analyze one retaliatory policy: a tariff. If, however, the country that imposes MQS anticipates that its trading partner is going to retaliate, it may impose a higher MQS.

Since MQS is usually not seen as a trade promotional policy, it is allowed by the current version of SCM Agreement. This means that it may be more difficult for an importing country that is facing a MQS to request retaliation at the WTO. However, this paper argues that some domestic policies such as MQS can be used strategically in an international context, and should not be ignored by the SCM Agreement.

To analyze the strategic nature of MQS in an international context, we consider a two-country, two-firm model, with demand in one of the countries only. We show that the exporting country (foreign) that has a firm producing the good of a low quality can use a MQS to improve the firm's profit and its welfare, at the expense of the firm in the importing country (home), even though such a policy will encourage both firms to improve the quality of their outputs. Even though the policy benefits the consumers in the home country, it could hurt the home country's welfare. This will induce home country to retaliate with a tariff. However, the outcome depends on the timing of the policies. Under the present WTO arrangement, it is possible that a country may make the first move and wait for the other country to react (complain to the WTO). In such a case, the first country will want to impose a MQS higher than that without retaliation.

The remainder of the paper is organized as follows: Section 2 considers a closed economy in which a monopolist chooses the quality level of its output to serve a local market. Section 3 extends the model to two countries, with one firm in each of the countries. How the two firms compete in quality and price is examined. An asymmetry between the countries is introduced, with the firms possessing different technologies of quality improvement and with market demand only in the country with an advanced firm. The use of minimum quality standard by the government of the country that has a firm with an inferior technology in quality improvement is investigated in Section 4. Section 5 shows how the advanced country can retaliate with a tariff. However, if the advanced country has to wait for the MQS before a tariff is imposed, the inferior country can take advantage of this sequence of policies and get a higher welfare. Section 6 provides some concluding remarks.

2 The Model

Consider a product with various quality levels. It can be produced by two firms, one in each of two countries. Label the countries home and foreign, and the firms home firm and foreign firm. Demand exists in the home country only, implying that any output of the foreign firm will be exported to the home country. In home, there is a continuum of consumers indexed by θ, uniformly distributed in the interval $[\underline{\theta}, \bar{\theta}]$. The parameter θ represents consumers' marginal willingness to pay for quality. Consumer θ has unit demand for the good and his utility function is:

$$U = \begin{cases} \theta s_i - p_i & \text{if buying one unit of the good with quality } s_i \text{ at price } p_i; \\ 0 & \text{otherwise.} \end{cases}$$

In this section, we focus on the home country, assuming no trade and thus no production by the foreign firm. So the home firm is a monopolist in the local market. In the home economy, there is a single firm, which is able to produce the product of a quality s_0 with a unit cost α. We assume that $2\underline{\theta} - \bar{\theta} \geq \alpha / s_0 > 0$. As explained below, the condition implies that the entire market is always fully covered by the product of the home firm, i.e., every consumer in the home market will choose to purchase one unit of the good in equilibrium. This section considers a closed home economy.

2.1 Product with a Fixed Quality

Assume for the time being that the quality of the product is fixed at s_0. The market equilibrium depends on whether the market range is big enough. Two cases can be considered.

Case (A): $\underline{\theta} < (\bar{\theta} + \alpha / s_0)/2$

Suppose that the home firm picks $\theta_0 \in [\underline{\theta}, \bar{\theta})$ and chooses to serve $[\theta_0, \bar{\theta}]$ of the market, setting the price of the output at $p_h = \theta_0 s_0$, where subindex "h" denotes variables of the home firm. Its problem is to choose the optimal value of θ_0 to maximize its profit, $\pi_h = (\theta_0 s_0 - \alpha)(\bar{\theta} - \theta_0)$, where $\bar{\theta} - \theta_0$ is the demand. The first-order condition gives $\theta_0^0 = (\bar{\theta} + \alpha / s_0)/2$.[3] The market price is equal to $p_h^0 = (\bar{\theta} s_0 + \alpha)/2$, producing a monopolist profit of $\pi_0^0 = (\bar{\theta} s_0 - \alpha)^2 /(4 s_0)$. Note that this case exists when $\underline{\theta} < \theta_0^0$, or $2\underline{\theta} - \bar{\theta} < \alpha / s_0$. The part of the market $[\underline{\theta}, \theta_0^0)$ is not served by the firm.

Case (B): $\underline{\theta} \geq (\bar{\theta} + \alpha / s_0)/2$

In this case, $\underline{\theta} \geq \theta_0^0$, and the monopolist prefers to serve the whole market. It will set the price of the product at $p_h^1 = \underline{\theta} s_0$, earning a profit of $\pi_h^1 = (\underline{\theta} s_0 - \alpha)(\bar{\theta} - \underline{\theta})$. In the rest of the present paper, we consider only Case B in which the monopolist, when alone in the market with a fixed quality level of its product, chooses to serve the whole market.

2.2 Product with Quality Determined Endogenously

Suppose that the monopolist is able to improve the quality of its product in the following way: By spending a cost of $c_h = c(e_h)$, the firm is able to improve the quality of the product by $e_h \in [0, \infty)$. The new quality level is $s_h = s_0 + e_h$. The quality improvement cost function satisfies the following conditions: (a) $c(0) = c'(0) = 0$; (b) $c(e_h)$, $c'(e_h) > 0$ for $e_h > 0$; (c) $c''(e_h) > 0$ for $e_h \geq 0$; (d) $c'(e_h)$ is sufficiently large when e_h is large. The last assumption is made to ensure that the firm will not want to choose a very large quality improvement value. A possible cost function c_h is illustrated in Figure 1.[4] With an improvement in the quality of the product, the monopolist still prefers to serve the whole market (Case B). So it will set a price at $\underline{\theta} s_h = \underline{\theta}(s_0 + e_h)$. Its problem becomes

$$\max_{e_h} [\underline{\theta}(s_0 + e_h) - \alpha - c(e_h)](\bar{\theta} - \underline{\theta}).$$

The first-order condition is

---

[3] The profit function is strictly concave in θ_0, ensuring that the second-order condition is satisfied.

[4] Ignore the curve labeled c_f for the time being.

$$c'(e_h) = \underline{\theta}. \tag{1}$$

A solution with $e_h \in (0, \infty)$ is guaranteed because the derivative of the profit function with respect to e_h is (a) positive at $e_h = 0$, and (b) negative when e_h is sufficiently large. Strict convexity of the cost function $c(e_h)$ implies that the solution represents a maximum and is unique. The equilibrium quality improvement is depicted by point H in Figure 1, at which the slope of the cost function is equal to $\underline{\theta}$.

3 International Rivalry

Suppose now that export by the foreign firm to the home country is allowed. For the time being, no government interventions are considered so that free trade exists. Variables of the home (foreign) firm are distinguished by a subindex "*h*" ("*f*"). Assume again that the range of the market is not too big so that either of them, when producing as a monopolist, will choose to serve the whole market.[5] Initially, both firms possess the same technology to produce the product of a quality level of s_0, and both firms decide whether to improve the quality of their outputs by paying a cost.

We consider the following two-stage game. In stage one, firm i chooses to improve the quality of its output by $e_i \in [0, \infty)$, after paying a cost of c_i, where $c_h = c(e_h)$, $c_f = \lambda c(e_f)$, and $\lambda > 1$. The parameter λ is used to represent the inferior quality improvement technology possessed by the foreign firm.[6] The quality level of the firm i's output is equal to $s_i = e_i + s_0$, $i = h, f$. In the second stage, the firms compete in the home market in a Bertrand way, with the price set by firm i denoted by p_i. Consumers, taking the quality levels and prices set by the firms as given, choose the output from the firm that produces a higher utility level. For example, consumer θ will choose the output of the home (foreign) firm if $\theta s_h - p_h > (<)\ \theta s_f - p_f$. Let $\hat{\theta}$ be the consumer who is indifferent to the product produced by the firms, i.e., $\hat{\theta} s_h - p_h = \hat{\theta} s_f - p_f$. By rearranging the terms, we have

$$\hat{\theta} = \frac{p_h - p_f}{s_h - s_f}. \tag{2}$$

[5] In other words, the condition for Case B exists, $2\underline{\theta} - \overline{\theta} \geq \alpha / s_0$.

[6] The technology gap may be due to more experience the home firm has. In general, firms tend to choose different quality levels of their products and the present assumption is one way to avoid symmetry between the firms.

Thus the necessary and sufficient condition for both firms supplying a positive output to the market is

$$\underline{\theta} < \hat{\theta} < \overline{\theta}. \tag{3}$$

The demand functions for the home and foreign firms are as follows, respectively:

$$q_h = \overline{\theta} - \hat{\theta} \tag{4a}$$

$$q_f = \hat{\theta} - \underline{\theta}. \tag{4b}$$

The profit functions of the home and foreign firms are given as follows, respectively:

$$\pi_h = [p_h - \alpha - c(e_h)]q_h \tag{5a}$$

$$\pi_f = [p_f - \alpha - \lambda c(e_f)]q_f. \tag{5b}$$

To obtain a subgame perfect equilibrium, the two-stage game is solved by backward induction. Differentiate each firm's profit function in (5) by its own price, taking the other firm's price level and the quality levels as given. Solving the reaction functions to get the second-stage equilibrium prices as:

$$p_h = \alpha + \frac{1}{3}[2c(e_h) + \lambda c(e_f) + (2\overline{\theta} - \underline{\theta})(e_h - e_f)] \tag{6a}$$

$$p_f = \alpha + \frac{1}{3}[c(e_h) + 2\lambda c(e_f) - (2\underline{\theta} - \overline{\theta})(e_h - e_f)]. \tag{6b}$$

The resulting profits of the firms are

$$\pi_h = \frac{1}{9}(e_h - e_f)(2\overline{\theta} - \underline{\theta} - g)^2 \tag{7a}$$

$$\pi_f = \frac{1}{9}(e_h - e_f)(g - 2\underline{\theta} + \overline{\theta})^2, \tag{7b}$$

where $g = g(e_h, e_f, \lambda) = [c(e_h) - \lambda c(e_f)]/(e_h - e_f)$ for $e_h > 0$ and $e_f \geq 0$.

It is clear that because the foreign firm is inferior in quality improvement, in equilibrium we must have $e_h > e_f$, which is the case we will focus on in this paper. The derivatives of $g(e_h, e_f, \lambda)$ are

$$g_h \equiv \frac{\partial g}{\partial e_h} = \frac{c'(e_h) - g}{e_h - e_f} \tag{8a}$$

$$g_f \equiv \frac{\partial g}{\partial e_f} = \frac{g - \lambda c'(e_f)}{e_h - e_f} \tag{8b}$$

$$g_\lambda \equiv \frac{\partial g}{\partial \lambda} = -\frac{c(e_f)}{e_h - e_f}. \tag{8c}$$

To determine the signs of the derivatives in (8), refer to Figure 1, where $c_h = c(e_h)$ and $c_f = \lambda c(e_f)$. Suppose that the home and foreign firms have chosen e_h^1 and e_f^1, respectively. So $g(e_h, e_f, \lambda)$ is equal to the slope of line FH. Consider the following condition:

$$g > \lambda c'(e_f). \tag{9}$$

Lemma 1. *Suppose that condition (9) holds. Then*

(a) $g > 0$;

(b) $e_h > e_f$;

(c) $c(e_h) > \lambda c(e_f)$;

(d) $g_h,\ g_f > 0,\ g_\lambda < 0.$

Proof. Note that because $c'(e_f) > 0$, part (a) follows immediately. Part (a) implies part (b), as evident from Figure 1. Part (c) comes from the definition of g and parts (a) and (b). Part (d) comes from equations (8).

The usefulness of Lemma 1 is that, as will be shown later, if both firms are producing positive outputs, the output quality chosen by the foreign firm e_f must be small enough so that condition (9) holds.

Recall the marginal consumer given by (2). Using function $g(e_h, e_f, \lambda)$ and the price equations (6), the marginal consumer can also be defined as

$$\hat{\theta} = \frac{\overline{\theta} + \underline{\theta} + g}{3}. \tag{10}$$

The necessary and sufficient condition (3) for a duopoly equilibrium with positive outputs by both firms reduces to

$$2\underline{\theta} - \overline{\theta} < g < 2\overline{\theta} - \underline{\theta}. \tag{11}$$

We now turn to the first stage, in which the two firms choose quality levels to maximize their own profits. Define the following function:

$$\Theta(e_h, e_f; \lambda) = (2\overline{\theta} - \underline{\theta} - g)(2\overline{\theta} - \underline{\theta} - 2c_h' + g), \tag{12}$$

where $c_h' \equiv c'(e_h)$. It is easy to show that the partial differentiation of home firm's profit function in (7a) with respect to e_h, taking e_f as given, is equal to $\Theta(e_h, e_f; \lambda)/9$. Thus the first-order condition is $\Theta(e_h, e_f; \lambda) = 0$, which, according to (12), implies two solutions,

$$2\overline{\theta} - \underline{\theta} - 2c_h' + g = 0 \tag{13a}$$

$$2\overline{\theta} - \underline{\theta} - g = 0. \tag{13b}$$

Note that the solution in (13b) implies zero profit of the home firm. Denote the partial derivatives of function Θ by

$$\Theta_h \equiv \partial\Theta / \partial e_h, \ \Theta_f \equiv \partial\Theta / \partial e_f, \text{ and } \Theta_\lambda \equiv \partial\Theta / \partial\lambda. \tag{14}$$

The second derivative of the profit function with respect to e_h is equal to $\Theta_h/9$, where $\Theta_h = (2\overline{\theta} - \underline{\theta} - g)(g_h - 2c_h'') - g_h(2\overline{\theta} - \underline{\theta} - 2c_h' + g)$, and $c_h'' \equiv c''(e_h)$. Using condition (13b), equation (14) reduces to $\Theta_h = 2g_h(c_h' - g) > 0$.
Suppose now that condition (13a) holds. Then $2\overline{\theta} - \underline{\theta} > g$, and

$$\Theta_h = (2\overline{\theta} - \underline{\theta} - g)(g_h - 2c_h'') < 0, \tag{15}$$

where the sign is due to the assumption that the quality improvement function $c(e_h)$ is sufficiently convex so that $2c_h'' > g_h > 0$. Thus the solution in (13b) gives a minimum and that in (13a) leads to a maximum. We now consider only condition (13a) but not (13b). Condition (13a) gives the reaction function of the home firm, $e_h = R_h(e_f)$.

The same analysis can be applied to the foreign firm. Denote the partial derivative of the foreign firm's profit function (7b) with respect to e_f (keeping e_h constant) by $\Phi(e_h, e_f; \lambda)/9$, where

$$\Phi(e_h, e_f; \lambda) = (g - 2\underline{\theta} + \overline{\theta})(g + 2\underline{\theta} - \overline{\theta} - 2c_f'), \tag{16}$$

where $c_f' \equiv \lambda c'(e_f)$. The first-order condition is $\Phi(e_h, e_f; \lambda) = 0$. From (16), two roots exist:

$$g + 2\underline{\theta} - \overline{\theta} - 2c_f' = 0 \tag{17a}$$

$$g - 2\underline{\theta} + \overline{\theta} = 0. \tag{17b}$$

The root given by (17b) corresponds to a minimum, with the foreign firm earning zero profit. The solution corresponding to (17a) gives a maximum, as long as $g_f - 2c''_f < 0$, where $c''_f \equiv \lambda c''(e_f)$.[7] Condition (17a) gives the foreign firm's reaction function $e_f = R_f(e_h)$, as long as the foreign firm is making a positive profit.[8] At this maximum, (11) implies that $g > 2\underline{\theta} - \overline{\theta}$. Alternatively, we can say that if it is known that the foreign firm produces a positive output, (17a) implies that condition (9) is satisfied, and by Lemma 1, g_h, $g_f > 0$.

Thus, the Nash equilibrium with positive outputs by both firms can be described by the following conditions:

$$\Theta(e_h, e_f; \lambda) = 0 \tag{18}$$

$$\Phi(e_h, e_f; \lambda) = 0. \tag{19}$$

Using the derivatives of function g and the first-order conditions of the firms, we can show that $\Theta_f = \Phi_h = 2(e_h - e_f)g_h g_f > 0$. Denote the free-trade Nash equilibrium by (e_h^f, e_f^f), which satisfies conditions (18) and (19). Once the quality improvements chosen by the firms are determined, the market prices and firms' profits can be obtained from equations (6) and (7).

In the above analysis, it is assumed that both firms produce positive outputs of the product. In general, when the technology gap between the firms is not big, i.e., λ is only slightly greater than unity, the firms will share the market approximately equally. We now want to see what difference it will make if the technology gap becomes larger, with λ being treated as a parameter.

Lemma 2. *An increase in the technology gap between the firms will increase home firm's profit but lower foreign firm's profit. However, the impacts on the consumer surplus and home welfare are ambiguous.*

Proof. Differentiating equations (18) and (19) with respect to λ yields

$$\begin{bmatrix} \Theta_h & \Theta_f \\ \Phi_h & \Phi_f \end{bmatrix} \begin{bmatrix} \partial e_h^f / \partial \lambda \\ \partial e_f^f / \partial \lambda \end{bmatrix} = \begin{bmatrix} (2\overline{\theta} - \underline{\theta} - g)c(e_f)/(e_h - e_f) \\ (g - 2\underline{\theta} + \overline{\theta})\{2c'(e_f) + [c(e_f)/(e_h - e_f)]\} \end{bmatrix}.$$

Solving these two equations, we get

[7] The second-order condition is satisfied: $\Phi_f = (g - 2\underline{\theta} + \overline{\theta})(g_f - 2c''_f) < 0$.

[8] If the optimal quality improvement level and the corresponding output implied by (17a) lead to zero profit, the foreign firm is indifferent to this outcome and no production. In this case, we assume that the foreign firm will choose not to produce.

$$\frac{\partial e_h^f}{\partial \lambda} = -\frac{c'(e_f)g_f + [\lambda c''(e_f)c(e_f)/(e_h - e_f)]}{2\lambda c''(e_h)c''(e_f) - c''(e_h)g_f - \lambda c''(e_f)g_h} < 0$$

$$\frac{\partial e_f^f}{\partial \lambda} = -\frac{c'(e_f)[2c''(e_h) - g_h] + [c''(e_h)c(e_f)/(e_h - e_f)]}{2\lambda c''(e_h)c''(e_f) - c''(e_h)g_f - \lambda c''(e_f)g_h} < 0.$$

Thus, we have

$$\frac{\mathrm{d}\pi_h^f}{\mathrm{d}\lambda} = \frac{\partial \pi_h^f}{\partial \lambda} + \frac{\partial \pi_h^f}{\partial e_f}\frac{\partial e_f^f}{\partial \lambda} > 0, \tag{20}$$

because $\partial \pi_h^f / \partial \lambda = 2c(e_f^f)(\bar{\theta} - \hat{\theta})/3 > 0$, $\partial \pi_h^f / \partial e_f = -(\bar{\theta} - \underline{\theta})(\bar{\theta} - \hat{\theta}) < 0$. We also have

$$\frac{\mathrm{d}\pi_f^f}{\mathrm{d}\lambda} = \frac{\partial \pi_f^f}{\partial \lambda} + \frac{\partial \pi_f^f}{\partial e_h}\frac{\partial e_h^f}{\partial \lambda} < 0, \tag{21}$$

because $\partial \pi_f^f / \partial \lambda = -2c(e_f^f)(\hat{\theta} - \underline{\theta})/3 < 0$, $\partial \pi_f^f / \partial e_h = (\bar{\theta} - \underline{\theta})(\hat{\theta} - \underline{\theta}) > 0$. Furthermore,

$$\frac{\mathrm{d}CS^f}{\mathrm{d}\lambda} = \frac{\partial CS^f}{\partial \lambda} + \frac{\partial CS^f}{\partial e_h}\frac{\partial e_h^f}{\partial \lambda} + \frac{\partial CS^f}{\partial e_f}\frac{\partial e_f^f}{\partial \lambda},$$

where $\partial CS^f / \partial \lambda = c(e_f^f)(2\underline{\theta} - \bar{\theta} - \hat{\theta})/3 < 0$, $\partial CS^f / \partial e_h = (\bar{\theta} - \underline{\theta})(2\underline{\theta} - \bar{\theta} - \hat{\theta})/2 < 0$ and $\partial CS^f / \partial e_f = (\bar{\theta} - \underline{\theta})(2\bar{\theta} - \hat{\theta} - \underline{\theta})/2 > 0$. The direct effect of λ on consumer surplus is always negative, but the indirect effect is ambiguous because of the opposite effects of high quality and low quality on consumer surplus. Thus, the overall effect of λ on consumer surplus is ambiguous *a priori*. Similarly, the overall effect of λ on the home welfare is ambiguous *a priori*.

Because of equation (21), let λ^c be the value of λ so that the resulting $\pi_f^f = 0$, i.e., λ^c is the value of λ that will lead to zero foreign profit. At λ^c, the foreign firm is indifferent to improving the quality of the product and producing nothing. In such a situation, the foreign firm is assumed to choose not to produce and export. The corresponding value of g is denoted by $g^c \equiv g(e_h^f(\lambda^c), e_f^f(\lambda^c), \lambda^c)$.

The Nash equilibrium can be illustrated in a simple diagram. In Figure 2, schedule AB represents condition (18) and schedule CE represents condition (19). Their slopes are given by

$$\left.\frac{\partial e_h}{\partial e_f}\right|_{\mathrm{AB}} = -\frac{\Theta_f}{\Theta_h} > 0$$

$$\left.\frac{\partial e_h}{\partial e_f}\right|_{\mathrm{CE}} = -\frac{\Phi_f}{\Phi_h} > 0,$$

where the analysis given above is used to determine the signs of the slopes. The diagram shows the case in which schedule CE is steeper than AB.[9] The diagram also shows schedule HK, which represents $g(e_h, e_f, \lambda^c) = g^c$, i.e., the locus of (e_h, e_f) that, when $\lambda = \lambda^c$, will give a value of g equal to g^c. Schedules CE and HK intersect at point D.

Based on the above analysis, the reaction curve of the foreign firm is represented by line segment OF, which is part of the vertical axis, plus DC, the part of CE above schedule HK. Note that on DC, the foreign firm is able to get a positive profit when reacting to the home firm's quality improvement. The resulting Nash equilibrium is at point N, at which DC and AB intersect.

Lemma 2 can be illustrated in Figure 2. An increase in λ will shift schedule AB down and schedule CE to the left. Let the new schedules be AB′ and C′E′, respectively, which intersect at point N′, $(e_h^{f\prime}, e_f^{f\prime})$, the new Nash equilibrium, with both firms making smaller quality improvement than before.

Since the Nash equilibrium depends on the value of λ, we can express the quality improvement levels chosen by the firms as the following functions $e_h^f = e_h^f(\lambda)$ and $e_f^f = e_f^f(\lambda)$, which depend negatively on λ. Graphically, if we increase λ gradually, the resulting Nash equilibria will trace out a locus shown in Figure 3. Let us call this locus the *quality competition* (*QC*) *schedule*.[10]

Along the QC schedule, the rate of change of function $g(e_h(\lambda), e_f(\lambda), \lambda)$ is

$$\left.\frac{dg}{d\lambda}\right|_{QC} = \frac{\partial g}{\partial e_h}\frac{\partial e_h}{\partial \lambda} + \frac{\partial g}{\partial e_f}\frac{\partial e_f}{\partial \lambda} + \frac{\partial g}{\partial \lambda} < 0.$$

Recall that when $g = g^c = 2\underline{\theta} - \bar{\theta}$, or $\lambda = \lambda^c$, the profit of the foreign firm is zero. In Figure 3, schedule HK represents the equation $g(e_h, e_f, \lambda^c) = g^c$, which gives the combinations of the firms' quality improvement levels, when given λ^c, so that the value of g remains at g^c.[11]

However, when $\lambda = \lambda^c$, there is a strategy for the home firm to earn a profit more than what point N′ represents. What it should do, as the following proposition shows, is to regard itself as a monopolist, as Section 2.2 describes.

---

[9] This is the usual "stability" condition. While in the present one-shot game stability has no meaning, the present condition gives "normal" comparative static results.

[10] The quality competition schedule is defined by the two parametric equations: $e_h^n = e_h^n(\lambda)$ and $e_f^n = e_f^n(\lambda)$. By lemma 2, it is positively sloped, and the value of λ increases along the schedule toward the vertical axis.

[11] There may be a question of whether the QC schedule and schedule HK do not cut each other at a point when e_h and e_f are non-negative. The answer is in the negation because if $g > g^c$, then when $e_f = 0$, $c'(e_f) = 0$ and π_f is increasing in e_f. This means that when $g > g^c$, the foreign firm will want to improve its output quality, and schedule QC will not cut the vertical axis first before cutting schedule HK.

Proposition 1. There exists a critical value λ^c so that if $\lambda < \lambda^c$, an international duopoly equilibrium exists with both firms earning positive profits. If $\lambda \geq \lambda^c$, then the home firm will behave as a local monopolist, with zero import from the foreign firm.

Proof. We have already analyzed the case in which $\lambda < \lambda^c$. When $\lambda = \lambda^c$, the foreign firm earns zero profit at the Nash equilibrium, and we assume that it will choose not to enter the market. When $\lambda > \lambda^c$, the foreign firm earns negative profit at a Nash equilibrium, and it is better off by not entering the market. As for the home firm, when $\lambda \geq \lambda^c$, the home firm can choose the monopolistic equilibrium, which will give it the highest possible profit. It does not have to worry about the possible entry of the foreign firm as it will get negative profit if it does try to enter the market.

Note that there is an alternative case not shown in Figures 2 and 3. If, however, point A is above point H, meaning that AB does not cut schedule HK. Then the Nash equilibrium is always above HK, implying that the foreign firm can always get a positive profit in a Nash equilibrium. Thus a duopoly equilibrium always exists.

4 Minimum Quality Standard

In this section, we examine the use of a minimum quality standard (MQS) policy by the foreign government while the home government still allows free trade. We want to analyze how the foreign government may use this policy to improve its national welfare.

Assuming that the foreign government is able to announce and precommit a policy before the firms compete, we extend the model introduced above to a three-stage model. For a reasonable analysis in this section, λ is assumed to be sufficiently small so that an international duopoly exists with or without a MQS policy. The second and third stages are similar to the two stages analyzed in the previous model, with the firms competing in quality and then in price. In the first stage, the foreign government sets a MQS for the output of the foreign firm, $\bar{s}_f$. Thus the product produced by the foreign firm has to be of quality not less than $\bar{s}_f$ before it is allowed to be exported. The policy constraint is binding (not binding), if $s_f^f = s_0 + e_f^f < (\geq)\ \bar{s}_f$.

As usual, the game is solved by backward induction. The present second and third stages are the same as the two stages of the previous model, except that the quality level of the foreign output is $\bar{s}_f$, if the policy constraint is binding.[12] This means

[12] As will be explained later, the optimal MQS chosen by the foreign government will be binding.

that the first-order condition of the foreign firm is no longer applicable. In the first stage, the foreign government solves the following problem: to choose a MQS $\overline{s}_f$ to maximize the national welfare, which is equal to the foreign firm's profits, making use of the reaction function of the home firm, $R_h(e_f)$.[13] Differentiate the foreign firm's profit function with respect to the quality level to get:

$$\begin{aligned}\frac{\mathrm{d}\pi_f}{\mathrm{d}s_f} &= \frac{\mathrm{d}\pi_f}{\mathrm{d}e_f} \\ &= \frac{\partial \pi_f}{\partial e_f} + \frac{\partial \pi_f}{\partial e_h}\frac{\partial R_h(e_f)}{\partial e_f} \\ &= \frac{1}{9}(g - 2\underline{\theta} + \overline{\theta})[2\underline{\theta} - \overline{\theta} - 2\lambda c'(e_f) + g] \\ &\quad + \frac{1}{9}(g - 2\underline{\theta} + \overline{\theta})[2c'(e_h) - g - 2\underline{\theta} + \overline{\theta}]\frac{\partial R_h(e_f)}{\partial e_f} \\ &= \frac{g - 2\underline{\theta} + \overline{\theta}}{9}\left[2c'(e_h) - 2\lambda c'(e_f) - 3(\overline{\theta} - \underline{\theta})\left(1 - \frac{\partial R_h(e_f)}{\partial e_f}\right)\right].\end{aligned} \tag{22}$$

Note that $\partial R_h(e_f)/\partial e_f$ is the slope of schedule AB in Figure 2. Evaluate the derivative in (22) at the free-trade Nash equilibrium to give

$$\left.\frac{\mathrm{d}\pi_f}{\mathrm{d}s_f}\right|_{s_f = s_f^f} = \frac{\partial \pi_f}{\partial e_h}\frac{\partial R_h(e_f)}{\partial e_f} = \frac{1}{3}(\overline{\theta} - \underline{\theta})(g - 2\underline{\theta} + \overline{\theta})\frac{\partial R_h(e_f)}{\partial e_f} > 0. \tag{23}$$

Condition (23) implies that the foreign government has an incentive to impose a MQS at least slightly higher than the free trade level. Because the quality improvement cost becomes prohibitively high when e_f is large, the foreign government will never want to impose a MQS too high. Thus we conclude that the optimal MQS for the foreign country is finite and higher than the free-trade level. At the maximum, $\mathrm{d}\pi_f/\mathrm{d}s_f = 0$, which, by condition (22), implies[14]

$$\partial R_h(e_f)/\partial e_f < 1. \tag{24}$$

Differentiate the home profit with respect to the MQS to give,

$$\frac{\mathrm{d}\pi_h}{\mathrm{d}s_f} = \frac{\mathrm{d}\pi_h}{\mathrm{d}e_f} = \frac{\partial \pi_h}{\partial e_h}\frac{\partial R_h(e_f)}{\partial e_f} + \frac{\partial \pi_h}{\partial e_f} = \frac{\partial \pi_h}{\partial e_f} < 0, \tag{25}$$

---

[13] The home firm's reaction function is defined in (13a).

[14] Note that in (22), $g > 2\underline{\theta} - \overline{\theta}$ and $c'(e_h) > \lambda c'(e_f)$.

where the first-order condition of the home firm has been used. Condition (25) implies that the home firm is hurt by the MQS.

From equation (22), it is easy to see how the MQS works: The equilibrium is moved from the free-trade Nash equilibrium to the Stackelberg leader point, with the foreign firm acting as a leader. Without any government intervention, the foreign firm can hardly achieve this equilibrium because any attempt to convince the home firm to produce an output with a higher standard is not credible. Now with the MQS, an announcement by the foreign firm to produce an output with a higher standard becomes credible. The present policy, like the Brander-Spencer type export subsidies (Brander and Spencer 1985), has the effect of improving the profit of the foreign firm while hurting the home firm, the so-called profit-shifting effect. However, two differences between the present policy and the Brander-Spencer type export subsidies can be noted: MQS does not appear to be a trade policy, and due to the asymmetry between the two firms, MQS does not work for the home country.[15]

The impact of the MQS $\bar{s}_f$ on consumer surplus of the home country is

$$\begin{aligned}\frac{\mathrm{d}CS}{\mathrm{d}s_f} &= \frac{\mathrm{d}CS}{\mathrm{d}e_f} \\ &= \frac{\partial CS}{\partial e_h}\frac{\partial R_h(e_f)}{\partial e_f} + \frac{\partial CS}{\partial e_f} \\ &= \frac{1}{2}(\bar{\theta} - \underline{\theta})[(2\underline{\theta} - \bar{\theta} - \hat{\theta})\frac{\partial R_h(e_f)}{\partial e_f} + (2\bar{\theta} - \hat{\theta} - \underline{\theta})] \\ &> \frac{1}{2}(\bar{\theta} - \underline{\theta})(\bar{\theta} + \underline{\theta} - 2\hat{\theta}) \\ &> 0,\end{aligned}$$

where the first inequality in equation (26) comes from the condition (24) and the second inequality in equation (26) comes from the fact that $\hat{\theta} < (\bar{\theta} + \underline{\theta})/2$.[16] Thus, a foreign MQS always benefits the home consumers. The total effect of the MQS on the home welfare is

---

[15] With a given market, the foreign firm wants the home firm to choose a higher standard of its output so that it can have an output with a higher quality in order to capture a bigger share of the market. Conversely, the home firm wants the foreign firm to choose a lower quality so that it can capture a bigger share of the market.

[16] With cost advantage, the home firm producing the higher quality product must earn higher profits than the foreign firm producing the lower quality product, otherwise the former can always get higher profits than the latter's duopoly profits by deviating to produce the lower quality product instead. Thus, $9\pi_h = (e_h - e_f)(2\bar{\theta} - \underline{\theta} - g)^2 > (e_h - e_f)(g - 2\underline{\theta} + \bar{\theta})^2 = 9\pi_f$, implying that $g < (\bar{\theta} + \underline{\theta})/2$ and $\hat{\theta} = (\bar{\theta} + \underline{\theta} + g)/3 < (\bar{\theta} + \underline{\theta})/2$.

$$
\begin{aligned}
\frac{\mathrm{d}W_h}{\mathrm{d}s_f} &= \frac{\mathrm{d}W_h}{\mathrm{d}e_f} \\
&= \frac{\partial CS}{\partial e_h}\frac{\partial R_h(e_f)}{\partial e_f} + \frac{\partial CS}{\partial e_f} + \frac{\partial \pi_h}{\partial e_f} \\
&= \frac{1}{2}(\bar{\theta} - \underline{\theta})[(2\underline{\theta} - \bar{\theta} - \hat{\theta})\frac{\partial R_h(e_f)}{\partial e_f} + (\hat{\theta} - \underline{\theta})] \\
&= \frac{1}{2}(\bar{\theta} - \underline{\theta})[(\hat{\theta} - \underline{\theta}) - (\bar{\theta} + \hat{\theta} - 2\underline{\theta})\frac{\partial R_h(e_f)}{\partial e_f}].
\end{aligned} \tag{27}
$$

The sign of $\mathrm{d}W_h / \mathrm{d}s_f$ is in general ambiguous and depends on, among other things, the value of $\partial R_h(e_f)/\partial e_f$. We have the following proposition:

Proposition 2. When the home country imports the low-quality good, a MQS on the product benefits the home country if the marginal cost function is weakly convex, i.e., $c'''(e_i) \geq 0$.

Proof. From (13a), $g = 2c'(e_h) + \underline{\theta} - 2\bar{\theta}$, so

$$
\frac{(\hat{\theta} - \underline{\theta})}{(\bar{\theta} + \hat{\theta} - 2\underline{\theta})} = \frac{\bar{\theta} - 2\underline{\theta} + g}{4\bar{\theta} - 5\underline{\theta} + g} = \frac{c'(e_h) - (\bar{\theta} + \underline{\theta})/2}{c'(e_h) + \bar{\theta} - 2\underline{\theta}}. \tag{28}
$$

From equation (22), we know that when $\mathrm{d}\pi_f / \mathrm{d}s_f = 0$, $c'(e_h) - \lambda c'(e_f) = 3(\bar{\theta} - \underline{\theta})[1 - \partial R_h(e_f)/\partial e_f]/2$. Thus

$$
\begin{aligned}
\frac{\partial R_h(e_f)}{\partial e_f} &= -\frac{\Theta_f}{\Theta_h} \\
&= \frac{g_f}{2c''(e_h) - g_h} \\
&= \frac{g - \lambda c'(e_f)}{2c''(e_h)(e_h - e_f) - c'(e_h) + g} \\
&= \frac{c'(e_h) - \lambda c'(e_f) + c'(e_h) + \underline{\theta} - 2\bar{\theta}}{2c''(e_h)(e_h - e_f) + c'(e_h) + \underline{\theta} - 2\bar{\theta}} \\
&= \frac{3(\bar{\theta} - \underline{\theta})(1 - \partial R_h(e_f)/\partial e_f)/2 + c'(e_h) + \underline{\theta} - 2\bar{\theta}}{2c''(e_h)(e_h - e_f) + c'(e_h) + \underline{\theta} - 2\bar{\theta}}.
\end{aligned}
$$

After rearranging terms, we get

$$\frac{\partial R_h(e_f)}{\partial e_f} = \frac{c'(e_h) - (\bar{\theta} + \underline{\theta})/2}{2c''(e_h)(e_h - e_f) + c'(e_h) - (\bar{\theta} + \underline{\theta})/2}. \tag{29}$$

From equation (27), we know that $\mathrm{d}W_h / \mathrm{d}s_f > 0$ if $(\hat{\theta} - \underline{\theta}) / (\bar{\theta} + \hat{\theta} - 2\underline{\theta}) > \partial R_h(e_f)/\partial e_f$, i.e.,

$$c''(e_h) > \frac{3(\bar{\theta} - \underline{\theta})}{4(e_h - e_f)}, \tag{30}$$

by comparing equations (28) and (29). If $c'''(e_i) \geq 0$,

$$c''(e_h) > \frac{c'(e_h) - c'(e_f)}{e_h - e_f} > \frac{c'(e_h) - \lambda c'(e_f)}{e_h - e_f} = g_h + g_f,$$

which implies that

$$\frac{\partial R_h(e_f)}{\partial e_f} = \frac{g_f}{2c''(e_h) - g_h} < \frac{c''(e_h) - g_h}{2c''(e_h) - g_h} < \frac{1}{2}.$$

Condition (30) is thus satisfied because

$$c''(e_h) > \frac{c'(e_h) - \lambda c'(e_f)}{e_h - e_f} = \frac{3(\bar{\theta} - \underline{\theta})}{2(e_h - e_f)}\left(1 - \frac{\partial R_h(e_f)}{\partial e_f}\right) > \frac{3(\bar{\theta} - \underline{\theta})}{4(e_h - e_f)}. \tag{}$$

Under the duopoly model in a closed economy, Crampes and Hollander (1995) show that if the quality response by the high-quality firm is less than the increase in quality by the low-quality firm (i.e., $\partial R_h(e_f)/\partial e_f < 1$ in terms of our notation), a MQS will increase the social welfare. However, when we consider an open economy in which the foreign firm exports to the home country, the necessary (but not sufficient) condition to make the MQS increase the home welfare is $\partial R_h(e_f)/\partial e_f < 1/3$, which is much stricter.[17]

Comparing our results with those in Das and Donnenfeld (1989), one can find two differences. First, it is easy to check that $\mathrm{d}q_f / \mathrm{d}s_f > 0$ and $\mathrm{d}q_h / \mathrm{d}s_f < 0$. Thus, a

[17] From equation (27), we know that $\mathrm{d}W_h / \mathrm{d}s_f > 0$ if $[(\hat{\theta} - \underline{\theta}) / (\bar{\theta} + \hat{\theta} - 2\underline{\theta})] > \partial R_h(e_f)/\partial e_f$. Due to the fact $\hat{\theta} < (\bar{\theta} + \underline{\theta})/2$ mentioned in footnote 16, $(\hat{\theta} - \underline{\theta}) / (\bar{\theta} + \hat{\theta} - 2\underline{\theta}) < 1/3$. Thus, $\partial R_h(e_f)/\partial e_f < 1/3$ is a necessary (but not sufficient) condition for a foreign MQS beneficial to the home country.

MQS increases the volume of exports to the home market while reduces the sales volume of the domestic good. However, a MQS reduces both firms' sales in Das and Donnenfeld (1989). Second, Proposition 2 shows that a MQS may benefit the home country. However, in Das and Donnenfeld (1989) a MQS always hurts the home country.

Proposition 2 provides some situations in which the home country may benefit from the foreign government's MQS policy. In fact, it also implies that the home government may increase its welfare by setting a MQS on the imports if the foreign government does not take any MQS policy. However, in Das and Donnenfeld (1989), the home government has no incentive to adopt a MQS policy because it always hurts the home country.

5 Minimum Quality Standard and Tariff

As explained, a MQS imposed by the foreign government has an adverse effect on the profit of the home firm. The home country thus has an incentive to retaliate, for example, with a tariff. It is well known that tariff is a policy to shift profit from a foreign monopolist to a domestic firm. As a result, a tariff can be used as a counteracting policy to protect the domestic firm. This section examines the interactions between the two governments when trying to protect their own firms. Two cases are considered: the case in which both governments choose their policies simultaneously, and the case in which the foreign government takes the first move.

5.1 Simultaneous Policies

We now modify the above three-stage game. In the first stage of the present game, the foreign government chooses a MQS and the home government chooses a tariff at the same time. In the second stage, taking the policy parameters as given, both firms choose qualities and then in the third stage they choose prices of their outputs, all in a non-cooperative way. As usual, the game is solved by backward induction. For the time being, we can assume that no MQS is imposed, or if one is imposed, it is not binding.

The third and second stages are the same as the second and first stages in Section 3, respectively, except that $\lambda c(e_f)$ is replaced by $\lambda c(e_f)+t$. Using a "tilde" to denote the variables when both governments choose policies simultaneously, the third-stage equilibrium prices are

$$\tilde{p}_h = \alpha + \frac{1}{3}\left[2c(e_h) + \lambda c(e_f) + t + (2\overline{\theta} - \underline{\theta})(e_h - e_f)\right] \tag{31a}$$

$$\tilde{p}_f = \alpha + \frac{1}{3}[c(e_h) + 2\lambda c(e_f) + 2t - (2\underline{\theta} - \overline{\theta})(e_h - e_f)], \tag{31b}$$

and the resulting profits of the firms are

$$\tilde{\pi}_h = \frac{1}{9}(e_h - e_f)(2\overline{\theta} - \underline{\theta} - \tilde{g})^2 \tag{32a}$$

$$\tilde{\pi}_f = \frac{1}{9}(e_h - e_f)(\tilde{g} - 2\underline{\theta} + \overline{\theta})^2, \tag{32b}$$

where $\tilde{g} = \tilde{g}(e_h, e_f, t, \lambda) = [c(e_h) - \lambda c(e_f) - t]/(e_h - e_f)$ for $e_h > 0,\ e_f \geq 0$. The new first-order conditions in the second stage are

$$\tilde{\Theta}(e_h, e_f, t, \lambda) = 0 \tag{33a}$$

$$\tilde{\Phi}(e_h, e_f, t, \lambda) = 0. \tag{33b}$$

Note that equations (33) are written as if the MQS is not binding. If it is, then e_f is equal to the one set by the government, and condition (33b) is not applicable. Conditions (33) give the reaction functions of the home firm and the foreign firm, $R_h(e_f, t)$ and $R_f(e_h, t)$, respectively. Solving conditions (33) gives the Nash equilibrium quality improvements, which are denoted by $(\tilde{e}_h(t),\ \tilde{e}_f(t))$. Note that $(\tilde{e}_h(t=0),\ \tilde{e}_f(t=0)) = (e_h^f,\ e_f^f)$, which is the free-trade Nash equilibrium derived in Section 3.

It is easy to show that $\tilde{\Theta}_t = \partial\tilde{\Theta}/\partial t < 0$ and $\tilde{\Phi}_t = \partial\tilde{\Phi}/\partial t < 0$, implying that in Figure 2 a rise in t will shift schedule AB down and DE to the left. Differentiating equations (33) with respect to t yields

$$\begin{bmatrix} \tilde{\Theta}_h & \tilde{\Theta}_f \\ \tilde{\Phi}_h & \tilde{\Phi}_f \end{bmatrix} \begin{bmatrix} \partial\tilde{e}_h/\partial t \\ \partial\tilde{e}_f/\partial t \end{bmatrix} = \begin{bmatrix} -\tilde{\Theta}_t \\ -\tilde{\Phi}_t \end{bmatrix},$$

which can be solved to give $\partial\tilde{e}_h/\partial t < 0$ and $\partial\tilde{e}_f/\partial t < 0$. Thus, if initially both firms are producing with positive outputs, a small rise in t (with the MQS not binding) will lead to a small decrease in the quality of the products produced by both firms.

We now analyze the first stage of the game. As in the previous case, the optimal MQS chosen by the foreign government will be binding. This means that the foreign firm's first-order condition (33b) and reaction function $R_f(e_h, t)$ do not exist. Substituting the reaction function of the home firm into equation (32b), we get the foreign firm's profit as a function of the MQS e_f and the tariff rate t.

The problem of the foreign government is to choose a MQS $\bar{s}_f$ to maximize the profits of the foreign firm, taking the specific tariff t as given. The first-order condition is

$$\frac{\mathrm{d}\tilde{\pi}_f}{\mathrm{d}s_f} = \frac{\mathrm{d}\tilde{\pi}_f}{\mathrm{d}e_f} = \frac{\partial \tilde{\pi}_f}{\partial e_f} + \frac{\partial \tilde{\pi}_f}{\partial e_h}\frac{\partial R_h(e_f, t)}{\partial e_f} = 0, \tag{34}$$

which gives the reaction function of the foreign government, $\bar{s}_f(t)$, in terms of t. To see how an interior solution for the foreign government exists, note that

$$\left.\frac{\mathrm{d}\tilde{\pi}_f}{\mathrm{d}s_f}\right|_{s_f = s_0 + \tilde{e}_f} = \frac{\partial \tilde{\pi}_f}{\partial e_h}\frac{\partial R_h(e_f, t)}{\partial e_f} > 0.$$

This implies that even in the presence of a tariff imposed by the home government, the foreign government still has an incentive to impose a MQS. The second-order condition $\mathrm{d}^2\tilde{\pi}_f / \mathrm{d}s_f^2 < 0$ is assumed to be satisfied. The slope of the reaction function of the foreign government $\bar{s}_f(t)$ is given by

$$\frac{\partial \bar{s}_f}{\partial t} = -\frac{\mathrm{d}^2\tilde{\pi}_f / \mathrm{d}s_f \mathrm{d}t}{\mathrm{d}^2\tilde{\pi}_f / \mathrm{d}s_f^2}.$$

The sign of $\mathrm{d}^2\tilde{\pi}_f / \mathrm{d}s_f \mathrm{d}t$ is in general ambiguous. However, if $c'''(e_i) \geq 0$, then $\mathrm{d}^2\tilde{\pi}_f / \mathrm{d}t\mathrm{d}s_f < 0$ and $\partial \bar{s}_f / \partial t < 0$,[18] meaning that the level of the MQS decreases as the home tariff increases. This result is different from Krishna (1987), indicating that a specific tariff raises quality and lowers imports when the marginal customer with higher willingness to pay has a higher valuation of an increment in quality.[19]

Proposition 3. When the foreign firm produces the low-quality good, the foreign government has an incentive to set a MQS on its export to increase the foreign firm's profit, whether or not the home government imposes a specific tariff. The specific tariff imposed by the home government, if exists, will decrease the quality levels of the home and foreign goods.

We now turn to the policy of the home government. Taking the foreign government's MQS $\bar{s}_f$ as given, the home government's problem is to choose a specific tariff t to maximize the home welfare, which is defined as $\tilde{W}_h \equiv \tilde{\pi}_h + \tilde{C}S + t\tilde{q}_f$. The first-order condition is

---

[18] Please see Appendix A for details.

[19] In our model, the valuation of an increment in quality by the customers buying the domestic (foreign) goods is $\partial p_h / \partial e_h = \hat{\theta} + \bar{\theta} - \underline{\theta}$ ($\partial p_f / \partial e_f = \hat{\theta} + \underline{\theta} - \bar{\theta}$), which increases as $\hat{\theta}$ increases. Thus, the marginal customer indexed by $\hat{\theta}$ has a higher valuation of an increment in quality no matter whether he purchases the domestic or foreign good.

$$\frac{\mathrm{d}\tilde{W}_h}{\mathrm{d}t} = \frac{\partial \tilde{\pi}_h}{\partial t} + \frac{\partial \tilde{C}S}{\partial t} + \frac{\partial \tilde{C}S}{\partial e_h}\frac{\partial R_h(e_f,t)}{\partial t} + \tilde{q}_f + t\left(\frac{\partial \tilde{q}_f}{\partial t} + \frac{\partial \tilde{q}_f}{\partial e_h}\frac{\partial R_h(e_f,t)}{\partial t}\right)$$
$$= \frac{(\overline{\theta}-\underline{\theta})[2c''(e_h)(e_h-e_f)+2c'(e_h)-(\overline{\theta}+\underline{\theta})]-2c''(e_h)t}{3(e_h-e_f)[2c''(e_h)-(\partial\tilde{g}/\partial e_h)]} \quad (35)$$
$$= 0.$$

Assuming that the second-order condition $\mathrm{d}^2\tilde{W}_h/\mathrm{d}t^2 < 0$ is satisfied, condition (35) provides the reaction function of the home government $t(\overline{s}_f)$, and its slope is given by

$$\frac{\partial t}{\partial \overline{s}_f} = -\frac{\mathrm{d}^2\tilde{W}_h/\mathrm{d}t\mathrm{d}s_f}{\mathrm{d}^2\tilde{W}_h/\mathrm{d}t^2}.$$

The sign of $\mathrm{d}^2\tilde{W}_h/\mathrm{d}t\mathrm{d}s_f$ is in general ambiguous. If, however, $c'''(e_i)\geq 0$, then $\mathrm{d}^2\tilde{W}_h/\mathrm{d}t\mathrm{d}s_f<0$ and $\partial t/\partial\overline{s}_f<0$,[20] meaning that the optimal tariff decreases as the level of MQS increases. Thus, if $c'''(e_i)\geq 0$, then $\overline{s}_f$ and t are strategic substitutes. It can be shown that $\mathrm{d}\tilde{W}_h/\mathrm{d}t(t=0)>0$, implying that at least a small positive tariff is welfare improving. Let us assume the existence of an interior solution $(\overline{s}_f^n, t^n)$, for equations (34) and (35).

Graphically, the above analysis can be illustrated by Figure 4. The home and foreign's reaction functions are illustrated by schedule AB and DE, respectively. The diagram shows the case in which $c'''(e_i)\geq 0$, meaning that both schedules are negatively sloped. For normal "stability" or normal comparative static results, schedule DE is steeper than AB. The Nash equilibrium is at point N, at which AB and DE cut each other. The diagram also shows several iso-welfare contours of the foreign government. One of them, labeled u_f^n, passes through point N, with a welfare level equal to u_f^n.

---

[20] Totally differentiating equation (35) with respect to s_f to give

$$\frac{\mathrm{d}^2\tilde{W}_h}{\mathrm{d}t\mathrm{d}s_f} = \frac{\partial(\mathrm{d}\tilde{W}_h/\mathrm{d}t)}{\partial e_h}\frac{\partial R_h(e_f,t)}{\partial e_f} + \frac{\partial(\mathrm{d}\tilde{W}_h/\mathrm{d}t)}{\partial e_f}$$
$$= \frac{2(\overline{\theta}-\underline{\theta})c''(e_h)[2(\partial R_h/\partial e_f)-1]+2c'''(e_h)[(\overline{\theta}-\underline{\theta})(e_h-e_f)-t](\partial R_h/\partial e_f)}{3(e_h-e_f)[2c''(e_h)-(\partial\tilde{g}/\partial e_h)]}$$

Assume that $c'''(e_i)$ is small enough so that we can ignore the term with $c'''(e_h)$. If $c'''(e_i)\geq 0$, $c''(e_h)>\partial\tilde{g}/\partial e_h+\partial\tilde{g}/\partial e_f$, which implies that $\partial R_h(e_f,t)/\partial e_f<1/2$. Thus, we can make sure that $\mathrm{d}^2\tilde{W}_h/\mathrm{d}t\mathrm{d}s_f<0$ and $\partial t/\partial\overline{s}_f<0$ if $c'''(e_i)\geq 0$.

5.2 The Foreign Government as a First Mover

As explained, under the current WTO rules, countries can appeal to the WTO for retaliation if it can be proved that some of its industries are hurt by policies set by another country. We now analyze the impacts of this rule using the present framework, with first the foreign government imposing a MQS, and then the home government retaliating with a tariff.

This case can be analyzed by introducing an additional stage to the previous game, making it a four-stage game. In the first stage, the foreign government chooses the MQS level for its own firm. In the second stage, the home government chooses a specific tariff level. In the third stage, the home firm chooses its quality level. In the fourth stage, the two firms compete in prices.[21]

Solving the game by backward induction, it is noted that the third and fourth stages of the present game are similar to the second and third stages of the previous game, implying that the results derived earlier can be applied here. The second stage consists of the home's problem: to choose the tariff as given by condition (35), and it is assumed that it is below the prohibitive tariff level. In the first stage, by taking into account the effects of the MQS level on the tariff, quality, and prices chosen by the corresponding agents in subsequent stages, the MQS level is chosen according to the following first-order condition:

$$\frac{\mathrm{d}\tilde{\pi}_f}{\mathrm{d}s_f} = \frac{\partial \tilde{\pi}_f}{\partial e_f} + \frac{\partial \tilde{\pi}_f}{\partial e_h}\left(\frac{\partial R_h(e_f,t)}{\partial e_f} + \frac{\partial R_h(e_f,t)}{\partial t}\frac{\partial t}{\partial \overline{s}_f}\right) + \frac{\partial \tilde{\pi}_f}{\partial t}\frac{\partial t}{\partial \overline{s}_f} = 0. \tag{36}$$

Compared with condition (34), condition (36) has an additional term:

$$\left(\frac{\partial \tilde{\pi}_f}{\partial e_h}\frac{\partial R_h(e_f,t)}{\partial t} + \frac{\partial \tilde{\pi}_f}{\partial t}\right)\frac{\partial t}{\partial \overline{s}_f} > 0, \qquad ()$$

where the sign is due to the assumption that $c'''(e_i) \geq 0$, which implies that $\partial t / \partial \overline{s}_f < 0$. Condition (36) can be solved for the optimal MQS in the present case, $\overline{s}_f^s$. Once this quality level is determined, the optimal tariff of the home country, and the quality and price levels set by the firms, can also be determined.

The above analysis can be illustrated in Figure 4, where AB is the reaction curve of the home government. Point S, at which a foreign welfare contour labeled u_f^s represents the highest welfare level the foreign country can get when being subject to the home government's reaction function. Thus point S represents the equilibrium in this case, and is nothing but the Stackelberg point with the foreign government acting as a leader. Denote the equilibrium by $(\overline{s}_f^s, t^s)$. The diagram shows that $\overline{s}_f^s > \overline{s}_f^n$ and $t^s < t^n$. This means that the foreign government's strategic

[21] Since the MQS is assumed to be binding, in the third stage the foreign firm will choose an output with a quality level same as the MQS level.

incentive to use a MQS policy is even larger if it can move before the home government, as a higher MQS will induce the home government to impose a lower tariff. Thus, we have the following proposition:

Proposition 4. If the cost asymmetry parameter λ is small enough and the marginal cost function is weakly convex, i.e., $c'''(e_i) \geq 0$, the foreign government as a Stackelberg leader will set a higher MQS level to induce the home government to impose a lower tariff than in the case in which the two governments act simultaneously.

The current WTO's dispute settlement procedure actually provides two advantages to the foreign government: (a) If it decides to impose a MQS, it can act first before the home government reacts. (b) The foreign government has the option of imposing a MQS and the option of imposing no MSQ.

Advantage (a) was analyzed above, and the result was summarized by Proposition 4. Advantage (b) can be analyzed here. If foreign chooses a MQS, it gets a welfare of u_f^s. If it does not choose a MQS, the result is free trade because home may have difficulty in justifying its use of a protective policy.[22] In Figure 4, the origin represents the free trade equilibrium ($\overline{s}_f = s_f^f$, $t = 0$), as described in Section 3. The foreign welfare level under free trade is illustrated by the contour passing through the origin, labeled u_f^f. Therefore foreign will choose a MQS if and only if $u_f^s > u_f^f$.

The choice between MQS and free trade can be illustrated in Figures 4 and 5. Figure 4 shows the case in which the iso-welfare curve u_f^s cuts the horizontal axis, implying that $u_f^s > u_f^f$, and that it is better for the foreign government to use a MQS policy in the first place even though the home government will impose a retaliatory tariff later. On the other hand, Figure 5 shows the case in which the iso-welfare curve u_f^s cuts the vertical axis, implying that $u_f^s < u_f^f$, and that for the foreign government a MQS policy hurts. The interesting point under this option is that if the foreign government chooses not to impose an MQS, no retaliation by the home government will exist. This means that free trade will prevail.

6 Concluding Remarks

We examined the use of minimum quality standard (MQS) for an open economy. We showed that in the presence of an international duopoly, there are situations in which the country with an inferior technology in quality improvement can use such a policy in a strategic way to shift part of the profit of the advanced firm toward its own firm, thereby improving its own national welfare. In this sense, MQS

[22] Of course home can impose a tariff. Foreign can then appeal to the WTO and ask for compensation. Analyzing such a case is beyond this paper.

is similar to other strategic trade policies such as export subsidies that are well known in the literature.

While export subsidies and many other types of subsidies are prohibited by the World Trade Organization (WTO) to be used to promote trade, it seems that MQS is not covered by the current WTO agreement on subsidies and countervailing duties because it does not directly involve government revenues. What we can learn from this paper is that there are some non-subsidy policies that can also be used strategically in an international context.

We also argued that the current system of remedies, i.e., countries need to challenge to the WTO's dispute settlement procedure in the presence of a prohibited subsidy, provides a first-mover advantage to the country that imposes a strategic trade policy in the first place.

Appendix A

Totally differentiating equation (34) with respect to t to yield

$$
\begin{aligned}
\frac{\mathrm{d}^2\tilde{\pi}_f}{\mathrm{d}t\mathrm{d}s_f} &= \frac{\partial(\mathrm{d}\tilde{\pi}_f/\mathrm{d}e_f)}{\partial e_h}\frac{\partial R_h(e_f,t)}{\partial t} + \frac{\partial(\mathrm{d}\tilde{\pi}_f/\mathrm{d}e_f)}{\partial t} \\
&= \left(\frac{\partial^2\tilde{\pi}_f}{\partial e_h\partial e_f} + \frac{\partial^2\tilde{\pi}_f}{\partial e_h^2}\frac{\partial R_h(e_f,t)}{\partial e_f} + \frac{\partial\tilde{\pi}_f}{\partial e_h}\frac{\partial^2 R_h(e_f,t)}{\partial e_h\partial e_f}\right)\frac{\partial R_h(e_f,t)}{\partial t} \\
&\quad + \frac{\partial^2\tilde{\pi}_f}{\partial e_f\partial t} + \frac{\partial^2\tilde{\pi}_f}{\partial e_h\partial t}\frac{\partial R_h(e_f,t)}{\partial e_f} + \frac{\partial\tilde{\pi}_f}{\partial e_h}\frac{\partial^2 R_h(e_f,t)}{\partial e_f\partial t} \\
&= \left(\underbrace{\frac{\partial^2\tilde{\pi}_f}{\partial e_h\partial e_f}}_{(+)} + \underbrace{\frac{\partial^2\tilde{\pi}_f}{\partial e_h^2}}_{(+)}\underbrace{\frac{\partial R_h(e_f,t)}{\partial e_f}}_{(+)}\right)\underbrace{\frac{\partial R_h(e_f,t)}{\partial t}}_{(-)} + \underbrace{\frac{\partial^2\tilde{\pi}_f}{\partial e_f\partial t}}_{(-)} + \underbrace{\frac{\partial^2\tilde{\pi}_f}{\partial e_h\partial t}}_{(-)}\underbrace{\frac{\partial R_h(e_f,t)}{\partial e_f}}_{(+)} \\
&\quad + \underbrace{\frac{\partial\tilde{\pi}_f}{\partial e_h}}_{(+)}\left(\underbrace{\frac{\partial^2 R_h(e_f,t)}{\partial e_h\partial e_f}\frac{\partial R_h(e_f,t)}{\partial t} + \frac{\partial^2 R_h(e_f,t)}{\partial e_f\partial t}}_{(?)}\right),
\end{aligned}
$$

where

$$
\begin{aligned}
&\frac{\partial^2 R_h(e_f,t)}{\partial e_h\partial e_f}\frac{\partial R_h(e_f,t)}{\partial t} + \frac{\partial^2 R_h(e_f,t)}{\partial e_f\partial t} \\
&= \frac{[2(\partial\tilde{g}/\partial e_h) + 3(\partial\tilde{g}/\partial e_f) - 4c''(e_h)]c''(e_h) + 2c'''(e_h)(\partial\tilde{g}/\partial e_f)}{(e_h - e_f)^2[2c''(e_h) - (\partial\tilde{g}/\partial e_h)]^3}.
\end{aligned} \tag{37}
$$

The sign of $\mathrm{d}^2\tilde{\pi}_f/\mathrm{d}t\mathrm{d}s_f$ is in general ambiguous. If it is negative, we can be sure that $\mathrm{d}^2\tilde{\pi}_f/\mathrm{d}t\mathrm{d}s_f < 0$. Assuming that $c'''(e_i)$ is small enough so that we can ignore the term with $c'''(e_h)$ in equation (37). If $c'''(e_i) \geq 0$, $c''(e_h) > \partial\tilde{g}/\partial e_h + \partial\tilde{g}/\partial e_f$ so that $2(\partial\tilde{g}/\partial e_h) + 3(\partial\tilde{g}/\partial e_f) - 4c''(e_h) < 0$. Therefore, the sign of (37) is negative, and $\mathrm{d}^2\tilde{\pi}_f/\mathrm{d}t\mathrm{d}s_f < 0$.

Appendix B

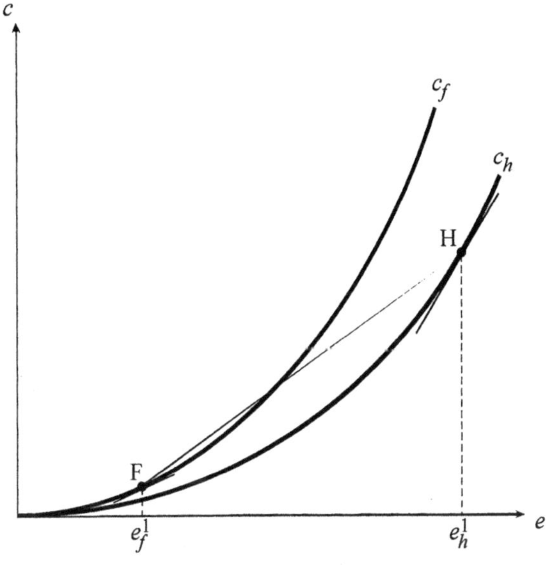

Figure 1. Quality Improvement Functions of the Firms

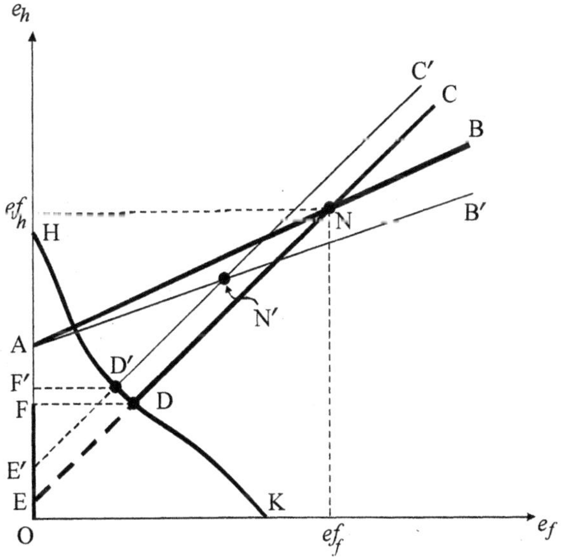

Figure 2. Nash Equilibrium With Quality Competition

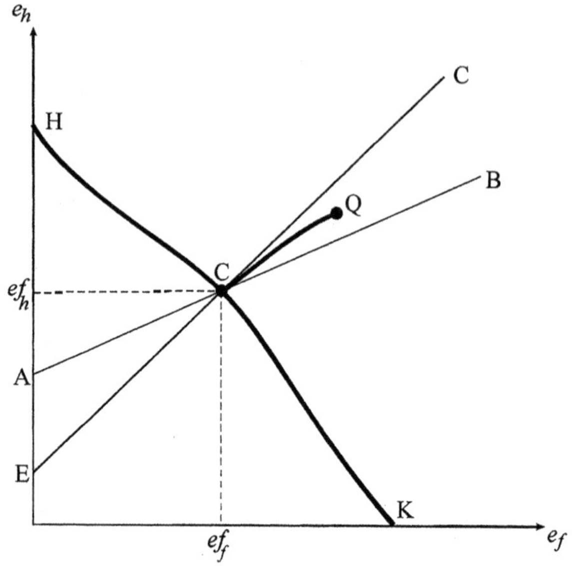

Figure 3. Quality Competition Schedule

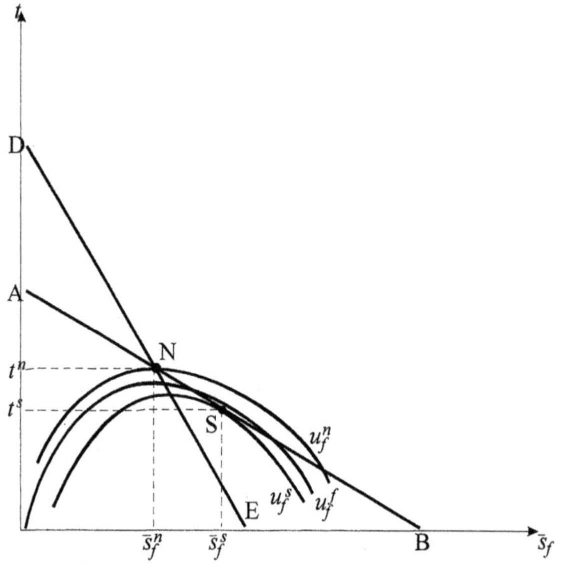

Figure 4. Policies of the Governments: MQS and Tariff

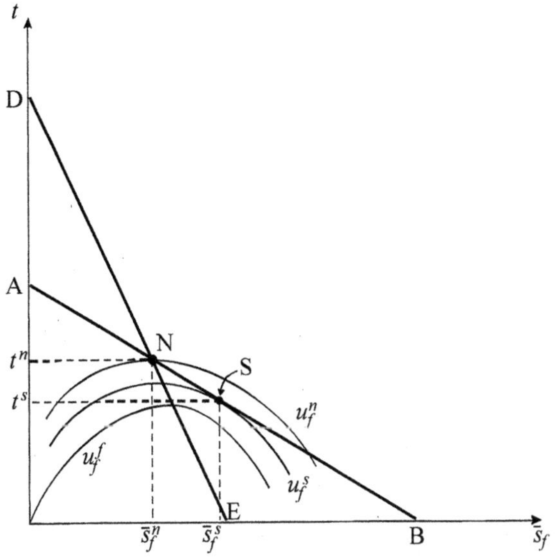

Figure 5. Policies of the Governments: Free Trade

References

Boom A (1995) Asymmetric international minimum quality standards and vertical differentiation. Journal of Industrial Economics XLIII : 101–119

Brander JA, Spencer BJ (1985) Export subsidies and international market share rivalry. Journal of International Economics 18 : 83–100

Crampes C, Hollander A (1995) Duopoly and quality standards. European Economic Review 39 : 71–82

Ecchia G, Lambertini L (1997) Minimum quality standards and collusion. Journal of Industrial Economics XLV : 101–113

Ecchia G, Lambertini L, Scarpa C (2001) On the regulation of vertically differentiated markets through minimum quality standards. Rivista di Politica Economica 91 : 163–202

Das SP, Donnenfeld S (1989) Oligopolistic competition and international trade: Quantity and quality restrictions. Journal of International Economics 27 : 299–318

Krishna K (1987) Tariffs vs. quotas with endogenous quality. Journal of International Economics 23 : 97–112

Lutz S (2000) Trade effects of minimum quality standards with and without deterred entry. Journal of Economic Integration 15 : 314–344

Polavarapu R, Vaidya A (1996a) Commercial policy with vertical product differentiation. Journal of Economic Integration 11 : 230–247

Polavarapu R, Vaidya A (1996b) Optimal trade policy with quality differentiated goods. International Trade Journal X : 379–406

Ronnen U (1991) Minimum quality standards, fixed costs, and competition. RAND Journal of Economics 22 : 490–504

Comment

Ngo Van Long

Department of Economics, McGill University, Montreal, Canada

This paper presents a model of the rivalry between a foreign firm and a home firm that produce vertically differentiated goods for same in the home country. The foreign firm suffers from a technology gap: its cost of improving quality is higher than that of the home firm. In equilibrium, therefore, the foreign firm will choose to produce at a lower quality level than the home firm.

The paper then asks the following question: is it in the interest of the foreign government to impose a minimum quality standard (MQS) on its exported good? The answer turns out to be yes. An increase in the quality level of the product of the foreign firm (above the Nash equilibrium level) will raise the foreign firm's profit. But then why does the foreign firm not choose such a quality level itself? The answer is that such a choice would not be credible. (This is similar to the reason why in a Cournot duopoly, a firm does not produce a greater quantity than the Cournot equilibrium quantity; it is not credible to produce the output level of a Stackelberg leader if one does not have the ability to precommit.)

An interesting result is that a MQS imposed by the foreign country on its export can raise the welfare level of both countries, even though it causes the home firm's profit to fall. The home country does not gain by imposing a MQS on its own good.

If the home country wants to protect the home firm, it can impose a tariff. When this occurs, the quality levels of both products fall (even if the foreign country can impose a MQS.

These are interesting results. One may however wonder whether the results are applicable to the case where each consumer may consume both low and high quality products. For example, one might consume cheap wines on normal days and high quality wines on special occasions.

Also, MQS on both home and imported goods may be imposed by the home country for reasons such as health and safety protection (e.g. toys must meet certain safety standard). Governments may have better information about safety than consumers, in addition there are externalities in the consumption of unsafe products (e.g. unsafe cars can harm pedestrians). Often, however, MQS imposed by advanced countries is perceived as a protectionist device. Politicians may impose MQS as a means of helping home firms make more profit, possibly at the expense of consumers. They may exaggerate the danger of consuming low quality (unsafe) products, in order to shift the surplus from consumers to the home firms. Consumers normally do not know whether the government exaggerate or not, because they are not as well informed as the government. A MQS on the imported good may reduce the probability that the good causes damages (to health, say). Damages may or may not occur in any given period, whether a MQS is imposed or not.

A model that would take these factors into account would be a Bayesian game, in which there are two types of politicians, good and bad. Good politicians care about conventional social welfare, while bad politicians want to help firms (so as to get kickbacks from them). Consumers do not know if a given politician is good or bad. They have beliefs, which get updated once damages are observed. Elections take place at the end of each period. Politicians do not give direct transfers to firms (even though this may be socially a less costly way to help firms), because they do not want o be perceived as bad politicians.

Such a model can be extended to allow for active foreign politicians, who might want to impose MQS on the foreign products. The set of equilibrium outcomes of this Bayesian game can be very rich, and some refinements may have to be imposed to restrict the set of outcomes.

Reforms of Quantitative Import Restrictions and Fair Wage Unemployment

Udo Kreickemeier

School of Economics, University of Nottingham, United Kingdom

1 Introduction

Consecutive rounds of negotiation under the auspices of the GATT have led over the past decades to a considerable decrease in average tariff rates, at least in the developed countries. For the OECD countries, the collected tariff revenue amounted on average to less than 2 percent of the value of imports in 1995, down from nearly 6 percent in 1975 (Ebrill et al. 1999).[1] Their role as dominant means of protection has been taken over in the developed countries by a vast array of nontariff trade barriers (NTBs), and one of the tasks for future WTO rounds is clearly to deal with reducing these NTBs.

In this paper, the focus is on NTBs which restrict imports by imposing a binding upper limit on import quantities. This encompasses, *inter alia*, the cases of pure import quotas and voluntary export restraints (VERs). The paper analyzes the welfare effects of changes in these quantitative import restrictions. It differs from the existing literature on trade policy reforms in that it explicitly considers the existence of involuntary unemployment. In particular, a multi-sector efficiency wage model is set out where unemployment arises in equilibrium because of the workers' fair wage conception: workers compare the wage they receive with what they consider a fair wage and adjust their work effort accordingly. As is typical for efficiency wage models, the relationship between effort and wages makes it optimal for profit maximizing firms to pay a non-market-clearing wage. The consideration of involuntary unemployment in the context of trade policy reform is arguably a worthwhile undertaking: The reluctance in many developed countries to consider further steps of trade liberalization may well be explained in part by concerns about the level of domestic employment.

The paper is organized as follows: Section 2 describes the equilibrium of the domestic economy, focusing in particular on the role played by the workers' fair wage consideration. In section 3, the welfare effects of piecemeal changes in the quantitative import restrictions are derived. Section 4 entails a graphical illustration and section 5 concludes.

---

[1] In many developing countries, there are still much higher tariff rates. For the Non-OECD countries, Ebrill et al. (1999, p. 14) report an average tariff share of almost 13 percent of the value of imports.

2 Equilibrium in the Domestic Economy

Consider a competitive open economy, consuming and producing $n+1$ tradable goods. There is a single export good, which is traded freely with the rest of the world.[2] In addition, there are n import goods which are subject to binding quantitative import restrictions. The export good serves as *numéraire*, and its domestic production is denoted by y_0. Production and domestic prices of the importables are denoted by the vectors y and p, respectively.[3] There are $m+1$ internationally immobile factors of production, where the vector v comprises m factors for which fully flexible factor prices ensure full employment of the exogenously given respective endowments. In addition, there is labor L for which equilibrium unemployment exists.[4]

Following Kreickemeier and Schoenwald (2002), unemployment is explained by a variant of the fair-wage effort hypothesis due to Akerlof and Yellen (1990). It is assumed that employees are able to choose their effort at work, and that the amount of effort supplied depends on their personal fairness conception. In particular, as in Akerlof and Yellen (1990), the effort that workers are willing to supply depends positively on the differential between the actual wage and a reference wage s. From a single worker's point of view, s is not constant but assumed to depend positively on the expected wage w^e and some fixed standard wage $\bar{w}$. The latter may either be determined by collective bargaining or be equal to a (non-binding) minimum wage. Each worker, employed or unemployed, supplies one unit of labor, and hence w^e equals labor income per head. It includes an income of zero for the unemployed, and therefore

$$w^e \equiv \frac{1}{\bar{L}}\sum_{i=0}^{n} w_i L_i \tag{1}$$

with w_i as the wage in sector i, L_i as the number of workers employed in that sector, and $\bar{L}$ as the economy's labor endowment. The expected wage hence captures two variables, which are commonly used as determinants of the reference wage in models of the fair wage type, namely the wage of those who are employed and the level of unemployment.[5] Formally, the reference wage is given by

---

[2] Alternatively, the export good may be reinterpreted as a bundle of freely traded goods with constant relative world market prices. In this case, not all of them have to exported. The assumption of a single export good is only made for notational and terminological convenience.

[3] Unless stated otherwise, vectors are column vectors, transposes are denoted by a prime.

[4] It is assumed that $m \geq n$, i.e. that there are at least as many factors as goods, in order to ensure differentiability of the restricted profit function introduced below.

[5] Agell and Lundborg (1995) consider the market wage and the level of unemployment, along with the rental rate of capital, as separate determinants of s. Albert and Meckl (2001a) consider only w^e, Albert and Meckl (2001b) have $\bar{w}$ as the single determinant of s. Schlicht (1992) uses $\bar{w}$ and the market wage as the two relevant variables, mentioning unemployment only in passing.

$$s = s\left(w^e, \overline{w}\right) \tag{2}$$

with s_{w^e}, $s_{\overline{w}} > 0$. In addition, $s(\cdot)$ is assumed to be linearly homogeneous in $\left(w^e, \overline{w}\right)$. The effort function is given by

$$\varepsilon_i = \varepsilon_i\left(\gamma_i\right) \tag{3}$$

where $\gamma_i \equiv w_i / s$ denotes the differential between the wage paid in sector *i* and the reference wage. In order to ensure the existence of a unique equilibrium, it is assumed that $\varepsilon_i(\cdot)$ takes on a value of zero up to some positive level of γ_i and is increasing and strictly concave above this threshold.

Firms are wage setters but they are assumed to treat the reference wage parametrically. Under this assumption, profit maximization can be thought of as a two-stage process, just as in the standard efficiency wage model of Solow (1979). In stage one, firms in each sector *i* set the wage rate such as to minimize the wage for labor in efficiency units w_i / ε_i. As the firms treat *s* parametrically, minimizing the cost of efficient labor from their point of view is equivalent to minimizing γ_i / ε_i. The first order condition of this optimization problem is given by

$$\frac{\partial \varepsilon_i\left(\gamma_i\right)}{\partial \gamma_i} \frac{\gamma_i}{\varepsilon_i\left(\gamma_i\right)} = 1 \tag{4}$$

This is a variant of the familiar Solow condition (Solow 1979), according to which the optimal wage is such that the elasticity of the effort function is equal to one. Here, the argument of the effort function is the differential between the actual wage and the standard of reference rather than the wage itself as in Solow (1979). Therefore, the condition yields an optimal mark-up on the standard of reference $s(\cdot)$, not an optimal wage.[6]

[6] A related condition appears in Albert and Meckl (2001a).

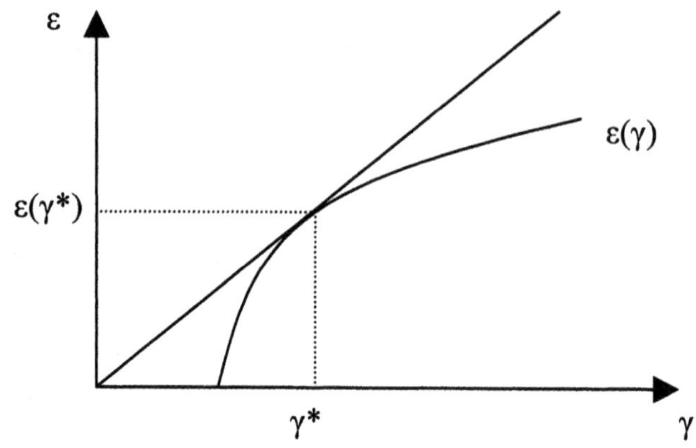

Figure 1. The Optimal Wage Differential

With homogeneous labor it is natural to assume identical effort functions in all sectors. This implies that firms choose to pay equal wages in all sectors of the economy, i.e., w_i=w, $\gamma_i = \gamma$, and in equilibrium

$$w = \gamma^* s\left(w^e, \overline{w}\right) \tag{5}$$

where γ^* is the profit-maximizing wage differential, depending solely on the effort function. A graphical representation is given in Figure 1, with $\varepsilon\left(\gamma^*\right)$ denoting equilibrium effort. As the latter depends solely on the effort function as well, it remains constant throughout the analysis. Hence, one can equivalently describe the model in terms of physical labor (L) or in terms of efficient labor (εL). We will use physical labor as this turns out to make the presentation more transparent.

In stage two, the production sector maximizes profits by choosing the labor input as well as all output quantities, treating parametrically prices of goods and factors, including w. The equilibrium can be described by the restricted profit function

$$\pi\left(p, v, L\right) = \max_{y_0, y}\left\{p'y + y_0 \mid \left(y_0, y, L, v\right) \text{ feasible}\right\} \tag{6}$$

where the functional value of $\pi(\cdot)$ gives the value of domestic production. The employment of L is determined endogenously by the condition that its value marginal product in all sectors be equal to the wage given in (5), i.e., $p_i \partial y_i / \partial L_i = w$ for $i \in (0, \ldots, n)$. It is assumed that the labor endowment $\overline{L}$ is sufficiently large to make it a non-binding constraint to the production sector.

In graphical terms, equilibrium in the labor market is shown in Figure 2. Employment L^* is determined as that particular point on the marginal value product curve for physical labor (VMPL) which makes the marginal value product, being the same for labor in all sectors, equal to the wage w^*. Along the VMPL curve the dependency of effort on w is taken into account, holding constant the reference wage s. As drawn, the VMPL curve is upward sloping for low values of w. This arises as a possibility because an increase in w decreases w/ε for wages below w^*, giving an incentive for the profit maximizing firm to increase employment not only of efficient labor but also of physical labor. It can be shown, however, that the equilibrium combination (w^*, L^*) must lie on the downward sloping part of the VMPL curve.[7] It is not uncommon in the efficiency wage literature to identify the VMPL curve with a labor demand curve, see, e.g., Weiss (1991, p. 20). As the representative firm is a wage setter, and hence only one point on the curve is relevant, this terminology is avoided here. Labor supply is given by the endowment $\bar{L}$, leaving $\bar{L} - L^*$ people unemployed in equilibrium. A change in importables prices, as considered below, leads to a shift of the VMPL curve. As will be shown there, the new equilibrium is characterized by a change in both wages and employment.[8]

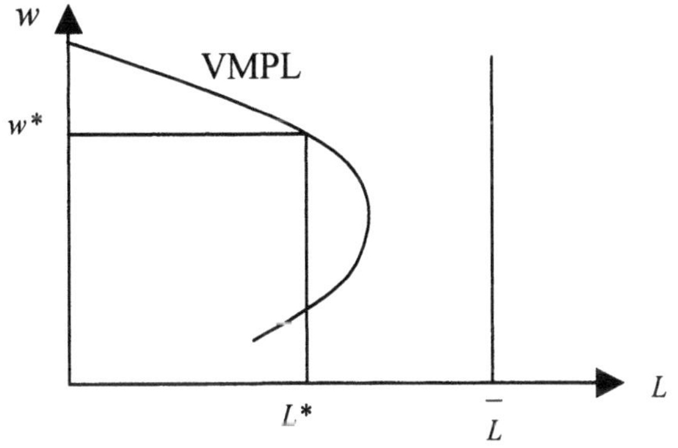

Figure 2. The Labor Market

Having described the influence of the workers' fairness conception on the production side of the economy, it remains to show how the supply of effort arises from utility maximization. Agell and Lundborg (1995, p. 338) argue that in a fair wage

[7] See Weiss (1991, p. 20) for a verbal statement of the argument and, e.g., Kreickemeier and Schoenwald (2002) for a formal derivation.

[8] As an aside, it may be worth noting that the VMPL curve would shift as well if a change in $\bar{L}$ was considered. This is due to the fact that the labor endowment influences w^e and hence s for a given level of w and L. However, as $\bar{L}$ is assumed to remain constant throughout, this effect plays no role in the analysis below. The argument is spelt out in greater detail in Kreickemeier and Schoenwald (2002).

model it is reasonable to assume that effort does not *per se* cause disutility: "If a worker perceives herself as underpaid, she tries to get even. In a fair wage context, the way to get even is to reduce effort – countering unfair pay with low effort increases utility. But the argument also goes in the other direction. If the pay is good, workers derive utility from supplying more effort; they enjoy work, at least up to some point."

This idea is captured formally in the indirect utility function

$$V = v(p, I) + h(\varepsilon^n) \tag{7}$$

with

$$h(\varepsilon^n) = \max_{\varepsilon}\left\{-(\varepsilon - \varepsilon^n)^2\right\} \tag{8}$$

Here, $v(\cdot)$ is the utility from consumption of goods, depending on prices of the non-*numéraire* goods p and income I. The second term, $h(\cdot)$, gives the maximum level of utility due to the choice of effort ε, given some effort norm ε^n. It is obvious that utility maximizing workers will always choose $\varepsilon = \varepsilon^n$, i.e., their optimal choice implies strict compliance with the effort norm. Hence, the effort function (3) follows in effect from assuming an effort norm function $\varepsilon_i^n = \varepsilon_i^n(\gamma_i)$ and have the representative consumer choose to comply with that effort norm in his utility maximizing supply of effort.

It follows immediately that $h(\cdot) = 0$, and overall utility is independent from equilibrium effort. There is a "disutility of norm violation" built into (8) which replaces the disutility of effort known from efficiency wage models of the non-fair wage type.[9] Inverting (7) with $h(\cdot) = 0$ yields the expenditure function

$$e(p, u) \equiv \min_{x_0, x}\{x_0 + p'x \mid f(x_0, x) \geq u\} \tag{9}$$

where x_0 and x are the demand for the *numéraire* and non-*numéraire* goods, respectively, and $f(\cdot)$ is the direct utility function belonging to $v(\cdot)$. In the following, (9) is used to describe the behavior of the representative consumer.

Using (6), the economy's budget constraint with quantitative import restrictions becomes

$$e(p, u) = \pi(p, v, L) + (1 - \beta)t'm \tag{10}$$

where m is the vector of imports and t is the vector of implicit tariffs. Following Anderson (1994), β denotes the fraction of quota rent which is lost for redistribution to domestic consumers. The polar case $\beta = 0$ denotes the situation where the complete quota rent is captured by the domestic government and redistributed to

[9] Brecher (1992) is an example for the latter strand of literature concerned with trade and efficiency wages. In his model, workers supply positive effort only because they lose their job if they are caught shirking.

the household sector. This is the textbook case of an import quota. With *β=1*, the quota rent in its entirety is lost for domestic consumers. This is the case with VERs, where the rent accrues to the foreign suppliers of importables. Alternatively, the quota rent may be wasted domestically in the form of bureaucratic costs of quota administration or costly rent-seeking activities.[10] As VERs are hence not the only situation where the polar case of *β=1* might be relevant, the term "quota" is used in the following for quantitative import restrictions with all possible rent retention shares, including the polar cases just mentioned.

3 Welfare Effects of Quota Reforms

Throughout the paper, the focus is on the case of a small open economy which cannot influence the world market prices for traded goods. Totally differentiating (10) gives in a first step

$$e_p' dp + e_u du = \pi_p' dp + \pi_L dL + (1-\beta)(t' dm + m' dt)$$

and eventually, using the derivative properties $\pi_L = w$, $\pi_p = y$, and $e_p = x$ as well as the small country assumption,

$$dI \equiv e_u du = -\beta m' dp + (1-\beta)t' dm + w dL \tag{11}$$

Here, $dI \equiv e_u du$ denotes the change in real income, which is the measure of welfare change employed below. Equation (11) shows that quota reforms in the present setting have three types of welfare effects. The first and second are the terms of trade effect and the volume of import effect, respectively, known from the full employment variant of the model (Neary 1988).[11] With *β=0* (full rent retention), the terms of trade effect vanishes because price changes of the importables constitute a pure domestic redistribution effect. With *β=1* (zero rent retention), the volume of import effect vanishes because changes in the quota rents are not welfare relevant. The third effect in (11) is an employment effect that is absent in the standard model. It stands out among the three in that it is independent from the rent retention share. It is seen in (11) that in the intermediate case *0<β<1* welfare increases *ceteris paribus* with an increase in employment, an increase in the volume of imports, and a decrease in the domestic prices of importables.

With import quotas, *dp* as well as *dL* are endogenous. In order to derive the relation between the welfare change and changes in the policy instruments, appropriate substitution must be made for both endogenous variables in (11). The

[10] See Krueger (1974) for the second argument.

[11] Clearly, $m' dp$ is not a "true" terms of trade effect because world market prices are constant by assumption. However, with quota rents not accruing to domestic consumers, a change in *p* is equivalent to a change in the world market price from the domestic economy's point of view. The terminology follows Neary (1988, p.719).

change in employment is substituted for by $dL = L_p'dp$. From $m = e_p - \pi_p$, it follows that changes in p and m are related in the following way:

$$dm = Sdp + e_{pu}du - \pi_{pL}L_p'dp$$

with $S \equiv e_{pp} - \pi_{pp}$. The matrix S denotes the price derivatives of compensated net import demand functions for the non-*numéraire* goods with L constant.. We assume that there is some substitutability between *numéraire* and non-*numéraire* goods, in which case S is negative definite (Dixit and Norman 1980, p. 130). Solving for dp gives

$$dp = \Psi^{-1}\left(dm - e_{pu}du\right) \tag{12}$$

with $\Psi \equiv S - y_L L_p'$. The elements of the matrix Ψ are the price derivatives of compensated net import demand, taking into account the output effects of the optimal change in L. The latter are captured by the matrix $y_L L_p'$ which is positive semidefinite, as shown in the appendix. Hence, the adjustment in L increases the price responsiveness of net import demand and Ψ is negative definite.[12] In analogy to the standard full employment model, goods i and j are said to be net substitutes (complements) in import demand if Ψ_{ij}, the respective element of Ψ, is positive (negative).

Substituting $dl = L_p'dp$ as well as (12) into (11) eventually gives the central equation for assessing the welfare effects of quota reforms:

$$\mu^{-1}dI = \left(\left(wL_p - \beta m\right)\Psi^{-1} + \left(1-\beta\right)t'\right)dm \tag{13}$$

with $\mu \equiv \left(1 + \left(wL_p - \beta m\right)\Psi^{-1}x_I\right)^{-1}$ and $x_I = e_{pu}/e_u$.

Here, x_I is the income derivative of demand and μ is the shadow price of foreign exchange. The latter measures the domestic welfare change effected by the transfer on one unit of the *numéraire* good from abroad and, following standard practice, is assumed to be positive. This assumption is most easily justified by noting that with a negative shadow price of foreign exchange, the small open economy would gain by giving transfers to the rest of the world. Clearly, in such a situation paradoxical results would be forthcoming.[13] The three welfare effects from equation (11) reappear on the right hand side of (13). One can see that the employment effect of a change in import quotas operates via the induced change in domestic goods prices measured by the matrix Ψ^{-1}. Clearly, as in the standard model of

[12] This result is remarkable because it does *not* follow from the Le Châtelier principle, which assumes a constant factor price. In contrast, w varies endogenously.

[13] See, e.g., Neary (1995, p. 540) for different justifications of this assumption, including the one given above. The derivation of the shadow price of foreign exchange in a similar but slightly simpler model with minimum wage unemployment is given in Kreickemeier (2001).

Neary (1988), the same holds true for the terms-of-trade effect while the volume of import effect directly depends on the change in import quotas.

Of central importance for the following is the interpretation of the elements of L_p which give the change in economy-wide employment following a change in domestic prices of the importables. As is shown now, it is possible to give an interpretation in analogy to Dixit and Norman (1980, p. 57), who in a standard full employment framework define sector *i* as being labor intensive in a general equilibrium sense if and only if $w_{p_i} > 0$. From (1) and (5), the level of employment in the present framework is given by

$$L(w^e) = \frac{\overline{L}}{\gamma^*} \frac{w^e}{s(w^e, \overline{w})} \tag{14}$$

where $w^e = w^e(p)$. It follows that

$$L_p = \frac{\overline{L}}{\gamma^*} \frac{(s - w^e s_{w^e})}{s^2} w_p^e \tag{15}$$

From the linear homogeneity of $s(\cdot)$, $s - w^e s_{w^e} > 0$. Together with (5), this implies

$$sign(w_{p_i}) = sign(w_{p_i}^e) = sign(L_{p_i}) \tag{16}$$

Intuitively, an increase (decrease) in aggregate labor income, and hence the expected wage w^e, is brought about in the present model by a combined increase (decrease) in the wage *and* the level of employment. Because of the fixed standard wage $\overline{w}$ as a variable in $s(\cdot)$, wages vary less than proportionately with changes in w^e, leaving room for changes in employment in the same direction. Hence, all partial derivatives in (16) can interchangeably be used as measures of labor intensity. In particular, we will say that sector *i* is labor intensive in a general-equilibrium sense if and only if $L_{p_i} > 0$. It is assumed in the following that all L_{p_i} keep their respective signs in the course of the reforms considered. That is, the analysis presumes the absence of factor intensity reversals.

In order to make the central point most transparent we focus on the cases of zero and full rent retention, respectively. With full rent retention, (13) collapses to

$$\mu^{-1} dI = (wL_p{}'\Psi^{-1} + t')dm \tag{17}$$

with $\mu \equiv (1 + wL_p{}'\Psi^{-1}x_I)^{-1}$. Now, let Ψ^{-1} be partitioned as

$$\Psi^{-1} \equiv (\Psi_1^{-1}, \dots, \Psi_n^{-1}),$$

where Ψ_i^{-1} is the $n \times 1$ vector of domestic price changes induced by a change in the quota on good *i*, holding constant all other import quotas. While $\Psi_{ii}^{-1} < 0$, the cross effects Ψ_{ij}^{-1} are negative (positive), if the respective goods are inverse net substitutes (complements) in import demand.[14] The welfare effect of a change in a single import quota m_i is given by

$$\mu^{-1}dI = \left(wL_p{}'\Psi_i^{-1} + t_i\right)dm_i \tag{17'}$$

Now, call the importables in (17') labor intensive on average if and only if the sum $-L_p{}'\Psi_i^{-1}$ is positive.[15] In this case, it is straightforward to see the following:

Proposition 1. With full rent retention, the piecemeal relaxation of an import quota up to the free trade level increases welfare continuously if and only if the importables are not labor intensive on average. If the importables are labor intensive on average, partial quota relaxation may be welfare increasing for a sufficiently low initial level of imports.

If the importables are not labor intensive on average, the term in brackets on the right hand side of (17') is a positive scalar, and hence a reform of the type $dm_i>0$ must lead to a welfare increase. Intuitively, the increase in imports leads to a change in the domestic prices of all importables which are such that there is an increase in the expected wage, a less than proportionate increase in w and hence an increase in employment. In addition, there is the positive volume of trade effect. In the opposite case of the importables being labor intensive on average, the volume of trade effect is unaltered but now the employment effect is negative. The price changes of the importables lead to a decrease in the expected wage, a less than proportionate decrease in w and hence a decrease in employment. For sufficiently high import levels, the volume of trade effect becomes negligible because the implicit tariff t_i approaches zero, and it is therefore sure that the employment effect dominates in this case. It is conceivable that the volume of trade effect dominates for a lower level of imports, implying a higher implicit tariff, and that hence a partial relaxation of the import quota increases welfare with the importables being labor intensive on average. *Ceteris paribus*, this is more likely the higher the implicit tariff of a prohibitive import quota.

With zero rent retention, (13) collapses to

$$\mu^{-1}dI = \left(wL_p - m\right)\Psi^{-1}dm \tag{18}$$

with $\mu \equiv \left(1+\left(wL_p - m\right)\Psi^{-1}x_I\right)^{-1}$. It turns out to be useful to distinguish between the relaxation of a single quota and the proportional relaxation of all quotas. If only

[14] It is possible for two goods to be at the same time net substitutes and inverse net complements, or vice versa, for each other. However, if *all* importables are net substitutes for each other, they are inverse substitutes as well (Hatta 1977, p. 1866).

[15] Note that with some of the goods being inverse net complements for good i, the respective weights $-\Psi_{ij}^{-1}$ would be negative. For analogous definitions of average factor intensities in a model with many importables, see Neary (1988).

the import quota on good i is changed, holding all other quotas constant, (18) becomes

$$\mu^{-1}dI = \left(wL_p{}'\Psi_i^{-1} - m'\Psi_i^{-1}\right)dm_i \tag{18'}$$

Comparing (18') to (17') shows, besides the above noted fact that the employment effects are identical for both cases, that the terms of trade effect in (18') is more complicated than the volume of trade effect in (17'). This is due to the fact that the volume of trade effect depends directly on the policy instrument m_i while the terms of trade effect depends on the induced changes of domestic prices.[16] Now, use the same definition as above and call the importables labor intensive on average if and only if $-L_p{}'\Psi_i^{-1}$ is positive. In this case, one can easily show the following:

Proposition 2. With zero rent retention and all importables being net substitutes for each other, the piecemeal relaxation of a single import quota up to the free trade level increases welfare continuously if the importables are not labor intensive on average. Otherwise, a piecemeal quota relaxation decreases welfare for a sufficiently low initial level of all restricted imports but may be welfare increasing for higher import levels.

If the importables are not labor intensive on average and all importables are net substitutes for each other, the term in brackets on the right hand side of (18') is positive, and hence a reform of the type $dm_i>0$ must lead to a welfare increase. Besides the employment effect, which is identical to the case of full rent retention, the increase in imports has a positive terms of trade effect, i.e., it leads to a decrease in the domestic prices of all importables. With labor intensive importables, the employment effect changes its sign, as above, while the terms of trade effect is unaltered. The terms of trade effect becomes negligible for sufficiently low import levels, and hence the employment effect dominates in this case. The higher the level of imports, the larger is the terms of trade effect, i.e., the welfare impact of a change in the domestic prices of importables. It is therefore conceivable that it outweighs the employment effect for sufficiently high import volumes and that hence, once a certain critical import level is reached, further relaxations of the quota increase welfare.

If all import quotas are changed proportionally, (18) becomes

$$\mu^{-1}dI = \left(wL_p{}'\Psi^{-1}m - m'\Psi^{-1}m\right)d\alpha \tag{18''}$$

with α being some scalar. Note that in (18'') the second term in brackets is minus a quadratic form in a negative definite matrix and therefore unambiguously positive, irrespective of whether the importables are substitutes for each other or not. For the following discussion, call the importables labor intensive on average if and

[16] This difference is well known from the full employment variant of the model, as discussed in Neary (1988).

only if the sum $-L_p'\Psi^{-1}m$ is positive.[17] In this case, it is immediate that the following holds:

Proposition 3. With zero rent retention, the proportional relaxation of all import quotas increases welfare continuously if the importables are not labor intensive on average. Otherwise, a proportional quota relaxation decreases welfare for a sufficiently low initial level of restricted imports but may be welfare increasing for higher import levels.

The explanation is analogous to the reform of a single quota above. As in the full employment model, the proportional change in all import quotas eliminates the possibility of a second-best paradox via the terms of trade effect by creating a "composite Leontief commodity" (Anderson and Neary 1992, p. 68). Therefore, the assumption on net substitutability, which had to be employed in proposition 2, can be dispensed with here.

Now, let a "trap" in the present context denote a situation where a welfare increasing piecemeal quota reform, be it proportional or not, leads the economy away from the global welfare maximum. Then, it is straightforward to see the following:

Proposition 4. Consider the case of zero rent retention and importables that are labor tensive in the appropriate average sense. Then, the economy may be caught in a low import trap if welfare with prohibitive quotas is lower than welfare with free trade. The economy may be caught in a high import trap if the opposite is true.

With labor intensive importables, welfare increasing piecemeal reforms will lead the economy towards prohibitive import quotas if the initial import level is sufficiently low. Clearly, the reform path leads into the "wrong" direction from a global point of view, and the economy is therefore in a low import trap, if free trade is welfare superior to a prohibitive quota. Similarly, consider an economy where, due to a sufficiently high initial import volume, welfare increasing reforms lead the economy towards free trade. The reform path leads into the "wrong" direction from a global point of view, and the economy is therefore in a high import trap, if a prohibitive quota is welfare superior to free trade.

4 A Graphical Illustration

For the case of a single importable, the above results lend themselves to a straightforward graphical illustration. To this end, possible runs of the function *I(m)* are

---

[17] Comparing this definition of average labor intensity to the one above, it is immediate that

$$-L_p'\Psi_i^{-1} > 0 \;\forall i \Rightarrow -L_p'\Psi^{-1}m > 0$$

$$-L_p'\Psi_i^{-1} < 0 \;\forall i \Rightarrow -L_p'\Psi^{-1}m < 0$$

and therefore neither definition is unambiguously more stringent than the other.

drawn for the cases β=1 and β=0, respectively. This follows Neary (1988), who derived this function for the standard case of a small open economy with full employment. Neary showed that with full rent retention and a single importable, welfare is a concave function of the quota level, while with zero rent retention it is "approximately" a convex function of the quota level. As the respective quota is the only distortion in Neary's model, it is obvious that in addition both functions must be monotonously increasing in the quota level. Furthermore, they coincide for the autarky and free trade points because the quota rent is zero in these cases.
In analogy to Neary (1988), the results are derived in the present context under the assumption that Ψ and x_I are constant. The same assumption is made here with respect to the employment effect wL_p.[18] In this case, the slope and curvature of $I(m)$ in the case of full rent retention can be derived from (17) as

$$\frac{dI}{dm} = \mu\left(wL_p\Psi^{-1} + t\right) \tag{19}$$

$$\frac{d^2I}{dm^2} = \mu\frac{dt}{dm} < 0 \tag{20}$$

Hence, one can see that welfare is a strictly concave function of the import quota. In addition, there is an optimum implicit tariff $t^o = -wL_p\Psi^{-1}$ which is positive if and only if the importable is labor intensive.[19]

With zero rent retention, the analogous results follow from (18) as

$$\frac{dI}{dm} = \mu\Psi^{-1}\left(wL_p - m\right) \tag{21}$$

$$\frac{d^2I}{dm^2} = -\mu^2\Psi^{-1} > 0 \tag{22}$$

where the derivation of (22) is given in the appendix. Welfare is a strictly convex function of the import level in this case, and there is a welfare minimizing critical import level $m^m = wL_p$ which is positive if and only if the importable is labor intensive.[20]

[18] It is shown in the appendix that wL_p may be increasing or decreasing in p, and that hence it is acceptable to assume it being constant, but it is more plausible that it increases. In this case, the results derived for the more critical situation of zero rent retention are strengthened, while those for the case of full rent retention are weakened.

[19] It is possible in principle that t^o exceeds the prohibitive implicit tariff, in which case it is obviously unattainable by using an import quota.

[20] It is possible for m^m to exceed the free trade import level.

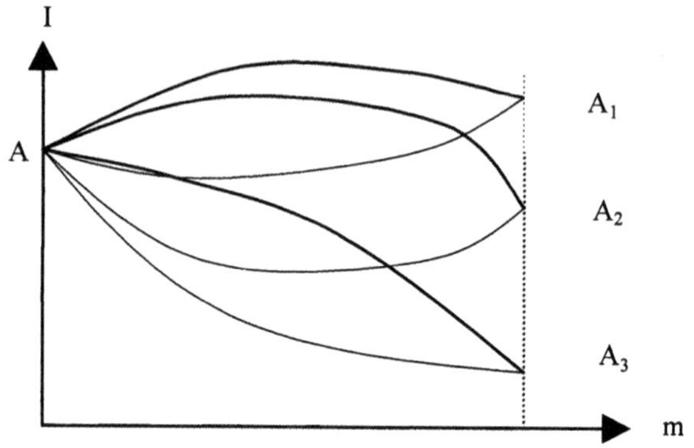

Figure 3. Possible Quota Effects on Welfare with L_p>0

Three possible runs of the function *I(m)* are given in Figure 3 for the more interesting case of L_p>0.[21] The thin lines denote the case of zero rent retention, and the bold lines denote the case of full rent retention. With zero rent retention, *I(m)* is decreasing in the neighborhood of the autarky point, while with full rent retention it decreases in the neighborhood of the free trade point. These are, as set out above, the points where the respective non-employment effects vanish. The reform paths AA_1 and AA_2 show situations where the optimum implicit tariff and the critical import level, respectively, lie between the free trade and the autarky point. The reform path AA_3 on the other hand shows a situation where the optimum implicit tariff exceeds the prohibitive tariff and the critical import level exceeds the free trade level of imports. The difference between the cases of zero and full rent retention is obvious from Figure 3: With full rent retention, the small open economy cannot be caught in a high or low import trap because of the concavity of the reform path. This is different with zero rent retention. A low import trap exists if the reform path is AA_1 and the economy starts off with an import level below the critical level that is illustrated by the minimum of AA_1. In contrast, AA_2 in combination with a starting point to the right of the reform path's minimum denotes a high import trap. Finally, no trap of any sort exists in the case of the monotonously decreasing reform path AA_3.

5 Conclusion

This paper has shown a straightforward way in which involuntary unemployment can be incorporated into an otherwise standard multi-sector model of trade policy

[21] With L_p<0, all reform paths are strictly increasing in the level of imports.

reform. Despite the complexity of the model with variable but non-market-clearing wages, the central results are clear. In particular, the important role played by the labor intensity of the import competing sector, which is familiar from standard trade models, is retained, although the chain of reasoning is different here. If the importables are not produced by labor intensive techniques domestically, piecemeal quota liberalization poses no problems. This is different with labor intensive importables, where the case for quota liberalization is weakened, but not necessarily eliminated. What the analysis makes transparent is the fact that employment effects matter, but they constitute in all cases only a part of the total welfare effect. One last aspect highlighted in the preceding analysis is the crucial role played by the rent retention share. It has been shown that if for some reason the rent is not distributed to domestic consumers, there exist plausible scenarios where welfare increasing piecemeal quota reforms lead the economy into the wrong direction, i.e., away from the optimum level of imports. Put differently, if the economy strives for the global welfare maximum, there may exist situations where there is no way around a "valley of tears" with intermediate reform stages involving welfare losses. This case cannot occur in the standard model with full employment.

Appendix

Positive Semidefiniteness of the Matrix $y_L L_p'$

From Young's theorem, $y_L = w_p'$, y_L is an $n \times 1$ matrix and w_p is a $1 \times n$ matrix. Using $w = \gamma^* s(w^e, \overline{w})$, it follows that

$$y_L = \gamma^* s_{w^e} (w_p^e)' \tag{23}$$

and hence, using (15),

$$y_L L_p' = \gamma^* s_{w^e} (w_p^e)' M w_p^e \tag{24}$$

with

$$M \equiv \frac{s_{w^e} \overline{L} \left(s - w^e s_{w^e} \right)}{s^2} > 0$$

The matrix $(w_p^e)' M w_p^e$ is a quadratic form in a positive scalar and therefore positive semidefinite.

The employment effect wL_p with a single importable

The welfare relevant employment effect of a change in the price of the importable, wL_p, does in general vary with the price level. Differentiation with respect to p gives

$$\frac{d\left(wL_p\right)}{dp} = w_p L_p + wL_{pp} \tag{25}$$

where

$$L_{pp} = \frac{\overline{L}}{\gamma^*} \frac{s\left(s - w^e s_{w^e}\right) w_{pp}^e - \left(s w^e s_{w^e w^e} + 2 s_{w^e}\left(s - w^e s_{w^e}\right)\right)\left(w_p^e\right)^2}{s^3}$$

One can see that the sign of (25) is indeterminate in general because L_{pp} can have either sign.

Convexity of $I(m)$ with zero rent retention

Differentiating (21) w.r.t. m gives, under the assumption that Ψ, wL_p and x_I are constant,

$$\frac{d^2 I}{dm^2} = \frac{-\left(\Psi + \left(wL_p - m\right)x_I\right) + \left(wL_p - m\right)x_I}{\left(\Psi + \left(wL_p - m\right)x_I\right)^2}$$

$$= \frac{-\Psi}{\mu^{-2}\Psi^2} = -\mu^2 \Psi^{-1} > 0$$

Acknowledgements

I thank Max Albert, Jürgen Meckl, Steffi Schoenwald, Henry Thompson, and participants at the 2002 Midwest International Economics Meeting in Evanston for helpful comments on earlier versions of this paper. The paper draws on chapter 4 of my unpublished PhD dissertation at the University of Mainz. I am indebted to my supervisor Karlhans Sauernheimer for numerous helpful comments and discussions throughout the process of completing the thesis. The usual disclaimer applies.

References

Agell J, Lundborg P (1995) Fair Wages in the Open Economy. Economica 62: 335–351

Akerlof G Yellen J (1990) The Fair Wage-Effort Hypothesis and Unemployment. Quarterly Journal of Economics 105: 255–283

Albert M, Meckl J (2001a) Efficiency-Wage Unemployment and Intersectoral Wage Differentials in a Heckscher-Ohlin Model. German Economic Review 2: 287–301

Albert M, Meckl J (2001b) Green Tax Reform and Two-Component Unemployment: Double Dividend or Double Loss?. Journal of Institutional and Theoretical Economics 157: 265–281

Anderson JE (1994) The Theory of Protection. In: Greenaway D, Winters LA (eds) Surveys in International Trade. Blackwell, Oxford, pp 107–138

Anderson JE, Neary JP (1992) Trade Reform with Quotas, Partial Rent Retention, and Tariffs. Econometrica 60: 57–76

Brecher R (1992) An Efficiency Wage Model with Explicit Monitoring. Journal of International Economics 32: 179–191

Dixit A, Norman V (1980) Theory of International Trade. Cambridge University Press, Cambridge

Ebrill L, Stotsky J, Gropp R (1999) Revenue Implications of Trade Liberalization. Occasional Paper 180, International Monetary Fund, Washington DC

Hatta T (1977) A Recommendation for a Better Tariff Structure. Econometrica 45: 1859–1869

Kreickemeier U (2001) The Shadow Price of Foreign Exchange with Minimum Wages. Economics Letters 72: 369–373

Kreickemeier U, Schoenwald S (2002) A General Model of Fair Wages in an Open Economy. GEP Research Paper 2002/34. University of Nottingham

Krueger A (1974) The Political Economy of the Rent-Seeking Society. American Economic Review 64: 291–303

Neary JP (1988) Tariffs, Quotas, and Voluntary Export Restraints with and without Internationally Mobile Capital. Canadian Journal of Economics 21: 714–735

Neary JP (1995) Trade Liberalisation and Shadow Prices in the Presence of Tariffs and Quotas. International Economic Review 36: 531–554

Schlicht E (1992) Wage Generosity. Journal of Institutional and Theoretical Economics 148: 437–451

Solow R (1979) Another Possible Source of Wage Stickiness, Journal of Macroeconomics 1: 79–82

Weiss A (1991) Efficiency Wages: Models of Unemployment, Layoffs and Wage Dispersion. Oxford University Press, Oxford

Comment

Henry Thompson

Economics, Comer Hall, Auburn University, Auburn, USA

Import restrictions in the form of quotas and voluntary export restraints (VERs) are common distortions in international trade. This paper examines the theoretical impact of relaxing quotas and VERs on welfare (real income) in a small open economy that has "fair wage" unemployment. The economy produces an export along with a number of imports using labor and various other factors of production. For clarity, the present review discusses results in terms of the 2x2 model with only one import and one other factor of production, capital.

The basic economic issue is that relaxing a quota or VER would increase real income except for a potential rise in unemployment. Workers supply effort according to their sense of a fair wage and firms hire according to the efficiency wage. Given unemployment, relaxing a quota or VER can be expected to affect its level. The model of the labor market in Kreickemeier's paper is very well developed but it may be useful to shift focus to the results of changing trade policy.

A binding quota or VER keep domestic production of the import artificially high and relaxing either will lower domestic price and production. The labor market will also be affected in the general equilibrium and the effect should depend in some part on the labor intensity of producing the imported product. The net effect on real income is the sum of three effects: terms of trade, volume of trade effect, and employment.

Consider a binding VER with no domestic distribution of the rent. If imports are capital intensive, relaxing the VER would raise labor demand as the economy shifts toward labor intensive production. Unemployment would fall as consumption of the imported product increases, generating an increase in real income. This result is in Proposition 1.

With labor intensive imports, relaxing the VER would lower labor demand and increase unemployment. The falling price of the import raises real income but rising unemployment has a negative effect. Real income would fall if the import level were initially high as stated in Proposition 1 since the impact on unemployment would be larger.

Results for relaxing a quota with its total rent distribution to the domestic economy are in Propositions 2 and 3. If imports are capital intensive, relaxing the quota increases labor demand, lowers unemployment, and increases real income. Gains due to lower unemployment and increased consumption outweigh the lost quota rent. As with the VER, there are unambiguous gains when imports are capital intensive.

If imports are labor intensive, however, real income might fall with a low import level and a relaxed quota. Higher unemployment and lost quota rent might outweigh the benefit of increased consumption with a low level of imports. Real income might rise if the import level is high due to the impact of increased consumption.

Compare the effects of relaxing a VER and quota when there is a low level of labor intensive imports. Relaxing a VER favors a gain in real income while relaxing a quota favors a loss. This is perhaps a surprise since there would be less quota rent lost when there is a low import level. The employment effect, however, dominates. This interplay of effects is developed in the paper.

Kreickemeier's results largely follow intuition based on the Stolper-Samuelson theorem although the model is much more sophisticated than this simple review suggests. There is a efficiency wage model is developed clearly, as are various complications arising from the assumption of numerous imported products and domestic inputs. Nevertheless, the model closely follows factor proportions intuition.

There is some practical concern over increasing unemployment in any move toward free trade. The labor market involves a good deal of psychology and the fair wage model contributes to an understanding of the intricacies of work effort and hiring practice. Perhaps political factors such as unionization and labor laws could be integrated into the model of the labor market. The model might be extended to allow for dynamic adjustment in unemployment using a specific factors model with adjustment costs. Both theory and experience suggest there are sizeable impacts of changing prices of traded goods on labor markets, making this line of research worthwhile.

Trade Games: Modelling WTO's Role in Trade Disputes

Earl L. Grinols and Roberto Perrelli

Department of Economics, University of Illinois, USA

1 Introduction

The disastrous beggar-thy-neighbor trade policies of the 1930s forced the world's leading countries after World War II to seek better institutions to guide post war international relations. The goals were to avoid future wars and to prevent a return to the depression conditions that prevailed before the war. The United Nations was formed and a triad of organizations, each devoted to an important component of international relations, proposed. The International Bank for Reconstruction and Development (World Bank) would oversee loans for the reconstruction of war torn countries and other countries seeking to better their circumstances, the International Monetary Fund would oversee exchange rate issues, and the International Trade Organization (ITO) would focus its attentions on the flow of goods in international trade. The General Agreement on Tariffs and Trade (GATT) was the agreement that the ITO would oversee. Its signatories represented a club of 23 countries, a third of them English speaking or Commonwealth related, dedicated in principal to the benefits of free trade among themselves. Due primarily to questions about national sovereignty relative to the authority of the ITO, the International Trade Organization was never accepted by enough countries to be viable, and it failed to materialize. In its place, periodic rounds of GATT negotiations expanded the agreements aimed at moving to free trade.

Several trends and findings emerged in the succeeding years. First, as countries perceived the benefits to themselves – often seen as acquiring for themselves access for their goods in developed country markets – the number of signatories to GATT grew. Increased membership came, however, at the cost of decline in the level of dedication to the disciplines of the organization. Many countries were more interested in mercantilistic accounting that placed a premium on access to developed country markets for their exports, but were less willing to adopt measures that would open their own markets. Second, the goal of converting all trade barriers into tariffs and then by degree reducing them was subverted by the increasing use of nontariff barriers. By the 1980s nontariff barriers were a well-recognized topic of discussion of the world trading system. Third, whereas GATT had started as a small group of like-minded countries for whom consensus might have been a reasonable operating procedure, it became increasingly clear as time passed that it was inadequate to adjudicating trade disputes for a large organization of countries, many of whom could block the formation of review panels, impede the adoption of panel reports opposed to their interests, and ignore GATT directives to correct trade practices that violated their GATT commitments. Large countries, or groups of countries, like the European Union felt less need to set their policy to be in accord with GATT directions, and often, on the contrary, viewed their actions in trade disputes as matters of national pride.

The experiences of the fifty years following 1945 convinced many nations, including the United States, that an international trade organization with stronger authority would provide benefits to the trading system that outweighed its costs. With U.S. backing, the World Trade Organization was negotiated into being in the Uruguay Round of international trade negotiations. It began operations in January 1995 with strong dispute settlement provisions that included fixed timetables for the process of accepting disputes for resolution, adopting panels to investigate and adjudicate them, adopting panel reports and appellate reports, and providing for sanctions in the case of countries that refused to bring infringing practices into compliance with WTO panel findings.

Consistent with these developments, recent economic literature has explored more assiduously the political economy motivations of international trade.[1] The hallmark of this trend is the endogenous approach to political economy and the application of formal models to trade institutions.[2] The impact of the WTO and the dispute settlement process is a priority of the literature. Rose (2002a,b) finds that countries that joined the WTO do not exhibit particularly different trade patterns after membership, nor are they necessarily more liberal with respect to protectionist measures than WTO non-members. This seems to cast doubt on the WTO's impact on increasing trade flows and the welfare of its members. Empirical evidence presented by Park and Eggers (2001) suggests that the number of trade disputes has increased significantly since the introduction of the WTO, involving more countries than before, while recent legal studies (Jackson (2001)) emphasize that WTO dispute settlement absorbs most of the effective work of member countries' diplomats and secretaries. The questions now before the world trading system have to do with the impact of the WTO on its various competencies. Will shorter timetables improve dispute settlement? Will smaller countries find their access to the dispute settlement process improved? Ultimately, will the new provisions increase satisfaction with the world trading system – now including 146 countries – by reducing the number of trade infringements, the number of trade disputes, and increasing compliance with negotiated disciplines?

This paper seeks to do two things in addressing these questions. First, by examining in a game theoretic context the decisions of the infringing and complainant countries to engage in proscribed trade behavior and to litigate for their WTO rights we provide a framework within which to discuss the impact of the WTO on international trade. This framework complements and augments others' direct at-

[1] E.g., Gould and Woodbridge (1998), Grinols (1989), Grossman and Helpman (1995), Helpman (1995), and Sevilla (1998).

[2] Grossman and Helpman (1994), Pack (1994), Rodrik (1995), Helpman (1997), Goldberg and Maggi (1999), Mitra (1999), Gawande and Bandyopadhyay (2000).

tempts to measure the impact of the WTO on variables such as trade flows. Second, after constructing the framework we simulate its implications to show that it can produce reasonable predictions. One implication is the observation in trade disputes involving the United States that smaller countries tend to engage in shorter duration trade disputes than larger ones. By reducing the costs of dispute settlement, the WTO may, *ceteris paribus* encourage not only more dispute cases, but more infringements from which cases arise. We find evidence that this is true, leading us to propose further use of the model and examination of the dispute-encouraging effects of the WTO.

Before providing a description of our model, a further word about its interpretation is in order. The finding that WTO dispute mechanisms may encourage more trade disputes and encourage them disproportionately by smaller trading countries need not imply more infringements and/or dispute cases involving small countries, only that forces working in the direction of fewer cases will be attenuated by counter forces of the type we identify. Our conception of trade infringements is based on the random arrival of "infringement opportunities" that are evaluated by the country in light of its expectations about the benefits of using the opportunity to violate its WTO obligations, its expectations about how the trade partner will respond, whether it believes the case will go to WTO litigation, and what its prospects of winning or losing the case will be. It is expected that smaller countries have smaller trade flows from which infringement opportunities come, have different constellations of benefits and costs to them of infringement, and thus, with respect to a larger country, have a number of sources of different experience in trade disputes that could lead them to be involved in disproportionately more or fewer trade disputes relative to their size or participation in the world trading system. In this paper we construct a framework in which these various differences can be treated, and discuss in this initial investigation one obvious route by which the effect of the WTO could be to increase dispute cases.

The paper is organized as follows: In section 2 we characterize trade disputes as a game played by two countries (the complainant, "infringee," and the defendant, "infringer") where each country acts to achieve its own objectives. In section 3 we calibrate the resulting game-theoretical model and examine its implications for the impact of cost on both the decision to infringe and the decision to litigate. We present some final remarks in section 4.

2 The Model

Trade disputes result from decisions made by countries about their opportunities to infringe, to seek redress for infringements, and to litigate using the WTO if other solutions have not been reached. These decisions entail costs and benefits and expectations about how the other country will respond. Presume that country β has infringed the WTO rights of country α and that country α evaluates the situation in order to decide whether it will pursue WTO remedies or decline to respond. WTO principles hold that negotiated resolution of disputes is the first objective. If jective. If the complainant, α, therefore negotiates a settlement offer with the defendant, β, that is preferable for α to full-length WTO panel adjudication, β can accept or reject it. We assume, therefore, that the complainant makes an offer to the defendant. A take it or leave it offer is the optimal bargaining format from the complainant's viewpoint and means that the entire surplus of an accepted offer accrues to the complainant. This aspect of the model could be modified if desired, at the cost of greater, and for our purposes unnecessary, complication.

Some defendants have higher settlement costs than others. Costs can be psychic or political as well as real costs. The complainant knows the probability distribution of defendant's settlement costs, but not the precise number, which is private knowledge of the defendant. This feature is meant to capture the fact that the complainant may not know for this particular dispute how important the issue is to the defendant. The defendant compares the offer to what it would receive if it refuses. If the offer is refused and the case is litigated under WTO auspices, the costs of litigating are assigned to each country according to the litigation outcome. The game just described is summarized in the steps below.

Stage 1: Defendant's Decision to Infringe. In stage 1 we assume that infringement opportunities with different characteristics arrive according to a probability distribution. Country β decides whether to use the opportunity the arrival provides to infringe α's WTO rights. If no infringement is chosen, the payoffs to both players are zero (retain status quo). The decision to infringe initiates the remainder of the process. An infringement represents a direct welfare loss to α measured by A and a direct welfare gain to β measured by B.

Stage 2: Complainant's Settlement Offer. Once there is an infringement, country α decides whether to respond or do nothing (drop the case). If the case is dropped, α loses A while β gains B. If α responds, it incurs costs, $C(t,L)$, which increase with time from acceptance, t, and depend on a measure of direct acceptance costs, L. It is in α's interest to solve the case as soon as possible because costs rise with dispute duration. Country α proposes a "take it or leave it" settlement offer S to country β that takes account of β's willingness to accede.

Stage 3: Defendant's Settlement Response. If β accepts the settlement offer, its payoff is $-S$ while country α receives S. In addition, β may incur other costs by accepting the settlement. These are measured by a random variable b, which we assume follows a Bernoulli distribution: β has low cost of settling, b_l, with probability p, or high cost, b_h, with probability $(1-p)$. Cost b is known to β, but is unknown to α, who must make decisions based on knowledge of its distribution only.

Stage 4: Complainant's Decision to Litigate. If β rejects the settlement offer, α must decide whether to proceed with litigation in the WTO or to drop the case. If α drops the case, it loses the costs $C(t_0, L)$ incurred at this stage. If α proceeds with the case, it pays costs to the end of the litigation process, $C(t, L)$ where $t_0 < t$. In addition, α risks having to pay adjudication costs if it loses the dispute.

Stage 5: Adjudication. The WTO tribunal decides which country wins the dispute. Because both countries know the type of case, both countries know *a priori* that α wins with probability ε, and loses with probability $(1-\varepsilon)$. We assume that ε follows a Bernoulli probability distribution. For realism, we assume that adjudication costs $D(t, M)$ are entirely paid by the losing country, increase with time t and with case complexity M. Finally, we assume that the tribunal is fair enough to impose a penalty on the losing country such that (i) if α wins, its welfare losses are compensated, and (ii) if β wins, its welfare gains are preserved.

Figure 1 displays the process just described. Payoffs to the left apply to α, payoffs to the right to β. Without loss of generality, we assume the parameters A, B, L, M, and the random variables b, ε, and t, are all positive real numbers. We also assume that $C(t, L)$ and $D(t, M)$ are continuous non-decreasing positive functions. To keep the notation compact, hereafter we denote $C(t_0, L)$, $C(t, L)$, and $D(t, M)$, respectively, as C_0, C, and D. We will also use the notation, $x = (A, B, C, D, L, M, \varepsilon, p, t)$.

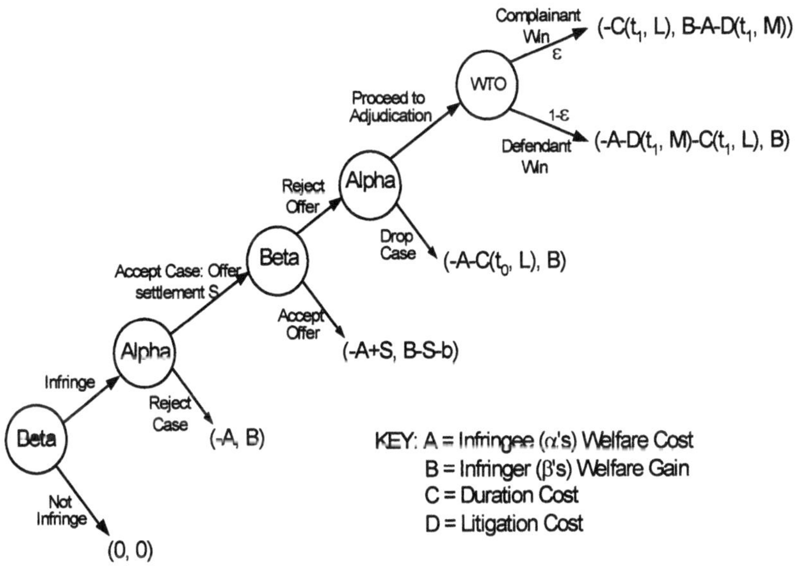

Figure 1. The Trade Adjudication Game

2.1 Solution

We solve the game by backward induction.

Stage 4. If α litigates, the complainant wins the case in stage 4 with probability ε, and defendant wins with probability $1-\varepsilon$. The country that loses the dispute pays adjudication costs D. We do not assume that the game is repeated because the uniqueness of trade disputes, their relative infrequency, changes in governmental regimes, changes in governmental constituencies, and the inability to bind future play, make inappropriate and unrealistic a focus on punishment and strategies that must be played out over repeated plays of the game. We do know, of course, that repetition of the solution to the game is a solution to the repeated game.

The value to the complainant country α of dropping the case is $-A - C_0$, where A is the direct welfare cost caused by the infringement, and C_0 is the cost function evaluated at time t_0. α's expected payoff from litigating is $(1-\varepsilon)(-A-D)-C$. Country α litigates, therefore, if and only if

$$LC(x) = \varepsilon\,(A + D) - D - \Delta C > 0 \tag{1}$$

In equation (1), $\Delta C \equiv C - C_0$ is the increment to the complainant's costs caused by extending the duration of the litigation process. Comparing α's expected payoff from litigation with its payoff from dropping the case, the constraint requires $LC(x) > 0$. Reducing adjudication costs D or duration costs ΔC make the credibility constraint $LC(x)$ easier to bind. For future reference we denote equation (1) as the litigation constraint function $LC(x)$.

Stage 3. S stands for the value of the settlement between α and β. If the defendant accepts to settle, the total value of this decision to α is $-A + S$, and to β is $B - S - b$, where b is the psychic, political, and/or reputational cost to β of accepting the offer. If the defendant rejects the settlement offer, the case is solved via adjudication, where α's expected payoff is $\varepsilon\,(A + D) - A - D - C$, and β's is $B - \varepsilon\,(A + D)$. Viable settlement requires that it be preferable to litigation for both countries. α requires an offer such that $S(\alpha) > \varepsilon\,(A + D) - D - C$, whereas β will only consider offers such that $S(\beta) < \varepsilon\,(A + D) - b$. α knows that defendants with high costs of settlement (b_h) will reject even more generous settlement offers. We assume inequalities (2) and (3):

$$\varepsilon\,(A + D) - b_h < \varepsilon\,(A + D) - D - C \tag{2}$$

$$< \varepsilon\,(A + D) - b_l \tag{3}$$

The term in the middle is the least S that is better for α than going straight to adjudication. The term on the right is the most S that β will be willing to pay if β has low settlement costs (b_l); going to adjudication would be preferred to paying an amount greater than this. The expression on the left is the highest S that β can afford to pay if its settlement costs are high (b_h). The assumption that the term in the middle lies between the two means there is room for mutually beneficial settlement with low-cost defendants. If the middle term exceeds both other terms, there is no mutually acceptable settlement and the game goes straight to adjudication. If the middle term is lower than both other terms, all cases are settled without need of WTO panels.

We presume that a nondegenerate equilibrium applies whereby α litigates cases if its settlement offers are rejected. If not, β infringes and α does nothing but proposes spurned settlements. Assumptions 2 and 3 rule these cases out.

If the complainant offers S lower than $\varepsilon (A + D) - b_l$ it will not improve the chances that the offer is accepted but *will* reduce what the complainant gets from the offer. Demanding *higher* payment than $\varepsilon(A + D) - b_l$ means the settlement will always be rejected. Asking $S = \varepsilon (A + D) - b_l$, however, will be accepted p percent of the time, when defendant β has low settlement cost b_l. The remaining $1-p$ percent of the time the offer will be rejected, the case will go to adjudication and the complainant's expected payoff will be $\varepsilon (A + D) - A - D - C$. Thus, α 's settlement offer is

$$S^* = \varepsilon (A + D) - b_l. \tag{4}$$

Notice that the rejection bound given by the right hand side of equation (4) can be negative. In that case, the defendant will reject *any* positive settlement. Another implication of the model is that according to the probability p of having low settlement cost b_l, defendant countries will tend to pay more in settlement, and will accept settlement more frequently.

Stage 2. The expected value to α of accepting a case is

$$\Pi(\alpha) \equiv p\,[-A + \varepsilon (A + D) - b_l] + (1 - p)[\varepsilon(A + D) - A - D - C] \tag{5}$$

where the first square-bracketed term is the value to α if the settlement offer S is accepted, and the second square-bracketed term is the value of WTO adjudication if settlement is rejected and the case is litigated. On the other hand, if α rejects the case its payoff is simply $-A$, the original welfare loss caused by the infringement. Thus, the complainant's decision to accept a case is $\Pi(\alpha) > A$, where $\Pi(\alpha)$ is given by equation (5).

Stage 1. At the beginning of the process, β takes account of α's litigation strategy. It therefore uses the arrival of a case to infringe only if it is in its *ex ante* interest. In particular, β infringes if and only if

$$IC(x) \equiv B - \varepsilon (A + D) > 0. \tag{6}$$

For future reference we denote the left hand side of equation (6) as the infringement function $IC(x)$ where $x = (A, B, C, D, L, M, \varepsilon, p, t)$. Vector x can be calibrated to assess the impact of changes in this framework.

Summary. Thus, we have learned the following. $x = (A, B, C, D, L, M, \varepsilon, p, t)$ characterizes the type of case. Upon the arrival of a potential case of type x, the infringer's (β) strategy is: If $B < 0$, do not infringe. If $B > 0$ and the case is such that α will reject it for prosecution ($LC(x) < 0$), infringe. If $B > 0$ and the case is such that α will accept it for prosecution ($LC(x) > 0$), infringe if and only if the infringement condition $IC(x) > 0$ is satisfied. Accept α's negotiated settlement $S^* = \varepsilon(A + D) - b_l$ if low-cost type, and reject otherwise. The complainant's (α) strategy is: Respond to a case if $\Pi(\alpha) > -A$, where $\Pi(\alpha) \equiv p\,[-A + \varepsilon(A+D) - b_l] + (1 -$

$p)[\varepsilon(A + D) - A - D - C]$. Ask negotiated settlement $S^* = \varepsilon(A + D) - b_l$ if the case is accepted. Litigate if the negotiated settlement is rejected and $LC(x) > 0$.
The solution therefore identifies an infringement constraint set, $IC = \{x|\ IC(x) > 0\}$ and a litigation constraint set, $LC = \{x \mid LC(x) > 0\}$. Changes in x that increase $LC(x)$ enlarge the set of rejected settlements that will be litigated. If both IC and LC regions grow, there will be more infringements and more litigation. Direct computation shows that a reduction in adjudication costs results in enlarged sets IC and LC. Both effects, therefore, point to more dispute cases. If the infringer's costs of losing are raised, this results in fewer decisions to infringe. However, presuming that the motivation provided by better WTO dispute settlement procedures dominates the discouraging effect on infringements – a not improbable outcome – then the model predicts more infractions and more litigation. In the next section we simulate the model to test its implications.

3 Monte Carlo Simulation

The model emphasizes the effect of the costs and benefits to participants of the dispute litigation process. Empirically, we observe that smaller countries are associated with shorter disputes, while larger countries are more likely to be involved in longer litigations. Disputes between the European Union and the United States are typically longer and more costly than disputes between Taiwan and the U.S., or South Korea and the U.S. This pattern can be explained by, among other factors, the smaller budgets and weaker bargaining power of smaller countries. Apparently, small countries have fewer reasons to keep battling over a trade case than a large country.

In this section we examine the implications of the game-theoretic model for a number of parameters that enter the vector x and focus on the effect that the pattern of shorter cases and associated lower costs suggests for infringements and litigations through a Monte Carlo simulation. Without loss of generality, one can think of a benchmark player (e.g. the U.S.), and examine the results of litigating against fictitious "small" and "large" countries. In our terminology, "large" opponents correspond to countries that trade heavily with the U.S., where trade volume is measured by the sum of exports to and imports from the US, divided by the US GDP. Conversely, "small" countries are those that do not constitute a large share of U.S. trade. One can easily think of European Union countries as examples of the former, and African countries and selected political and military allies, such as Taiwan and South Korea, which rely more heavily on the US assistance in regional conflicts, as the latter.

We distinguish the two types of opponents by their respective duration of trade disputes. To model duration, we propose a Weibull cumulative distribution function with shape parameter a and scale parameter b:

$$F(t) = 1 - \exp[-(t/b)^a] \tag{7}$$

Without loss of generality, we assume that both types of countries have the same shape ($a = 2$), and they differ simply by the scale parameter ($b = 7$ for small countries, and $b = 21$ for large countries). This is an attempt to replicate the empirical findings of trade dispute process: in this setup, because the mean of a Weibull distribution is given by $E(T) = b\Gamma(1 + 1/a)$, the average duration of disputes against "small" countries is close to 6 months, whereas the average duration of disputes against "large" countries is approximately 18 months. This is a rough approximation to the true empirical distribution of durations. More interesting, the Weibull distribution presents long right tail, which allows the existence of outlying cases with extremely long durations.

The Monte Carlo simulation proposed here starts with the calculation of the vector of case characteristics, $x = (A, B, C_0, C, D, b_l, \varepsilon, p)$. For simplicity, we assume that A and B are random draws from a normal probability distribution with mean $\mu = 100$ and standard deviation $\sigma = 10$. In a more realistic experiment, the distributions of A and B would be tied more closely to information on actual case values, which are unavailable to us. Next we select forms for the costs of litigating and adjudicating, $C = [1 - \exp(-t/360)]L$, and $D = [1 - \exp(-t/360)]M$, where t is the lifespan of trade disputes, measured in days. The increasing functional form for costs implies that L and M are the upper bounds of the respective cost functions. Both C and D rise as $t \to \infty$ toward their respective upper bounds, L and M. A variation of the model could allow L and M to be random draws from a probability distribution. Here we retain simplicity by assuming that they are a non-decreasing function of welfare costs, $L = \max(A)$ and $M = \max(B)$ where the maxima are taken over our sample of dispute durations.

The remaining terms in x are parameters in the simulation. We assume that ε ranges from .20 to .80 (a complainant has the greater likelihood of winning a case if $\varepsilon > .5$), $C_0 = k\,C$, where $k \in \{.10, .15, .20\}$ is relatively small, meaning that costs at the beginning a dispute are small relative to the costs of the entire process, $p \in \{.10, .15, .20\}$ indicates that the probability of two parties reaching settlement by negotiation outside the WTO is not great and $p - k > 0$.[3] b_l appears in the acceptance condition, but not the infringement condition or the litigation condition, which are the focus of our simulation. Without loss of generality, therefore, we assume that b_l is zero. Recall that litigations are cases that satisfy both the infringement and litigation conditions.

Whether the defendant country β infringes, and whether the complainant country α decides to litigate depend on whether $IC(x) > 0$ and $LC(x) > 0$, respectively. To estimate the outcome of these two conditions for "small" and "large" opponent countries, we draw a sample of case durations t_i, $i=1, \ldots, n$ from a Weibull (a,b)

---

[3] This is a technical condition to simplify the interpretation of the simulation. The acceptance condition can be displayed as: $LC(x) + p\,(C + D) + \Delta C - pb_l - C = LC(x) + (p - k)\,C + pD > 0$. This condition is always satisfied in the reported simulations when the litigation condition is satisfied. Infringement opportunities that satisfy the infringement condition and the litigation condition, therefore, become infringements; p percent of them are settled between infringer and complainant, and $1 - p$ percent of them become trade disputes.

distribution that approximates the observed empirical distribution of case lifespans as described above.[4] Next we draw two random vectors of size n from a normal distribution with mean 100 and standard deviation 10, corresponding to the estimated welfare effects A_i and B_i. The reader can view these disputes as having value of $100 million, with the infringer and complainants sometimes receiving slightly more and sometimes slightly less. The upper bound of litigation costs are $L = \max(A_i)$, and of adjudication costs $M = \max(B_i)$, where the maxima are taken over the samples drawn. This information is then used to construct n row vectors x_i, whose components include A_i, B_i, the cost functions $C_i = [1 - \exp(-t_i/360)]L$ and $D_i = [1 - \exp(-t_i/360)]M$, $b_i = 0$, and ε and p chosen as previously described. For each x_i, we compute the inequality constraints $IC(x_i)$ and $LC(x_i)$. The experiment is completed after we compute the indicator functions $IIC \equiv [I(IC(x_i)>0)=1]/n$ and $ILC \equiv [I(LC(x_i)>0)=1]/n$, which provide the percentage of times each of the constraints is satisfied.

To achieve statistical significance, the comparison should be repeated a large number of times and for different combinations of parameters (see, for example, Efron and Tibshirani (1986) bootstrap approach). Here we vary ε and p as previously described. We also consider different specifications of the litigation costs, $C_0=kC$. For each value of ε and specification of p and C_0, we run the procedure described five thousand times for "small" countries, and five thousand times for "large".

The results are shown in Table 1. We restrict our discussion to the case of p = 15%, 20%, and k = 15%, 20%. Other combinations of the parameters produce results that are qualitatively similar. On the top of the table we present the results for small countries (these simulate the effect of lowered costs of trade disputes for opponents that have shorter disputes), while to the right we present the results for disputes of larger countries (longer dispute durations).

Start first in the middle left panel, p = 20%, k = 15 %. The left-most column shows the probability that the complainant country wins the trade dispute case. Columns to the right show the percentage of infringement opportunities that result in infringements and that satisfy the litigation condition. The right hand column shows the percentage of cases that satisfy both the infringement litigation condition. This column therefore measures the effect of the parameters on the number of case opportunities that result in trade disputes cases. For example, if the probability that the complainant wins a case is 50 percent, 95.5 percent of infringement opportunities satisfy the infringement constraint and become infringements, and 31.8 percent satisfy the litigation condition. Increases in ε lower the benefits to the infringer of the infringement and decrease monotonically the number of case opportunities that satisfy the infringement constraint. Larger ε increases monotonically percentage of cases that satisfy the litigation condition. These are intuitive results, given that we assume the litigating countries are rational players of the trade game. The remarkable feature is that small countries that engage in shorter duration disputes are much more sensitive to variations in ε than large countries

[4] Based on the history of US trade disputes under WTO auspices, we adopt n = 100 as an approximation of the actual sample size.

(longer duration) when they are complainants, and much less sensitive when they are defendants. Increasing ε from 50 percent to 0 percent causes the litigation constraint to be satisfied more than 90% of the time, whereas the same constraints are satisfied only about 40% and 67% of the time, respectively, for large countries. The reverse situation happens for the infringement constraint, where small countries are less sensitive to the odds of losing a dispute than large countries. This suggests that small countries tend to infringe and to litigate more often than large countries, regardless of the odds of the complainant winning the case (ε).

Table 1. Impact of Costs, Duration, and Probability of Successful Litigation on the Decision to Infringe, the Decision to Litigate and the Number of Trade Disputes from a Given Pool of Infringement Opportunities

Small countries				Large countries			
p=15%, k= 15%				p=15%, k= 15%			
ε [%]	IC [%]	LC [%]	Disputes [%]	ε [%]	IC [%]	LC [%]	Disputes [%]
20	100.0	0.4	0.4	20	100.0	0.0	0.0
30	100.0	5.8	5.8	30	100.0	0.1	0.1
40	99.9	17.7	17.7	40	95.6	1.9	1.9
50	95.5	30.6	30.5	50	56.3	2.9	2.9
60	72.2	46.7	43.0	60	18.5	6.6	5.9
70	40.7	68.6	36.9	70	6.1	11.0	4.8
80	17.9	88.7	17.8	80	2.0	21.5	1.9
p=20%, k= 15%				p=20%, k= 15%			
ε [%]	IC [%]	LC [%]	Disputes [%]	ε [%]	IC [%]	LC [%]	Disputes [%]
20	100.0	3.5	3.5	20	100.0	1.0	1.0
30	100.0	10.4	10.4	30	100.0	1.0	1.0
40	99.9	21.1	21.1	40	96.5	1.9	1.9
50	95.5	31.8	31.8	50	62.9	3.3	3.3
60	73.3	49.4	45.7	60	25.4	7.6	6.7
70	42.6	68.8	39.0	70	8.2	16.5	5.8
80	20.3	88.8	20.2	80	2.6	33.1	2.6
p=20%, k= 20%				p=20%, k= 20%			
ε [%]	IC [%]	LC [%]	Disputes [%]	ε [%]	IC [%]	LC [%]	Disputes [%]
20	100.0	1.6	1.6	20	100.0	0.0	0.0
30	100.0	6.9	6.9	30	100.0	2.0	2.0
40	99.9	18.3	18.3	40	97.0	3.0	3.0
50	95.9	32.4	32.3	50	66.2	7.5	7.5
60	73.0	49.5	45.2	60	29.0	13.6	12.1
70	40.6	72.7	37.2	70	11.4	22.8	9.7
80	17.9	93.9	17.8	80	4.1	39.7	4.1

The other interesting result has to do with the number of times both *IC* and *LC* constraints are satisfied. These results are presented on the last column of Table 1 labeled "Disputes." There we see a quadratic response of number of trade disputes to the probability of the complainant winning the case (ε). More specifically, *IC* and *LC* jointly bind more often around $\varepsilon = .6$, and less often at low or high values of ε. This quadratic effect captures the feature that there is a balance between the incentives to infringe and to litigate according to the position of the opponent country: higher ε would be preferred by complainants, and lower ε by defendants. As we are considering a pool of opponents that includes both complainants and defendants, the maximum likelihood of both *IC* and *LC* binding is about 0.6. Also interesting is that small countries have both constraints binding much more often (45%) than large countries (12%) have at $\varepsilon = 0.6$. Such findings reinforce our previous results.

The impact of a decrease in the probability p that the infringer will accept the complainant's settlement offer is seen by comparing the middle tables to the tables at the top of the chart. Lower p lowers the percentage of cases that satisfy the litigation constraint, and so lessens the tendency of large or small countries to litigate. The result is a decline in the number of trade disputes. For example, if the probability that complainant wins a trade dispute is 0.8, the share of opportunities that become trade disputes is 20.2% for small countries. This share falls 12 percent to 17.8 if p falls to 0.15. For large countries, the effect is a 27 percent drop in trade disputes from 2.6 to 1.9 percent of opportunities.

The effect of an increase in costs, from $k = 0.15$ to $k = 0.2$ is displayed in the bottom two tables. For small countries, the number of opportunities that become disputes falls. For cases where the probability that the complainant wins is small, this is due primarily to a reduction in the decision to litigate (the share of cases satisfying *LC* declines), but for cases where the probability that the infringer wins is high, it is due to a reduction in the decision to infringe. For large countries, the effect of higher dispute costs is to reduce the number of trade disputes for small ε, but to increase them for large. The latter effect operates through the decision by large countries to litigate a larger percentage of cases.

The simulation shows that a game approach to the decisions to infringe and litigate, even in a simple game that is designed to contain only the core objectives of complainants and defendants, are not monotonic in the variables that matter to the country participants. Countries that know trade disputes will be shorter and less costly will take this information into account and tend to infringe and litigate more frequently, given the same set of original circumstances. Table 1 displays the range of variations that result from adjustments in the probability that a country wins the trade dispute, the size of the dispute costs, and the probability that a settlement offer will be accepted. The relative contribution of countries' tendency to infringe more and to litigate more can be read from the table. Finally, it is important to bear in mind that infringement opportunities may vary between large and small countries. Thus, the tables should be considered predictions that are *conditional* on the set of potential cases. If case opportunities are proportional to the volume of trade, and small countries tend to have trade volumes that are ten percent those of larger countries, for example, then the number of infringements implied by the *IC* columns will have to be adjusted by a factor of 0.1. The interplay of other variables can also be worked out as needed.

4 Conclusion

We have described an infringing country's decision to infringe another country's WTO rights and the infringed-against country's decision to pursue remedies under WTO auspices as the outcome of a game wherein the infringer (defendant) and infringee (complainant) take into account the benefits and costs to themselves of their decision and their expectations about how the opponent will respond. The complainant attempts to settle disputes with a settlement offer that is sometimes accepted by the infringer and sometimes rejected. When the settlement offer is rejected, cases go to litigation where they are settled with probability $\varepsilon < 1$ in favor of the complainant. Potential infringement opportunities arrive on a random basis, are evaluated by the infringer, and the decision is made to use the opportunity to infringe when an infringement condition $IC(x) > 0$ is satisfied. Cases go to litigation when a litigation condition $LC(x) > 0$ is satisfied.

We simulated the outcomes of the game that results for the effect of various parameters on the decision to infringe and the decision to litigate. The model delivers the prediction that by reducing the costs of litigation leads to an increase in infringements and the number of disputes that are litigated. This finding implies that small countries, *ceteris paribus*, have a differential incentive compared to large countries to increase the fraction of infringement opportunities that become infringements and that this results in a greater number of cases litigated. The implication is that the WTO dispute settlement contains incentives that run counter to the objective of reducing trade disputes and increasing compliance with internationally agreed trading rules. Refinements to the model and closer attention to selecting parameters that more closely describe the circumstances of members of the WTO should be able within the context of the game-theoretic approach to predict and identify the effects of changes to WTO rules. A game-theoretic representation of the dispute process, therefore, provides promising and potentially rich avenue for future research.

References

Efron B, Tibshirani R (1986) Bootstrap Methods for Standard Errors, Confidence Intervals, and Other Measures of Statistical Accuracy. Statistical Science 1(1): 54–75

Gawande K, Bandyopadhyay U (2000) Is Protection for Sale: Evidence on the Grossman-Helpman Theory of Endogenous Protection. Review of Economics and Statistics 82: 139–152

Goldberg PK, Maggi G (1999) Protection for Sale: An Empirical Investigation. American Economic Review 89: 1135–1155

Gould DM, Woodbridge GLW (1998) The Political Economy of Retaliation, Liberalization and Trade Wars. European Journal of Political Economy 14: 115–137

Grinols EL (1989) Procedural Protectionism: The American Trade Bill and the New Interventionist Mode. Weltwirtschaftliches Archiv 125: 501–521

Grinols EL Perrelli R (2002) Politics, the WTO, and Trade Disputes: Evidence from US Cases. Pacific Economic Review 7: 335–357

Jackson JH (2001) The Role and Effectiveness of the WTO Dispute Settlement Mechanism. In: Dollins SM, Rodrik D (eds) Brookings Trade Forum: 2000. Brookings Institution Press, Washington, pp 179–219

Mitra D (1999) Endogenous Lobby Formation and Endogenous Protection: A Long Run Model of Trade Policy Determination. American Economic Review 89(5): 1116–1134

Pack H (1994) Productivity or Politics: The Determinants of the Indonesian Tariff Structure. Journal of Development Economics 44: 441–451

Park YD, Eggers B (2000) WTO Dispute Settlement 1995–99: A Statistical Analysis. Journal of International Economic Law, pp 193–204

Rodrik Dani (1995) Political Economy of Trade Policy. In: Grossman GM, Rogoff K (eds) Handbook of International Economics: Vol. III. Elsevier Publishers, Amsterdam, pp 1457–1496

Rose A (2002) Do We Really Know that the WTO Increases Trade?, NBER Working Paper 9273

Rose A (2002) Do WTO Members have More Liberal Trade Policy?, NBER Working Paper 9347

Sevilla CR (1998) Explaining Patterns of GATT/WTO Complaints. Weatherhead Center for International Affairs, Cambridge

United States Trade Representatives (2000) Section 301 Table of Cases USTR, February

World Trade Organization (2000) Overview of the State-of-Play of WTO Disputes. WTO, February

Comment

Henryk Kierzkowski

Graduate Institute of International Studies, Geneva, Switzerland

The application of economics to legal matters has proven a gold mine yielding high returns over the last decade or so. The process of exploitation will continue as new problems emerge. Earl Grinols and Roberto Perrelli show how new opportunities for interdisciplinary research can be created and exploited.

Casting international trade disputes and litigation within the WTO framework as a game comes naturally to the economists. The basic idea should also have a natural appeal to the lawyers, trade negotiators and international organization officials. After all, they may be like Monsieur Jourdain in Molière's play who was delighted to discover that he had been speaking prose all his life. In order to be useful, the game theory has to be capable of explaining some important features regarding international trade relations. Two such stylised facts seem worth modelling:

- Joining the WTO does not necessarily make a country liberal. In fact, WTO members are no less protectionist than WTO non-members.
- We have witnessed a sharp increase in the number of trade disputes after the creation of the WTO. The trade-dispute tendency can be observed especially among small countries.

The unintended, one would hope, dispute-encouraging effect of the WTO may come from the reduction of costs of dispute settlement. This effect works particularly strongly to the advantage of small countries.

But how do we define a small country? In the traditional trade theory this was done by reference to a country's power of influencing international terms of trade. A small country can change the volume of its imports or exports without any impact on their prices in the world market. This definition is no longer clear-cut in the world of imperfect competition. Models of non-competitive market behaviour that have become so popular with the advent of the new thread theory assign some pricing influence to *all* countries involved in international trade.

Since the small-large country distinction plays such a crucial role in the Grinols and Perrelli paper, it merits a deeper discussion then the one offered by the authors. They state that "smaller courtiers have smaller trade flows from which infringement opportunities come." And how do infringement opportunities come about? Basically by a random process. The smallness is thus associated with the size and importance of trade flows. There is some merit to this view; it flows naturally from the definition of a small country used in the traditional trade literature.

However, consider the United States' main origins of imports as reported in The Economist's World in Figures, 2002:

- Canada: 19.3 % of total
- EU15: 19.1 % of total
- Japan: 12.8 % of total
- Mexico: 10.7 % of total
- China: 8.0 % of total

Would anyone seriously suggest that the above ranking would correspond the way the United States would line up the above countries on its scale of importance. Surely, Canada is not bigger in the eyes of its neighbour to the South than the EU15. Neither is Mexico bigger than China.

Without getting into a hair-splitting exercise, it seems important to define who is small and who is large. There is no obvious way of settling this discussion but a large country will not bash a small country every time the latter commits a trade infringement. And the bigger the difference in their sizes, the more can a small country get away with. And if you reduce the cost of dispute settlements you will in general encourage more trade infringements and in particular infringements by small courtiers.

To my mind, the basic asymmetry comes possibly from different national welfare functions applied by large countries vis-à-vis those who punch in the same weight category and the ones who are much weaker opponents. To put it in an extreme way: A truly big country cannot afford to lose a fight with a strong opponent. At the same time, it may not "afford" to win, or even start, a fight with a truly small country. I would very much encourage Earl Grinols and Roberto Perrelli to pursue this line of investigation.

There is another aspect of the paper which could be greatly extended, even though it would certainly not be easy. As it stands, the model assumes that infringement opportunities arrive on a random basis. Would it mean that commercial policies become random with case-by-case response to some external shocks? If this indeed were claimed, I would find such a proposition hard to swallow.

If it is a game, trade policy is not a one-shot event; it is a repeated game. I know, it is easy to say it but much more difficult to come up with a tractable model. Luckily, not everything is lost. The very rich literature of the 1980s on wage indexation, government-trade union bargaining and the credible conduct of monetary policy produced results such as "tit-for-tat strategy", or "overlook a first infringement but hit hard when a second violation happens".

I applaud the approach taken by Earl Grinols and Roberto Perrelli. Perhaps my suggestions can encourage them to go further in their research.

Modelling the Impact of China's WTO Membership on Its Investment and Growth: A New Flexible Keynesian Approach

Tran Van Hoa

Department of Economics, University of Wollongong, Australia

1 Introduction

The standard theories of economics, international finance, transnational corporations, and within the accounting framework of the United Nations System of National Accounts (SNA93) or earlier stipulate that investment plays a crucial role in influencing microeconomic decisions and macroeconomic activity, national output growth and economic development. Investment also helps to shape fiscal and monetary policy (Dornbusch and Fischer 1990) and economic reforms in many developed, newly industrialized and especially developing countries (World Bank 1991). Corporate and private strategies for business development and expansion in a home or host economy depend on this crucial role in a Wiener-Granger causal sense. As a result, a rigorous study and discussions of the movements or trends of these economic aggregates and their empirical relationships either in a historical context or in future predictions are amply justified.

With its formal accession to the WTO in November 2001, China expects, as a result in the medium and long term, enhanced trade, investment and economic growth in that sequential order. The purpose of our paper is therefore to contribute to this important nexus study by exploring empirically the interdependence of the various 'engines of growth' and by using a new modelling approach integrating the static CGE and dynamic multi-equation Keynesian theories and the SNA93 framework.

To achieve our purpose in a novel way, the paper departs from the applied econometric modelling approaches using conventional multiple regressions, Haavelmo's simultaneous equations, Zellner's SUR, or subjective or data-inconsistent CGE/GTAP, and makes use instead of a fairly simple and flexible economy-wide modelling approach based on the calculus of differential analysis in economics (Van Hoa 1992a, 1992d) to provide the fundamental equations in the reduced form for macroaggregates of interest. The success of this new approach is assessed via its modelling performance, analytic and empirical.

Finally, the paper is a contribution to applications of recent advances in the econometric theory of forecasting and impact studies to better formulate forward planning/impact policy and strategies either in finance, economics, or business.

These advances consist of our new empirical Bayes or two-stage hierarchical information – 2SHI – (Van Hoa 1985, 1986a, 1993b, Van Hoa and Chaturvedi 1988, 1990, 1997) theories that have average MSE or Wald risk properties superior to other conventional methods including the OLS, the maximum likelihood, or the explicit (Baranchik 1973) positive Stein-like (Anderson 1984) methodologies.

The implications from our paper are twofold. First, if the modelling success of our new approach is relatively superlative – in terms of its empirical fit and turning point predictions – then its superiority in impact studies for say China's WTO membership is confirmed, historically or in an *ex ante* sense. Secondly, if, based on the same model and dataset, a substantial improvement in impact outcomes is achieved by our 2SHI methods in relation to other conventional procedures currently in use, then our findings will, in addition, point to a new direction of rigorous modelling and impact study methodology not only for China's WTO membership but also for other applications in finance, economics, and business analysts in their corporate and individual planning to investment and growth.

2 Trends in China's Main Economic Activities (1960-1999)

In the investment area, China has actively sought foreign direct investment (FDI) and technology to promote its modernization efforts and accelerate its export trade capabilities since its opening up in 1978. The total amount of incoming FDI rose from almost zero in that year to a high of about $110 billion in 1993 and $320 billion in 1999. Thus, China has become the world's third (second until 1998) largest recipient of FDI, and the largest recipient among developing countries. The FDI volume has hovered around $40-50 billion in each of the past several years. China also expects significantly increased inflows over the next five years following its WTO accession in November 2001. This accession would bring about the removal of a number of restrictions on foreign investment (OECD 2001).

At present, China is on the threshold of crucial developments and policy decisions concerning FDI, and keen to increase the level, quality and source diversity of incoming FDI, particularly FDI from the OECD member countries. The Chinese government also continues its efforts to adjust its policy and institutional framework, as well as investment promotion policies, to the requirements of the changing international and domestic circumstances (OECD 2001) such as globalization and China's reforms.

Previous efforts by the OECD and China's Ministry of Foreign Economic Cooperation and Trade (MOFTEC) resulted in a conference in Xiamen, Fujian, in September 2000 to discuss the driving forces and economic effects of FDI on China's development, to exchange information and experiences on best FDI promotion practices, and to elaborate China's future FDI plans and policies. Our study below supplements these efforts from a methodological perspective and having important implications for more effective impact studies of China's WTO membership consistent with historical data over three decades.

Figure 1 summarizes the annual (1960-1998) movements of China's six main SNA macroaggregates: GDP, private consumption, gross fixed investment, government expenditure, exports, and imports (all at current prices). All these aggregates show an exponential growth path from 1960 to 1998 recording the well-known fast pace of China's recent development. The largest component of GDP is private consumption, followed by investment, exports and imports (generally with a trade surplus). Despite the role played by the government in the economy, its share in SNA is the lowest as seen in Figure 1. Significantly, there is a slight sign of the Asia crisis' impact only in so far as exports and imports are concerned. Also, there seems to be a link between the trends of these macroaggregates.

While the impact of China's WTO membership can be studied via increased exports and imports alone, the apparent link between them and the rest of the economy's activities in an SNA93 context makes the task of study more complicated.

More specifically, to decompose this link into a more precise form for say a study of the impact of increased trade and investment from China's WTO membership or for other policy analysis, we have a number of options. These options can involve (a) a descriptive analysis of the graphs of these macroaggregates, their means, standard deviations and cross-correlations, or their shifts (instability) over time. We can also look at (b) the econometric interaction between trade and investment and other relevant causal economic activities in the economy. We adopt the second approach because of the inherent Marshallian nature of economic activities in which all are interrelated or interdependent.

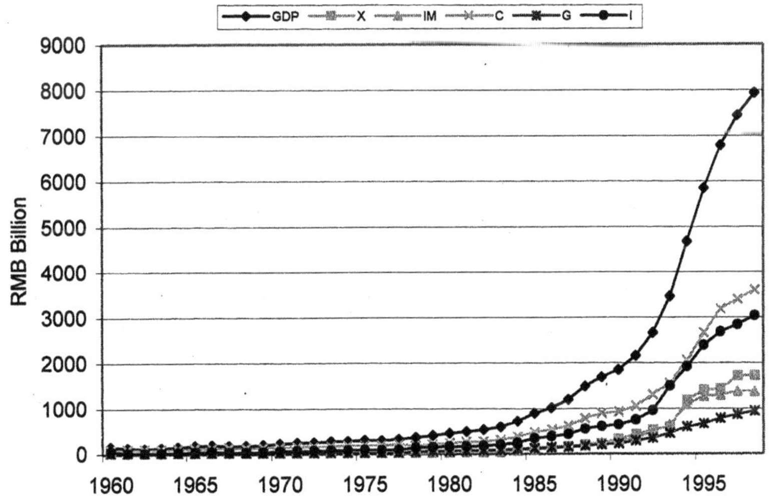

Figure 1. China's Main Macroaggregates (in local currency)
Source: World Bank World Tables (2001)

3 Modelling China's Economy: A Multi-Sectoral Flexible CGE-Keynesian Approach

Modelling an economy can take many approaches and forms with varying degrees of success from both a theoretical and empirical context. In an economy with interdependent sectors and activities, any of our six macroaggregates in-focus for China above could be argued to be dependent on many varied internal and external, economic and non-economic factors and in a linear, nonlinear, or mixed functional form. Consider for illustration in this paper a simple well-known generic five-equation Keynesian macroeconomic model of an open economy in an arbitrary functional form as

$$C = C(Y,C\text{-}1) \tag{1'}$$

$$I = I(Y, Y\text{-}1, R, R\text{-}1) \tag{2'}$$

$$X = X(Y, YW, PCN, PUS) \tag{3'}$$

$$IM = IM(Y, YW, PCN, PUS) \tag{4'}$$

$$Y = Y(C, I, G, X, IM) \tag{5'}$$

or its usual linear form

$$C_t = \alpha 11 + \alpha 12 Y_t + \alpha 13 C_{t-1} + u1_t \tag{1}$$

$$I_t = \alpha 21 + \alpha 22 Y_t + \alpha 23 Y_{t-1} + \alpha 24 R_t + \alpha 25 R_{t-1} + u2_t \tag{2}$$

$$X_t = \alpha 31 + \alpha 32 Y_t + \alpha 33 YW_t + \alpha 34 PCN + \alpha 35 PUS_t + u3_t \tag{3}$$

$$IM_t = \alpha 41 + \alpha 42 Y_t + \alpha 43 YW_t + \alpha 44 PCN + \alpha 45 PUS_t + u4_t \tag{4}$$

$$Y_t = C_t + I_t + G_t + X_t - Im_t \tag{5}$$

where C = private final consumption expenditure, Y = gross domestic product or GDP, I = private gross fixed investment, G = government expenditure, X = exports of goods and services, IM = imports of goods and services, YW = US income (as a proxy for world income), PCN = general price deflator in China, PUS = general price deflator in the US (as a proxy for world prices), and R = US prime rate (as a proxy for world interest rate). The α's denote the structural parameters, and the u's the error terms. All value variables are expressed in terms of their constant 1995 prices.

The model (1)-(5) is a dynamic macroeconomic model (Pindyck and Rubinfeld 1991) for an open economy and takes into account (a) a partial adjustment process in consumption behaviour encompassing the hypotheses of relative and permanent income, liquid assets, wealth, and life cycles in the sense of Duesenberry, Friedman, and Modigliani, (b) a flexible accelerator investment behaviour, augmented by foreign capital borrowings (see for further detail Van Hoa and Harvie 1998) and user's costs, (c) trade openness through exports and imports regulated by foreign and domestic demand conditions and price relativities and (d) relevance of the government sector expenditure especially in transition economies.

In this model, the WTO membership impact is assumed to be transmitted through increased trade and investment, and this itself will be transmitted to increased growth and private consumption. In the model, consumption, investment, exports, imports and GDP are endogenous, and there are 9 exogenous and predetermined variables.

It can be verified that, using the order condition for identifiability or mathematical consistency in the theory of econometrics, all equations in the model are over-identified. As a result, the endogenous variable equations for say investment, consumption and growth can be written, instead of their linear form given traditionally in (1)-(5), in their complete differential form (see Allen 1960) in the reduced form as (see Van Hoa 1992a and 1992d, Harvie and Van Hoa 1993)

$$I\%_t \cup C\%_t \cup Y\%_t = a_{i1} + a_{i2} C\%_{t-1} + a_{i3} Y\%_{t-1} + a_{i4} R\%_t + a_{i5} R\%_{t-1} + a_{i6} YW\%_t + a_{i7} PCN\% + a_{i8} PUS\% + a_{i9} G\%_t + e_{i_t} \quad (6a/b/c)$$

where U is a union symbol, I%, C%, Y%, R%, YW%, PCN%, PUS%, and G% indicate the rate of change of I, C, Y, R, YW, PCN, PUS and G respectively, a's indicate the reduced form parameters, and e's are the new error terms with I referring the I, C or Y equation.

The three equations in (6) characterize the investment, consumption and growth relationships from the illustrative five-equation macroeconomic model given in Eqts (1)-(5). In contrast to the conventional unidirectional analysis, the impact of enhanced trade due to China's WTO membership on investment, consumption and growth can be only seen indirectly through the exogenous and predetermined variables. By conventional definition, the impact parameters from these equations are in fact either static (or dynamic) elasticities associated with either current (or lagged) variables included in it.

The derivation of (6) by means of total differentiation of an arbitrarily functional relationship is simple and, more importantly, consistent with the procedure usually adopted for the neoclassical macroeconomic models of the applied or CGE kind. In these neo-classical models, the endogenous and exogenous variables in the economy are linked by a (usually first order) approximate transmission mechanism in terms of the elasticities. There are however at least five important differences between our equations given in (6) above and the specifications from applied or CGE Johansen-class models.

First, in our case, the important linking elasticities have to be estimated for the model as a whole using economic time-series data and possibly other extraneous (prior) information such as policy switches or external non-economic factors. Our equations given in (6) thus are completely data-based, although clearly we do not preclude the use of prior or extraneous information (in the form of an oil crisis or a major war for example) in the equations in other theoretical or judgemental contexts.

Secondly, in view of the above arguments, our model is capable of accommodating sub- and add-factors as well as structural change and other institutional considerations (for a discussion supporting the use of these factors in macroeconomic policy models, see Johansen 1982).

Thirdly, our equations must be mathematically consistent as required by the identifiability conditions for complete systems of structural simultaneous equations in the theory of econometrics.

Fourthly, by its construct, our modelling approach encompasses a wide class of linear and nonlinear multi-equation econometric models in which the exact functional form of each of the individual structural equations is, as usual, unknown or needs not be specified.

Finally, for an important group of economic variables whose first differences in logs are approximately equivalent to the rates of change, our equations by their construct include as the special cases the Granger-Wiener short-term causality if these rates of changes are I(0) and the co-integration or long-term equations of the Engle-Granger (1987) class (see Van Hoa 1993c, and Harvie and Van Hoa 1993, for further detail) if the rates of change are I(1).

To evaluate the performance of the equations of interest in (6) in our macroeconomic model (1)-(5) and our new impact study methodology using real-life data from China in recent years, we have fitted the I%, C% and Y% equations (6) to data for the period 1966 to 1998. This will optimally produce the necessary elasticity estimates. These estimates can then be used in a comparative study which is based on stochastic simulation to measure the relative MSE performance or operational accuracy of our modelling equations. These equations can finally be used for a study of the impact of China's WTO membership under different and plausible scenarios of shocks or policy regimes.

4 Impact and Forecasting Study: Alternative Methodologies

The equations in differential and reduced form as given in (6) can be written more generally with a sampling size T and k independent variables (possible causes) in matrix notation as

$$\underset{(T\times 1)}{y} = \underset{(T\times k)}{Z}\ \underset{(k\times 1)}{\beta} + \underset{(T\times 1)}{u} \qquad (7)$$

where y = I%, C% or Y%, Z = the rate of changes of the exogenous and predetermined variables (both static and dynamic), ß = the parameters, and u the disturbance satisfying all standard statistical assumptions.

We now define our evaluation criterion (Wald risks) for an arbitrary estimator βa for β in (7) as Wald risk ≡ MSE(βa) = (βa-β)'W(βa-β) where W is positive definite.

Under Wald risks, we can estimate (7) which is essentially a general linear model (7) for structural or behavioral analysis or for direct forecasting and policy studies (see Pindyck and Rubinfeld 1991) by using the OLS or, at a more efficient level, any of the explicit (Baranchik 1973) Stein or Stein-rule methods as described below.

More specifically, using (7), the basic and most well-known method to produce estimates and forecasts of y (or I%, C% and Y%) is the OLS estimator of ß (denoted by b) and written as

$$b = (Z'Z)^{-1}Z'y \tag{8}$$

A more sophisticated and efficient method is the explicit Stein estimator of ß (Baranchik 1973) and given by

$$\hat{\beta}s = [1 - c(y-Zb)'(y-Zb)/b'Z'Zb]\, b = [1 - c(1-R^2)/R^2]\, b \tag{9}$$

where c is a characterizing scalar and defined in the range $0 < c < 2(k-2)/(T-k+2)$, and R^2 is the square of the sample multiple correlation coefficient.

A still more efficient method is the explicit positive-part Stein estimator of ß (Anderson 1984) defined as

$$\begin{aligned} \hat{\beta}{+s} &= [1 - \min\{1\,,\ c(y-Zb)'(y-Zb)/b'Z'Zb\}]\, b \\ &= [1 - \min\{1\,,\ c(1-R^2)/R^2\}]\, b \end{aligned} \tag{10}$$

A new method to obtain estimates and forecasts of ß in (7) with better properties has been proposed (see Van Hoa 1985, Van Hoa and Chaturvedi 1988, 1990, 1997). It is in a class of explicit improved Stein-rule or empirical Bayes [also known as two-stage hierarchical-information (2SHI)] estimators for some linear regression models. This estimator includes the explicit Stein and the double k-class (Ullah and Ullah 1981) estimators as subsets (Van Hoa 1993b). Other applications of the Stein, Stein-rule, and 2SHI estimators to linear regression models with non-spherical disturbances and to Zellner's seemingly unrelated regression model have also been made (see Van Hoa et al. 1993a, in the case of regressions with non-spherical disturbances, and Van Hoa 1992b, and 1992d, in the case of seemingly unrelated regressions).

The explicit 2SHI estimator is a *bona fide* or fully operational estimator and defined as

$$\hat{\beta}h = [1 - c(1-R^2)/R^2\} - c(1-R^2)/\{R^2(1+c(1-R^2)/R^2)\}]\, b \tag{11}$$

and its positive-part counterpart (Van Hoa, 1986a) is given by

$$\hat{\beta}{+h} = [1 - \min\{1\,,\ c(1-R^2)/R^2\} - \{1/((R^2/c(1-R^2)) + 1)\}]\, b \tag{12}$$

While all the estimators given above can be applied to the general linear model (7) for structural and forecasting analysis, their relative performance in terms of historical, *ex post* or *ex ante* (Pindyck and Rubinfeld 1991) forecasting MSE can differ. Thus, it is well-known that, in MSE and for $k \geq 3$ and $T \geq k + 2$, $\hat{\beta}$ s dominates (that is, it performs better in forecasting MSE) b, and $\hat{\beta}$ s is dominated by $\hat{\beta}$ +s (Baranchik 1973, Anderson 1984). However, it has also been demonstrated (Van Hoa 1985, Van Hoa and Chaturvedi 1988) that, in MSE, $\hat{\beta}$ h dominates both b and $\hat{\beta}$ s, and more importantly, $\hat{\beta}$ +h dominates $\hat{\beta}$ +s (Van Hoa 1986a).

A further important path-breaking result of the 2SHI theory has recently been proved (see Van Hoa and Chaturvedi, 1997): *the dominance of the 2SHI over the OLS and Stein exists anywhere in the range* $0 < c < 2(k-1)/(T-k)$. This indicates that the 2SHI method produces better (in terms of smaller Walk risk or generalized Pitman nearness) estimates and forecasts even if the estimating and forecasting equation has only one independent variable in it. *The condition for the optimal Stein dominance in the linear equation up to now requires that* $0 < c < 2(k-2)/(T-k+2)$ (see Anderson 1984).

While some application of these forecasting methodologies to predictions of economic activities in some developed countries such as Australia (see Van Hoa 1992d) has been made, the extent of the significance of the MSE dominance, or equivalently, the informational gain or relative forecasting success between the alternative estimators above has not been investigated explicitly within an open trade theoretical framework and an empirical context using more recent economic data for the major economies in East Asia. This issue is taken up in the study below for one of the fastest growth economies in the world in recent years but with highly fluctuating investment and being very sensitive to foreign trade and capital flows in the region (see Van Hoa and Harvie 1998).

Another interesting feature of our study is that, since all data are annual and have, as usual, a small sample size, our study is therefore designed to look at the finite sample performance of alternative impact study methods, an area neglected in numerous studies of this kind.

Finally, since the poor quality of economic data from the Asian countries and other less developed countries (LDC) economies is well known, one by-product of our study is that we in fact investigate the performance of the alternative forecasts in the case of serious measurement errors on the variables of the macromodel of an economy however it is defined.

The substantive findings reported below are based on the five-equation macroeconomic model described earlier in (1)-(5), and the appropriate estimating equations (6) to produce elasticity parameters or the equations to study the impact of China's WTO membership on its investment, consumption and growth as given in (6). In addition, a number of well-known methods is used to compare their relative performance for better decision analysis.

5 Modelling China's Economy: Performance of Alternative Methodologies

In our study, we have fitted the three equations (investment, consumption and growth) in differential and reduced form (6a-6c) of the model (1)-(5) to annual data from China. The original dataset is from 1961 to 1998, but the effective sample period is 1962 to 1998, giving, when the dynamic (lag) structure is taken into account, a sample size of up to 37 observations for each variable. In our comparative study, only the OLS or ML, the positive-part Stein, and the positive-part 2SHI forecasts of investment are used to produce elasticities for impact study.

The data for our study are in real terms at the constant 1995 prices and obtained from the 2000 World Bank World Tables Industrial Countries and East Asia databases, using Australia's data express (DX) extracting procedure. The performance of our reduced form equations is determined solely from their good fit, correct turning point predictions and improved forecasting MSE.

The possible effects of structural instability (economic dynamism) and uncertainty (due to financial or economic crises) on China's investment, consumption and growth have also been taken into account. This is achieved by modelling these macroaggregates in the short (one year), medium (two years) and long-terms (3 or more years), and also subjecting our impact to wide fluctuations (measurement errors) over the study period.

The simulation results from this study (not shown here) support the analytical results discussed in Section 3 in all scenarios (see also other evidence in Appendix). More specifically, our methodologies indicate that they are specially suited to study the impact of the factors affecting China's trade, investment, consumption and growth especially in the long term.

6 Measuring the Impact of China's WTO Membership on Investment, Consumption and Growth

6.1 Possible Impact on China's Investment

In order to study the impact of China's WTO membership on the country's investment, it is necessary to study the determinants (whether WTO-induced or not) as focused in our specified model that have directly or indirectly affected this investment in an historical context. The relevant determinants of investment based on our simple model (1)-(5) are given in Equation (6a). The impact of the WTO membership on China's investment is transmitted directly via enhanced trade (exports and imports) but indirectly through these determinants at the end of the transmission mechanism. A good equation in this case would then be able to provide better outcomes for future impact or *ex ante* studies on investment.

The historical forecast movements of China's investment are econometrically efficient and emulate well its actual fluctuations (peaks and troughs) during the period under study, 1962-98 (see Figure 2). While there are some underestimations of the actual peaked investment in the early 1960s, there is also some indication of more minor overestimation in the recent years due possibly to other relevant but omitted (internal or external) factors from our model. Of special interest to us is however the ability of our estimated model to mimic not only the trends but also the turning points of the observed investment data over nearly four decades, even though we conceded earlier that our model is simply an illustration of the performance of our new modelling methodologies for impact study. On this evaluation criterion, our forecasts and impact findings would be regarded as reliable.

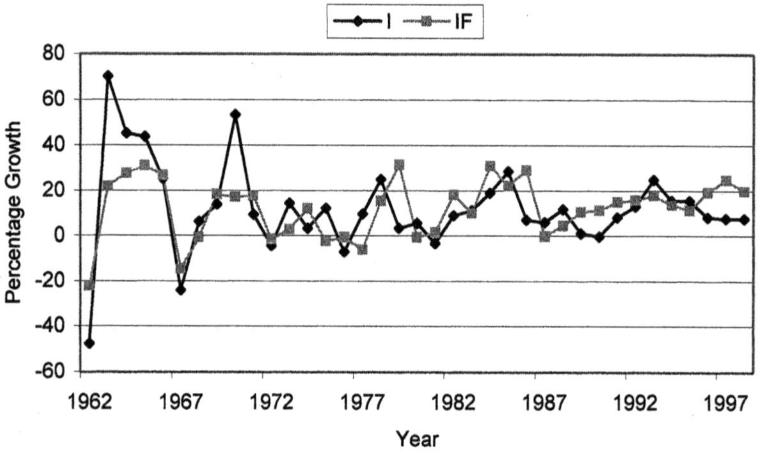

Figure 2. Modelling China's Investment for WTO Membership Impact Study

6.2 Possible Impact on China's Private Consumption

Modelling China's private consumption (6b) for impact study and based on our illustrative Keynesian model (1)–(5) has not been as successful in accurately predicting the peaks and troughs as in the case of investment (see Figure 3). This may be understandable in the sense that this underestimation of consumption occurred during the period of great constitutional changes. These changes include the opening up of China to the world in 1972, the internal turmoil of 1989, and the Gulf War of the early 1990s. In addition, expected conspicuous consumption (due to great anticipations of the country's reform) in China has been fairly high in the decades of high growth (1980s and early 1990s), and political stability in the country.

The consumption explanation needs further clarification. In fact, it is our observation that in economies of fairly sustained high growth rates, sometimes over-hyped expectations of better things seem to override unrealistically other considerations (see also Hewitt 2001). It is within this context of consumer's behaviour that our model which is based on the Keynesian-Friedman-Modigliani theory should be amended to take this observation into account in future modelling and impact studies.

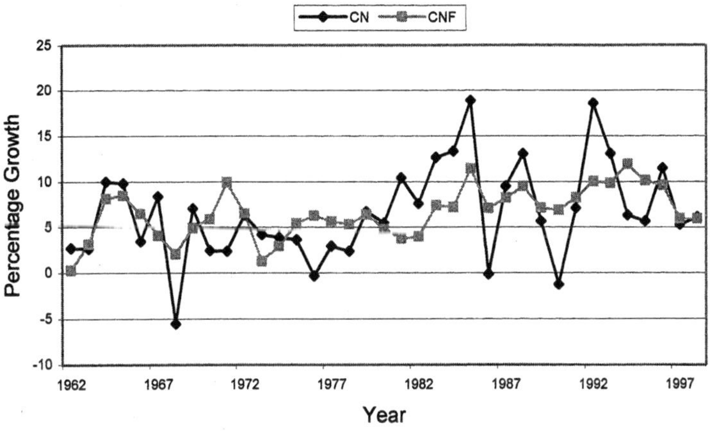

Figure 3. Modelling China's Private Consumption for WTO Membership Impact Study

6.3 Possible Impact on Growth

In contrast to the performance of the private consumption equation (6b) discussed above, our estimated equation (6c) for China's growth over the period of nearly 4 decades (1962-98) appears to fare very well (see Figure 4). These findings thus indicate that the equation is particularly suitable for WTO membership impact study. It should be noted that the sampling period is a period of great upheavals in the country that also was subject to big changes or shocks outside it. Some of these shocks are well-known such as the opening up of China to the outside world, the two great oil crises of 1974 and 1981, the crash of the stock market in the US in 1987, the Gulf War in 1991, China's internal turmoil in 1989, and the Asia crisis of 1997. While these shocks and the consumer's hype may have affected our estimated private consumption, they are capably and fully accommodated in our estimated growth equation.

Thus, in spite of these so-called perceived outliers in the data, our estimated growth equation still could mimic almost all fluctuations (including the peaks and troughs) of China's spectacular and widely fluctuating output growth during 1962-98. On the basis of these findings, our model as given in (1)–(5) should be capable of calculating fairly accurately the impact of China's WTO membership on the country's principal economic objective: its increasing standard of living or welfare. The impact is transmitted significantly through the variables specified for the model and given in the reduced form equation (6c).

It should be noted that, there is no reason why other relevant variables or the sub- and add-factors in the sense of Jorgensen (1982) cannot be integrated into the model (1)-(5) for a better study of the impact of the WTO membership on China's growth or standard of living in the future.

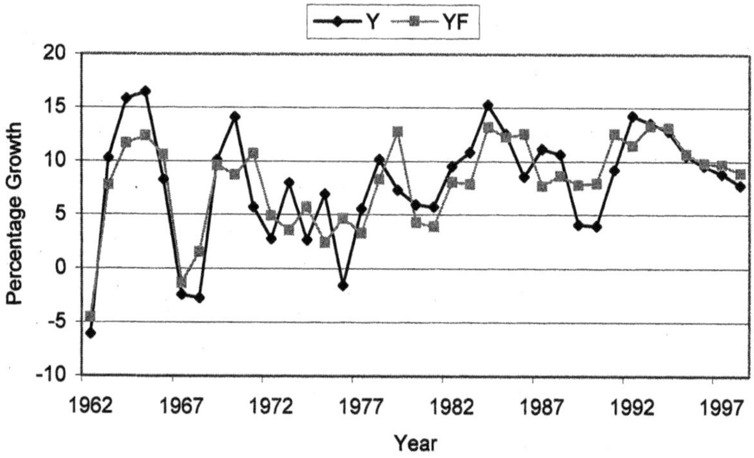

Figure 4. Modelling China's Growth for WTO Membership Impact Study

Case Study

WTO Membership Impact (via 10% Price Reduction and 10% Government Spending Boost) on China's Growth

The impact model: Below we have used our estimated reduced form equation (6c) for China's growth to study the perceived impact of the country's 2001 WTO membership on its standard of living or growth rates over a number of years. The analysis is historical but its translation to impact studies for the post-WTO accession period is straightforward. The methodological justification for this argument is that good historical or *ex post* outcomes will produce good *ex ante* results (Pyndyck and Rubinfeld 1991).

The scenario: As a result of the WTO membership, it is assumed that opening up the Chinese market to the outside world and accompanying reform (and change of culture) will reduce the general price level (the CPI) in China by 10 per cent. This will boost domestic spending due to reduced commodity prices and increase government revenue and subsequent increased government spending. Assume that the spending boost is also 10 per cent. Assume also that the impact started in 1991 for historical studies (or equivalently in 2002 for ex ante studies). The estimated impact of the WTO membership on China's growth rate under this scenario is depicted in Figure 5.

The outcomes: In Figure 5 we have plotted the WTO-membership-induced impact of a 10 per cent reduction in China's CPI and a 10 per cent increase in the government expenditure. This impact seems to have a mixed effect initially on China's growth rate. The effect becomes clearer and more uniform after a few years.

For example, in the first two years after the change (that is, the WTO membership), there would be a slow-down (that is, lower but still very much positive rates) in China's growth. This may be due to challenges of restructuring in policy and over-hyped community perception in the country. But six years after the change, China's growth was seen to attain an increase of 10.1 per cent higher than that in the no-change (no WTO membership) state. And seven years after the change, China's growth will be 16.5 per cent higher than that in the no-change state. The effects of China's WTO membership are, from our study, beneficial and of a long-term nature. In addition, the effects would continue to grow over time, especially when the compound flow-throughs of other economic, financial or administrative reforms introduced as a result of China's WTO membership are taken into account in modelling and in policy analysis.

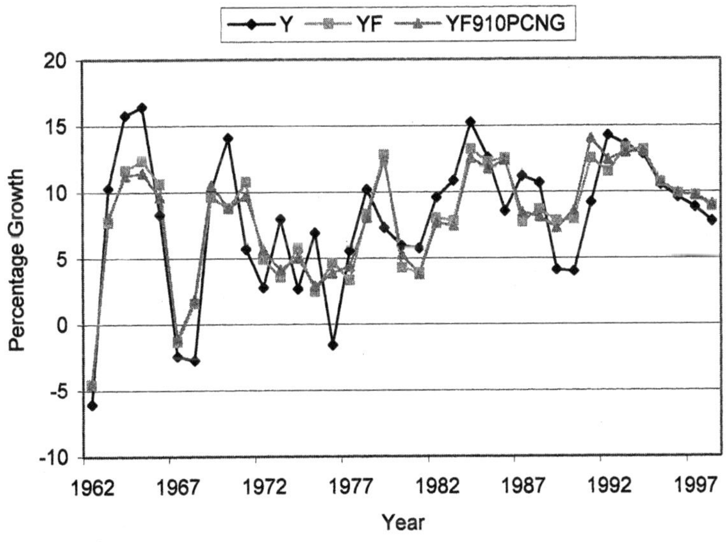

Figure 5. Impact of China's WTO Membership on Growth

References

Allen RGD (1960) Mathematical Analysis for Economists. Macmillan, London

Anderson TW (1984) An Introduction to Multivariate Statistical Analysis. 2nd Edition. Wiley, New York

Baranchik AJ (1973) Inadmissibility of Maximum Likelihood Estimators in some Multiple Regression Problems with Three or More Independent Variables. Annals of Statistics 1 : 312–321

Chaturvedi A, Van Hoa T (1997) The dominance of the 2SHI estimator under generalized Pitman nearness. Communications in Statistics 26(5) : 1227–1238

Dornbusch D, Fischer S (1990) Macroeconomics. 5th Edition. McGraw Hill, Sydney

Hewitt D (2001) Chinese Hope for Consumer Revolution. BBC News, November 12, 2001. Internet: http://news.bbc.co.uk/1/hi/world/asia-pacific/1651880.stm

Engle RF, Granger CWJ (1987) Co-integration and Error Correction: Representation, Estimation and testing. Econometrica 55 : 251–276

Harvie C, Van Hoa T (1993) Long Term Relationships of Major Macrovariables in a Resource-Related Economic Model of Australia: a Cointegration Analysis. Energy Economics 15 : 257–262

Johansen L (1982) Econometric Models and Economic Planning and Policy: Some Trends and Problems. In: Hazewinkle M, Rinnooy Kan AHG (eds) Current Developments in the Interface: Economics, Econometrics, Mathematics. Reidel, Boston

OECD (2001) Foreign Direct Investment in China, Internet: www/oecd/org/oecd/pages/

Pindyck RS, Rubinfeld DL (1991) Econometric Models and Economic Forecasts. McGraw-Hill, Sydney

Van Hoa T (1985) The Inadmissibility of the Stein Estimator in Normal Multiple Regression Equations. Economics Letters 19 : 39–42

Van Hoa T (1986a) The Inadmissibility of the Stein Estimator in Normal Multiple Regression Models: Analytical and Simulation Results. 15th Anniversary of the NBER-NSF Seminar on Bayesian Inference in Econometrics, ITAM. Mexico City, 16–18 January 1986

Van Hoa T (1986b) Effects of Monetary and Fiscal Policy on Inflation: Some Evidence from the J-Test. Economics Letters 22 : 187–190

Van Hoa T, Chaturvedi A (1988) The Necessary and Sufficient Conditions for the Uniform Dominance of the Two-Stage Stein Estimators. Economics Letters 28 : 351–355

Van Hoa T, Chaturvedi A (1990) Further Results on the Two-Stage Hierarchical Information (2SHI) Estimators in the Linear Regression Models. Communications in Statistics (Theory and Methods) A19(12) : 4697–4704

Van Hoa T (1992a) Modelling Output Growth: A New Approach. Economics Letters 38 : 279–284

Van Hoa T (1992b) Energy Consumption in Thailand: Estimated Structure and Improved Forecasts to 2000 (in Thai). Thammasat Economic Journal (Thailand) 10 : 55–63

Van Hoa T (1992c) A Multi-equation Model of Energy Consumption in Thailand. International Journal of Energy Research 16 : 381–385

Van Hoa T (1992d) A New and General Approach to Modelling Short-Term Interest Rates: With Application to Australian Data 1962–1990. Journal of Economics and Finance: Proceedings 16 : 327–335

Van Hoa T, Chaturvedi A, Shukla G (1993a) Performance of the Stein-rule Estimators when the Disturbances are Misspecified as Spherical. Economic Studies Quarterly (Japan) 44 : 601–611

Van Hoa T (1993b) The Mixture Properties of the 2SHI Estimators in Linear Regression Models. Statistics and Probability Letters 16 : 111–115

Van Hoa T (1993c) Effects of Oil on Output Growth and Inflation in Developing Countries: The Case of Thailand 1966:1 to 1991:1. International Journal of Energy Research 17 : 29–33

Van Hoa T, Chaturvedi A (1997) Performance of the 2SHI Estimator under the Generalized Pitman Nearness Criterion. Communications in Statistics (Theory and Method) 26(5) : 1227–1238

Van Hoa T, Harvie C (1998) Causes and Impact of the Asian Financial Crisis. Macmillan, London

Ullah A, Ullah S (1978) Double k-class Estimators of Coefficients in Linear Regression. Econometrica 46 : 705–722

World Bank (1991) The Challenge of Development, World Development Report. Oxford University Press, Oxford

World Bank (2000) World Tables, World Bank, Washington DC

Appendix: Performance of the 2SHI Estimator Under the Generalised Pitman Nearness Criterion

Tran Van Hoa* and Anoop Chaturvedi**[1]

* Department of Economics, University of Wollongong, Australia
** Department of Mathematics and Statistics, University of Allahabad, India

1 Introduction

In 1985, Van Hoa proposed a family of 2SHI (two stage hierarchical information) estimators for the coefficient vector of the linear regression model. These 2SHI estimators were demonstrated to dominate in average mean squared errors (MSE) the OLS and the Stein estimators. A number of applications of the 2SHI estimators in empirical economic studies based on static and dynamic regression models where the 2SHI dominance was calculated have also been reported (see Van Hoa 1992a, 1992b, 1993).

In 1990 and 1993, Van Hoa and Chaturvedi extended the 2SHI further and considered a more general family of 2SHI estimators. They obtained the conditions for the dominance of the 2SHI estimator over the OLS and Stein rule estimators under a quadratic loss function. In those studies, the criterion of relative MSE or risks in the sense of Wald was adopted.

The MSE criterion is only one of many criteria that can be used in the studies of this kind. The Pitman nearness criterion is another concept that has been developed and used by several researchers for a comparison of alternative estimators, see Keating and Mason (1985), Rao et al. (1986), Khatree (1987) and Peddada (1987), to cite a few. A special feature of this criterion is that it does not require the existence of the moments of the estimator and is less sensitive to the tail behaviour of the sampling distributions of the estimator. Rao et al. (1986) and Keating and Mason (1988) considered a Generalized Pitman Nearness (GPN) criterion and analysed the performance of the Stein rule estimator in comparison to the Maximum Likelihood Estimator (MLE) for the mean of the multivariate normal distribution using extensive numerical studies. Sen et al. (1989) derived the dominance condition for the Stein rule estimator over the MLE under a GPN criterion (see also Keating and Czitrom (1988) and Mason et al. 1990).

[1] This work was carried out during the second author's visit to the Department of Economics, University of Wollongong, as a Visiting Lecturer. The financial support and research facilities from the Department are greatly appreciated.

The main objective of the present paper is to establish the dominance of the 2SHI estimator over the OLS estimator and the Stein rule estimator under a GPN criterion. Since the technique adopted in Sen et al. (1989) is quite involved and leads to fairly complicated expressions, we have adopted a simple methodology based on the small disturbances approximations.

2 The Model and the Estimators

Consider the linear regression model

$$y = X\beta + \sigma u, \tag{1}$$

where y is a Tx1 vector of observations on the dependent variable, X is a Txk matrix of observations on k independent variables with full column rank, β is a kx1 vector of unknown regression coefficients and u is a Tx1 random vector following a multivariate normal distribution $N(0,I_T)$ independent of X and σ^2 (>0) is the disturbance variance.

In 1990 and 1993, Van Hoa and Chaturvedi generalized the work by Van Hoa (1985) and proposed the following family of explicit 2SHI estimators $\hat{\beta}_h$ for the coefficient vector β:

$$\hat{\beta}_h = \left[1 - cw\frac{(1-R^2)}{R^2} - c(1-w)\frac{(1-R^2)}{R^2\left\{1+c^*(1-R^2)/R^2\right\}}\right]b, \tag{2}$$

where $b = (X'X)^{-1}X'y$ is the OLS estimator of β, $R^2 = (b'X'Xb/y'y)$ is the coefficient of determination corresponding to a no intercept model and w ($0 \leq w \leq 1$), c(≥ 0) and c* (≥ 0) are the characterizing scalars.

We can equivalently write the estimators $\hat{\beta}_h$ as:

$$\hat{\beta}_h = \left[1 - cw\frac{(y-Xb)'(y-Xb)}{b'X'Xb} - c(1-w)\frac{(y-Xb)'(y-Xb)}{(b'X'Xb+c^*(y-Xb)'(y-Xb))}\right]b, \tag{3}$$

It can be verified that, when c*=0 or w=1, the 2SHI estimator $\hat{\beta}_h$ reduces to the following Stein rule estimator $\hat{\beta}_s$.

$$\hat{\beta}_s = \left[1 - \frac{(y-Xb)'(y-Xb)}{b'X'Xb}\right]b. \tag{4}$$

3 Comparison of the Estimators

For the comparison of the estimators, let us consider the quadratic loss function

$M(\hat{\beta}) = (\hat{\beta} - \beta)'X'X(\hat{\beta} - \beta)$. Then, following Rao et al. (1986), the formal definition of the GPN criterion is given as follows:

3.1 Definition

For any two estimators $\hat{\beta}$ and $\tilde{\beta}$ of β, under the loss function above, the estimator $\hat{\beta}$ is said to be Pitman closer to the estimator β if

$P[M(\tilde{\beta}) - M(\hat{\beta}) > 0] > \frac{1}{2}$.

3.2 Theorem

Under the assumption of small disturbances variance, up to order 0(σ), we have

$$P\left[M(b) - M(\hat{\beta}_h) > 0\right] = \frac{1}{2} + \frac{\sigma}{(2\pi\tau)^{\frac{1}{2}}}\left[(k-1) - \frac{c}{2}(T-k)\right]. \tag{5}$$

$$P\left[M(\hat{\beta}_s) - M(\hat{\beta}_h) > 0\right] = \frac{1}{2} + \frac{\sigma}{(2\pi\tau)^{\frac{1}{2}}}\left[(k-1) - c(T-k)\right] \tag{6}$$

See Proof at the end of this Appendix.

The above theorem implies that, up to the order of our approximations, under the GPN criterion, the 2SHI estimator $\hat{\beta}_h$ dominates the OLS estimator b whenever

$$0 < c < \frac{2(k-1)}{(T\ \ k)},\ k>1; \tag{7}$$

whereas, $\hat{\beta}_h$ dominates the Stein rule estimator $\hat{\beta}_S$ whenever

$$c > \frac{2(k-1)}{(T-k)},\ k>1. \tag{8}$$

The dominance conditions (7) and (8) show that under the GPN criterion the 2SHI estimator dominates both the OLS estimator as well as the Stein rule estimator whenever c lies in interval [(k-1)/(T-k), 2(k-1)/(T-k)] and k>1. Thus, if k>1, it is possible to improve upon the Stein rule estimator by using the 2SHI estimator.

4 Simulation Results on the Performance of the 2SHI

The performance, by means of a simple simulation study, of the 2SHI estimator over the OLS and Stein estimators in some linear regression models is given in the table below. The 27 different models are the reduced form equations of growth in

Australia derived from a standard 4-equation Keynesian macroeconomic model for an open economy. These models are characterized by different representative values of (a) the weight w, (b) the sample size T, and (c) the disturbance variance σ^2. In these models, w=(0.2, 0.5, and 0.8), T=(10,14 and 16), k=8, and $c=c^* = 1.5(k-1)/(T-k)$. The raw data for X are actual annual economic data on GDP, consumption, investment, government expenditure, exports and imports and obtained from the international 1995 DX database. The magnitude of σ^2 are defined over the range (0.01, 1, and 100). The simulation results are based on the averages from 100 statistical trials (larger numbers of trials have been tried but the findings remain basically unchanged). The dominance between say b and $\hat{\beta}_S$, denoted by $R(b/\hat{\beta}_S)$, is computed as $100[M(b)-M(\hat{\beta}_S)]/M(\hat{\beta}_S)$ where M(b) and $M(\hat{\beta}_S)$ are the average loss of b and $\hat{\beta}_S$ respectively. The calculation of the relative risk is similar for $R(b/\hat{\beta}_h)$ and $R(\hat{\beta}_S/\hat{\beta}_h)$.

From these simulation results, the 2SHI estimator dominates both the OLS and Stein estimators in all models. The smallness of σ as discussed above in the paper can have a fairly wide range of values, from 0.1 to 10 in our simulation study. The dominance does not seem to be greatly affected by these different values of σ.

Table 1. Forecasting Performance of the 2SHI Estimators Over the OLS and Stein: Ex Post Simulation Results

Average R^2 (for all models)	0.980	0.972	0.962	0.962	0.816	0.807	0.941	0.722	0.733
Weight w =	0.2								
T=		10			14			16	
σ^2	0.01	1	100	0.01	1	100	0.01	1	100
R(b/ $\hat{\beta}_s$)	4.51	4.85	6.97	3.85	18.71	19.80	4.80	20.42	19.02
R(b/ $\hat{\beta}_h$)	22.18	23.48	25.01	20.80	95.67	115.74	26.41	122.95	119.49
R($\hat{\beta}_s$)/ $\hat{\beta}_h$)	16.90	17.78	16.86	16.32	64.83	80.07	20.61	85.15	84.42
Weight w =	0.5								
T=		10			14			16	
σ^2	0.01	1	100	0.01	1	100	0.01	1	100
R(b/ $\hat{\beta}_s$)	11.39	11.95	12.87	9.97	48.07	53.14	12.53	56.24	53.97
R(b/ $\hat{\beta}_h$)	21.91	22.92	24.74	20.64	92.94	112.42	26.16	119.14	116.84
R($\hat{\beta}_s$)/ $\hat{\beta}_h$)	9.45	9.80	10.52	9.70	30.30	38.70	12.11	40.26	40.84
Weight w =	0.8								
T=		10			14			16	
σ^2	0.01	1	100	0.01	1	100	0.01	1	100
R(b/ $\hat{\beta}_s$)	18.24	19.22	20.73	16.51	70.10	84.81	20.93	84.72	91.80
R(b/ $\hat{\beta}_h$)	22.25	23.54	27.98	20.82	97.85	116.87	26.44	119.83	121.25
R($\hat{\beta}_s$)/ $\hat{\beta}_h$)	3.39	3.62	6.00	3.70	16.32	17.35	4.56	19.01	15.36

Proof of Theorem

Let us define

$$z = (X'X)^{-\frac{1}{2}} X'u \,,$$
$$\delta = (X'X)^{\frac{1}{2}} \beta \,,$$
$$\tau = \delta'\delta$$
$$v = u'\left[I_T - X(X'X)^{-1} X' \right] u \,.$$

Then $z \sim N(0, I_k)$ and $v \sim \chi^2$ distribution with (T-k) degrees of freedom independently of z. Then, to order $0(\sigma^2)$, we have

$$(b-\beta)'X'X(b-\beta) - (\hat{\beta}_h - \beta)'X'X(\hat{\beta}_h - \beta) = 2c\sigma^3 \,\frac{v}{\tau}\left[\delta'z + \sigma\left\{ z'z - \frac{2}{\tau}(\delta'z)^2 - \frac{cv}{2} \right\} \right],$$

which is greater than zero as long as

$$\eta = \frac{1}{\sqrt{\tau}}\left[\delta'z + \sigma\left\{ z'z - \frac{2}{\tau}(\delta'z)^2 - \frac{cv}{2} \right\} \right]$$

is greater than zero. Let $f(\eta)$ denote the pdf of η. Then to order $0(\sigma)$

$$P\left[M(b) - M(\hat{\beta}_h) > 0 \right] = \int_0^\infty f(\eta)\, d\eta \,.$$

To obtain the pdf $f(\eta)$ we observe that, to order $0(\sigma)$, the characteristic function of η is given by:

$$\begin{aligned}
\psi(t) &= E\left[\exp(it\eta) \right] \\
&= E\left[\exp\left\{ \frac{it}{\sqrt{\tau}}\left(\delta'z + \sigma z'z - \frac{2\sigma}{\tau}(\delta'z)^2 - \sigma\frac{cv}{2} \right) \right\} \right] \\
&= E\left[\exp\left(it\frac{\delta'z}{\sqrt{\tau}} \right)\left\{ 1 + \frac{it\sigma}{\sqrt{\tau}}\left(z'z - 2\frac{(\delta z)^2}{\tau} - \frac{cv}{2} \right) \right\} \right] \\
&= \exp\left(-\frac{1}{2}t^2 \right)\left[1 + \frac{i\sigma}{\sqrt{\tau}}\left\{ t(k-2) + t^3 - c\frac{(T-k)}{2}t \right\} \right]
\end{aligned}$$

Now, utilizing the inversion formula

$$f(\eta) = \frac{1}{2\pi}\int_{-\infty}^{+\infty} e^{-it\eta}\psi(t)\, dt$$

along with the results that

$$\frac{1}{2\pi}\int_{-\infty}^{\infty}\exp\left(-it\eta-\frac{1}{2}t^2\right)dt=\phi(\eta)\ ,$$

$$\frac{1}{2\pi}\int\int_{-\infty}^{\infty}t\exp\left(-it\eta-\frac{1}{2}t^2\right)dt=-i\eta\phi(\eta)\ ,$$

$$\frac{1}{2\pi}\int_{-\infty}^{\infty}t^3\exp\left(-it\eta-\frac{1}{2}t^2\right)dt=-i(3\eta-\eta^3)\phi(\eta)\ ,$$

where $\phi(.)$ denotes the pdf of a standard normal variate, we get the following approximate expression for $f(\eta)$:

$$f(\eta)=\phi(\eta)\left[1+\frac{\sigma}{\sqrt{\tau}}\left\{\eta(k+1)-\eta^3-\frac{c}{2}\eta(T-k)\right\}\right].$$

Thus, to order $0(\sigma)$, we obtain

$$P\left[M(b)-M(\hat{\beta}_h)>0\right]=\int_0^{\infty}f(\eta)d\eta$$

$$=\frac{1}{2}+\frac{\sigma}{(2\pi\tau)^{\frac{1}{2}}}\left[(k-1)-\frac{c}{2}(T-k)\right],$$

which leads to (5).

Following Van Hoa and Chaturvedi (1993), to order $0(\sigma^4)$, we can write

$(\hat{\beta}_s-\beta)'X'X(\hat{\beta}_s-\beta)-(\hat{\beta}_h-\beta)'X'X(\hat{\beta}_h-\beta)$

$$=2cc^*(1-w)\sigma^5\frac{v^2}{\tau^2}\left[-\delta'z-\sigma\left\{z'z-\frac{4}{\tau}(\delta'z)^2-cv\right\}\right],$$

which is greater than zero if and only if

$$\gamma=\frac{1}{\sqrt{\tau}}\left[-\delta'z-\sigma\left\{z'z-\frac{4}{\tau}(\delta'z)^2-cv\right\}\right]$$

is less than zero.

Now, to order $0(\sigma)$, the characteristic function of γ is given by:

$$\psi^*(t)=\exp\left(-\frac{1}{2}t^2\right)\left[1+i\frac{\sigma}{\sqrt{\tau}}\left\{(k-4)t+3t^3-cv\right\}\right]$$

Hence, using the inversion formula, the pdf of γ, to order $0(\sigma)$, is given by

$$f^*(\gamma)=\phi(\gamma)\left[1+\frac{\sigma}{\sqrt{\tau}}\left\{(k+5)\eta-3\eta^3-cv\eta\right\}\right].$$

Therefore, to order 0(σ), we have
$P[M(\hat{\beta}_S) - M(\hat{\beta}_h) > 0] = P[\gamma<0]$

$$= \int_{-\infty}^{0} f^*(\gamma)d\gamma$$

$$= \frac{1}{2} - \frac{\sigma}{\sqrt{2\pi\eta}}\left[(k-1) - c(T-k)\right],$$

which gives the result (6).

References

Keating JP, Czitrom V (1989) A Comparison of James Stein Regression with Least Squares in the Pitman Nearness Sense. Journal of Statistical Computation and Simulation 34 : 1–9

Keating JP, Mason RL (1985) Pitman's Measure of Closeness. Sankhya, Series B 47 : 22–32

Keating JP and Mason RL (1988) James Stein estimation from an Alternative Perspective. American Statistics 42 : 160–164

Khattree R (1987) On Comparison of Estimates of Dispersion Using Generalized Pitman Nearness Criterion. Communications in Statistics (Theory and Methods) 16 : 263–274

Khattree R, Peddada SD (1987) A Short Note on Pitman Nearness for Elliptically Symmetric Estimators. Journal of Statistical Planning and Inference 16 : 257–260

Mason RL, Keating JP, Sen PK, Blaylock NW (1990) Comparison of Linear Estimators using Pitman's Measure of Closeness. Journal of American Statistics Association 85 : 579–581

Rao CR, Keating JP, Mason RL (1986) The Pitman Nearness Criterion and its Determination. Communications in Statistics (Theory and Methods) 15 : 3173–3191

Sen PK, Kubokawa T, Saleh AK (1989) The Stein Paradox in the Sense of Pitman Closeness. In : Annals of Statistics 17 : 1375–1386

Van Hoa T (1985) The Inadmissibility of the Stein Estimator in Normal Multiple Regression Equations. Economic Letters 19 : 39–42

Van Hoa T (1992a) Energy Consumption in Thailand: Estimated Structure and Improved Forecasts to 2000 (in Thai). Thammasat Economic Journal 10 : 55–63

Van Hoa T (1992b) A New and General Approach to Modelling Short Term Interest Rates: With Applications to Australian Data 1962–1990. Proceedings of the Journal of Economics and Finance 16 : 327–335

Van Hoa T (1993) Estimation and Inference in Dynamic Econometric Equations. Proceedings of the American Statistical Association, Section on Bayesian Statistical Science, 241–248

Van Hoa T, Chaturvedi A (1990) Further Results on the Two Stage Hierarchical Information Estimators in the Linear Regression Models. Communications in Statistics (Theory and Methods) 19 : 4697–4704

Van Hoa T, Chaturvedi A (1993) Asymptotic Approximations to the Gain of the 2SHI over Stein Estimators in Linear Regression Models when the Disturbances are Small. Communications in Statistics (Theory and Methods) 22 : 2777–2782

Comment

Sweta C. Saxena

Graduate School of Public and International Affairs, University of Pittsburgh, USA

This is an interesting paper on a pressing issue. The topic is fascinating, and China is no doubt occupying the minds and hearts of academicians and policymakers around the world. China became the 143rd member of the WTO in December 2001, after negotiating the terms of its entry for 15 years. Given the potential size of the Chinese market, this may mark a watershed entry in the history of world trade. Jimmy's paper is concerned with the impact of China's WTO membership on the Chinese investment and growth. His paper uses a new two-stage hierarchical information (2SHI) estimation technique to estimate the investment, consumption and GDP growth from a new flexible Keynesian model.

The paper uses a well-known generic five-equation Keynesian macroeconomic model of an open economy in linear form to arrive at the following estimable model:

$$I\%_t = a_{11} + a_{12}C\%_{t-1} + a_{13}Y\%_{t-1} + a_{14}\Delta R_t + a_{15}\Delta R_{t-1} + a_{16}YW\%_t + a_{17}PCN\% + a_{18}PUS\% + a_{19}G\%_t + e_{1t} \tag{6a}$$

$$C\%_t = a_{21} + a_{22}C\%_{t-1} + a_{23}Y\%_{t-1} + a_{24}\Delta R_t + a_{25}\Delta R_{t-1} + a_{26}YW\%_t + a_{27}PCN\% + a_{28}PUS\% + a_{29}G\%_t + e_{2t} \tag{6b}$$

$$Y\%_t = a_{31} + a_{32}C\%_{t-1} + a_{33}Y\%_{t-1} + a_{34}\Delta R_t + a_{35}\Delta R_{t-1} + a_{36}YW\%_t + a_{37}PCN\% + a_{38}PUS\% + a_{39}G\%_t + e_{3t} \tag{6c}$$

where I%, C%, Y%, YW%, PCN%, PUS% and G% indicate the rate of change of investment, consumption, Chinese GDP, US GDP (proxy for world income), price deflator in China, price deflator in US (proxy for world prices) and government expenditures, respectively. ΔR stands for change in US prime rate (as a proxy for world interest rates).[1] The author estimates this model using a 2SHI estimation

[1] There is a typo in the paper, where the US interest rate is taken as a percentage change, like the other variables.

technique, which is claimed to be an improvement above the SUR or CGE estimation techniques.

To get an understanding of the model suggested in this paper, I will use alternative estimation techniques to compare my results with those of the author's. Since the paper's innovation is in the new technique used to estimate the model, my first instinct is to estimate the model using Seemingly Unrelated Regression (SUR). For this estimation, I obtain the data on GDP, consumption, investment, inflation and government expenditures from the World Bank's World Development Indicators (WDI), 2003 CD-Rom. I estimate the author's model (6a-6c) using SUR for data from 1962 to 1998 (to match the author's estimation period in the paper). The parameters are used to predict the output, investment and consumption growth rates. The results are shown in the figures 1–3 below:

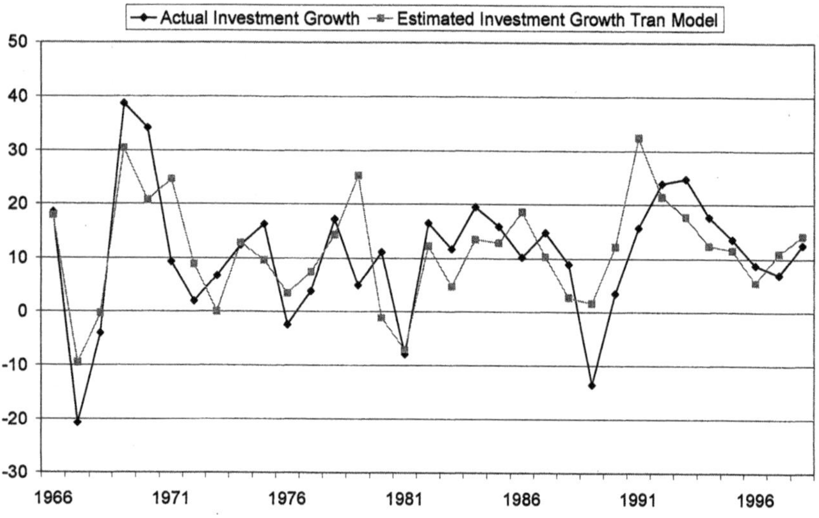

Figure 1. China's Investment Growth

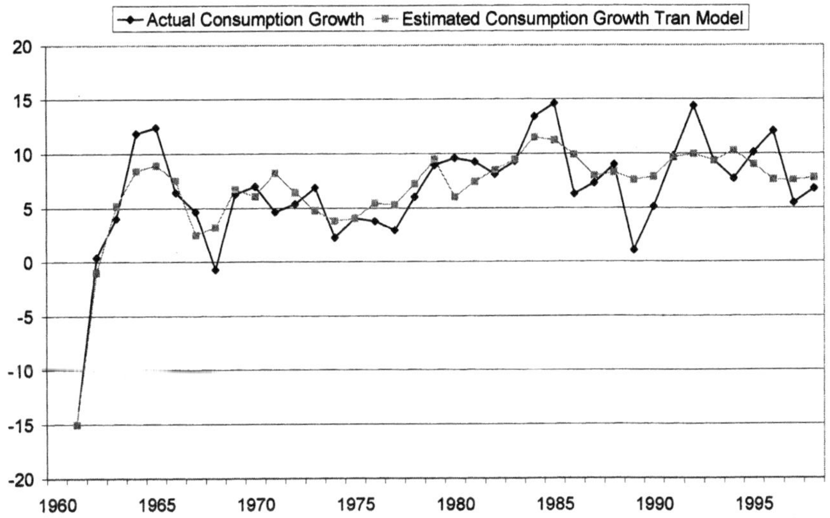

Figure 2. China's Consumption Growth

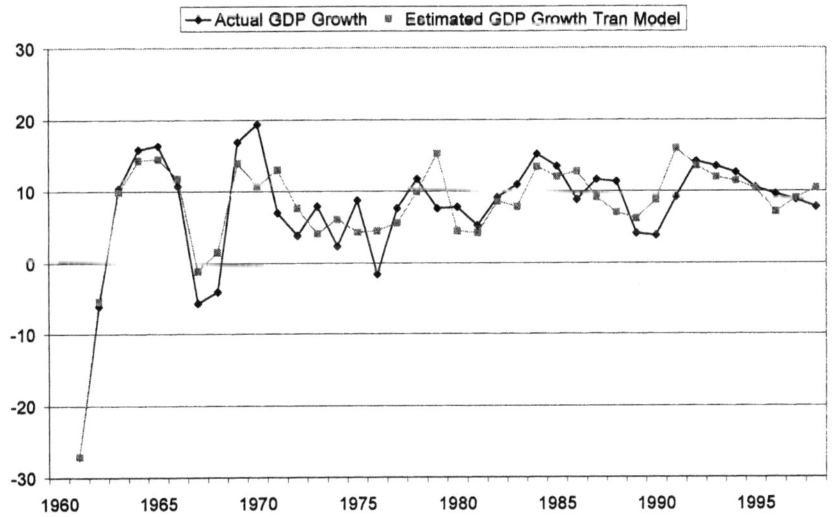

Figure 3. China's GDP Growth

Comparing the Figures above with Figures 2-4 in the paper, we find that the estimated growth rates for investment, consumption and GDP are very similar to that from Tran Van Hoa's 2SHI model. In fact, the trends in the estimated series are exactly the same.

The author does not directly account for trade in his model as he is interested in the movements in consumption, investment and income, which according to economic theory share a common stochastic trend. If this is indeed the case, an error correction model, which accounts for the long term co-movements in macroeconomic series, would provide a more efficient framework of analysis. The author recognizes this and hence writes that

> *"an important economic group of economic variables whose first differences in logs are approximately equivalent to the rates of change, our equations by their construct include as the special cases the Granger-Wiener short term causality if these rates of changes are I(0) and the co-integration or long-term equations of the Engle-Granger (1987) class [...] if the rates of change are I(1)."*

However, if the three series are indeed non-stationary and cointegrated, then estimating a model in changes only would lead to misspecification of the model.

According to the standard unit root tests, GDP, C and I are non-stationary and the Johansen Cointegration Test shows that the three series are cointegrated, with one cointegrating vector. Hence, I estimate an error correction model (ECM), using two lags to capture the business cycle, and use dummies for oil shocks, the Asian crisis, the Gulf war, US stock market crash and internal political conflict of 1989 (which the author mentions in the paper, but doesn't explicitly include in his estimations). The parameters from the ECM model were used to estimate the investment, consumption and GDP growth rates. The results are depicted in Figures 4-6.

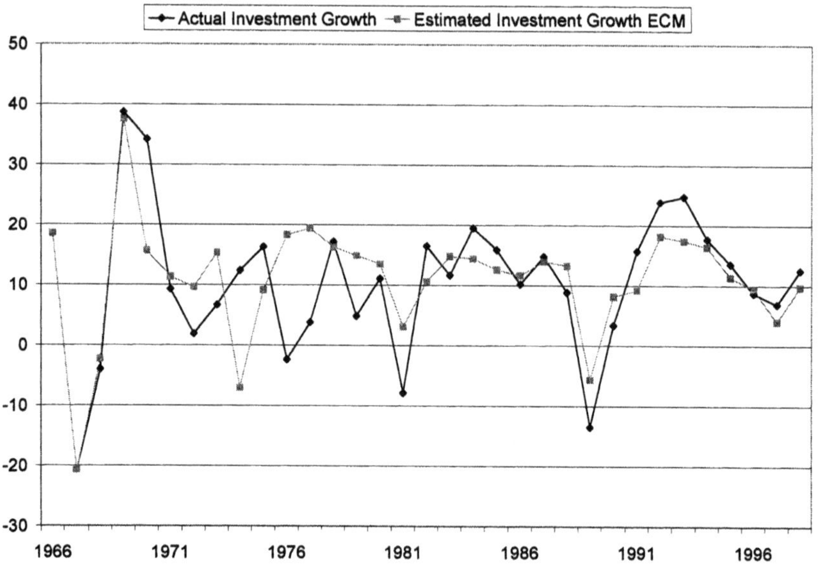

Figure 4. China's Investment Growth

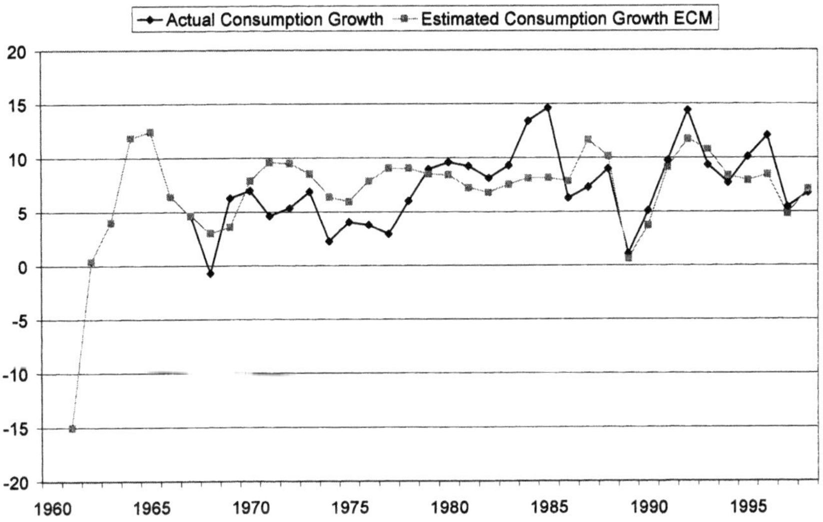

Figure 5. China's Consumption Growth

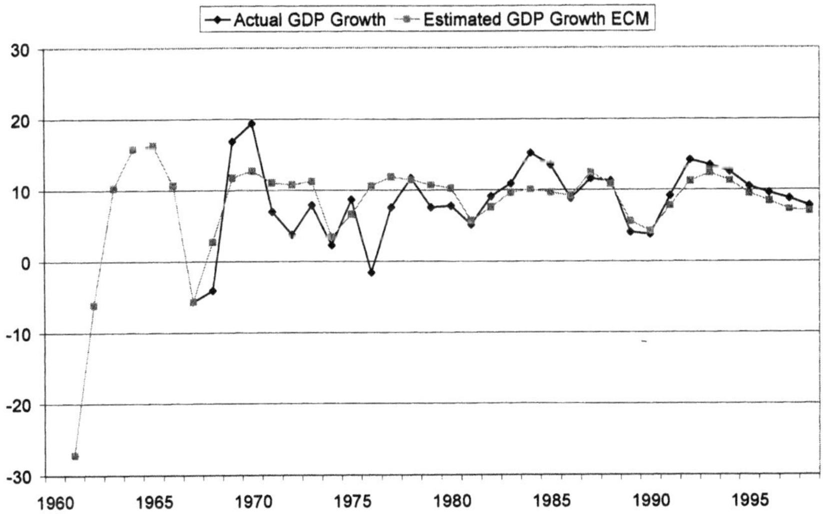

Figure 6. China's GDP Growth

The charts above clearly show that the fitted values from the error correction model follow the actual data more closely than the ones estimated from the author's model (6a–c). The fall in the GDP, consumption and investment in 1989 is identified correctly and the fitted values move closely thereafter. This shows that the ECM model does a better job of predicting these variables.

Sometimes we are interested in seeing if our models predict the variables in the right direction, even if not necessarily by the exact magnitude.

Table 1. Probability of Fitted Values Moving in the Same Direction as the Actual Data

Variable	Tran's model	ECM model
Investment Growth	0.70	0.79
Consumption Growth	0.62	0.70
GDP Growth	0.59	0.89

The table above shows that, compared to the error correction model, the author's model performs no better/worse for investment and consumption. However, the difference between the two models in predicting the GDP growth in the right direction is statistically significant at 1 percent level in favor of the ECM.

Lastly, the author prefers to not use CGE model to predict the impact of WTO membership on China's growth, but uses an ad hoc method by assuming

> *"that the opening up the Chinese market to the outside world and accompanying reform [...] will reduce the general price level (the CPI) in China by 10 percent. This will boost domestic spending due to reduced commodity prices and increase government revenue and subsequent increased government spending. Assume that the spending boost is also 10 percent. Assume also that the impact started in 1991 for historical studies (or equivalently in 2002 for ex-ante studies)."*

It would be extremely helpful to see how the model in equations 6a-c accounts for any structural changes that would accompany the membership into the WTO. This is important because the predictions from the author's model (with and without the assumptions) are quite close (Chart 5) and this could lead a skeptic to believe that the 2SHI estimation has no particular advantage over the other techniques – like SUR or CGE models. But skepticism is what keeps our profession alive!

WTO Dispute Settlement in Action: An Economic Analysis of Four EU-US Mini Trade Wars

Fritz Breuss

Research Institute for European Affairs, Vienna University of Economics and Business Administration, Austria and Austrian Institute of Economic Research (Wifo), Vienna, Austria

1 Introduction

One of the unique features of the WTO compared to other international organizations is dispute settlement (DS). Whether the WTO DS system is more successful than the former GATT is an open question. Some critics see a "bias" in the system because the developed countries (primarily the G4 countries Canada, EC, Japan and US) account for over 60% of all complaints (Horn et al. 1999). Others call for institutional and/or procedural changes (Bronckers 2001). In preparation for the 5th Ministerial Conference in Cancun, Mexico in September 10-14, 2003, the WTO member states have made several proposals for such more formal legal changes. In principal, one should believe that everything related to international trade is a fundamental economic issue. But interestingly, until recently the field of dispute settlement was primarily a research area of lawyers. Economic theory has produced a few explicit contributions to explain the working of GATT/WTO (e.g. Hungerford 1991, Rodrik 1995, Staiger 1995, Bagwell and Staiger 1999, Spagnolo 2001) and the system of dispute settlement (e.g., Maggi 1999). But the actual working, possible failures and the economic implications of the WTO DS system have been examined by only a few economist as yet (e.g. Anderson 2002, Breuss 2003).

World trade consists of a web of bilateral relations in which large (powerful) and small (powerless) countries participate. From optimal-tariff theory one knows that for a large player in world trade the optimal tariff is positive, whereas it would be zero for a small country. WTO's major principles, reciprocity and nondiscrimination are simple rules that, when used together, can deliver an efficient outcome. Both rules can help to neutralize externalities resulting from terms-of-trade effects (Bagwell and Staiger 1999, p. 237). Another strand of modern trade and tariff literature – building on the literature of endogenous tariff formation (see e.g. Mayer 1984) – deals with the politico-economic explanation of trade wars. Grossman and Helpman (1995) build on a strategic interaction between interest groups and politicians in the domestic arena and strategic interaction between governments in the international arena. Such models can be used to analyze the rise and fall of the Bananas dispute between the EC and the US (see Breuss 2003). Many authors have shown that as a rule large countries will win trade wars (e.g. Whalley 1985, chapter 14, McMillan 1986, Kennan and Riezman 1988, Breuss 2003).

Since its inception in 1995, 299 bilateral disputes have been raised under the WTO Dispute Settlement Understanding (DSU). As complainants, 25.3% of which concern the EC, 24% the USA, and the rest is distributed to other countries, each involved not more than 9%. As respondent, 21.9% concern the EC, 19.9% the USA, and the rest concerns other countries, each not more than 8% (Horn et al. 1999). Presently there are 27 active WTO disputes involving the EC, in 15 of these cases the EC is the complaining party while in the remaining 12 cases the EC is on the defending side (see European Commission 2003). Those 27 cases relate to the EC's relations with 8 of its trading partners (Argentina, Australia, Brazil, India, Korea, Peru, Thailand and the US). Dispute Settlement activities against the US continue to represent the vast majority of EC's dispute settlement cases. The EC has presently 13 active WTO disputes underway with the United States. In 11 of these cases it is the Community which is the complaining party, being the defendant only in 2 cases (Hormones and EC Steel Safeguards; see Tables 6 to 8 in the Appendix).

In the following analysis we concentrate on the four most prominent disputes between the EU and the US. The cases are: Hormones, Bananas, FSC and Steel. Out of the large number of DS cases, in only three occasions the WTO-DS authorities (Arbitrators) allowed the complainant party to introduce retaliatory measures against another WTO member. The three cases are the Hormones case, the Bananas case (now settled) and the FSC case (countervailing measures not yet implemented). In the Steel case, on July, 11, 2003 the WTO Panel against the US steel safeguards concluded that the safeguard measures imposed by the United States on the imports of certain steel products are inconsistent with the WTO Safeguards Agreement and GATT 1994. The case was brought to the WTO by the EC, Japan, Korea, China, Switzerland, Norway, New Zealand and Brazil. A fifth trade dispute may arise on genetically-modified material (GMO). In May 2003, the United States, Argentina and Canada filed a WTO case against the EC over its illegal five-year moratorium on approving agricultural biotech products. The US as the world's leading supplier of biotech crops have a strong interest in the settlement of this case. Some movement in the GMO issue might be brought about with the adoption of two European Commission proposals by the European Parliament on July 2, 2003 concerning the genetically modified food and feed and the traceability and labeling of GMOs. By the formal adoption of these proposals by the Council of Ministers on July 22, 2003 the European legislative framework for GMOs is in place. This is a clear EU system to trace and label GMOs and to regulate the placing on the market and labeling of food and feed products derived from GMOs. It will be interesting to hear the WTO decision on this trade dispute.

First, by analyzing each of the four EU-US trade disputes the WTO Dispute Settlement system is critically evaluated. Each dispute has its unique legal and economic history. Second, for the first time we try to quantify the welfare and trade implications of these trade conflicts which – in line and in contrast with former studies on hypothetical large trade wars – we call "mini" trade wars. The analysis is done by simulations with the GTAP5 world CGE model which is designed for our purpose to a 12 regions, 7 sectors and 5 factors of productions model (see Table 9 in the Appendix).

2 The Hormones Case

2.1 A Brief Historical Background

In 1996, the USA and Canada held formal consultations in the framework of the WTO dispute settlement mechanism[1] with the EU regarding its legislation covering the ban on hormones (17 beta-oestradiol, progesterone, testosterone, zeranol, trenbolone and melengestrol acetate) for growth promoting purposes in livestock. Following requests from the two countries, in April 25, 1996, WTO panels were set up (WT/DS26: US complainant, third parties: New Zealand, Canada, Australia) to assess the conformity of the EC measures with its WTO obligations (relevant WTO Provisions: GATT (III or XI), SPS (2, 3, 5), TBT (2), Agriculture (4)). The EC measures (prohibiting the importation of meat and meat products that have been treated with growth hormones) were found not in conformity with a number of WTO rules. The EU objected to the conclusions of the panels in September 1997, which were consequently submitted for review to the Appellate Body (AB). On February 13, 1998 the report of the AB found that the EC had provided "general studies which do indeed show the existence of a general risk of cancer; but they do not focus on and do not address the particular kind of risk at stake here [...] those general studies are in other words relevant but do not appear to be sufficiently specific to the case at hand". Due to the lack of specific scientific verification for the EC measures, the AB recommended that the EC bring its measures into conformity with its obligations under the SPS Agreement. The Arbitrator granted the Community a "reasonable period" of 15 months (until May 13, 1999) to collect further significant scientific studies in this case. The 17 studies the EC supplied, however, were not significant enough to proof the risk of cancer. On May 13, 1999, the EC decided to ban all imports of US beef and beef products including those that have not been treated with hormones – as of June 15, 1999.

Therefore, the USA, on May 17, 1999, had requested the Dispute Settlement Body (DSB) of the WTO to authorize the suspension of the application to the EC and its Member States to tariff concessions. A similar request was made by Canada on May 20, 1999. On July 12, 1999, the WTO Arbitrator determined the level of nullification or impairment suffered by the USA and Canada (WTO 1999c).

---

[1] The legal basis for WTO Dispute Settlement is the "Understanding on rules and procedures governing the settlement of disputes", Appendix 2 of the WTO Agreement, signed at the Marrakesh ministerial meeting in April 1994.

2.2 How to Calculate the Level of Damage?

On May 17, 1999, the USA had requested the Dispute Settlement Body (DSB) of the WTO to authorize the suspension of the application to the EC and its Member States to tariff concessions covering trade in an amount of US$ 202 million per year. The EC, however, calculated only a loss of US exports to the EC by US$ 53 million. A similar request was made by Canada on May 20, 1999, for an amount of CDN$ 75 million per year. The EC objected to the level of suspension proposed by the US and Canada. As the large differences between the calculated (estimated) levels of suspension proposed by the US government (US$ 202 million per year) and the EC (only US$ 53 million per year) demonstrate, it is not easy to calculate the damage a country suffers from trade-restricting measures. In the report on the Hormone case EC versus USA (WTO 1999b, at para. 36ff., similarly in the Canada decision, see WTO 1999c), the Arbitrators set out guidelines for the calculation of nullification and impairment. They find the proposed figures by the USA are to high, they should only be "equivalent" to the level of nullification and impairment (Art. 22.4 DSU) caused by the hormone ban of the EC. The problem is to determine an anti-monde scenario which would tell what would annual US exports of hormone-treated beef and beef products to the EC be if the EC had withdrawn the ban on May 13, 1999.

The task of estimating the level of damage for the US exporters, involves an estimation procedure in several steps (WTO 1999b, at para. 43):

1. For each product category, the Arbitrators estimate the total value of US beef or beef products – hormone treated or not – that would enter the EC annually if the ban would have been withdrawn on May 13, 1999 (*"hypothetical exports"*).
2. To estimate the nullification and impairment caused by the hormone ban, the Arbitrators deduct from that total value the current value of US exports of HQB (US high quality beef) and EBO (US edible beef offal), i.e., those that have not been treated with hormones (*"current exports"*). The arbitrators assume that these "current exports" are representative of the exports that will occur in the future with the ban in place.
3. The end result provides the estimated value of hormone treated HQB and EBO exports that would enter the EC but for the ban's continuing existence beyond May 13, 1999. The calculations are base on exports at the f.o.b. stage (excluding insurance and freight) and also on f.o.b. prices.

These estimations more or less include only unknown variables. Not only the level of "current exports" could be agreed upon between USA and EC, but also the "hypothetical exports" cannot be calculated with certainty. In order to calculate the damage for HQB, additionally further assumptions have to be made concerning the volume of the tariff quota (the EC market for HQB exports from the USA and Canada – with or without the ban – is limited by a tariff quota of 11,500 tons at an in-quota tariff rate (TQR) of 20% ad valorem. Then the US share was estimated at 92% (the rest goes to Canada). A further unknown variable is the expected price (this was taken from US suggestions of US$ 5,342 per ton, although the Arbitrators admit that this price is higher than current unit values of US beef entering the EC!). With these three parameters at hand one can calculate the "hypothetical exports", given that the TRQ is exhausted (TRQ fill is one). By reducing the current US exports by 25% the value of the "current exports" is estimated. The subtraction of the "current exports" from the "hypothetical exports" gives the damage for HQB as US$ 32.7 million. A similar exercise (with even more arbitrary adjustments) is made to estimate the damage for EBO (worth US$ 84.1 million). Together, this gives the total level of nullification and impairment for the USA of US$ 116.8 million per year (see Table 1). Only slight changes in the assumed parameters (US share, price, reduction factor etc.) would change the results ad libitum!

On July 12, 1999, the WTO Arbitrators determined the level of nullification or impairment suffered by the United States in the matter European Communities – Measures Concerning Meat and Meat Products (Hormones) at US$ 116.8 million per year (WTO, 1999b) and CND$ 11.3 million per year (WTO, 1999c), respectively. Furthermore, the suspension by the USA of the application to the EU and its member States of tariff concessions and related obligations under GATT 1994 covering trade in a maximum amount of US$ 116.8 million per year would be consistent with Article 22.4 of the DSU (WTO 1999b, at para. 83 and 84). The retaliatory tariff measures by the USA are set in this case in the same sector as the noncompliance has taken place, namely in the agricultural sector and concern a variety of EC agricultural products[2]. The EC feared that the USA would resort to a "carousel" type of suspension where the concessions and other obligations subject to suspension would change every now and then, in particular in terms of product coverage. The arbitrators in its report (WTO 1999b, at para. 22), however, assumed that the USA will not implement the suspension of concessions in a "carousel" manner!

Since July 1999, the USA have taken countervailing measures worth US$ 467.2 million (US$ 116.8 million over four years). This amounts to 0.05% of the total EU exports to the USA each year, or 0.11% of agricultural EU exports to the USA each year. As the Hormones case is not yet resolved, the sanctions taken by the US are still in place.

[2] The list of agricultural products for suspension of concessions proposed by the USA, can be found in Appendix II of WTO (1999b).

Table 1. Calculation of the Level of Nullification and Impairment in the USA-EC-Hormone Case

High Quality Beef (HQB)								
[(11,500	* 1)	* 0.92	* 5,342]	-	(31,804,779	*0.75)		**= US$ 32,664,776 Total**
TRQ	TRQ fill	US share	price/t (fob)		current exports (fob)	25% for "test & hold"		
Edible beef offal (EBO)								
[(65,568	*	0.816	* 1,689)	-	(2,460,759	*0.75)]	*0.95	**=US$ 84,095,731 Total**
av. 86-88 exports 18.4% adjustment for decline in consumption for the ban			price/t (f.o.b.)		current exports (fob)	25% reduction for "test & hold"	5% reduction for pet food usage	
Total: HQB + EBO								**=US$ 116,760,507**

Source: WTO (1999b), Appendix I.

2.3 Economic Impact of the Hormones EU-US "Mini" Trade War

The welfare and trade implications of this "mini" trade war between the EU and the USA are analyzed with the help of model simulations with the GTAP5 CGE world model with 12 regions, 7 sectors and 5 factors of production (see Table 9 in the Appendix). However, there are a lot of economic problems and peculiarities surrounding the implementation of the retaliatory measures of the decisions by the WTO Arbitrators into a general equilibrium model:

- *Amount of suspension:* In the hormones case, what does it mean when the "Arbitrators decide that the suspension by the United States of the application to the European Communities and its member States of tariff concessions and related obligations under GATT 1994 covering trade in a maximum amount of US$ 116.8 million per year would be consistent with Article 22.4 of the DSU" (WTO/DS26/ARB, p. 17)? Does this mean the US can reduce their imports in the sector "Meat" from the EU by US$ 116.8 million per year or does it imply that the US may increase their import tariffs on meat from the EU until the revenues reach US$ 116.8 million each year? Because of this ambiguity we simulate two alternative scenarios of retaliations (one targeting the imports and one targeting the tariff revenues).
- *Trade loss equivalent and economic welfare:* The other problem is that the damage is calculated by the WTO Arbitrators as a nominal damage and the retaliatory measures are defined as a simple static value of imports. Such a procedure, however, completely neglects the reactions of importers on increased tariffs! As Anderson (2002) demonstrates (see also Figure 1 in the Appendix), the trade loss equivalent never translates into equivalent damage to economic welfare, except by coincidence. In general, both the complainant and the respondent will suffer a welfare loss by retaliation. Therefore, when a complainant (in the hormones case the US) implements retaliatory measures by imposing (prohibitive) measures by raising the import tariffs by 100% on an arbitrary list of products, this not only hurts the respondent (in this case the EU) by reducing its export chances, it also hurts the complainant (its consumers) and therefore one often speaks in this context of a situation of "shooting oneself in the foot" (see e.g. Mavroides 2001, p. 46 for such a phrase).

Three Scenarios

The dimension of the trade disputes are calibrated in the GTAP5 model according to the amounts of damage calculated by the WTO arbitrators in each of the four trade disputes.

(I) In the *first scenario,* the EU imposes a trade regime (in the Hormones case the ban on US exports of beef to the EC market as of May 13, 1999) which does not comply with WTO rules (violates several agreements). The trade restriction (increase of import tariffs) in the GTAP5 model is so calibrated (by increasing import tariffs) that the meat imports of the EU from the USA are reduced by US$

116.8 million. This is equal to the estimated level of nullification and impairment by the WTO DS decision.

(II) In the *second scenario,* the USA retaliates against the EU according to the decision of the WTO arbitrators. However, due to the ambiguity of their decision two sub-scenarios are calculated:

(IIa) In this scenario the USA reduces its imports from the EU by US$ 116.8 million distributed on several sectors according to the retaliation list of products (see Appendix II in WTO, 1999b). We implemented these retaliations in the sectors "meat", "food", "other primary products" and "manufacturing".

(IIb) In this scenario the USA reduces imports from the EU in order to collect import tariff revenues amounting to US$ 116.8 million. The implementation is done in the same sectors of the model as in scenario (IIa).

(III) In the *third scenario* we simulate the economic impact of the combined implementation of measures and counter-measures of the scenarios (I) and (IIb), which is what we call the "mini" trade war.

Simulation Results

The simulation results of the GTAP5 model are presented in Table 2 and can be summarized as follows:

1. All the effects are small due to the low amount of impairment involved relative to total trade between both partners. The trade restrictions amounting US$ 116.8 million per year add up only to 0.05% of the total EU exports to the USA each year or 0.11% of agricultural EU exports to the USA.
2. Nevertheless, the ban on hormone treated US beef seems to have the effect of "shooting the EU themselves in the foot", as this scenario (I) leads to slight welfare losses (measured by the total welfare measure of GTAP5, covering allocation and terms of trade effects), whereas the US loses only slightly. Obviously, the EU population weighs health higher than simply more consumption of beef (which is implied in the traditional welfare measure). Therefore, a simple welfare measure may be misleading. However, the EU can improve their terms of trade, whereas the US loses here. Trade between both partners slightly decreases.
3. The retaliation by the USA (scenario IIa and IIb) leads to welfare losses for the EU, whereas for the USA only negative allocative effects occur. Their terms of trade improve. Again, one could say that the tariff-imposer USA is "shooting in its foot"! Bilateral trade volume declines. Real GDP decreases, nominal GDP increases slightly in the US due to additional tariff revenues, more so in scenario (IIb) than in (IIa).

Table 2. “Mini“ Trade War EU versus USA: Hormones Case

Scenarios	Welfare Total*) (as % of GDP)		Welfare Allocation (as % of GDP)		Terms of Trade (% of change)	
	EU	USA	EU	USA	EU	USA
(I)	-0.000539	-0.000264	-0.000750	-0.000001	0.000676	-0.002122
(IIa)	-0.000334	0.000129	0.000003	-0.000028	-0.001097	0.001288
(IIb)	-0.001389	0.000443	-0.000129	-0.000123	-0.004100	0.004667
(III)	-0.001929	0.000179	-0.000879	-0.000124	-0.003424	0.002545
	Exports with Partner (%-change)		GDP, nominal (%-change)		GDP, real (%-change)	
(I)	-0.008001	-0.028448	0.001249	-0.001964	-0.000750	-0.000001
(IIa)	-0.061330	-0.012093	-0.002345	0.001747	0.000003	-0.000028
(IIb)	-0.239540	-0.045044	-0.008696	0.006235	-0.000129	-0.000123
(III)	-0.247541	-0.073499	-0.007447	0.004272	-0.000879	-0.000124

*) Total welfare = allocation plus terms of trade plus other effects.
(I) = EU bans MEAT imports from the USA amounting to US$ 116.8 million.
(IIa) = USA reduces imports from EU by US$ 116.8 million according to retaliation list of products.
(IIb) = USA reduces imports from EU in order to collect import tariff revenues by US$ 116.8 million according to retaliation list of products.
(III) = EU versus USA trade war: Scenarios (I) + (IIb) combined.
Source: Own simulations with the GTAP5 world CGE model.

4. The “mini” trade war between the USA and the EU is given when both scenarios (I) and (IIb) are simulated together – which in reality takes place in this trade dispute. This leads to a slight welfare loss in the EU and a slight gain in the USA (due to terms of trade improvements[3]). Trade between each other declines, so does real GDP, stronger in the EU than in the US. In this case US exports to the EU already decline by 0.2%. Overall, the EU is the loser of this “mini” trade war.

Since the Hormones case is not yet resolved, the sanctions amounting to US$ 116.8 million per year are still maintained by the US government. So the estimated welfare and trade effects calculated on the basis of an annual measure must be quadrupled already.

Although in Table 2 we presented only the economic impact of this “mini” trade war for the two parties involved (EU and USA), the retaliation measures taken by the complainant US against the respondent EU affect, however, also third countries via trade diversion. This “externalities” of WTO-allowed retaliation was not considered by the designers of the WTO dispute settlement system. In scenario (III) the third country effects are the following: Measured by total welfare only Korea would suffer a slight welfare loss, whereas in the other nine regions (inclusive ROW) there would be a slight welfare gain.

3. The Bananas Case

3.1 The Genesis and the End of the Banana Dispute

In 1993 the EU accepted a regime for the importation, sale and distribution of bananas (Common Market Organization for bananas), established by Council Reg. No. 404/93 on the common organization of the market in bananas and subsequent EC legislation, regulations and administrative measures, including those reflecting the provisions of the Framework Agreement on Bananas (the “BFA”), which implement, supplement and amend that regime. The idea behind this import regime with a complicated tariff-quota system was first, to have a common trade regime for EC’s Single Market and second, to prefer ACP countries (including former EC member states colonies) at the expense of traditional bananas supplier from Latin America and the USA.[4]

---

[3] The fact that the USA and the EU are more or less equally large world trade players (with a market share of around 20% each) lead to the theoretical effects, derived from the theory of optimal tariffs (see Johnson 1958), that they can influence the terms of trade. Improvements occur if one of these two regions either makes a protectionist first mover step (increases tariffs) or in case of a mutual retaliatory game the terms of trade improvements depend on the asymmetry of measures taken (see Breuss 2003 for an extensive discussion of the implications of trade wars).

[4] For a comprehensive documentation and analysis of the Banana Dispute, see Breuss et al. (2003).

Ecuador, Guatemala, Honduras, Mexico and the USA filed a complaint against this import regime for bananas (with the third parties Saint Lucia, Dominican Republic, Nicaragua and Jamaica) at the WTO by starting formal consultations with the EC in February 1996. Following request by the complainants, in April, 1996 WTO panels were set up (WT/DS27). This import regime was found to be illegal by the WTO in 1997. DSB recommendations were implemented in a revised scheme by the EC on January, 1999 (by EC Reg. 1637/98 and 2362/98). Complainants contended that the new EC regime continued to violate WTO obligations. The main criticisms were the setting aside of a quantity reserved solely for ACP imports (fails to conform to the "non-discrimination requirements" of Article XIII of GATT 1994), and the allocation of licenses on a "historical" basis (i.e., reflecting past sales, which violates Articles II and XVII of GATS). According to WTO, this did not eliminate the "drag-on" discrimination vis-à-vis third-country operators. In the Bananas case several WTO provisions are relevant or agreements are violated, respectively: GATT (I, II, III, X, XI, XIII), Licensing (1, 3), Agriculture, TRIMS(2) and GATS (II, XVI, XVII).

The USA requested suspension of concessions of a considerable amount which – after the EC requested arbitration – was arbitrated by the WTO on April 19, 1999. The DSB of the WTO authorized the USA to suspend concession made in the Uruguay Round. In addition to the USA sanctions against the WTO-illegal EC import regime for bananas, the Arbitrators (WTO 2000) decided in favor of Ecuador and authorized this country to retaliate against the EU. Ecuador was allowed to suspend concessions under the TRIPS agreement.

Only after nearly a decade, the Banana dispute had been resolved. In the long-standing Bananas case, the second phase of the Understanding concluded with the US and Ecuador has been implemented as foreseen on January 1, 2002, with the entry into force of Council Regulation (EC) No 2587/2001. That meant that the EU adjusted its Common Organization of the Market in Bananas, coming into force as of January 1, 2002. As a consequence of the earlier agreement with the USA and Ecuador, the US government lifted its sanctions as of July 1, 2001 already. In accordance with Article 16(1) of Regulation No (EC) 404/93 (as amended by Regulation No (EC) 216/2001)), the European Communities (EC) hence will introduce a Tariff Only regime for imports of bananas no later than January, 1, 2006 (see the notification of the mutually agreed solution, WTO 2001a).

3.2 A Scandal in Calculating the Level of Damage?

The estimation of an "equivalent" level of nullification or impairment suffered by EC's import regime for bananas is even more complicated (and hence, more problematic) than in the Hormones case. On the one hand, more agreements are relevant in this case (GATT, GATS, TRIPS, etc.), on the other the calculation of the "hypothetical" exports are more difficult because the EU changed its regime continuously and at the time of determination the damage, nobody knew the new EU regime as a counterfactual base for calculations.

To tackle this problem, the Arbitrators in the decision for the United States (WTO 1999a at para. 6.3 to 6.27) set out general and special considerations concerning the calculation of compensation:

1. Retaliation duration: Compensation and the suspension of concession are only *temporary measures* (Art. 22.1 DSU). According to the USA and agreed upon by WTO, countermeasures should only *induce compliance.*
2. Direct or *"indirect" benefits*: Besides the estimation of the direct damage (which is complicated enough), the USA argued that they suffered also an "indirect" damage. US exports to Latin America (e.g., fertilizers) used in the production of bananas that would be exported to the EU under a WTO-consistent regime should be counted in setting the level of suspension (Article XXIII:1 of GATT 1994; GATS does not contain analogous provisions).[5]
3. The damage of *services*: The EU argued that the revision of the UN Central Product Classification (CPC) system affects the interpretation of the scope of its market access on "wholesale trade services". WTO concludes that for the calculation of nullification or impairment by reference to losses of actual or potential service supply, it does not matter whether the lost services relate to trade in bananas from the USA, or from third countries, to the EU, or to bananas wholesaled within the EU, provided that the services suppliers harmed are commercial present in the EU and US-owned or US-controlled.
4. *Company-specific effects vs. overall country effects*: Originally, the USA requested only compensation for the losses incurred by one company. The WTO, however, regards it necessary to calculate the aggregate net effects on all US suppliers of wholesale services to bananas wholesaled in the EU.

On January 14, 1999, the United States requested the DSB to authorize suspension of tariff concessions covering trade in an amount of US$ 520.0 million per year (see WTO 1999a, at para. 1.1). The EU objected to the level of suspension on the ground that is was not equivalent to the level of nullification or impairment of benefits suffered by the USA. More so, the EU contends that with respect to trade in goods the nullification or impairment suffered by the USA can only be negligible or nil since there is no actual trade and little prospect for potential trade in bananas between the USA and the EU (WTO 1999a, at para. 6.8).

In contrast to the Hormone case, the calculation of the levels of suspension of concessions are much less (or not at all) transparent (see WTO 1999a, at para. 7.1 to 7.8). The principle of estimating the level of damage is, however, the same. The value of relevant EC imports from the USA under the present banana import regime (the "actual situation") is compared with their value under a WTO-consistent regime (a "counterfactual" situation). The USA proposed very high counterfactual figures assuming a regime change in favor of them. In response, the EU argued (correctly) that there could be many possible WTO-consistent counterfactuals with rather different outcomes as to the potential damage for the USA. Two examples

[5] These indirect damages were, however, not accounted for in the calculations of the level of compensation by the Arbitrators of the WTO in the EU-USA Bananas case.

were a tariff-only regime (which will be implemented only in 2006!) and the current tariff quota regime with a first-come, first-served licensing system.

The WTO requested the USA to provide calculations for four "counterfactuals" to the actual EC revised regime (in parenthesis the proposed figures provided by the US government):

1. A tariff-only regime, without tariff quotas, but including an ACP tariff preference (US$ 326.9 million),
2. A tariff-quota system with license allocations based on the first-come, first-served method (US$ 619.8 million),
3. The complete allocation of a tariff-quota system with country-specific allocations to all substantial and non-substantial ACP and non-ACP suppliers (US$ 558.6 million),
4. The base US counterfactual, which assumed a continuation of a 857,700 ton quantity for ACP imports and an expansion of the MFN tariff quota to 3.7 million tons (US$ 362.4 million).

The EU believed that none of these counterfactuals would involve higher profits for US suppliers than the current revised regime. The WTO sees the relevant effect not on US suppliers' profits but rather on the value of relevant imports from the USA. The Arbitrators could either pick out one figure between the range of possible estimated damages supplied by the USA (from US$ 326.9 million to US$ 619.8 million) or nil as asserted by the EU, or make own calculations. They did the latter by assuming as a reasonable counterfactual, a global tariff quota equal to 2.553 million tons (subject to a 75 Euro per ton tariff) and unlimited access for ACP bananas at a zero tariff. Import licenses would be allocated differently in order to remedy the GATS violations (WTO, 1999a, at para. 7.7 and 7.8). Then they calculated the relevant US imports of the revised EC banana regime (the "actual" situation), compared them with the counterfactual (the "counterfactual" situation), and based on the assumption that the *aggregate volume* of EC banana imports is the same in the two scenarios. This implies that EC banana production and consumption, and the f.o.b., c.i.f., wholesale and retail prices of bananas, also is the same in the two scenarios. This in turn implies that the *aggregate value* of wholesale banana trade services after the f.o.b. point, and the aggregate value of banana import quota rents, is the same in the two scenarios. Both values are calculated from the price and quantity data made available to the WTO (which, however, are not quoted in the decision). The only difference between the scenarios is in the shares of those aggregates that are enjoyed by US and other *service* suppliers. The WTO assumes away the volume of responsiveness of producers, consumers and importers to EC domestic price differences, since there are none. Then the Arbitrators simply calculated the difference between the two scenarios in (a) the US share of wholesale trade services in bananas sold in the EU and (b) the US share of allocated banana import licenses from which quota rents accrue.

As a result, the Arbitrators determined that the level of nullification and impairment is US$ 191.4 million per year. On April 19, 1999 the DSB of the WTO authorized the USA to suspend concessions worth US$ 191.4 million per year (WTO 1999a). The non-transparent way in which the Arbitrators dealt with this calculation exercise is near to the border of a scandal. In sharp contrast to the Hormones case (see Table 1), where each commentator can simply reproduce the different steps which lead to the final amount of the level of nullification and impairment, the Arbitrators refused to document the steps on the way to the final result.

The USA carried this trade sanctions out by setting 100% customs duties on an equivalent amount of trade for a variety of EC products. First, the USA requested authorization to suspend concessions under Art. 22.3(b) or (c). The EC claimed that this would be a cross-sectoral request and that the USA had not fulfilled the procedural requirements foreseen in Art. 22.3(d and e). The Arbitrators did not share the EC's view (see, WTO 1999a at para. 3.8 to 3.10). In order to make the decision legally easier and quicker, the Arbitrators concluded, based on Art. 22.3(a) that the Appellate Body has found that in the Bananas case nullification occurred in the "same sector(s)". That means that violations under the GATT and the GATS in the original dispute were closely related and all concerned a single import regime in respect of one product, i.e., bananas. In DSU legal terms (Art. 22.3(f(i)), US retaliations by imposing tariffs on industrial goods concern the "same sector(s)" (i.e., all goods!) as the bananas belong to! In economic terms, however, it makes a difference in which sectors a country retaliates against violations in, say the agricultural sector (bananas). Among specific sectors that suffered the most were bed linen, bath products (for example UK company "The Body Shop" and French company "Le Laboratoire du Bain"), folding cartons and boxes for luxury goods (e.g., German company "Karton Druck"), lead acid batteries (e.g., Italian company FIAM), luxury handbags and wallets (e.g., French company "Louis Vuitton" and Italian company "Gucci"), lithographs and coffee-making machines.[6] The "carousel" method, announced by the US government, whereby the products subject to sanctions would have been rotated every 6 months, however, was not applied.

In addition to the US sanctions against the WTO-illegal EC import regime for bananas, the Arbitrators (WTO 2000) decided in favor of Ecuador and determined that the level of Ecuador's nullification and impairment is US$ 201.6 million per year. Ecuador is allowed to suspend concessions under the TRIPS agreement. Ecuador was allowed to apply sanctions in form of "cross-retaliation" according to Art. 22.3.c (suspension of concessions under another covered agreement as in the Bananas case, namely those concerning the agricultural sector)[7]. Ecuador, however, decided not to implement sanctions against the EU. A classical case of the "biased" position of small and poor countries vis-à-vis large and powerful trade regions, like the EU.

Since March 1999, the USA has taken countervailing measures worth US$ 478.5 million (US$ 191.4 over 2½ years; March 1999 to July 2001). This amounts

---

[6] For the complete list of products involved, see: http://europa.eu.int/comm/trade/miti/dispute/bana.htm

[7] For the calculation of the level of nullification and impairment, see WTO (2000) at para. 166-170). For the legal discussion about the novelty of "cross-retaliation", see Bronckers (2001), pp. 59-61 and Vranes (2000, 2003b).

to 0.08% of the total EU exports to the USA each year, or 0.19% of agricultural EU exports to the USA each year. With a world market share of some 23% the EU is the world's second biggest banana importer, following the USA (30%).

3.3 Economic Impact of the Bananas EU-US "Mini" Trade War

The welfare and trade implications of this "mini"-trade war between the EU and the USA are again analyzed with the help of model simulations with the GTAP5 CGE world model as in the Hormones case.

Three Scenarios

(I) In the first scenario, the EU has in place its import regime for bananas which is protectionist according to WTO worth US$ 191.4 million per year; in the model simulations, these measures are assumed to be taken in "bananas" sector. (The Arbitrators of the WTO, however, calculated the level of damages for US firms on the assumption that they occurred only in the wholesale trade service sector for bananas!). The restrictive EU Banana regime is implemented in the GTAP5 model by assuming that in the banana sector the EU imports from the USA are reduced by the amount of damage calculated by the WTO arbitrators (US$ 191.4 million per year). Technically this is reached by calibrating an adequate increase of EC tariffs on bananas imports from the USA.

(II) In the second scenario, the USA imposes trade sanctions according to the WTO DSB decisions worth the same amount. As we have the same ambiguity in the WTO arbitrators decision as to the correct meaning of the retaliatory sanctions:

> *"In light of the foregoing considerations, the Arbitrators determine that the level of nullification or impairment suffered by the United States in the matter European Communities –Regime for the Importation, Sale and Distribution of Bananas is US$191.4 million per year. Accordingly, the Arbitrators decide that the suspension by the United States of the application to the European Communities and its member States of tariff concessions and related obligations under GATT 1994 covering trade in a maximum amount of US$ 191.4 million per year would be consistent with Article 22.4 of the DSU." (see WTO 1999a, p. 43),*

we simulate two sub-scenarios:

(IIa) In this scenario the US reduces imports from EU by US$ 116.8 million according to the retaliation list of products. As the products of retaliation concern all manufactured goods we reduce US imports from the EU in the "manufactures" sector by US$ 191.4 million.

(IIb) In this scenario the US reduces imports of manufactures from the EU in order to collect import tariff revenues amounting to US$ 191.4 million.

(III) In the third scenario we calculate the economic effects of the "mini" trade war in the case of the banana dispute between the EU und the USA. This scenario consists of the combined implementation of the measures of the scenarios (I) and (IIb).

Simulation Results

The simulation results of the GTAP5 model are presented in Table 3 and can be summarized as follows:

1. Again, due to the small dimension of the levels of trade restrictions and/or amount of impairment, the effects are small. The trade restrictions amounting US$ 191.4 million per year add up only to 0.08% of the total EU exports to the USA each year or 0.19% of agricultural EU exports to the USA.
2. The EC import regime for bananas (scenario I) is similar to the Hormones case, as this acts as "shooting the EU themselves in the foot" insofar, as it ends in a loss in consumer welfare (misallocation) but due to terms of trade gains in a slight overall welfare improvement of the EU. Total trade between the partners is dampened. Total real GDP in both regions decline. In a partial-equilibrium analysis of EC's banana regime, Badinger et al. (2002) come to similar conclusions concerning the EU as a whole. The overall welfare loss over the period 1993-1998 amounted to Euro 68 million or 0.001% of GDP[8].
3. The retaliation by the USA (scenario IIa and IIb) leads to welfare losses in the EU, but to slight gains in the USA. This is again due to terms of trade gains in the US. Bilateral exports shrink and also real GDP declines in both regions.
4. The "mini" trade war between the USA and the EU leads to a welfare losses in both regions, but higher in the EU. The USA can improve its terms of trade. Bilateral trade was hampered quite a bit. Real GDP declines in both regions. Overall, the EU is again the loser of this "mini" trade war.

The third-country (welfare) externalities of scenario (III) are for all nine regions in the GTAP5 simulations positive. Only if looking at the allocation components of the welfare measure, Turkey suffers slightly from the "mini" bananas trade war between the EU and the USA.

---

[8] The special topic of the Badinger et al. (2002) study, however, is not the estimation of the welfare impact of the EC import regime for bananas for the EU as a whole, but the estimation of the welfare implications for the individual EU countries. It turns out that countries with formerly free trade regimes for bananas are welfare losers (Austria, Finland, Germany and Sweden). Also the group of tariff imposing countries (Belgium-Luxembourg, the Netherlands, Denmark and Ireland) is losers. From the countries which are supplied by ACP countries, Italy is a winner and United Kingdom is a loser. Counties with own bananas production are partly winners (France and Greece) and partly losers (Portugal and Spain).

Table 3. „Mini" Trade War EU versus USA: Bananas Case

Scenarios	Welfare Total*) (as % of GDP)		Welfare Allocation (as % of GDP		Terms of Trade (%-change)	
	EU	USA	EU	USA	EU	USA
(I)	0.000201	-0.000756	-0.000139	-0.000171	0.001079	-0.004780
(IIa)	-0.000671	0.000177	-0.000143	-0.000024	-0.001732	0.001558
(IIb)	-0.002685	0.000709	-0.000571	-0.000097	-0.006929	0.006233
(III)	-0.002483	-0.000048	-0.000709	-0.000268	-0.005850	0.001453
	Exports with Partner (%-change)		GDP, nominal (%-change)		GDP, real (%-change)	
(I)	-0.013515	-0.065884	0.003328	-0.004246	-0.000139	-0.000171
(IIa)	-0.105096	-0.018708	-0.003803	0.002279	-0.000143	-0.000024
(IIb)	-0.420391	-0.074826	-0.015214	0.009115	-0.000571	-0.000097
(III)	-0.433907	-0.140710	-0.011886	0.004869	-0.000709	-0.000268

*) Total welfare = allocation plus terms of trade plus other effects.
(I) = EU blocks BANANAS imports from the USA amounting to US$ 191.4 million.
(IIa) = USA reduces imports from EU by US$ 191.4 million according to retaliation list of products.
(IIb) = USA reduces imports from EU in order to collect import tariff revenues by US$ 191.4 million according to retaliation list of products.
(III) = EU versus USA trade war: Scenarios (I) + (IIb) combined.
Source: Own simulations with the GTAP5 world CGE model

The same caveats as observed in the Hormones case are applicable in the Bananas case. Besides the ex post controlling problem about the level of collecting the "right" (equal) amount of retaliatory tariff revenues which have been granted to impose by WTO, we see in this case clearly the "biased" applicability of DS measures if they come along in the form of tariffs. Large countries (the USA) are able to confront another large country or trading bloc (the EU), whereas small and/or poor (LDC) countries (in this case, Ecuador) are unable to go ahead with such sanctions. Why then did the EU give in at all? First, the next WTO negotiations (the Doha Round) are in preparation in which the EU wants to be a fair partner with special interest (e.g., in the agricultural sector). Second, obviously the EU was eager to sustain the credibility of the binding nature of the DS system. If not, other WTO members in future cases could have argued that the EU itself did not regard the DS decisions as binding. Third, the USA have promised to use its sanctions only as a temporary measure in accordance with Art. 22.1 DSU.

4. The FSC Case

4.1 A Special Kind of Export Subsidization

On November 28, 1997, the EU requested for consultations on the US Internal Revenue Code (sections 921-927) and related measures establishing special tax treatment for "Foreign Sales Corporations" (FSC). The FSC scheme provides for an exemption to the general tax rules which results in substantial tax savings for US companies exporting through FSCs. The EC argued that the exemptions from the US direct (income) taxes of a portion of FSC income related to exports and of dividends distributed to US parent companies constitute *export subsidies* contrary to Article XVI GATT 1994 and Article 3.1(a) of the ASCM. The case was filed at WTO under WT/DS108 and touches provisions on Subsidies (3) and Agriculture (8, 9, 10).

The USA decided to introduce the FSC scheme in 1984 as a replacement of its old export promoting tax scheme, the so-called DISC that was condemned by a GATT panel in 1981. The EC contested the legality of the FSC scheme. After unsuccessful rounds of consultations the EC decided to request the establishment of a WTO Panel in September 1998. In the WTO Panel report (October 8, 1999), the FSC was found to constitute a prohibited *export subsidy* under the Subsidies Agreement and (in relation to agricultural products) an export subsidy in violation of the Agriculture Agreement. The US appealed to the WTO Appellate Body on November 26, 1999. The AB confirmed on February 24, 2000, all the findings of the Panel as to the WTO compatibility of the FSC. The USA was given until October 1, 2000, at the latest to implement the WTO recommendations and rulings.

As the implementation deadline was exceeded without a satisfactory change in the FSC regulations, on November 17, 2000, the EU has requested the WTO to authorize trade sanctions on the USA up to a maximum amount of US$ 4.043 billion in the FSC trade dispute. This amount is based on the value of the subsidy granted by the USA under the FSC scheme according to the figures in the fiscal year 2001 US Budget proposal. The USA continue to provide a significant illegal export subsidy to more than half of total US exports, to the direct detriment of European companies. The US sectors that benefit the most from FSC are: chemical, pharmaceutical, mechanical machinery, electrical equipment and transport equipment; these are sectors where US and EC companies fiercely compete. The EU has also submitted to the WTO an indicative list of those products that would be eligible for sanctions. The list of products avoids premature and unnecessary effects on trade flows while at the same time complying with WTO obligations. The EU argues in its "Background on latest developments in the FSC trade dispute" of November 17, 2000[9], that the list includes chapters of the Common Customs Tariff where the EU has found that there are products that could be subjected to sanctions without negatively affecting the EU industry and consumers as the degree of dependency from the USA is low and there are alternative sources of supply available either within the EU or in third countries. If no imports stem from the USA, how would the EU then be able to collect the demanded tariff revenues amounting to around US$ 4 billion per year? The latest Panel decision of August 20, 2001 (WTO 2001b) confirms the EU position that also the revised US FSC regulation ("FSC Repeal and Extraterritorial Income Exclusion Act of 2000"), set into force on November 15, 2000, is still not consistent with the SCM Agreement and the Agreement of Agriculture. Additionally, the legislation maintains in place the FSC regime at least until the year 2002.

4.2 The Level of Damage – Easier to Calculate?

At first sight, it seems that in contrast to the Hormones and the Bananas cases, the calculation of the damage for EC firms should be simpler, because the US budget pays for the FSC subsidies and must therefore provide respective amounts in the budget plans.

On August 30, 2002, the WTO arbitrators estimated the damage of nullification for the EU amounting to US$ 4,043 million (WTO 2002). However, this was only a compromise: "Having regard to the figures reached on the basis of the calculation, we note that the final amount of subsidy following the United States approach is US$ 3,739 million, whereas the final amount following the European Communities approach is US$ 5,332 million. We see merits and shortcomings in both calculations. We also recall that we are not expected to calculate an exact amount but to determine whether the amount of countermeasures proposed by the European Communities, in the amount of US$ 4,043 million, is appropriate. In these circumstances, we find that the amount of $4,043 million, which falls within the range of reasonable values calculated on the basis of the parties' respective methodologies, can be considered to be a reasonable approximation of the actual value of the subsidy for the year 2000." (WTO 2002, p. 39-40).

[9] The background information on the FSC case in view of the EU can be found on: http://mkaccdb.eu.int/miti/dsu

There is a further problem: Although the FSC regulation is non-discriminatory – meaning that not only the exports to the EU are targeted – only the EU complained at the WTO against this export subsidization scheme. In order to evaluate the whole impact of the FSC one should also implement the costs for Non-EU countries. However, as no other third country, except the EU filed a complaint against the USA, there is no decision by the WTO as to the damage to Non-EU countries, we restrict our calculations of the economic impact only on the EU-US trade relations.

As of May 7, 2003, the WTO authorized the EU to apply countermeasures of up to 4 billion USD against the USA (see EU homepage). The WTO Dispute Settlement Body authorized the EU to increase customs duties up to the level of 100%, for a total of US$ 4 billion of US trade. This move clears the way for the EU to impose countermeasures to be applied on a detailed list of products notified to the DSB (see WTO 2003a). If the United States may not comply until autumn 2003, the EU will start the legislative procedure for the adoption of countermeasures by 1 January 2004. This would amount to 1.8% of the total EU exports to the USA each year, and hence, in comparison to the other mini trade wars would have a bigger impact on the bilateral trade relations.

4.3 Economic Impact of the FSC EU-US "Mini" Trade War

As the EU not yet implemented the countermeasures the calculation of the welfare and trade implications of this "mini"-trade war between the EU and the USA is hypothetical. However, it might become reality as of January 1, 2004, if the US does not comply. The FSC case is quantitatively by far the most important case for both sides. Again we analyze this case with the help of model simulations with the GTAP5 CGE world model as in the previous cases.

Three Scenarios

(I) In the *first scenario* the US subsidizes exports to the EU (but in principle to all third countries) by the estimated amount of US$ 4 billion. The implementation into the GTAP5 model is done in practically all 7 sectors so as to increase the export subsidies in order to reach an increase of US exports to the EU by US$ 4 billion.

(II) In the *second scenario* the EU retaliates with the same amount. But due to the ambiguity of the WTO decision, again we differentiate into two sub-scenarios. These scenarios are still hypothetical, as the EU not yet introduced the countervailing measures.

(IIa) In this scenario the EU reduces imports from the USA amounting to US$ 4 billion according to the list of retaliation of products. In our model simulations this means an increase of import tariffs in the sectors meat, food, steel, other primary goods, steel and manufactures.

(IIb) In this scenario the EU reduces imports from the USA in the same sectors as in scenario (IIa) in order to collect import tariff revenues equivalent to US$ 4 billion.

(III) In the *third scenario* we simulate the – now not so small – "mini" trade war between the EU and the US in the FSC case. For this purpose we implement the scenarios (I) and (IIb) simultaneously into the model.
As mentioned above, in reality the FSC regulation of the US not only stimulates exports to the EU but also to other third countries. As those, however, did not apply for sanctions at the WTO, we can only measure the possible economic impact for the EU-US relations.

Simulation Results

The simulation results of the GTAP5 model are presented in Table 4 and can be summarized as follows[10]:

1. As the amount of the WTO-illegal subsidies involved is much higher than in the former cases (Hormones and Bananas), the impact is also larger in terms of welfare, trade and terms of trade. The retaliatory measures amount to US$ 4 billion which is 1.8% of the total EU trade with the USA. In scenario (I), the isolated effects of the WTO-illegal FSC scheme is simulated. Export subsidies have the classical text book effects. Welfare and terms of trade decreases in the subsidizing country in support of exports. The EU gains in welfare, mainly due to the relatively strong improvement of the terms of trade. US exports to the EU increase by 1.74%. Also EU exports to the US increase slightly. Overall, there is a slight increase in real GDP.
2. In scenario (II) the variant (IIb) where the EU targets import tariff revenues of US$ 4 billion exhibit stronger effects than variant (IIa). Overall welfare in the EU increases, mainly due to the terms of trade gains. The introduction of retaliatory tariffs, however, deteriorates allocation in the EU. The USA loses welfare. The trade restrictions result in a decline in bilateral exports, whereby the US exports to the EU would shrink dramatically (by 8.5%). Real GDP declines in both countries.
3. The trade war in the FSC case (scenario (III)) would be – due to the high volume of trade policy measures involved – no longer a "mini" trade war. Overall, it seems as the EU would gain this trade war at the expense of the USA. EU welfare and its terms of trade would increase; those of the US would decrease. The former export stimulating effect of the FSC scheme would be more than neutralized in this trade war. Bilateral exports would decline, those of the EU

---

[10] In earlier calculations of the economic impact of the major trade disputes between the EU und the USA, the welfare and trade results were only slightly different to the present calculations. The slight differences might be due to the different CGE models used. Her we use a 12x7x5 CGE world model. In the previous calculations we used a 3 regions, 7 sectors model with 2 factors of production (see Breuss 2003 p. 166).

by 1.5% and those of the USA by 6.8%. There would be a Trade Creation effect within the EU because the intra-EU trade would be stimulated by 0.7%.

Besides the impact of the FSC "trade war" on both parties (EU and the US) it is also interesting to study the externalities of this dispute in other third countries. By using a 12 country/region CGE model we can study these third-country effects. It turns out that all other nine regions plus the ROW would slightly improve total welfare in case of scenario (III). However, two countries (Canada and Mexico) and the ROW would have slight negative allocative effects. However, scenario (I) – the simulation of the impact of the FSC scheme of the US alone – leads to welfare losses all over the regions in the GTAP5 model (except for the EU, due to terms of trade gains).

Contrary to the first two cases the FSC induced trade war between the EU and the USA would be of a considerable dimension and it would involve nearly all sectors of both economies with not easy appreciable consequences on welfare, allocation, efficiency, labor markets and change in sectoral competitiveness in both countries. The larger the retaliatory level at stake the plainer one sees the problems with the present practice of sanctions by the WTO-DS system. Without a detailed computable general equilibrium model (CGE) for both countries one is simply not able to evaluate all the economic interactions and consequences of such a trade war.

5 The Steel Case

5.1 An Evolving Conflict with Unknown Level of Damage

On March 20, 2002, the US imposed severe restrictions on steel from the rest of the world with import tariffs as high as 30%. These safeguard measures applied to imports from all countries, except for products of Canada, Israel, Jordan and Mexico, and also for products of developing countries when they are members of the WTO[11]. Given that this left the EU – the world's largest steel producer, with 159 million tons of crude steel (19% of world production) in 2001 - as the only remaining sizeable steel market, this created a serious risk that the EU would be flooded by steel shut out of the US market. The extent of possible trade diversion is estimated by the European Commission as high as 15 million tons per year, 56% of current EU import levels. EU steel imports are already at record levels (imports in 2001 stand at 26.6 million tones, compared to 15.4 million tons in 1997, an overall increase of 73% over the last 4 years).
The EU reacted to the US safeguard measures for steel imports by two actions: (a) introduction of own safeguard measures to avoid trade diversion to the EU market; (b) request of a decision by the WTO (panel).

[11] For details of the measures and the coverage of products, see www.whitehouse.gov/

Table 4. „Mini" Trade War EU versus USA: FSC Case

Scenarios	Welfare Total*) (as % of GDP)		Welfare Allocation (as % of GDP		Terms of Trade (%-change)	
	EU	USA	EU	USA	EU	USA
(I)	0.010163	-0.002143	0.002144	0.000686	0.028071	-0.035651
(IIa)	0.007094	-0.015304	-0.001326	-0.000983	0.026789	-0.115756
(IIb)	0.032990	-0.069634	-0.005256	-0.004452	0.122031	-0.524867
(III)	0.043128	-0.071750	-0.003120	-0.003760	0.150102	-0.560518
	Exports with Partner (%-change)		GDP, nominal (%-change)		GDP, real (%-change)	
(I)	0.239033	1.739642	-0.031311	0.053677	0.002144	0.000687
(IIa)	-0.390677	-1.888334	0.075005	-0.102136	-0.001327	-0.000982
(IIb)	-1.772778	-8.532730	0.341510	-0.464057	-0.005273	-0.004431
(III)	-1.533745	-6.793090	0.310199	-0.410380	-0.003130	-0.003744

*) Total welfare = allocation plus terms of trade plus other effects.
(I) = USA subsidizes exports to EU by US$ 4,043 billion over all sectors.
(IIa) = EU reduces imports from USA by US$ 4 billion according to retaliation list of products.
(IIb) = EU reduces imports from USA in order to collect import tariff revenues by US$ 4 billion according to retaliation list of products.
(III) = EU versus USA trade war: Scenarios (I) + (IIb) combined.
Source: Own Simulations With the GTAP5 World CGE Model.

a. The European Commission on March 27, 2002, adopted temporary safeguard measures on steel. This regulation measures (Commission Regulation EC No. 560/2002 of 27 March 2002, OJ L85/1) to 15 steel products (the list can be found at the trade portal of the homepage of the EU: http://europa.eu.int/comm/trade/goods/steel/pr_270302.htm). According to the European Commission the safeguard establishes a generous level of steel imports – within which the measures will not apply – based on the highest recent level of imports (2001). Beyond these levels, tariffs will apply varying from 14.9% (for Rebars) to a maximum of 26% (for Alloy Hot Rolled Flat Products)[12]. These temporary measures lasted for a maximum of 6 months. Although the measures are non-discriminatory, in accordance with WTO rules, developing countries were effectively excluded from the measures. They will also not apply to imports from Russia, Ukraine and Kazakhstan. On September 27, 2002, after a detailed investigation, the European Commission adjusted the safeguard measures and restricted it to seven out of the original 21 products. The EU adopted definitive safeguard measures on seven steel products[13]. The tariff quotas for the 7 products permit imports to continue at their traditional levels. Only above these quotas would any safeguard duties become payable at a rate between 17.5% and 26.0%. The tariff quotas will be abolished when the US measures are repealed, and in any event will be progressively liberalized over the next three years. The "short list" of retaliatory (safeguard) import tariffs amounted to € 380 million, the "long list" amounted to € 600 million.
b. The second front on which the EU fights the US steel protectionism is the establishing of a panel at the WTO. The EU requested WTO consultations with the US on its safeguard measures on March 2002. These proved unfruitful. A number of WTO members made similar requests and, on April, 11 and 12, joint dispute settlement consultations were held in Geneva, between the EU, Japan, Korea, China, Switzerland and Norway on one side and the United States on the other. At the meeting of the WTO Dispute Settlement Body (DSB) on May 22, 2002, the EU requested the establishment of a Panel in view of the failure to reach a solution through consultations. Although the United States blocked this request, WTO rules do not allow any further procedural devices for delay and a Panel was therefore established the special meeting on June 3, 2002.
   Following the establishment of a WTO panel on United States – "Definitive Safeguard Measures on Imports of Certain Steel Products" (WT/DS248 (EC) of June 3, 2002, seven other countries requested a panel, which was established under WT/DS249 (Japan) and WT/DS251 (Korea) on June 14, 2002,

---

[12] For each of the fifteen individual products, quota limits were calculated by taking the average import level for the last three years (1999-2001) and adding 10 per cent. The overall effect was to establish the total imports of these products to around the 2001 level. The quotas were allocated using a "first come first served" approach on the basis of customs declarations requiring exporters to prove they have steel ready to export.

[13] Five of these products are primary steel products, whilst the remaining two are more sophisticated finished products. More than 70,000 people are employed in the manufacture of these seven products in the Community.

WT/DS252 (China), WT/DS253 (Switzerland) and WT/DS254 (Norway) on June 24, 2002, WT/DS258 (New Zealand) on July 8, 2002 and WT/DS259 (Brazil) on July 29, 2002. On July 25, 2002 the Director-General appointed Ambassador Stefán Jóhannesson, Mr. Mohan Kumar and Ms Margaret Liang as panelists. The WTO, on July 11, 2003, issued the reports of a panel (requested by the EC, Japan, Korea, China, Switzerland, Norway, New Zealand and Brazil (Co-complainants)), which concluded that the safeguard measures imposed by the United States on the imports of certain steel products (10 steel product groupings) are inconsistent with the WTO Safeguards Agreement and GATT 1994 (see WTO 2003b). In this panel report of nearly 1000 pages the WTO not only evaluated the US safeguard measures against WTO law but also criticized fundamentally the US trade legislation and supplied an extensive analysis of the world steel market and those in the United States in particular. If the US were to appeal, the resolution of this dispute would be delayed until before the end of the year 2003.

As a counter-action the United States requested a Panel against the EU safeguard measures. On September 16, 2002 a WTO Panel (WT/DS260/4, request of 19 August 2002) was established following a request by the United States against the provisional safeguard measures taken by the EC with regard to imports of certain steel products. The US claims that these measures are inconsistent with the EC's commitments and obligations under the General Agreement on Tariffs and Trade 1994 ("GATT 1994") and the Agreement on Safeguards ("Safeguards Agreement"). The measures in question (collectively, the "Safeguard Measures") include Commission Regulation (EC) No 560/2002 of 27 March 2002, as amended by Commission Regulation (EC) No 950/2002 of 3 June 2002, and Commission Regulation (EC) No 1287/2002 of 15 July 2002, as well as any other amendments thereto or extensions thereof, and any related measures.

So far there is no estimation of the damage the EU and the USA have suffered from the counter-safeguard actions in the steel sector. However, on August 23, 2002 the European Commission welcomed the batch of exclusion of steel products of interest to the EU exporters from the US safeguard measures. This reduced the overall impact of the US WTO illegal safeguard measures which will exempt more than 50% of EU exports. Article 8.1 of the WTO Safeguard Agreement requires countries adopting such measures to offer offsetting compensation so as to "maintain a substantially equivalent level of concessions". When the US safeguard measures were announced, the Commission estimated that they would affect more than US$ 2 billion of EU steel exports. By the new exemptions the level of damage by the EU then would amount to roughly US$ 1 billion. This would be equivalent to 0.4% of the total EU exports to the USA.

5.2 Economic Impact of the Steel EU-US "Mini" Trade War

On the one hand there is until now only a WTO decision on the illegality of the US safeguard measures but not on those of the EU. On the other hand the level of damage on neither party (US and EU) has been determined yet. Therefore we make only some provisional and hence hypothetical simulation experiments with the GTAP5 CGE world model as in the previous cases.

Three Scenarios

(I) In the *first scenario* we simulate the impact of the safeguard measures by the US implemented at March 20, 2002, amounting to an estimated "damage" for the EU by US$ 1 billion. First, the USA increases import tariffs on steel imports from seven industrial countries/regions (EU, EFTA, Turkey, Brazil, China, Japan and Korea; LDCs, and the NAFTA countries Canada and Mexico are exempted from the safeguard measures) resulting in additional import tariff revenues in the USA by around US$ 391 million. According to estimations by the EU Commission the US safeguard measures have caused a potential damage in the EU of around US$ 1 billion in form of reduced steel exports to the US market. Therefore we calibrate the US safeguard measures in order to target a US$ 1 billion steel import reduction from the EU.

The asserted trade diversion effects (reallocation of steel exports from the US market to the EU market) cannot be detected – at least in the aggregate steel sector[14] in the GTAP5 model simulations. An indication that the trade diversion effect must not be large is that the European Commission reduced the number of products for which the EU introduced counter safeguard measures from originally 21 to only 7 steel products.

(II) In the *second scenario* we simulate the introduction of counter-safeguard measures by the EU at an amount of the "long list" by US$ 600 million. These import tariffs are introduced in a non-discriminatory way on steel imports from the USA, Canada, Mexico, Brazil, China, Japan and Korea (excluding EFTA, Turkey and the LDCs). The import tariffs are calibrated for steel imports so as to reach a reduction of EU steel imports from third countries amounting to US$ 600 million ("long" list).

(III) In the *"mini" trade scenario* we combine the scenarios (I) and (II).

Simulation Results

The simulation results of the GTAP5 model are presented in Table 5 and can be summarized as follows:

1. In scenario (I) the steel safeguard measures introduced by the US have the following implications: With the exception of the EFTA and Turkey all coun-

[14] The products concerned by the safeguard measures are very specific and cannot be captured properly in the GTAP5 model.

tries/regions targeted by the US safeguard measures suffer a welfare loss. The EU suffers a welfare loss due to misallocation and terms of trade losses. The US improves their terms of trade but suffers allocation losses, resulting in an overall welfare gain. Both countries suffer a slight real GDP loss. Bilateral trade will decline, more so the exports of the EU to the US than the other way round.
2. In scenario (II) the counter-safeguard measures by the EU have the following effects: The overall welfare of the EU increases (those of the US decreases) due to the terms of trade improvements resulting from the retaliatory import tariffs on steel products. However, there are negative allocation effects. Bilateral trade between the EU and the USA declines. Real GDP will slightly decrease in both countries. The safeguard measures of the EU will lead to a trade creation effect in so far as the intra-EU imports increase.
3. The welfare implications for the other regions are as expected. Those regions which are exempted from the safeguard measures by the EU – EFTA, Turkey, LDCs – will gain welfare, the others will lose.
4. The mini-trade war scenario (scenario (III) – with our hypothetical amounts of damages implemented – would have the following outcome: There would be welfare losses on both sides of the Atlantic ("shooting in their own feet"). The terms of trade would improve in the US and decline somewhat in the EU. However, bilateral trade would decline by 5% and 3% respectively. Real GDP would be slightly down in both countries. A further implication of the "mini trade" steel war between the EU and the USA is that EU exports will be diverted from the US to other world regions. The same is true for the US, although not in such an intensity as in the case of the EU.
5. The third-country impact on welfare is similar to that of scenario (II). However, now, also Canada and Mexico can gain welfare in case of an EU-US steel trade war.

Although the US government already made considerable concessions by excluding nearly half of the products initially sheltered, the new Steel dispute is still not yet settled. Also a decision by the WTO Dispute Settlement Body can be expected in the near future as how large the real damage on both side of the Atlantic will be.

6 How to Improve the WTO-DSU Sanctions Mechanism?

The WTO DS system is in place since 1995 and has already gathered a considerable amount of practice. Most of the cases dealt with ended with the implementation of the trade policy measures which comply with WTO rules as demanded by the WTO DSB. Until now, only three cases ended with the authorization for trade sanctions (the Hormones, the Bananas and the FSC case). In the present three cases the rivals are the USA and the EU as well as Canada and the EU, and Ecuador and the EU respectively.

Table 5. „Mini" Trade War EU versus USA: Steel Case

Scenarios	Welfare Total*) (as % of GDP)		Welfare Allocation (as % of GDP		Terms of Trade (%-change)	
	EU	USA	EU	USA	EU	USA
(I)	-0.003174	0.001096	-0.000614	-0.000412	-0.008291	0.013025
(II)	0.001407	-0.001559	-0.000233	-0.000115	0.005293	-0.011616
(III)	-0.001766	-0.000463	-0.000847	-0.000527	-0.002998	0.001410
	Exports with Partner (%-change)		GDP, nominal (%-change)		GDP, real (%-change)	
(I)	-0.467466	-0.110962	-0.016206	0.013390	-0.000614	-0.000412
(II)	-0.066176	-0.193604	0.012271	-0.010098	-0.000233	-0.000115
(III)	-0.533642	-0.304573	-0.003936	0.003291	-0.000847	-0.000527

*) Total welfare = allocation plus terms of trade plus other effects.
(I) = USA introduces safeguard measures for steel imports (import tariffs by 30%; steel import reduction from EU by US$ 1 billion)
(II) = EU introduces counter-safeguard measures for steel imports (import tariffs for 7 products; steel import reduction from third countries by US$ 600 million)
(III) = EU versus USA trade war EU-USA: Scenarios (I) + (II) combined.
Source: Own simulations with the GTAP5 world CGE model.

There are a lot of legal and economic reasons for reforming the WTO-DSU system. In the run-up to the Fifth Ministerial Conference of the WTO at Cancun (Mexico, September 10-14, 2003) the progress of the Doha Round will be reviewed. Also the DSU system will be reformed. In the following we concentrate primarily on the economic peculiarities of the present DSU system (see also Anderson 2002). Based on the present practice and the findings of our economic evaluation one can draw the following conclusions:

- *The calculation of damages:* The present cases showed that the estimation of the correct level of the suspension of concessions "equal to the nullification or impairment" is practically impossible. The calculation always involves the comparison between the actual situations with one hypothetical in which the trade measures would be WTO-legal. In both cases one has to estimate practically all parameters. A small change in the assumption of only one parameter results in considerable changes of the final result. As such calculations always have to be made under uncertainty one should at least do this exercise under two conditions: (a) The Arbitrators should make sensitivity analyses when fixing the level of impairment; (b) much more transparency is necessary (a good example is the Hormone case, a very bad example is the Bananas case). The concept of equivalence draws more on notions of fairness than on economic accuracy. As Anderson (2002) demonstrated theoretically (see also Figure 1 in the Appendix) and we calculated via model simulations in this paper, "trade loss equivalence would never translate into equivalent damage to economic welfare, except by coincidence". This can be seen by the unclear statements of the WTO arbitrators when specifying the value of the damage. The so estimated damage is always a static approximation to a possible loss by the complainant. If he is allowed to introduce retaliatory import tariffs in the amount of the "damage" this will enhance reactions by importers and will reduce the targeted tariff revenues. Also in an other respect the WTO dispute settlement system is flawed. Not only does it favor larger countries because they have better access to this procedure than smaller and poor countries. It only looks at future actions. Past wrongs go uncompensated. Trade retaliation under WTO only target non-compliance after the "reasonable period of time" has elapsed following a Panel or Appellate Body finding against a respondent's wrong policy regime. The damage done in preceding years to the complainant's export industry is simply ignored by DSU procedures. Further more, by retaliating it is the complainant's import-competing industries that enjoy temporary assistance because of the prohibitive retaliatory tariffs imposed. This does not help the export industry that has been denied market access by the respondent's wrong policy in the first place.
- *Controlling:* Besides the problem of calculating the level of damage a country suffers from another not complying with WTO rules, a question – overlooked by the DS architects – concerns controlling. Once the amount of impairment is set by the Arbitrators in the WTO DS procedure, who controls ever whether the country who has the allowance to retaliate (e.g. in the case of hormones and bananas the USA) really only cashes in the amount decided by the WTO? In

reality it is nearly impossible to split up the tariff revenues in "normal" and "retaliated" tariff revenues or if one takes into account the ambiguity of the WTO Arbitrators wording the amount (value) of imports.

- *Questionable system of compensation:* The present sanctions practice of the WTO DSB is to allow complainants to impose tariff measures. Theory and the empirical evidence (via simulations with CGE trade models) suggest that import tariffs may lead to a trade war. Trade wars can only be won by large (and hence, powerful) countries. This is the result of optimum tariff theory and more recent theoretical analysis (see Grossman and Helpman 1995, Breuss 2003). That means that small (and more so, poor LDCs) countries are discriminated in two respects. On the one hand, due to a lack of legal resources they can make less use of the WTO DS system. On the other hand, if they are authorized to retaliate against a large country or trading bloc (like the EU), they do no implement such sanctions (e.g., Ecuador in its "cross-retaliation" case against the EU) either because they fear to lose the trade war or to lose the necessary aids from the large country (e.g., from the EU) or they hope for preferential treatment in debt negotiations in the Paris Club. Countermeasures in form of retaliatory tariffs are hence bad policy. They amount to "shooting oneself in the foot" (see Mavroidis 2001, p. 46). Through countermeasures, at least a small and poor WTO member imposes an additional cost on society. Precisely because of the budgetary constraints, adoption of countermeasures is simply not an option for the poorer WTO members. The present system of compensation in the WTO illustrates the disadvantageous position of LDCs. Even "cross-retaliation" in the area of TRIPS, which may have seemed to more promising from the perspective of compliance-seeking developing countries, does not offer them the relief they hoped for, as can be seen in Ecuador's experience in the Bananas dispute with the EU (see Bronckers 2001, p. 61, Breuss et al. 2003).
- *Retaliations have incalculable impacts:* Retaliatory measures via import tariffs have a whole series of incalculable and unpleasant impacts. The Hormones, the Bananas and the FSC cases have demonstrated that retaliatory measures tend to injure a motley assembly of exporters and importers, often smaller companies, who rarely, if ever, have an interest in the original dispute (e.g., Bananas against luxury bags from "Gucci". As Bronckers (2001, p. 62) reports, "these companies have a point when arguing that any damages paid for WTO violations by a non-complying country ought to be paid from public funds, rather than by an arbitrary selection of individuals". If the group of small companies has also a small lobbying power the responsible Commission and the Member states of the EU are not inclined to change a WTO-illegal regime[15]. Besides these anecdotal remarks one can strictly prove from general equilibrium analysis of trade policy measures that the imposed tariffs on a randomly selected list of products (sometimes aggravated by a "carousel" method) can have implications which are not foreseen by WTO Arbitrators if they do not dispose of a

---

[15] As Bronckers (2001, p. 62) mentions, various European companies, struck by US retaliatory measures, had considered filing damage claims against the European institutions pursuant to Article 288 EC Treaty.

very detailed CGE world trade model. The larger the retaliatory measures (e.g. demonstrated in the FSC case) the bigger the negative allocative impact on the different sectors and the larger the allocative inefficiency caused. As long as such model devices are not at hand, the WTO DSB decisions on retaliatory tariffs are irresponsible. Not only, they disadvantage small and poor WTO members but also they can not fully estimate the economic consequences for the parties involved in the dispute directly, but also indirectly the impact on third countries not participating in the dispute (third country externalities). Furthermore, even if one accepts the estimated level of trade sanctions, presently, nobody is controlling whether the sanctioning country really collects exactly the amount it is allowed to, or more. Practically, this is an impossible game, as an administration cannot clearly differentiate which part of tariff revenues is retaliatory in nature and which is normal. Additionally, who controls the distribution of these retaliatory tariff revenues to the companies suffered damage? Tariffs are therefore very bad instruments for countermeasures. Although "the right to request financial reparation for a wrongful act, including damages incurred in the past, is a basic principle of international law in case compliance is not possible" (Bronckers 2001, p. 62), the question is the method in which sanctions should be executed.

- *From tariff to transfer sanctions:* Due to the negative and often incalculable impact a much more efficient and easier retaliation instrument than tariffs would be direct transfers (lump-sum penalties) from the government of the non-complying country to the government of the country having got the authorization of compensation by WTO. The latter government could than easily redistribute the received transfers to the companies which suffered the concrete loss. Whether transfers as retaliatory measures would also be covered by the present DSU legislation is an open question. Article 22.1 DSU never speaks about tariffs explicitly but only on "compensation and the suspension of concessions or other obligations". Suspension of concessions implies, however, tariffs as the major part of concessions in former GATT rounds consists of tariff reductions. One could (newly!) interpret "other obligations" as the duty of countries not complying with WTO rules to pay transfers to the countries hurt by the non-compliant action. This should be a recoverable claim, determined by the usual DSU procedure. The problem, however, is that the complainant would interfere into the national autonomy of the respondent which is excluded from the present WTO system.

  A somewhat other suggestion was put forward by Anderson (2002). He pleads for compensation instead of retaliation. A complainant unhappy with the respondent's policy reform should be entitled to seek compensation until satisfactory reforms are implemented. Compensation could come in the form of a temporary lowering of the respondent's import barriers on some other products, which should be offered on a most-favored-nation (MFN) basis. Instead of the restrictive effect of retaliation to both countries involved in the trade dispute, compensation in this form would simply mean trade liberalization. According to Anderson (2002) the concept of compensation would not only favor the complainant but also third countries and by granting compensation, the respondent would gain greater control of procedures. With retaliation, by contrast, the complainant can keep pressure on the respondent until the latter complies.

Overall, the sanctions – as intended in Article 22.1 DSU they should only be temporary – had at least succeeded in the Bananas case. Here, the EU came to an agreement with the USA in implementing a new regime which satisfies both sides. In the Hormones case, the EU is still belated in abolishing the ban on imports of US beef. The matter is complicated insofar as (a) it is difficult to proof that hormone treated meat can cause cancer (the time of experience is to short), and (b) the European consumers simply refuse to eat hormone treated meat. If this were really true, then no ban on US meat would be necessary, given that the meat sold in European shops is label as hormone treated. In the FSC case, the EU is allowed to impose retaliatory measures. It is, however, waiting for compliance of the US government. If implementing the US$ 4 billion measures this would hamper bilateral trade more than any other trade dispute. Still open is the outcome of the steel dispute. In any case there are not signs that the transatlantic trade relations are improving. On the contrary, the recent file of the US government against the EU over its illegal five-year moratorium on approving agricultural biotech products (GMOs) underlines that the pessimists could become right.

References

Anderson K (2002) Peculiarities of Retaliation in WTO Dispute Settlement, CEPR Discussion Paper Series, No. 3578

Badinger H, Breuss F, Mahlberg B (2002) Welfare Effects of the EU's Organization of the Market in Bananas. Journal of Common Market Studies 40 : 515–526

Bagwell K, Staiger RW (1999) An Economic Theory of GATT. The American Economic Review 89 : 215–248

Bievre, Dirk De (2002) Redesigning the Virtous Circle: Two Proposals for world Trade Organization Reform. Journal of World trade 36 : 1005–1014.

Breuss F (2003) WTO Dispute Settlement in Practice – an Economic Assessment. In: Breuss F, Griller S, Vranes E (eds.): The Banana Dispute – An Economic and Legal Analysis. Springer, Wien, NewYork, pp 131–184

Breuss F,Griller S, Vranes E (eds.) (2003) The Banana Dispute – An Economic and Legal Analysis. Springer, Wien NewYork

Bronckers MCEJ (2001) More Power to the WTO? Journal of International Economic Law 4 : 41–65

Dimaranan BV, McDougall RA (eds) (2002) Global Trade, Assistance, and Production: The GTAP 5 Data Base, Purdue University

European Commission (2003), General Overview of Active WTO Dispute Settlement Cases Involving the EC as Complainant or Defendant, Brussels, Ref. 177/03, 26 March

GATT (1994) The Results of the Uruguay Round of Multilateral Trade Negotiations: The Legal Texts, Geneva

Grossman GM, Helpman E (1995) Trade Wars and Trade Talks. Journal of Political Economy 103 : 675–708

Horn H, Mavroidis PC (2001) Economic and Legal Aspects of the Most Favoured Nation Clause, CEPR Discussion Paper, No. 2859, London

Horn H, Mavroidis PC, Nordström H (1999) Is the Use of the WTO Dispute Settlement System Biased?, CEPR Discussion Paper, No. 2340, London

Hungerford TL (1991) GATT: A cooperative equilibrium in a noncooperative trading regime? Journal of International Economics 31 : 357–369

Johnson HG, (1953) Optimum Tariffs and Retaliation. The Review of Economic Studies, 21 : 142–153; revised version in: Johnson HG, (1958) International Trade and Economic Growth: Studies in Pure Theory, George Allen & Unwin Ltd, London pp 31–55

Kennan J, Riezman R (1988) Do Big Countries Win Tariff Wars?, International Economic Review 29 : 81–85

Maggi G (1999) The Role of Multilateral Institutions in International Trade Cooperation. The American Economic Review 89 : 190–214

Mavroidis PC (2001) Remedies in the WTO Legal System: Between a Rock and a Hard Place. In: Matsushita M, Mavroides PC, Schonbaum TJ (eds) The WTO Law and Practice, London

Mayer W (1984) Endogenous Tariff Formation. The American Economic Review 74 : 970–985

McMillan J (1986) Game Theory in International Economics. Harwood Academic Publishers, Chur London Paris New York

Rodrik D (1995) Political Economy of Trade Policy. In: Grossman GM, Rogoff K (eds) Handbook of International Economics Vol III, Elsevier, Amsterdam Lausanne New York Oxford Shannon Tokyo pp 1457–1494.

Spagnolo G (2001) Issue Linkage, Credible Delegation, and Policy Cooperation. CEPR Discussion Paper, No. 2778, London

Staiger RW (1995) International Rules and Institutions for Trade Policy. In: Grossman GM, Rogoff K (eds) Handbook of International Economics Vol III, Elsevier, Amsterdam Lausanne New York Oxford Shannon Tokyo, pp 1495–1551

Vranes E (2000) Principles and Emerging Problems of WTO Cross Retaliation. Europäische Zeitschrift für Wirtschaftsrecht 10 : 10–15

Vranes E (2003a) From Bananas I to the 2001 Bananas Settlement: A Factual and Procedural Analysis of the WTO Proceedings. In: Breuss F, Griller S, Vranes E (eds) The Banana Dispute – An Economic and Legal Analysis. Springer, Wien New York, pp 11–37

Vranes E (2003b) Cross Retaliation under GATS and TRIPS – An Optimal Enforcement Device for Developing Countries? In: Breuss F, Griller S, Vranes E (eds) The Banana Dispute – An Economic and Legal Analysis. Springer, Wien New York pp 113–130

Whalley J (1985) Trade Liberalization among Major World Trading Areas. The MIT Press, Cambridge, Massachusetts, London

WTO (1999a) European Communities – Regime for the Importation, Sale and Distribution of Bananas – Recourse to Arbitration by the European Communities under Article 22.6 of the DSU: Decision by the Arbitrators (USA case), World Trade Organization, WT/DS27/ARB, 9 April

WTO (1999b) European Communities – Measures Concerning Meat and Meat Products (Hormones) – Recourse to Arbitration by the European Communities under Article 22.6 of the DSU: Decision by the Arbitrators (USA case), World Trade Organization, WT/DS26/ARB, 12 July

WTO (1999c) European Communities – Measures Concerning Meat and Meat Products (Hormones) – Recourse to Arbitration by the European Communities under Article 22.6 of the DSU: Decision by the Arbitrators (Canada case), World Trade Organization, WT/DS48/ARB, 12 July

WTO (2000) European Communities – Regime for the Importation, Sale and Distribution of Bananas – Recourse to Arbitration by the European Communities under Article 22.6 of the DSU: Decision by the Arbitrators (Ecuador case), World Trade Organization, WT/DS27/ARB/ECU, 24 March

WTO (2001a) European Communities – Regime for the Importation, Sale and Distribution of Bananas – Notification of Mutually Agreed Solution, World Trade Organization, WT/DS27/58, 2 July

WTO (2001b) United States – Tax Treatment for "Foreign Sales Corporations, Recourse to Article 21.5 of the DSU by the European Commission, World Trade Organization, WT/DS108/RW, 20 August

WTO (2002) United States – Tax Treatment for "Foreign Sales Corporations, Recourse to Arbitration by the United States under Article 22.6 of the DSU and Article 4.11 of the SCM Agreement: Decision of the Arbitrator, World Trade Organization, WT/DS108/ARB, 30 August

WTO (2003a) United States – Tax Treatment for "Foreign Sales Coroprations: Recourse by the European Communities to Article 4.10 of the SCM Agreement and Article 22.7 of the DSU, WT/DS108/26, 25 April

WTO (2003b) United States – Definitive Safeguard Measures on Imports of Certain Steel Products, WT/DS248/R, WT/DS249/R, WT/DS251/R, WT/DS252/R, WT/DS253/R, WT/DS254/R, WT/DS258/R, WT/DS259/R, 11 July

Appendix

Table 6. The WTO Dispute Settlement Cases, 1995-2002, Total and Breakdown by types of Countries

	Defendants				
Complainants	U.S.	EC	DCs	Others	Total
U.S.	-	30	29	15	74
EC	22	-	27	9	58
DCs	37	27	38	8	110
Others	22	8	13	14	57
Total	81	65	107	46	299

Source: De Bievre, Horn, and Mavroides, Messerlin, WTO

Table 7. The EC-U.S. Dispute Settlement Cases, 1995-2002, Sectors targeted

	U.S. as complainant	EC as complainant	Total
Agrifood	10	3	13
Steel	2	6	8
Textiles	-	2	2
Chemicals	-	1	1
Electronics	3	1	4
Services	8	1	9
Various	7	4	11
U.S. laws	-	4	4
Total	30	22	52

Source: Messerlin, WTO

Table 8. The EC-U.S. Dispute Settlement Cases, 1995-2002, Instruments Targeted

	U.S. as complainant	EC as complainant	Total
Tariffs	4		4
Import regime	3	3	6
Customs issues	3		3
Antidumping	-	4	4
CVDs	1	2	3
Safeguards	1	3	4
Export measures	1	-	1
Norms	1	-	1
Service regulations	3	1	4
TRIPs	8	1	9
Gov.procurement	-	1	1
U.S. laws	-	7	7
Total	30	22	52

Source: Messerlin, WTO

Table 9. Model Structure of the GTAP5 World Model Used in the Simulations

12 Countries/Regions	7 Commodities/Sectors	5 Factors of Production
USA, Canada, Mexico, EU, EFTA, Turkey, Brazil, Latin America, China, Japan, Korea, ROW	Bananas, Meat, Food, Other Primaries, Steel, Manufactures, Services	Land, Unskilled Labor, Skilled Labor, Capital, Natural Resources

Source: Dimaranan and McDougall (2002)

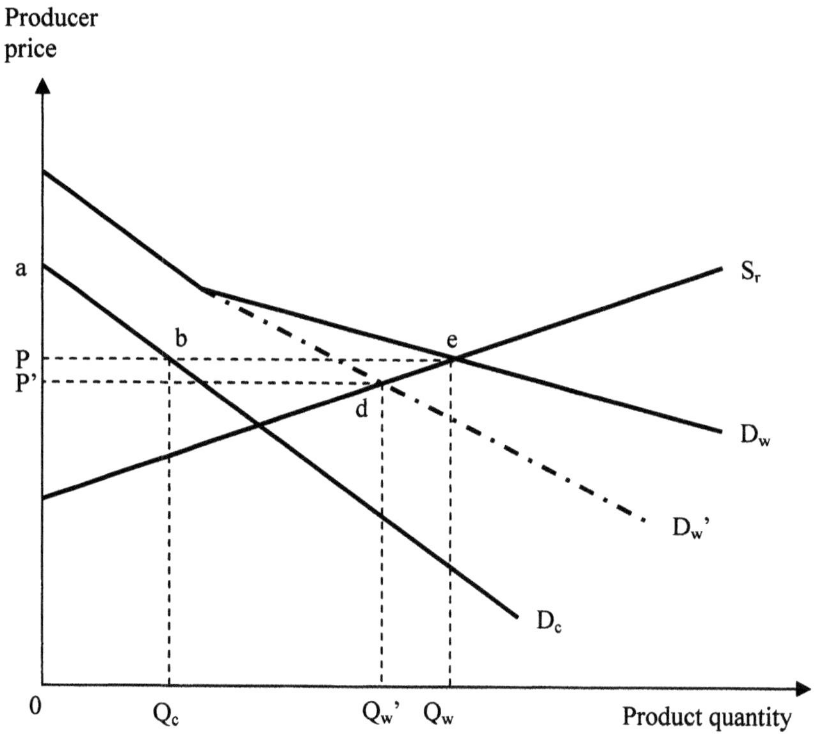

Figure 1. The Effects of Retaliation for the Complainant and the Respondent
Source: Anderson (2002)

D_c is the complainant's (e.g. the US in the bananas case) import demand curve for a product imported from the respondent (e.g. luxury goods from the EU). D_w is the world's import demand for it. If S_r is the respondent's excess supply curve for that product; then in the absence of distortions and assuming perfect competition, the international price of the product will be P and the quantity traded will be Q_w, of which Q_c goes to the complainant.

Retaliation means in the extreme a prohibitive (100%) tariff which reduces Q_c to zero. This will cause the global demand for the respondent's exported product to

Retaliation means in the extreme a prohibitive (100%) tariff which reduces Q_c to zero. This will cause the global demand for the respondent's exported product to shrink to D_w'. This horizontal shift will be by less than the full extent of D_c because the complainant will demand more close substitutes in the world market, driving up their price and hence shifting out to some extent the demand curve of the rest of the world for the respondent's export product. The international price of that product will fall to P' and the volume of the respondent's exports will fall from Q_w to Q_w', that is, by less than OQc.

The gross value of the imports to be prohibited is the area PbQ_cO, whereas the respondent's net loss of export earnings from this product is the smaller area PeQ_wQ_w'dP'.

The respondent's economic welfare loss because of the trade prohibition is just the area PedP', since the area under the respondent's export supply curve between points d and e represents costs of production which would not be borne if the respondent's export volume was reduce by Q_w'Q_w.

The economic welfare loss to the respondent is larger absolutely, and relative to the gross value of trade curtailed, the steeper (i.e. the less price elastic) is S_r, the respondent's export supply curve, between the free market equilibrium point e and the constrained equilibrium point d. Hence the ratio of PedP' to PbQ_c0 would vary across products.

This underscores the point that ensuring the reduction in the value of imports from the respondent, due to retaliation, matches the reduction in the value of imports from the complainant, due to the WTO-inconsistent measure being used by the respondent, will not be (except by coincidence) the same as ensuring equivalent losses in economic welfare for the other party due to the import restriction each is imposing.

Comment

Nicole Pohl

Department of Economics, Franklin & Marshall College, Lancaster, USA

In his analysis Fritz Breuss argues that there are three shortcomings of the WTO dispute settlement system that deserve particular attention from an economic point of view:

1. the bias of the system in favor of larger trading nations,
2. difficulties in calculating the damage that a country suffers,
3. the fact that retaliation by increasing tariffs – while putting pressure on the defending country – leads to overall negative effects from an economic point of view.

In his paper, Fritz Breuss focuses mostly on the second and third point. Using the GTAP5 world CGE model, he tries to quantify the welfare and trade implications of trade conflicts using four prominent disputes between the European Union and the U.S.: the hormones case, the bananas case, the dispute about foreign sales corporations, and – with some more preliminary conclusions – the more recent steel dispute. Choosing these cases, he focuses on a particular subset of cases, all of which (except the steel case which is still too recent) have resulted in WTO authorizations for sanctions. Quantifying the welfare and trade implications of trade wars, his model takes into account the effects of protectionist and retaliatory actions on exports, on nominal and real GDP, the terms of trade effect and welfare allocation effects. The latter are however not well defined for readers who are not familiar with the model. It would also generally be desirable to introduce some of the basic features of the model at least briefly.

The negative effects of tariff wars have been demonstrated by various trade models and have become part of the standard literature on international trade. Negative assessments of this measure of last resort are also due to the fact that the sectors in which retaliation occurs are mostly chosen politically. In many cases the sectors that benefit from retaliation are often not the ones that were harmed in the first instance. The steel dispute has also shown that counter-reactions not only concern WTO authorized retaliatory moves, but also the use of safeguard measures. The latter – as evidenced by the reaction of the EU to the U.S. tariff - are the result of fears that the initial protectionist move (in this case by the U.S.) not only prevents exports but will also lead to trade distortions.

Breuss comes to the conclusion that the calculations of the level of impairment and nullification done by the panels depend on various unknown variables and are highly sensitive to even slight changes in the assumed parameters. This is related to difficulties in determining an appropriate counterfactual or hypothetical scenario that would apply without the protectionist measures and that is compared to the actual situation with protectionist measures in place in order to determine the damage. And even if we accept the calculations themselves, WTO rules do not make it clear how the respective suspensions should be realized by the complaining country (by reducing imports by the same amount or by increasing import tariffs by that amount). For a welfare analysis, this is particularly relevant, as retaliatory reactions will cause complex adaptation dynamics that are difficult to predict. These consequences include reactions by firms in the countries under consideration, but, secondly, they also comprise what Breuss calls "externalities" or effects on third countries that are for instance based on trade diversion and that are caused by the initial protectionist measure as well as for retaliatory steps. Thirdly, effects not only on the sectors under consideration, but also on those sectors that use the respective products as intermediate inputs or that are linked to the respective industry in other ways have to be taken into account. The more complex those linkages are, the more sectors and the more countries will potentially be involved in a dispute. Breuss comes to the conclusion that estimates of the correct level of concessions are "practically impossible" and that the process suffers from control problems, once retaliatory measures are in place. One may add that the increasing importance of health concerns in agricultural trade for which a solid scientific basis is lacking and where cultural differences are at times taken as an argument (see for instance the current dispute about genetically engineered food) may make the respective calculations even more difficult if not impossible, as welfare assessments would have to include non-pecuniary benefits of protection from imports, too.

These two points, the difficulty to calculate the damage and the lack of control over retaliatory measures, make the WTO's dispute settlement not only an ill defined process and one that suggests a much higher degree of objectivity and clarity than is actually available. If one assumes that better systems are not at hand currently, they characterize the system as one that requires a very careful sensitivity analysis concerning the choice of parameters and assumed reactions. The work done by the WTO's panels is often not transparent enough to assess in how far this actually happens. Breuss does not postulate to offer better methods of calculating damage and levels of nullification in his paper, but demonstrates the variations in the relevant amounts to be determined under various scenarios. He concludes that the current system is not based on claims of accuracy, but on aims related to fairness.

In terms of possible alternative solutions for retaliatory tariffs, Breuss suggests a transfer system as a major conclusion of his paper. He argues that such a system could reduce the risk that trade wars spread across sectoral boundaries and that might be easier to control and less harmful in terms of its welfare effects. This suggestion is only explained relatively briefly at the end of his paper. Altogether we have doubts whether he makes a convincing point for such a system, as it would not allow the complainant to maintain pressure on the defending country. Alternatively, he also mentions suggestions by other authors to require a country that has been found in violation of WTO rules to actually lower its import barriers.

While this clearly corresponds closer to the overall spirit of the WTO, it seems to struggle with enforcement problems in a similar way as his transfer solution.

Altogether, Breuss suggests that the WTO's dispute settlement system is most problematic in cases where the initial steps of settlement and deterrence have failed and where the WTO is in fact not able to enforce its rules, but has to help the complainant get some form of compensation. One has to see clearly that this only concerns a relatively small number of cases and is therefore not helpful to make suggestions about the overall success of the dispute settlement system. The cases discussed are cases where the WTO system has already failed. However, for those cases where Breuss' criticism applies, one is tempted to ask whether the resources invested in determining the level of nullification are well allocated and whether retaliation does not cause more harm than good. In terms of the level of nullification and damage, the limits of reasonable amounts seem to be provided by the range between the estimates given by the complaining party (who will have a fairly high estimate) and the defending party (with a fairly low estimate). This range can be very broad. And even if one is able to determine a reasonably fair amount for nullification, it is – according to Breuss' argumentation – questionable if this will be the amount that will be reached through retaliatory measures that are difficult to control. So, Breuss is right in saying that the system is far from optimal in those respects. He seems to conclude in his paper that alternative mechanisms will have to be found. Evaluating this suggestion, it may be helpful to reconsider the aims pursued by the mechanisms in question. Generally, these or alternative measures are needed if we assume that they contribute to the WTO's ability to enforce its rules. Saying this, one has to take into account that it is by no means clear why countries give in to WTO decisions and whether or in how far retaliatory threats contribute to compliance. Peer pressure might be a force that is just as important as the fear of retaliation. At the same time, one may assume that the possibility of retaliation is based on an understanding of fairness for the complaining party, although the domination of the process by interest groups may make this doubtful. Rhetoric during the recent dispute about tariffs in the steel sector have also demonstrated that the parties involved were quite aware of the global costs involved in a trade dispute between the EU and the U.S. To the extent that such awareness is there, potential the costs of retaliatory action might actually have a deterring function.

Where Breuss' conclusions bring us depends on our assessment of the need for and usefulness of the enforcement mechanism that is currently provided by possibilities of retaliation. Assuming that some sort of enforcement mechanism is needed and that the current system is not a good choice, we find at the same time, that it is extremely difficult to find alternatives that are practically feasible, although there are some that may be economically more beneficial. This is mostly due to the fact that there is a need for the complaining party to control the process and to be able to keep up pressure. It is also related to the fact that governments may not necessarily be dominated by the desire to achieve a fair allocation of resources and thus compensate those sectors that had initially been hurt. Instead, trade policy has become more of a political gamble instead of a process of rational economic decision-making.

List of Contributors

Kenzo Abe	Graduate School of Economics, Osaka University, Japan
Fritz Breuss	Vienna University of Economics and Business Administration and Austrian Institute of Economic Research (Wifo), Austria
Anoop Chaturvedi	Department of Mathematics and Statistics, University of Allahabad, India
Volker Clausen	Department of Economics, University of Duisburg-Essen, Campus Essen, Germany
Roland Döhrn	Rhine Westphalia Institute of Economic Research, Essen, Germany
Theo Eicher	Department of Economics, University of Washington, Seattle, WA, USA
K.C. Fung	Department of Economics, University of California, Santa Cruz, CA, USA
Earl L. Grinols	Department of Economics, University of Illinois, Champain-Urbana, IL, USA
Günter S. Heiduk	Institute of International and Regional Economic Relations, University of Duisburg-Essen, Campus Duisburg, Germany
Tran Van Hoa	Department of Economics, University of Wollongong, Australia
Henryk Kierzkowski	Graduate Institute of International Studies, Geneva, Switzerland
Udo Kreickemeier	School of Economics, University of Nottingham, UK
Kala Krishna	Department of Economics, The Pennsylvania State University, University Park, PA, USA
Pei-Cheng Liao	Department of Accounting, National Taiwan University, Taipei, Taiwan
Ngo Van Long	Department of Economics, McGill University, Montreal, Canada
Andréa M. Maechler	Department of Economics, University of California, Santa Cruz, CA, USA
Keith E. Maskus	Department of Economics, University of Colorado, Boulder, CO, USA
Abhiroop Mukhopadhyay	Department of Economics, The Pennsylvania State University, University Park, PA, USA
Julian Emami Namini	Department of Economics, University of Duisburg-Essen, Campus Essen, Germany
Thomas Osang	Department of Economics, Southern Methodist University, Dallas, TX, USA

Roberto Perrelli	Department of Economics, University of Illinois, Champaign, IL, USA
Nicole Pohl	Department of Economics, Franklin & Marshall College, Lancaster, PA, USA
Pascalis Raimondos-Møller	Department of Economics, Copenhagen Business School, Denmark
Roberto A. de Santis	European Central Bank, Frankfurt/M, Germany
Sweta C. Saxena	Graduate School of Public and International Affairs, Pittsburgh, PA, USA
Henry Thompson	Economics, Comer Hall, Auburn University, Auburn, AL, USA
Huilan Tian	Division of Management, University of Toronto at Scarborough, Canada
Kar-yiu Wong	Department of Economics, University of Washington, Seattle, WA, USA
Alan D. Woodland	Discipline of Econometrics and Business Statistics, University of Sydney, Australia
Ian Wooton	Department of Economics, University of Strathclyde, Glasgow, UK
Cemile Yavas	Department of Economics, The Pennsylvania State University, University Park, PA, USA